Hume, Reason and Morality

Covering an important theme in Humean studies, this book focuses on Hume's hugely influential attempt, in Book 3 of his *Treatise of Human Nature* to derive the conclusion that morality is a matter of feeling, not reason, from its link with action.

Claiming that Hume's argument contains a fundamental contradiction that has gone unnoticed in modern debate, this fascinating volume is a refreshing combination of historical-scholarly work and contemporary analysis that seeks to expose this contradiction and therefore provide a significant contribution to current scholarship in the area.

Sophie Botros begins by pointing out that a contradiction concerning whether reason can influence action, or is wholly powerless, occurs in the intermediary premiss. She then moves on to draw out the consequences for recent meta-ethics of the failure to acknowledge this contradiction. Finally, highlighting the root of the argument's power in an article of naturalistic dogma, she suggests how it may be possible to restore to our moral concepts their traditional and integral link with both truth and motivation.

A significant and thought-provoking addition to this popular field of study, *Hume, Reason and Morality* is undoubtedly an important resource for moral philosophers interested in meta-ethics and practical reason, as well as Humean scholars.

Sophie Botros is an Honorary Research Fellow in the Department of Philosophy at Birkbeck College, University of London. She previously taught at the Universities of Essex and Stirling and at King's College, London, and has written on ethics, ancient philosophy, and philosophy of action in leading philosophical journals.

Routledge Studies in Eighteenth Century Philosophy

Hume, Reason and Morality

A legacy of contradiction

Sophie Botros

Routledge
Taylor & Francis Group

LONDON AND NEW YORK

First published 2006
by Routledge
2 Park Square, Milton Park, Abingdon, Oxon OX14 4RN

Simultaneously published in the USA and Canada
by Routledge
270 Madison Ave, New York, NY 10016

Routledge is an imprint of the Taylor & Francis Group

© 2006 Sophie Botros

Typeset in Garamond by
Taylor & Francis Books

Printed and bound in Great Britain by
Biddles Ltd, King's Lynn

British Library Cataloguing in Publication Data
A catalogue record for this book is available from the British Library

Library of Congress Cataloging in Publication Data
A catalog record for this book has been requested

ISBN10 0-415-33180-3   ISBN13 9-780-415-33180-7

T&F Informa

Taylor & Francis Group is the Academic Division of T&f Informa plc.

This book is dedicated to my father, Labib Botros, and to A. R. Jonckheere.

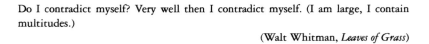

Do I contradict myself? Very well then I contradict myself. (I am large, I contain multitudes.)

(Walt Whitman, *Leaves of Grass*)

Contents

Acknowledgements

Several of the attempts to save Hume from contradiction dealt with in Chapter 1 were originally suggested to me by David Wiggins to whom I am indebted for reading an early draft of the chapter.

Early drafts of part of Chapter 2 were read at the Birkbeck College Philosophy Department Staff Seminar, and again at the Centre for Politics, Law and Society, University College, London. Part of Chapter 7 was read at a meeting of the Birkbeck Philosophy Society. I would like to thank the members of these seminars and meeting for their helpful comments. I would also like to thank my former colleague at Essex University, Will Cartwright, for an enlightening discussion of the issues raised in the last section of Chapter 8.

I am grateful to three anonymous referees at Routledge whose judicious and insightful comments on my original outline led to changes in the structure of the book.

My greatest debts however are to A.R. Jonckheere, my most effective and accomplished critic, and to Paul Johnson, without whose understanding, encouragement and moral support, the book would never have been written.

Abbreviations

T	*A Treatise of Human Nature*, ed. David Fate Norton and Mary J. Norton, Oxford: Oxford University Press, 2000.
Abstract	*Abstract of the Treatise*, in Norton and Norton (2000)
E	*An Enquiry Concerning the Principles of Morals, in Enquiries Concerning Human Understanding and Concerning the Principles of Morals*, ed. L.A. Selby-Bigge and P.H. Nidditch, Oxford: Clarendon Press, 1975.

Notes on the Text

In accordance with the Norton and Norton version of the *Treatise*, passages are referred to by Book, Part, Section and Paragraph, thus 3.1.1:22. I only use 'T' where the context is ambiguous.

In the text I have designated the agent as 'she' to avoid confusion.

Introduction

This book claims that there is a contradiction at the heart of one of the most potent arguments in moral philosophy. The argument is among a cluster used by David Hume in Book 3 of *A Treatise of Human Nature* to demonstrate that 'moral distinctions [are] not deriv'd from reason'. In this argument, he seeks to derive the conclusion from morality's practicality. The contradiction occurs in the second premiss – formulated no less than nine times – and concerns whether reason can, or cannot, influence action. Not only has this contradiction been almost universally ignored, but it has even been reproduced, without comment, in recent meta-ethical debate as a kind of orthodoxy. My clarification of the confusions thus engendered will lead to the undermining of the traditional opposition between cognitivism, claiming that moral judgements are beliefs, and non-cognitivism that they are desires, as these theories bear on moral action. It will also bring to light the source of the argument's power in an article of naturalistic dogma. This will finally suggest how, using Wittgensteinian ideas to resist the simple dichotomy *either* naturalism *or* metaphysical obscurantism, it may be possible to restore to moral concepts their traditional and integral link with both truth and motivation.

The main device that I use in the book to explore the contradiction, and its consequences, is to treat the 'practicality' argument *as if* there were compressed within its apparently unitary structure two arguments, depending on which of the contradictory readings of the second premiss is given. I call the argument with a second premiss claiming that reason can, and does, influence action, though only alongside desire, the 'moderate' version. The argument whose second premiss denies that reason has, or could have, any motivating role[1] is the 'extreme' version. This strategy bears fruit not only in the discussion of Hume, but also when applied to the contemporary scene. For what initially seemed like a jumble of interpretations are plausibly sorted into 'moderate' and 'extreme' versions of the argument.

The chief drawback with the 'moderate' version is that, as it stands, it is invalid. Indeed, many recent reinterpretations of the argument are best seen as attempts to redress this invalidity by philosophers who have automatically, and without being fully aware of it, assumed this version. Their solution is often simply to read back into Hume's *first* premiss a necessary, or 'internal', link between moral judgements and motivation, though in fact the relation that Hume claims to hold is much looser.

The 'extreme' version, though being immediately valid, suffers from another problem. This is the apparent obscurity, if not absurdity, of the claim – to cite one of Hume's more spectacular statements of the second premiss – that 'reason is perfectly inert'. But if it is difficult to see what Hume himself might have meant by this declaration, or who therefore could have been his target, the problem is intensified when it is appealed to by a recent philosopher such as Bernard Williams (1981). In trying to solve the puzzle of the identity of Williams' opponents here, I gradually lay bare the deeper structure of assumptions which has invisibly shaped, and even sometimes dictated, the form of contemporary meta-ethical debate in this area.

As far as the source of the contradiction itself is concerned, it lies, I argue, in a scepticism – I call it an unappeasable scepticism – which Hume, towards the end of Book 1, both passionately endorses and violently repudiates. He does this by using the device of the 'philosopher secluded in his closet' and the 'honest gentleman' in the midst of his domestic affairs. Through this almost theatrical contrast, Hume is able to rebel against the idea that our beliefs might ultimately be without foundation at the very same time as he is ruthlessly pushing the limits of his scepticism ever further out, beyond belief, to undermine demonstrative reasoning itself.

A final word on my method. My chapters on Hume's *Treatise* are not a measured progression through the text following the order in which Hume treats his topics. I am rather engaged on a journey of discovery which takes us sometimes forward, sometimes back. I thus plunge, as it were, cold, into Book 3 where our problem initially lies, and then I find myself pushed backward, through Book 2, to Book 1 because I am not able to resolve it any other way. This method suits a writer such as Hume much better than the more 'linear' alternative that is usually followed. For in those extraordinary sections towards the end of Book 1 where Hume confronts his scepticism head-on, and his viewpoint then oscillates back and forth between the 'philosopher in his closet' and 'the honest gentleman', engaged in backgammon and other such pursuits, we glimpse Hume's different 'voices', providing a counter-point of incomparable richness, so grievously lost in that tame set of views known officially as 'Humeanism'. To explain away Hume's inconsistencies is not the best way of rendering service to a philosopher, part of whose greatness lies in the very contradictions on which his multi-faceted genius thrives.[2]

Part I

Hume's Practicality Argument

1 A Contradiction, Not an Ambiguity

It is astonishing how reluctant philosophers have been to *look* at Hume's formulations of the second premiss of the practicality argument. Had they done so, they would surely have fallen prey to conflicting intuitions as to whether he holds that reason can (and does) influence action, or could not conceivably do so. Often – and quite contrarily – they have preferred a blinkered certainty, either emphatically maintaining that, for Hume, reason definitely has a motivating role or, just as emphatically, that it has not, and could not have, such a role.

Even those who can be coaxed into a more sustained attention tend to view the crucial passages through the kind of hazy lens which shields Hume from the apparently harsher judgement that he simply contradicts himself. For them, if his phraseology has given us this impression, it is unfortunate, but really it is our own fault; we have unreasonably, and uncharitably, demanded a degree of precision which is inappropriate in the context, and which leads to distortion. Sheltering behind one particular formulation, that 'reason *alone* can never have any influence . . . on actions' (also favoured by writers appealing to Hume's argument in the debate as to whether moral judgements are beliefs or desires), they will admit only to an ambiguity in Hume's language. Even this more concessive position, I argue below, ought not to be granted. A *prima facie* contradiction underlies Hume's formulations of his second premiss, and an ambiguity is not a contradiction.

In Section 1, I focus exclusively on the formulations themselves, first setting out the evidence on which my interpretation rests, and then dealing with objections. Only when it becomes clear that the formulations themselves cannot provide a basis for interpreting the premiss in one way rather than the other, shall I extend my investigation back to Book 2, and consider whether matters can be remedied by appeal to the theory of motivation in which the practicality argument is embedded. This will occupy the rest of the chapter.

1 The formulations: *Treatise* 3.1.1:6–16

(i) The contradiction

In the short interval between *Treatise* 3.1.1 6 and 16 Hume formulates his practicality argument in no less than seven different ways, at the same time varying the arrangements of the premisses and conclusion. Premiss 2 is recast on its own twice more. Differences in verbal expression do not of course necessarily indicate a corresponding difference in sense. For instance, when Hume rephrases premiss 1, 'morals have an influence on the actions and affections', as 'morals excite passions, and produce or prevent actions', this would seem merely to be elegant variation: something we should expect from a literary stylist of Hume's calibre.

We cannot, however, be equally confident that the meaning of the *second* premiss stays constant through its various reformulations. The main problem is that, though on first stating it, Hume qualifies 'reason' with *'alone'* – thus 'reason alone can never have any such influence [on action]' – he does not consistently do so. In fact, he qualifies 'reason' in this way again only in his ninth formulation of the premiss. Admittedly, on two other occasions he substitutes related adverbs, namely, 'in itself', in one, 'of itself' in the other. Of the remaining five formulations of the premiss, however, in three, he omits any adverb, and so apparently ceases to convert what is otherwise an outright denial of reason's influence over action into a statement setting limits to that influence. For instance, in his third and seventh formulations, he states flatly that 'reason has no influence [on our passions and actions]', while in the sixth he tells us that it 'can never immediately prevent or produce any action'. In the two formulations not yet mentioned, the categorical nature of these denials of reason's influences is, if anything, reinforced by the introduction of a new type of adverb. Thus, in the fifth, he prefaces his claim that reason 'can never either prevent or produce any action or affection', with the description of it as *'perfectly* inert', while in the eighth, where he reproduces the whole argument for the sixth time, premiss 2 states uncompromisingly that 'reason is *wholly* inactive' (my italics).

(ii) But it is not an actual *contradiction*

Now it is doubtful whether anyone could keep all these different formulations in mind at the same time without at least provisionally sorting them into two groups – those which seem to suggest that reason has a role in motivation, and those that seem to suggest it has (and could have) none. It is just as doubtful whether anyone could steadily contemplate the two groups without experiencing a twinge of unease about how they are meant to fit together. If a respectful veil is not immediately drawn over this reaction, a little breathing space can still be purchased by observing that, fleeting impressions aside, when one actually scrutinizes Hume's wording, one will see that there is no *actual* contradiction. For that, it will be explained, Hume would have had to say not just that 'reason alone can never have any influence [on action]' (which he does say) but that 'reason alone *can sometimes* have such an influence' (which he does not say). Alternatively, he would have had to say not just that 'reason has no such influence' (which he does say) but also that 'reason *has* an influence' (which he does not say).

We can agree that Hume is not involved in an *explicit* contradiction. Nevertheless the claim, that reason alone can never have any influence on action, would seem, taken in its most natural sense, to imply that reason *has* an influence (when combined with something else), that it *becomes* active (when something else is added) or again, in the words of one important commentator, Harrison (1976: 11), that it 'moves us to action in *some way or other*'. But then Hume's initial formulation of premiss 2 *implicitly* conflicts with those later reformulations according to which reason has (or can have) *no* influence on action. This difficulty is only exacerbated by his emphatic declarations that reason is 'perfectly inert', and 'wholly inactive'.

(iii) The formulations are too ambiguous

But to allege even an implicit contradiction is to assume, it will now be objected, that both the claim that reason *alone* can never have any influence, and the claim that reason has (or can have) no influence, are themselves tolerably clear, when in fact at least one, or even both, are ambiguous.

A useful definition of 'ambiguity' is given by W. Empson:[1] 'We call [a statement] ambiguous when we recognize that there could be a puzzle as to what the author meant, in that alternative views might be taken without sheer misreading.' Keeping this definition before us, let us now consider a statement with a relevantly similar form to 'reason alone can never influence action', for example, 'physical strength alone can never get a mountaineer to the summit', and ask whether it could plausibly be said to have two corresponding meanings. But it would be odd indeed to suggest that, though the statement might initially be read as implying that physical strength is only one of several factors required for success in mountaineering, each decisively affecting the outcome, one would soon see that it could equally plausibly be taken to imply that physical strength plays, and can play, no role, so that the mountaineer might as well be a puny weakling.

Perhaps, however, such a statement is felt to be ambiguous, not in being susceptible to *two* interpretations, but in conveying only a half-formed idea, and in this way thwarting the would-be interpreter. This would, of course, cast Hume in the odd role of someone who has just not thought through his second premiss and, rather like a first year philosophy student for whom clarifying a complicated idea is just too much, exhaustedly and prematurely gives up altogether. But even leaving this aside, to say that statements such as 'reason alone can never have any influence on action', or again 'physical strength alone can never get a mountaineer to the summit' are in a sense *incomplete* – they leave the hearer wondering what more is required – is not to say that they fail to have any determinate meaning, and are essentially inchoate. Moreover, what is left open is the identity of this further factor – in the mountaineering claim, perhaps 'consummate skill' or 'extreme determination, not whether what *is* mentioned – the subject of the claim – might be dispensed with altogether.

But it is not, it will now be suggested, Hume's *qualified* denials of reason's influence over action that are ambiguous in being susceptible to two different interpretations, but his *un*qualified ones. It is, therefore, these which ought to be brought under the umbrella of the qualified denials. Of course, it will be acknowledged, one obvious way that the claim that reason has, or can have, no influence over action, might be taken is that, no matter what it is combined with, reason will never motivate us. But the claim might equally be taken to be denying only that reason can have this influence *on its own,* being wholly dependent on something else for its power. To take a different example, mightn't a person deny that she did the shopping, not because she didn't do it, but because she didn't, and couldn't have done it *on her own*: without help, she would have been absolutely incapable of carrying all her purchases home? But this seems a strained interpretation: one would have expected her, unless she deliberately aimed to mislead the person addressed, to have, in these circumstances, qualified her denial in the appropriate way.

(iv) A plea for a relaxed attitude

But though, it will be admitted, it would ordinarily be inappropriate to read a simple denial, such as Hume's, as though it were really qualified, is not this permissible given the context? For doesn't the word 'alone', or 'in itself', or 'of itself', hover somewhere in the paragraphs in which the apparently unqualified denials occur, and is not this an indication that Hume relied on our being relaxed enough to take the qualification for granted? In fact, the answer to the textual question is strictly 'no': the qualifying adverb occurs nowhere, for instance, either in paragraph 8, or in paragraph 10, where the practicality argument is recast three times, but with, in each case, a flat denial of reason's influence as its second premiss.

(v) Hume is sometimes careless

A further way of settling the troubling inconsistency might be to put it down to carelessness on Hume's part, and on the supposition that a writer is more likely to be led by carelessness to omit, than to insert, a word, again to propose reading the apparently outright denials of reason's influence as though they were not really denials at all. Hume holds, it will be said, that reason *has* an influence: all he means is that it isn't the *sole* determining factor in the production of action, but he sometimes unwittingly leaves out the crucial adverb. But the dangerous precedent thus set of our not necessarily having to take Hume at his word is a high price to pay in order to avoid an acknowledgement of even the *appearance* of contradiction, whether or not it may later be resolved. (I do not yet[2] consider the possibility that an unresolved contradiction might prove invaluable as testimony to the existence of deep and fruitful tensions in a philosopher's thought, of which he himself maybe either dimly, or even acutely, conscious.)

(vi) Hume is a rhetorician

But suppose we were to countenance this appeal to carelessness, there is the further question whether we ought to allow the unqualified denials, simply on the basis of a flimsy observation about the psychology of writers, to be assimilated to the qualified ones, rather than vice versa. There is, after all, no explicit indication in the text that those formulations of the second premiss, which merely qualify reason's influence, should be taken as more definitive than those which apparently flatly deny it: in fact, as we have seen, the latter slightly preponderate over the former. Then, again,

Hume's characterizations of reason as 'perfectly inert' (para. 8), and 'wholly inactive' (para. 10), conveying as they do, the distinct and vivid impression of a faculty incapable of being roused to activity in any circumstances whatsoever, seem deliberate and considered. If it is now suggested that we discount them (see Baillie, 2000: 89) as mere 'rhetoric',[3] we shall be left with what is surely a strange, and unacceptable, reading of passages in which Hume is constructing one of the most potent arguments in all moral philosophy. For it represents these passages as marred, on the one hand, by pockets of carelessness in which Hume simply *forgets* to qualify his denials of reason's influence and, on the other, by pockets of rhetoric in which, letting his love of a fine line run away with him, he is deliberately prepared to say the opposite of what he means.

(vii) He could never have been so absurd as to assert reason's powerlessness!

One final consideration – suggested by Harrison's treatment (1976) of premiss 2 – for nevertheless rejecting the claim that Hume denies any motivating role to reason is that this would simply be a nonsensical view for *anyone* to hold. Thus, Harrison, in reaching his conclusion that Hume concedes that reason 'moves us to action *in some way or other*' (ibid.: 11, my italics), states that 'Hume of course never maintains anything so absurd as the proposition that my beliefs do not affect my behaviour' (ibid.: 5); and again that Hume's premiss could hardly have been 'that reason does not move us to action' since that '*is obviously false*' (ibid.: 11, my italics).

It is salutary then to point out that not all Humean scholars have found it similarly inconceivable that anyone could absolutely refuse to accord a role to reason in motivation. Indeed, that this is precisely what Hume is doing in premiss 2 has its distinguished adherents, just as does the opposing interpretation. David Fate Norton (1993: 163), for instance, takes Hume's claim that 'reason alone can never produce action' to entail that reason has 'no motivational force'. Again, he states that 'reason', for Hume, 'is perfectly inert, and quite unable to motivate agents to act'. Stroud (1977: 160) suggests that, for Hume, reason not merely has no influence over action but could not conceivably have. He explains that, for Hume, reason could only cause the 'aversions' and 'propensities' which cause action if it was, like them, a Humean 'original existence', but it is not (something about which we shall have more to say later).

I have now examined a series of possible – though in my view increasingly flimsy – grounds for favouring, on the basis of its various formulations alone, one or other of the conflicting interpretations of premiss 2. I have also attempted to show how unsatisfactory in each case was the proposal for dealing with those formulations which did not fit in with the chosen interpretation, whether this involved assimilating, or just discounting, them. In fact, however, as I observed at the outset, it is not usual to find in the literature, whichever interpretation is favoured, any such attempt to explicitly rule out the competing interpretation, or even any apparent awareness that a reconciliation of divergent formulations is necessary. Harrison is quite untypical in adverting to the interpretation he does *not* favour, and offering, if somewhat perfunctorily, a reason for rejecting it.

Even he, however, only dismisses this interpretation against a larger background of assumptions concerning Hume's theory of motivation, which such an interpretation would upset. These assumptions are that Hume is an instrumentalist who allows, as Harrison puts it, that 'action is the product of belief and desire in conjunction and can be changed by a change in either', but who insists that 'belief without desire is ineffective': it can move us to action but only by being 'relevant to the satisfaction of some passion, desire or need' (1976: 5–6).

(viii) It would not fit in with his theory of motivation

This reliance on the standard instrumental view of Hume's theory of motivation is still more marked in those who, adopting the same interpretation as Harrison – that reason does influence action – treat even more perfunctorily the possibility of the alternative interpretation. Baillie, for instance, assures us (2000:89) that 'once we get past the rhetoric, a careful and comprehensive reasoning of the *Treatise* shows that when Hume says that reason is inert, he's not denying it *any* causal role in motivating the will'. But this 'careful and comprehensive reasoning', either does not go beyond appeal to the standard instrumentalist reading, or else is never forthcoming.

Foot (1963: 73) differs from both Harrison or Baillie in not even broaching the possibility of the alternative interpretation. Despite selecting, from among Hume's formulations, two apparently flat denials of reason's influence, and asking what is meant by them, she fails to draw attention to the obvious fact that, taken at their face value, they conflict with the instrumentalist theory of motivation commonly attributed to him (and, indeed, with some of his other formulations of the premiss). Instead, she expounds this theory as though simply spelling out what is already implicit in the perhaps overly compressed formulations:

> Reason can tell us, for instance, that a certain action will have a particular effect, or again, that a certain object exists within our reach; but if the effect is indifferent to us, the thing not wanted, the discovery of fact which Hume calls 'a conclusion of reason' will make no difference to what we do.

She presumably supposes that this explanation justifies her in amending Hume's wording when he declares that 'reason is perfectly inert', for she adds: 'and so [Hume] says, reason *alone* is 'perfectly inert'; it may of course influence actions, but only when we happen to have certain desires' (my italics).

Now clearly Hume's theory of motivation *is* crucial to the interpretation of the second premiss of his practicality argument. Indeed, Hume refers us back for a defence of this premiss (in particular for his claim that reason is 'perfectly inert') to his original exposition of the theory in 2.3.3 where he says he has 'prov'd' the claim. But with both interpretations of premiss 2 still in play at the end of our discussion of its various formulations, we must surely wonder whether we can afford to be so certain of Hume's instrumentalism that we may simply override any remark suggesting reason's total powerlessness. In Section 2, therefore I turn back to Book 2, and to Hume's original exposition of his theory of motivation, to seek an answer to this question.

2 Hume's theory of motivation

(i) Five theses of instrumentalism, and Hume's response

I shall take it as uncontroversial that instrumentalists hold the following five theses: (1) that reason *can* influence action; (2) that it is not, however, sufficient for action since it requires the help of desire; (3) that it is necessary for action; (4) that reason's role differs from desire's in providing information relevant to our having, and satisfying, the desires, which provide our ends; and (5) that this role is nevertheless, like desire's, causal.

Now Hume explicitly affirms (1) when, at 3.1.1:12, he describes the two ways in which, as he clearly states, 'reason can have an influence on our conduct'. As regards (2), and the denial of reason's sufficiency, he states, in expounding his theory of motivation (2.3.3:3), that 'reason alone can never produce any action, or give rise to volition'. He goes on to explain that we only act when, having before us 'the prospect of pain or pleasure from any object, we feel a consequent emotion of aversion or propensity, and [so] are carry'd to avoid or embrace what will give us this uneasiness or satisfaction'. In other words, desire or passion is also required. That reason is nevertheless, together with this 'emotion of aversion or propensity' *necessary* – thesis (3) – is implicit in his next remark where he writes that 'as our reasoning varies [so] our actions receive a subsequent variation'. It is, therefore, he seems to be saying, not just the character of our feelings or desires that explains what we do, but also our *beliefs* concerning how these desires may be satisfied. Also, negatively, one might read (3) into the fact that Hume never states that desire *alone*, any more than he states that reason, or belief, alone, can produce action. That Hume holds thesis (4) is suggested by his description (in the same paragraph) of reason as 'tak[ing] place to discover this relation [of cause and effect]', and so of 'direct[ing]' the 'impulse' to act which arises independently of it. That reason's role here is nevertheless causal, thus meeting (5), is suggested by his remark at 3.1.1:16 where he says that 'reason and judgement may be the mediate cause of an action, by prompting, or by directing a passion'.

Unfortunately in order to present Hume's theory of motivation as consistently instrumentalist in this way, we have had to be highly selective in our use of quotations. On such an interpretation, Hume would seem to hold that reason and desire, though making qualitatively different contributions to action are, as its individually necessary and jointly sufficient conditions, equally important causal partners in the process. But what, then, are we to make of those other passages which also form part of the theory's exposition, but in which reason is sharply contrasted with passion, or desire, as wholly lacking the 'efficacy' of a motive, and bereft of any 'original influence [on the will]'?

(ii) Reason is inert because it cannot arouse desire

Now those writers who have acknowledged the significance of these passages in anticipating Hume's later descriptions of reason as 'perfectly inert' and 'wholly inactive', and yet wish to cling to the instrumental reading, have suggested two main ways of reconciling them with the causal remarks. One way is to suggest, as does Parfit (1997: 105), that all Hume means by claiming that 'reason is, and must be, wholly inert or inactive' is that it is incapable of itself of producing the requisite desire, not that it is incapable, when combined with an *independent* desire, of producing action. But this interpretation is hardly acceptable even on its own terms. For the account which Parfit offers of reason's inertia would allow us, oddly, to call *desire* inert also. Hume does not, after all, claim that *desire can* produce the *belief* required for action. As Harrison (1976: 6) points out, 'On the question whether desire without belief is ineffective, Hume does not express an opinion.' Whatever therefore is meant by desire's 'efficacy', in contrast to reason's inertia, it doesn't seem to mean having the power all by itself to give rise to the *other* necessary condition for the production of action.

(iii) Reason is inert because it cannot provide an impulse

The second solution has two variants, both of which at least avoid the problem of making too little of the contrast Hume draws in passages, such as 2.3.3:4, between reason and desire. One variant is to suggest, as does Basson (1958: 90) that, though 'Hume is willing to admit that knowledge and belief do influence our conduct . . . they are not [for him] a special kind of influence, called motives . . . and cannot be motives'. On this view, then, it is in not being, despite its causal role in action, that special thing called a 'motive' that reason, unlike desire, can be said to be inert.

But this interpretation does not receive unqualified support from the text. If it were correct, Hume ought to say that reason can never be a motive not, as he does say, that reason *alone* can never be a motive (2.3.3:1). For if the word 'alone' in 'reason alone does not influence action' implies, as we earlier argued it must, that reason does influence action, by parity of reasoning, the occurrence of 'alone' in 'reason alone can never be a motive to any action of the will' should imply that reason *is* such a motive (if only in conjunction with desire) not that it *isn't*.

The other variant may seem more promising. It involves substituting 'impulse' for 'motive' on grounds that Hume denies, in a roughly parallel way, that reason can give rise to an *impulse*, but does not here compromise his denial by qualifying 'reason' with 'alone'. Moreover he uses this denial, with its implication that reason lacks the 'efficacy' of an impulse, such as desire, to delimit a role – an instrumental one – for reason. He thus writes that the impulse to action 'arises not from reason but is only directed by it' (2.3.3:3). Later he describes reason, in 'directing' our impulses, as a 'cause' of action. Consequently, we can suggest that reason is inert in lacking the dynamism of an impulse without depriving it, as that which 'directs' desire, of a certain causal influence of its own over action.

But we should not forget that the idea of reason 'directing' an impulse is a metaphor, and so it is not automatically clear how it should be explicated. There are to be sure, as we've seen, remarks that suggest that reason's directive function is *causal* (3.1.1:16), and others which imply that direction is a form of *influence*. An example of the latter would be where he states even of 'abstract or demonstrative reasoning' that it 'never influences action, *but only as it directs* our judgement concerning causes and effects' (2.3.3:2, my italics).

But still other remarks, for instance, the one almost immediately following this, suggests something different. He observes (2.3.3:3) that we are never remotely interested in knowing that an 'object' causes, or is the effect of, another, where we do not desire to obtain, or avoid, either object. He then goes on: 'Where the objects themselves do not affect us, their connexion can never give them any influence; and t'is plain that as reason is nothing but the discovery of this connexion, it cannot be by its means that the objects are able to affect us'. Now it is hard not to read this passage as contrasting reason, as merely the impassive and inert 'discovery of a connection', with something which, because it can *affect* us, *has* such an 'influence' (namely, the 'original influence' just denied to reason). It might be suggested that if we were to distinguish 'influencing' from 'affecting', there would be just enough room to allow that reason *has* an influence, as a result of something *else*, desire, *affecting* us. But though Hume does indeed use both terms, it is not clear that *he* means something different by them. I will take it therefore that Hume's talk of 'direction', far from being the key to such a reconciliation, seems a further manifestation of the problem.

(iv) Desire as the outcome of reason

Even if these attempts at reconciliation were, as they clearly are not, satisfactory thus far, they would still have a further hurdle to overcome. For they crucially depend on the possibility of driving a wedge between reason's having the purely instrumental role of informing us about means – which Hume is said to allow – and its being an active force of some kind – which he is said to deny. In fact, we can find remarks of Hume's which precisely do not restrict reason's role to that of informing us how to satisfy a desire we *already* possess, nor even to producing the kind of secondary desire for that which is a means to satisfying our primary desire. For these remarks suggest that reason can 'excite' even such primary desires *itself*. Reason does this, Hume tells us at 3.1.1:12, by informing us that 'a proper object of' desire – a fruit, say, that 'I fancy to be pleasant and delicious' – lies within easy reach. Moreover, it can also, he adds, cause that desire, or 'longing' to vanish when on closer inspection we find the fruit to be 'really disagreeable'.[4] These remarks are echoed when in 3.1.1:16, having allowed that 'reason and judgement may, indeed, be the mediate cause of an action', he distinguishes the two ways in which it might do this: by 'prompting' *or* by 'directing' a passion.

The remarks quoted so far are from 3.1.1 where Hume is referring back to his theory of motivation, as developed in Book 2. However, these later remarks, though perhaps plainer in their import, and leaping to the eye more readily, only reflect a strand in his thinking which is already present in the original exposition. If we look again, for instance, at the account he gives (2.3.3:3) of the process whereby motivation takes place (and which we referred to earlier), we shall see that it is 'the prospect of pain or pleasure from any object', which leads to us feeling 'an emotion of aversion or propensity' so that we are 'carry'd to avoid or embrace what will give us this uneasiness or satisfaction'. But 'to have the prospect of pain or pleasure from any object' is surely to make a judgement about the object. Admittedly it is a judgement concerning pain or pleasure, and where it is to be found, but it is hardly therefore itself a *feeling* of pain or pleasure. Later in the paragraph he states the point even more succinctly: 'Tis from the prospect of pain or pleasure that the aversion or propensity arises towards any object'.

Consider once more then Parfit's claim that Hume, in describing reason as 'inert', just means that reason cannot *itself* give rise to desires or passions. But the remarks of Hume just quoted, if taken at their face value, now plainly contradict this claim. According to both variants of the second proposed resolution, reason does not, as we saw, contribute the 'active' force, or 'energy', required for action, which is contributed by desire. But if this were true, and yet reason, as the third set of remarks suggests, gives rise to desire, it would seem to follow that 'an active principle' *could* 'be founded on an inactive', yet Hume when coming at 3.1.1:16 to formulate the practicality argument, explicitly denies that this is possible.

The temptation when faced with these new remarks, bewilderingly at odds as they seem to be not only with the claim that reason has no influence at all on action but even with the claim that it has a bare instrumental force, is naturally enough to try to brush them off.[5] Surely 'excites', it will be urged, as it occurs in these remarks, only signifies for Hume the rousing of *an already existing* desire or passion.[6] But it is surely preferable to concede with Penelhum (1975: 129) what is, after all, the plain implication of these remarks – that for Hume a particular desire is 'sometimes the outcome of reason', or that just seeing, say, a pear can sometimes make me want it – than to have to invoke in his name this pre-existing, free-floating, desire for pears, or more nebulously still for pleasure, waiting to propel me towards a pear whenever I see one, provided an indefinite list of conditions is fulfilled: that it doesn't look unripe, or rotten, that I am not full, have no stomach ache, etc.

Moreover, Hume's use of 'excites' elsewhere supports Penelhum's policy of taking what Hume says at face value. For instance, when formulating his practicality argument, he speaks, as we saw earlier, of 'morals excit[ing] passions, and produc[ing] or prevent[ing] actions' in order to *contrast* 'morals' with reason which, he writes, 'of itself is utterly impotent in this particular'. But here the context clearly requires that 'excites' means brings a passion into existence, and not merely rouses an already existing passion.

In fact, far from being easy to shrug off these remarks, the impression given by them of what one might almost call, if it did not sound so paradoxical, reason's 'activity' can seem strong enough to warrant our searching out other passages which might indicate that passion, or desire, can *in its turn* affect our beliefs, hence at least putting it on a motivational par with reason. If, indeed, we extend our search back from the exposition of the theory of motivation in Book 2 of the *Treatise* to Book 1, such passages can be found. At 1.3.10:4, for instance, we find Hume maintaining that desires and emotions 'are very favourable to' our beliefs, and gives as an example the person whose fearful disposition makes him specially ready to credit reports of dangers. However, Hume has already in this context discussed how *belief* (by raising 'a simple idea to an equality with our impressions') influences our passions, and seems himself therefore merely to be attempting to show that desire is no *less* powerful. Moreover, his remark (1.3.10:4) that a belief is 'almost absolutely requisite to the exciting our passions' apparently entails just the opposite, 'The assistance', he firmly concludes, is 'mutual betwixt the judgement and passions.'

We are at last in a position to see something of the real shape and extent of the task of reconciliation that faces anyone striving to be true to everything Hume says. It is not, as we can now see, just a matter of interpreting reason's inertia so as to preserve the sharp contrast with desire, as an 'active' force. That would be relatively simple. But this inertia must somehow also incorporate the idea of reason's having a causal role comparable to, if qualitatively different from, desire's. If that weren't enough, it now turns out that this role is not even to be restricted to providing information about means, or even to producing the relevant secondary desire, but involves the capacity to engender (and extinguish) primary desires themselves.

In Section 3, I examine a final attempt, that of E. Millgram (1995: 75–93) to make a tolerable synthesis of these awesomely disparate elements. This attempt breaks new ground in embracing more of these elements than the two earlier attempts. It is also novel in what it chooses to drop. For Millgram, on the basis of his reading of the 'slave' metaphor, claims that Hume is such an uncompromising sceptic about practical reason that he cannot be counted an instrumentalist.

3 Humean 'original existences' and the inertia of reason

(i) Unsceptical instrumentalists

There is an ambiguity in instrumentalism (and in the account as I outlined it) concerning how far agents are necessarily committed to the conclusions of their means–end reasoning. Suppose, for instance, I desire an apple that I see hanging from the branch of a nearby tree, and realize that all I have to do is to stretch out my arm, and pluck it down, and suppose I have no competing desires. Instrumentalists are typically not explicit as to whether, on their view, I must, on pain of irrationality, desire to stretch out my arm and pluck down the apple, or whether I can, without irrationality, continue to desire the apple, yet not desire to pluck it down.

Now I am tempted to think that it is because the latter view seems to them so implausible that they just do not bother to entertain it. Millgram, however, portrays them as deliberately adhering to the former view in preference to the latter. Thus, on his account, they invoke Kant's adage that 'he who wills the end must will the means', precisely in order to emphasize that an agent is *rationally constrained* to desire what she believes to be the means to her desired end. But given, therefore, this endorsement of its 'critical and coercive' function, instrumentalists, he argues, are hardly sceptics about practical reason at all. Certainly they think that *only* means–end reasoning is practical reasoning, but *a fortiori* they think it *is* a form of practical reasoning. Hume, however, says Millgram, drawing particularly upon the claim that 'Reason is, and ought only to be the slave of the passions, and can never pretend to any other office than to serve and obey them', rejects even means–end reasoning as a legitimate form of practical reasoning. For Hume, I can, according to Millgram, desire an apple, realize that all I have to do is to pluck it from the tree, have no competing desires, and yet, without irrationality, fail to be motivated to perform the requisite action. Millgram states the real meaning behind Hume's metaphor thus:

> at their whim, the passions send reason searching for information about their objects and the ways of obtaining them. But that information, once obtained, exercises no coercive force whatsoever over the passions: the slave does not issue commands to its masters, or tell them what to do with the information it has gleaned. The passions will do whatever they like, and when they do, their slaves will not be the ones to call them to account.
>
> (ibid.: 80)

On the other hand, Millgram is keen to stress that this view of reason as lacking any dictatorial power over us is nevertheless compatible with its having a causal role in producing action. Thus, he writes:

> What Hume is saying here . . . is that once reasoning has arrived at the judge-ments that are its conclusions, those judgements must be supplemented with passions in order to 'produce any action, or give rise to volition'. And this inter-action of judgement and passion does not count as reasoning.
>
> (ibid.: 80)

Indeed, he thinks that there is no incompatibility at all between attributing this scepticism to Hume and yet taking him to hold that 'my desires are sensitive to my reasoning' (ibid.: 79) so long as this sensitivity is explained in terms of the merely *causal* effectiveness of my judgements. In other words, if my judgements do have an impact on my desires and passions, this is, for Hume, a fortunate accident of my constitution as a human being (Millgram gestures here towards evolutionary advan-tage) and nothing to do with the authority of reason.

It is unclear, however, whether his sceptical interpretation requires, on his view, that the impact of my judgements on my desires be limited to those secondary ones which are relevant to the fulfilment of primary desires, or whether my judgements can be envisaged as themselves arousing the latter. As in the above quotation, Millgram speaks as though these judgements always require, for Hume, supple-mentation by passions or desires, arising independently of the judgements. But he elsewhere concedes that judgements can 'provoke as well as accompany desires', and when he mentions Hume's example in which I come to desire a fruit because I judge it to be pleasant and delicious, he gives no indication that this might be problematic for his sceptical interpretation. Perhaps he takes it (as we earlier suggested was implausible) that for Hume there must here be a pre-existing, free-floating, desire which the judgement only lends direction to. The desire for this *particular* fruit then becomes the kind of secondary one on which Millgram chiefly concentrates.

(ii) Millgram's first attempt to corroborate his 'sceptical' reading

It is not necessary here to offer a justification of Millgram's construal of *instrumentalism*: indeed, it seems to me to be substantially correct, and in what follows I will refer to the – highly counter-intuitive – position he wishes to attribute to Hume as 'anti-instrumentalist'. What must concern us, however, is why we should endorse this 'sceptical', or 'anti-instrumentalist', reading of the 'slave' metaphor. For Millgram, the odd 'lack of fit' between Hume's picture of passion as 'a reclining pasha who sends reason scurrying off to bring back this or that object of desire' and the instrumentalism usually attributed to him is immediately striking. He acknowledges, though, that one cannot rest content with first impressions, and since this reading is so pivotal to his case for Hume's being a sceptic, and not an instrumentalist, he seeks to confirm it by a more indirect route. He suggests that Hume's claim is presented as the conclusion of two adjacent arguments, and that unless it is taken to entail reason's absolute powerlessness to produce practical conclusions, neither argument will be valid. Consider then the first argument which Millgram reconstructs from the text:

1 'The understanding exerts itself after two different ways, as it judges from demonstration or probability'. With only minimal anachronism, we can rephrase this as the claim that all reasoning is either mathematical reasoning, or empirical reasoning about matters of fact.
2 'Abstract or demonstrative reasoning . . . never influences any of our actions'. That is, mathematical reasoning on its own does not produce practical conclusions.
3 Empirical reasoning on its own (or supplemented with mathematical reasoning) does not produce practical conclusions.
4 Therefore, 'reason alone can never produce any action, or give rise to volition'. That is reasoning (or the understanding) does not produce practical conclusions.

(ibid.:77)

For anyone impressed by our discussion in Section 1, the immediate and glaring obstacle to assessing Millgram's claim concerning the validity of this argument is that he evidently treats a qualified denial of reason's ability to produce practical conclusions as equivalent to a categorical one. Indeed, in (2) and (4) both versions of the denial figure alongside each other. The only difference is that, in (2), it is Millgram's paraphrase that carries the qualification whereas, in (4), it is the quotation from the *Treatise*. But isn't this simply to ignore what ought to be staring him in the face: that Hume's qualified denials of reason's influence are one of the major stumbling blocks to his 'sceptical' reading?

One way of easing the difficulty might be to suggest that, in (2) and (3), 'on its own' is just there to indicate that the two types of reasoning of which, according to Hume, reasoning in general is made up, are being considered separately, and in turn. Once it has been established that neither type can 'on its own' influence action, they will be considered together and the qualification dropped. But if this were how Hume is using his terms 'alone' and 'of themselves', then they need not impugn the essentially categorical nature of his ultimate denial that 'reason' can produce practical conclusions. Let us look in more detail at 2.3.3:2–4 from which the argument has been reconstructed, and see whether we can dissolve in this way the force of the Humean qualifications.

A case can certainly be made for saying that Hume (unusually) is using 'alone' at the beginning of paragraph 2 (2.3.3:2) in a way that doesn't impugn the categoricity of his denial of reason's practical influence. For having divided 'the understanding' into two categories – abstract and empirical – he inserts 'alone' after 'reasoning' in the statement 'I believe it scarce will be asserted that the first species of reasoning alone is ever the cause of any action.' In doing this, he seems only to be indicating his intention to consider the two species of reasoning separately, and in turn. Moreover the grounds he goes on to offer for this assertion strongly suggest a categorical reading. Having declared that 'the proper province' of abstract reasoning is the 'world of ideas', whereas volition 'place[s] us in the '[world] of realities', he adds that precisely because they belong to these different worlds, the two are 'totally remov'd from each other'.

However, it is doubtful whether Millgram, given his project of reconciliation, based as it is on the distinction between reason as having a coercive function and as merely being a cause, can afford to welcome this 'two worlds thesis', as I shall call it. For it makes it seem inconceivable that abstract reasoning, having no foothold at all in the 'world of realities', could in any circumstances, and whatever its concomitants in that world, have even a *causal* impact on the events and actions which take place there. Nor is it easy to brush aside, as a temporary lapse on Hume's part, this picture of abstract reasoning as inexorably sealed off in one realm, with passion and action in another. For the picture is re-evoked in subsequent paragraphs though now extended to empirical reasoning or to reasoning in general. Thus, in paragraph 3 – from which Millgram distills his (3) – the impression is given that only desire can galvanize us into action, and that the inert impassive 'discover[y]' of empirical facts is no part of this process. In paragraph 5 (see below) only 'ideas', are said to be amenable to reason, desires and passions as 'original existences' are claimed to be wholly beyond reason's reach.

With regard to the present paragraph, however, the excursion into extreme scepticism proves brief. Moreover, it is followed by remarks where Hume's use of a qualifying adverb *does* seem to impugn the allegedly categorical nature of his denial of reason's practical influence, and which consequently may not appear sceptical *enough* to support Millgram's interpretation. For when Hume illustrates his claim that ''tis not *of themselves* that [mathematics and arithmetic] have any influence', his example suggests that what has been taken as crucially absent in this claim is not merely (as earlier) empirical reasoning, but a '*design'd end or purpose*', without which *neither* empirical, nor mathematical, reasoning, can bear on action. His point here (evidently incompatible both on one extreme with his claim that reason can itself excite passions and on the other with his claim that it is 'perfectly inert') seems to be, not that abstract reasoning never influences action, but that like empirical reasoning it can only do so, if the agent needs it in order to work out how best to achieve an end. As he writes:

> A merchant is desirous of knowing the sum total of his accounts with any person: Why? But that he may learn what sum will have the same effects in

paying his debt, and going to market, as all the particular articles taken together. Abstract or demonstrative reasoning, therefore, never influences any of our actions, but only as it directs our judgement concerning causes and effects.

(2.3.3:2)

Millgram might reply that he does not have to depend upon reading 'alone' as indicating that one type of reasoning is being considered separately from the other type. In any case, he might add, it is clearly impossible to dissolve in this way the force of 'alone', in Hume's summary of his position at 2.3.3:4 – from which Millgram's (4) is derived. For Hume writes, 'reason alone can never produce any action, or give rise to a volition'. But his subject here is now reasoning *in general* so that there can be no question of reading 'alone' as we suggested. There seems therefore no alternative to construing 'alone' here as indicating that reason *can* influence action, though only when supplemented by desire, thus generalizing the claim made specifically of abstract reasoning in paragraph 2.

But, Millgram might now add, provided we take 'influence' both here and in the earlier 'merchant' passage, to indicate simply that reason of whatever kind can, when supplemented by desire, have a causal role in action, then it is possible both to attribute to reason this 'influence' and at the same time deny it the power to produce practical conclusions. For only the latter will signify a power to *dictate* desires and passions. Our myopic fixation on individual words and phrases, such as whether 'alone' does or does not qualify reason, has led us, he might charge, to miss his whole point. For once we distinguish reason's *dictating* our passions (which Hume unlike the instrumentalists rules out), from its merely *causing* them (which he grants), it will easily be seen that it comes to much the same whether or not Hume includes his qualification. Thus, if Hume categorically denies that reason can influence action – that is, whatever it is supplemented with – he has the question of its power to *compel* uppermost in his mind. If, on the other hand, he states that reason *alone* (or of itself, or on its own) cannot influence action, he means that it requires supplementation by desire (over which it has no control) if it is to *cause* action. But to emphasize reason's dependence on these other independent factors if it is to have a causal impact, far from being incompatible with the denial of its *necessary* connection with desire and action, actually entails this denial.

The trouble with thus invoking the distinction between compulsion (or necessity) and causation in order to iron out the discrepancy between Hume's qualified and categorical denials of reason's influence, is that there is no remark, in the passages from which the first argument is reconstructed, on which to hang the distinction. (This is not to mention the fact that the 'two worlds' talk seems actually to rule out even the causal relation which is being asserted.) However, to import the distinction into these passages would be already to assume the method of reconciliation which the argument itself, if successful, is supposed to open up.

Millgram may prefer at this point to propose the second argument as the real basis for Hume's rejection of a necessary (but not a causal) link between reason and passion or action. In scrutinizing this argument, however, we shall be acutely aware that it must now bear the whole burden of corroborating Millgram's 'sceptical', or 'anti-instrumentalist' reading of the 'slave' metaphor.

(iii) A second attempt: the negative aspect of 'original existences'

Millgram gives the argument as follows:

1   'A passion is an original existence'; 'original' is being contrasted with 'representative', so what this means is that passions do not represent anything.
2   Since truth and falsity require representation (the agreement or 'disagreement of ideas, consider'd as copies, with those objects, which they represent'), passions cannot be true or false.
3   Reason concerns itself only with truth and falsity.
4   Therefore, a passion cannot be opposed (or, for that matter, endorsed) by reason; practical states of mind cannot be produced by reasoning.

One thing that can be said in favour of this reconstruction is that it *is* an accurate representation of the relevant paragraph: i.e. paragraph 5. Nevertheless the argument presents insuperable difficulties for anyone aiming to use it to pin on Hume a consistent form of scepticism about practical reason, let alone the particular 'anti-instrumentalist' version which interests Millgram. Oddly, most of these difficulties, as the subsequent paragraphs (paras 6 and 7) bear out, lie in the argument's fecundity. For no less than two different sets of sceptical implications flow from it, depending on whether one focuses on the negative, or the positive, aspect of passion's status as a Humean 'original existence'.

The more sceptical implications flow, as we shall later see, from the *positive* aspect, and are precisely those which, foreshadowed in the 'two worlds' view of paragraph 2, throw doubt on whether Hume consistently held that even a *causal* relation was possible between reason and passion. But Hume's treatment of the, *less* sceptical, implications of the *negative* aspect – on which Millgram concentrates – suggests, that even when he draws back from the 'two worlds' view, it is not to embrace 'anti-instrumentalism'. For, as we saw, such a reading would have him not only asserting that a causal relation holds between reason and passion but, equally crucially, denying a *necessary* relation. What we actually find, however, is a Hume still apparently uncommitted to the causal relation, but not now because he wishes to deny the existence of *any* relation, but rather because he is flirting – or seems to be flirting – with the possibility of a *necessary* relation here. But this would obviously be unthinkable were he really an 'anti-instrumentalist'. Moreover, it is supposed to be precisely this necessary relation that, according to Millgram, the second argument is designed to exclude. Now admittedly, Hume's flirtation is intermittent, being punctuated by what can only be called defiant assertions of passion's opacity to reason, replete with examples illustrating this opacity. However, his point, even here, as we shall now see, only coheres with the 'anti-instrumentalist' reading if it is given an inappropriate and erroneous modern slant.

Millgram's second argument can be slightly expanded as follows. To say that desires and passions are 'original existences' is at least to characterize them negatively as not aiming to represent anything, (1). Thus, unlike beliefs, which *are* representative – e.g. my belief that 'grass is green' represents grass *as* green – they cannot be compared with what they represent in order that they may be declared either true or false, (2). Since reason, for Hume (3.1.1:9), is only the 'discovery of truth and falsehood', and has no other function or mode of operation, (3), desires and passions are immune to reason (4).

In fact, it is already a pretty radical departure from our ordinary understanding to characterize desires and passions in this way as lacking a representative dimension. For were they really to do so, they would resemble pains or other such bodily sensations which plainly do not entail beliefs. But not only do desires, as *we* understand them, typically have an *object*, whereas pains and the like are not *about* anything, but we desire that object *under a particular description* which gives our reason for wanting it. To take Hume's own example, I desire the fruit I see from far off because 'I fancy it to be pleasant and delicious'. Likewise, with the possible exception of so-called 'nameless' fear, or dread, when we are frightened, we are frightened *of something*. Moreover, this 'transparency' to reason of passions and emotions is enshrined in the idea that they have 'formal objects'. Thus, my fear of flying, as opposed to my (irrational) phobia about flying, is only properly comprehensible if I really believe (even irrationally) that flying is dangerous.

It is this logical dependence of desires, and emotions, on beliefs that allows us to talk without strain of fear evaporating when it is realized that what was feared is not really dangerous, or again of desire ceasing when it is realized that the desired object does not fulfil the description under which it was desired. Hume himself remarks that when a person realizes that the fruit which from far off she desired is, on closer inspection 'really disagreeable', she will simply cease to desire it. But were fear and desire to altogether lack cognitive content, this kind of talk would be as odd as if I were to claim that I got a headache when, and only when, I had a certain belief, and that my headache could be made to disappear but only provided the belief was refuted.

Now Hume is clearly aware of this discrepancy between his negative characterization of passions as non-representative, and their apparent responsiveness to reason. His attitude, however, to this responsiveness is, as I have intimated, complicated and fluctuating. At the start of paragraph 6, he regards it as posing a difficulty for his account which must be dealt with. He tries to persuade us therefore that it isn't really a responsiveness *of the passions* at all, but of the 'judgement or opinion' which 'accompany' them. Thus, according to him, when reason 'pronounces' the judgement associated with a passion false, it is the judgement, which disintegrates, the accompanying passion simply collapsing with it in a kind of domino effect.

By the middle of the paragraph what started out as essentially a defensive move has evidently turned into an attack. For he has now come to see the limitedness of this responsiveness of passions to reason (which he has just told us is really of the accompanying beliefs) as an opportunity to press home the positive claim that passions are independent of reason. But no sooner has he embarked on this defiantly sceptical course than he applies his brakes sharply, speaking of 'unreasonable' passions as those which are *'founded on'*, rather than (as before) merely 'accompany'd by', false judgements. Thus, he appears to recreate the very impression of logical relatedness between judgement and passion which the earlier use of 'accompanied by' was designed to dispel. The passions, and desires, moreover, which he goes on to cite as evading the 'unreasonable' epithet, are not, as one might perhaps have expected, those lacking *any* foundation in judgement, but those founded on *true* judgements. It may seem bizarre, Hume admits, that I should prefer 'my total ruin' to 'the least uneasiness of an Indian or person wholly unknown to me', or again that I should 'prefer even my own acknowledg'd lesser good to my greater, and have a more ardent affection for the former than the latter'. But so long as the factual judgements are correct on which my preference is based, this preference is not 'contrary to reason'. Though Hume returns at the end of the paragraph to his original claim that 'unreasonable' passions are merely 'accompanied by' false judgements, he has hardly followed a consistent policy in expunging their representative dimension, but has wavered backward and forward under the guise of demonstrating their independence of reason.

But, Millgram might object, the sceptical import of the paragraph can be preserved, if we will simply turn a blind eye to Hume's talk of the passions being 'founded on' judgements, as a kind of temporary aberration, and mentally replace it with his earlier 'accompanied by'. After all, does not Hume switch back and forth between these different expressions throughout this and the subsequent paragraph, suggesting that for him nothing important hangs on the substitution of one for the other? Also, though he holds that passions based on false beliefs can be 'condemned by the understanding', he does not say that passions based on *true* beliefs can be *justified* by it. On the contrary, he plainly states that the understanding can *'neither justify nor* condemn' these passions. But this is surely a clear indication that they are, for him, beyond reason's reach, and are so because, like pains and other such sensations, they lack a cognitive content.

Hume's scepticism, it might now be concluded, amounts to a denial that there is a *necessary* link between reason and the passions. The *causal* link Hume posits between them, and which explains the passions' apparent sensitivity to reason, is (necessarily) between logically distinct items. Consequently, far from this link being inconsistent with Hume's scepticism it *entails* such a scepticism. Of course, human nature being what it is, 'the prospect of pain . . . from any object' will cause 'the emotion of aversion' just as '[the prospect of] pleasure' will cause '[the emotion of] . . . propensity', and a 'trivial good' will generally 'produce' a lesser desire in us than a significant one. But it does not follow *logically* from the fact that I perceive that the fruit before me is ripe, and so expect that eating it will be a pleasant experience, that I *must*, even in the absence of competing desires, desire it. As Millgram puts it: 'judgements are causally effective in producing and removing passions' (1995: 78) but 'these connections between reasoning and the passions are not enough to make the reasoning genuinely practical' (ibid.: 79). I want now to show that Millgram's case against Hume being an instrumentalist involves unwarrantedly extending – and with far-fetched results – this already unacceptable interpretation.

Suppose, to recap on the 'anti-instrumentalist' position, I was originally led to desire a pear because I thought it looked ripe, and would be sweet and juicy. I soon, however, discover that it isn't ripe, and so won't be sweet and juicy, nor is there anything else in my eyes to recommend it. Now whereas, according to Millgram, an instrumentalist would hold that I must in these circumstances cease to desire the pear, Hume, Millgram claims, holds that I might still continue to desire the pear. Again, suppose I desire a pear, and believing that the only place I can get one is at the supermarket two blocks away, acquire a desire to go there. I learn, however, that they are out of stock. Millgram's Hume, unlike the instrumentalist, allows that I may still continue to desire to go there, even though there is nothing else for me to go there *for*.

In attributing this anti-instrumentalist stance to Hume, Millgram cites Hume's claim both in this passage (para. 6), and later at 3.1.1:12, that it is only in 'a figurative and improper way of speaking' that we can call passions associated with false judgements unreasonable. In fact, however, Hume is talking here solely of cases where the person experiencing the passion *does not know* his judgement is false; his passion is called unreasonable *because* (and only because) it is based on a *false* belief. Millgram's cases are crucially, if subtly, different – and one might say much more modern – being about the *recalcitrance* of certain of my passions and desires *even when I know* that the judgement on which they were originally based, and which justified them, is false.

Indeed, it is worth observing that Hume may well be thought to have considerably more good sense here than Millgram's interpretation would allow. For though we might balk at calling it 'unreasonable', as Hume does, for someone, to feel, say, pride, on the basis of a false belief concerning her achievements – a belief which it is nevertheless in the circumstances entirely reasonable for her to have – the phenomenon is well known and commonplace. However, the kind of behaviour that Millgram would have Hume countenancing here is so bizarre – so perverse – as to only seem plausible at all if it is conflated with certain types of neurotic or addictive responses, or if unconscious motives are invoked. The idea of someone continuing, even when he finds out it will taste bitter, to desire a fruit which he only desired in the first place because he thought it would be sweet, and not bitter, is incomprehensible unless we invoke psychological forces operating within him that he knows nothing about. Likewise the person who goes on wanting to do something which he *once* thought was the means to a desired end, *even* when he knows it can lead nowhere, and even though he still passionately wants the end, has more in common with the obsessive-compulsive hand washer, whose plight is precisely that she knows her hands are clean, than with any ordinary person.

But it is not just that Hume does not mean by 'unreasonable' passions recalcitrant ones, he evidently supposes (not being acquainted with modern psycho-analysis) such recalcitrance to be inconceivable. Thus, when he comes to talk in the subsequent paragraph 7, of what *does* happen when a person finds out that the judgement on which her passion, or desire, is based is false, it is precisely to exclude this recalcitrance:

> *The moment* we perceive the falshood of any supposition, or the insufficiency of any means our passions *yield to* our reason *without any opposition*. I may desire any fruit as of an excellent relish; but *whenever* you convince me of my mistake, my longing ceases. I may will the performance of certain actions as means of obtaining any desir'd good; but as my willing of these actions is only secondary, and *founded on* the supposition, that they are causes of the propos'd effect; *as soon as* I discover the falshood of that supposition, they *must* become indifferent to me.
>
> (my italics)

But if a passion's recalcitrance is excluded in such a pointed way, if it 'yields', and *must* yield, 'without any opposition', once the 'falshood' of the underlying 'supposition' is realized, we can surely only conclude that Hume means what he says when he describes passions as 'founded on' judgements, and that, for him, the two are linked necessarily.

At this point Millgram will perhaps retort that, if Hume's illustrations show anything at all, it is that, as the Humean slogan goes, *'any* desire can go with *any* belief'. Surely then there is nothing to stop us extrapolating from this distinctive Humean claim to the possibility of recalcitrant desires. Hume's examples do indeed suggest that there are no constraints on the type of description under which we can *originally* desire a thing (though even here, significantly, he does not countenance desires untied to *any* description). But this is not quite the same as to say that, though we originally desired a thing only because, say, we expected it to taste sweet, and not bitter (we hate bitter things), we might still continue to desire it, even after we discover that it will taste bitter. If, however, despite granting these distinctions, Millgram is still intent on extrapolating from the illustrations in paragraph 6 to the possibility of recalcitrant desires, we are owed, I think, an answer to the question why Hume, in the subsequent paragraph, apparently does everything in his power to block such an extrapolation.

(iv) The positive aspect of 'original existences'

Since desires and passions, as Humean 'original existences', lack a representative dimension, it can apparently make no sense to talk of comparing them with the facts in order to ascertain their truth value. It follows that they are not, and cannot be, directly amenable to reason, which Hume states, is simply 'the discovery of truth or falshood'. This does not, for him, rule out their being *caused* by those beliefs, or judgements, on which reason *can* decisively operate. Indeed, as we have seen, Hume provides examples of this causal interaction. But if reason shows a given judgement to be false, and this judgement was in the first place what caused us to have a certain desire, or passion, it would seem that reason *can* after all have an impact – at least an indirect causal one – on these desires and passions.

But this leaves something vital out of the story. For, as I intimated earlier, when Hume characterizes desires and passions as 'original existences' he is not just characterizing them *negatively* as non-representative. The Humean notion of an 'original existence' has a *positive* dimension. This is brought out when, implicitly comparing passions to beliefs, he writes (para. 5): 'When I am angry I am actually possest with the passion, and in that emotion have no more a reference to any other object, than when I am thirsty, or sick, or more than five foot high.' Crucially therefore, if passions *were* representative they would only be *copies* of 'original existences', whereas they *are* themselves the 'original facts and realities' (3.1.1:9) of which *beliefs*, or *ideas*, are the copies. But this distinction between ideas, on the one hand, and such 'original facts or realities', on the other, is precisely that lying, as we saw, at the heart of Hume's 'two worlds' view; but between these two worlds even causal interaction seemed inconceivable.

Stroud (1977: 160) offers a gloss on Hume's thinking here. If something is 'compleat [in itself]' as only 'original existences' or 'modifications of existence' are, it has a location in space and time. But then it can only be causally affected by something else which has a location in space and time: in other words, another 'original existence' or 'modification of existence', which is likewise therefore 'compleat in itself'. But how can reason as 'just the totality of objects of reason, a set of propositions [having] no location in space and time', be thus 'compleat in itself'? But then how can it have a causal influence, even indirectly, on desire, passion, or action which *are* 'compleat in themselves'?

One can do no more than speculate as to the answer to the question why Hume seems intent on blocking any extrapolation from examples, apparently illustrating the independence of passion from judgement, to the possibility of recalcitrant passions. Is it perhaps that Hume, alarmed by the extreme scepticism that he has backed himself into, has temporarily bracketed passions with the relevant judgements in order not to have to deal with the destructive consequences of his 'two world' view for the causal relation that he has posited between reason and passions? If this were correct, the claim that passions 'yield', and must yield absolutely, and without resistance, to reason would be poised between two wholly different meanings. Bracketing the passions along with the relevant judgement, the 'yielding' in question would appear to be of the logical kind which occurs when the judgement itself is found to be false. Thinking, however, of passions as belonging to the 'world of realities', their lack of resistance would now signify the utter inconceivability of their having any effect at all at the level of ideas. This effacement, indeed, would only be matched by that of reason from the 'world of realities', of which Hume writes in a surprisingly similar vein: 'having no original influence, 'tis impossible it can withstand any principle which has such an influence, *or ever keep the mind in suspense a moment*' (para. 4, my italics).

I have here merely floated a suggestion – a suggestion which will hardly be attractive to those intent on finding a consistent reading of the passages discussed, and who will look upon it as not merely fanciful, but as a premature admission of defeat. In fact, though the last attempt has foundered, we are still nowhere near the end of the road in our search for a reconciliation of the apparently conflicting strands in Hume's thought. There are important leads that ought to be followed up: most crucially concerning the distinction, if any, between reason and belief. For instance, is belief really to be brought under the umbrella of reason as 'an object of reason' or is it rather itself 'an original existence' like the passions? And if the latter, might it not be suggested, as a way of resolving the original contradiction, that, though it is *reason* of which Hume is speaking when he states that it *cannot* move us to action, it is *belief* he has in mind when he states that it *can* do so (if only with desire or passion)? But to get to grips with this issue it would be necessary to extend our inquiry back, beyond Book 2, to Book 1. In the next chapter, I prefer to explore a less costly option. Returning to Book 3, and the practicality argument itself, I ask whether the more obscure reading of premiss 2 – that 'reason cannot conceivably move us to action' – might simply be eliminated on grounds that the argument's validity can be sustained by using just the reading that 'reason can move us to action, but only with the help of desire'.

2 Validity and the 'Moderate' Version

1 A requirement for validity

An example of a pair of formulations of the practicality argument, with implicitly contradictory second premisses, are the first and sixth, which Hume sets out at 3.1.1:6 and 10 respectively. Together with my italicized paraphrases, making the contradiction explicit, they can be reconstructed as follows:

> Premiss 1: Morals have an influence on the actions and affections.
> Premiss 2: Reason alone can never have any such influence. [*Reason has an influence, but only with the help of desire, which in turn requires reason.*]
> Conclusion: It follows they [morals] cannot be deriv'd from reason.

> Premiss 1: Conscience or a sense of morals [is an] active principle.
> Premiss 2: Reason is wholly inactive. [*Reason has, and can have, no influence over action.*]
> Conclusion: [Reason] can never be the source of [conscience or a sense of morals].

With these versions of the argument before us, however, our proposed strategy of seeing whether its validity can be sustained, just by using the first – or as I shall now call it – 'moderate' reading of the second premiss, may immediately seem unfeasible. For the version in which the second premiss is thus 'moderately' interpreted – let us call it the 'moderate' version – is, as it stands, *in*valid. Its first premiss says no more than that moral judgements have an influence on action, yet its second premiss states as much of reason. Admittedly, reason, even on this reading, only influences action with the help of desire but, for all premiss 1 says – it doesn't, after all, say that moral judgements influence action *all on their own* – moral judgements might also require this help. Indeed, so obvious is this invalidity that writers such as Harrison (1976: 11),[1] espousing (our) 'moderate' version, have been led to comment on Hume's puzzling confusion over what his first premiss needs to be in order to entail the conclusion: 'The proposition [Hume] needs to prove a conclusion – that moral beliefs *alone* move us to action – and the proposition he adduces evidence for – that moral beliefs *do* move us to action – are totally different.'

By contrast, the second, or 'extreme', version of the argument is already, and without further ado, valid. For here the first premiss does unequivocally assert of moral judgements what the second premiss denies of reason, namely that it has an influence on action, and so moral judgements and reason are contrasted in just the way required for the conclusion to follow from the premisses. Why, then, should we even bother to try and patch up the 'moderate' version?

As we saw earlier, this version, reflecting the instrumentalist strand in Hume's thought, is based on a theory of motivation with which we are not only familiar, but to which, since it is the dominant theory today, we may well already subscribe. By contrast, the claim entailed by the second premiss on the 'extreme' reading, namely that reason can have no influence at all on action, is at least obscure, if not, as many hold, absurd or 'obviously false' (Harrison, 1976: 11). Before therefore embarking on the lengthy task of trying to illuminate this claim – perhaps by uncovering a network of ideas against the background of which it would make sense – and then somehow defending it, we should be certain that the 'moderate' version of the argument cannot be salvaged.

One requirement for the practicality argument's validity is, in fact, already implicit in the contrast just drawn between the 'moderate' and 'extreme' versions. It is, moreover, one to which both are subject: the first premiss must at least assert of the relation between moral judgement and action what the second premiss denies of that between reason and action. On the 'extreme' version, whose second premiss denies any role to reason in action, this requirement – let us call it (i) – can be met, and the argument's validity secured, simply by taking premiss 1 to make the uncontroversial claim that moral judgements have *some* role in moving us to action.

On the 'moderate' version, however, whose second premiss concedes a necessary role to reason, or belief,[2] this requirement has to be qualified. For whatever the first premiss asserts about moral judgement's relation, it will now have to be possible for the second premiss to deny of belief's relation, to action, while still leaving room for belief to have this necessary role. Let us call this modified requirement (i[1]). To fulfil it, premiss 1 will have to assert that a specially close relation holds between moral judgement and action. This relation will have in fact to be so close that a similar relation can be denied to hold between belief and action, without ruling out their being causally connected.

But it should by now be apparent that, even were this requirement to be fulfilled – suppose, for instance, that premiss 1 was amended so that it entailed that moral judgements could, on their own, influence action – the 'moderate' version would still be invalid. For even if it were true (by premiss 2) that no belief could, on its own, influence action (but required desire), the conclusion would only be that moral judgements could not be matters of belief alone, not that they could not involve belief at all.

Before hastening to the argument's rescue with a further requirement – possibly even more difficult to fulfil than the first – it is worth considering whether there is not some way, compatible with Hume's intentions, of weakening his conclusion to the point where the premisses, once restated so as merely to fulfil requirement (i[1]), would already entail this conclusion. In other words, could it plausibly be maintained that Hume only means to deny that morality is a matter of belief *alone*?

But, it might sceptically be asked: do we need, or indeed can we ever have, a straight answer to this question? Certainly, a glance at the literature suggests that it has become acceptable for writers, attributing to Hume the 'moderate' version, to vacillate over its conclusion. Thus, while evidently wishing to endorse on his behalf the stronger conclusion (which, as we have seen, only follows on the 'extreme' version), they convert it to the weaker one at crucial junctures in their expositions. An example[3] is Mackie (1980: 51). He first gives Hume's conclusion as 'morality is not based on reason', and again as 'moral distinctions are not derived from reason', Drawing attention to the ambiguities surrounding Hume's use of reason, he nevertheless goes so far as to entertain the possibility that it maybe meant to cover having any beliefs whatsoever. In this case, Hume's conclusion could be 'an explicitly non-descriptive (emotive or prescriptive) analysis of moral judgements'. A little later, however, (ibid.: 53), with a 'moderate' reading of premiss 2 clearly in view – 'knowledge, beliefs and reasoning (of any kinds) *alone* do not influence action' – he restates the conclusion. But now it has the following form: 'the state of mind [expressed by a moral judgement] . . . does not consist *wholly* of knowledge, beliefs, and reasoning of any kinds' (my italics). This is strictly compatible with moral judgements being just a combination of reason and desire, or even with them being essentially matters of reason.

But the indecision of writers like Mackie over what Hume's conclusion either is, or ought to be, in order to secure the argument's validity, on their 'moderate' version, may well seem a consequence of that more fundamental failure to recognize the original contradiction in Hume's formulations of the second premiss, discussed in my previous chapter. It is as though they are vaguely aware that, were they to espouse unequivocally, rather than as they do merely equivocally, the 'moderate' reading of the second premiss, they would have to admit that the argument, even with a strengthened first premiss ('moral judgements *all on their own* influence action'), only entailed the 'weaker' conclusion. But they really wish to subscribe (as Humeans themselves) or to represent Hume as subscribing, to the stronger conclusion, which *would*, after all, be justified without more ado, were they to espouse the 'extreme' reading. Since, however, they have not fully emancipated their 'moderate', from this 'extreme', reading of premiss 2, they shuffle backwards and forwards between the two formulations of the conclusion. This vacillation, it goes without saying, is not open to us.

2 Don't weaken the conclusion!

(i) Morality – not a matter of reason alone

At least one bit of evidence, taken from his original exposition of the practicality argument, may seem to suggest that Hume would be content with the 'weaker' conclusion that morality is not a matter of belief *alone*. In formulating the argument for the third time (3.1.1:7), his conclusion is merely this: ''Tis in vain to pretend that morality is discover'd *only* by a deduction of reason' (my italics).

The difficulty is that he states the conclusion in this weaker form on only one out of the seven occasions on which he completely formulates the argument.

Moreover, when he does so, it is not apparently in order to ensure the argument's validity, when the second premiss is construed 'moderately'. For on the occasion in question his second premiss happens to be a flat denial of reason's influence over action, and as we can see from the complete formulation set out below, the argument as a whole is now *in*valid precisely because the conclusion has this weaker form:

Premiss 2: Reason has no influence on our passions and actions.

Conclusion: 'Tis in vain to pretend that morality is discover'd only by a deduction of reason.

Premiss 1: [Morality is] an active principle [and an active principle can never be founded on an inactive].

(ii) Reason enters by the back door

There is, we are now likely to be reminded, another source of evidence for how strongly Hume might want the conclusion of his practicality argument to be taken: this is the positive account of morality he expounds in the following, and subsequent, sections (strictly, from 3.1.1:26 onwards). It will be admitted, of course, that his initial pronouncements, in this constructive phase, suggest a wholly sentimental picture. Hume writes (3.1.2:3) that 'the distinguishing impressions, by which moral good or evil is known, are nothing but particular pains and pleasures', and again that 'To have the sense of virtue, is nothing but to *feel* a satisfaction of a particular kind from the contemplation of a character.' Nevertheless does he not, it will be asked, in his subsequent detailed working out of the positive account (and possibly under pressure of being true to ordinary moral experience) let reason in again by the back door?

Two areas have been flagged as problematic for attributing to Hume a *wholly* sentimental account of morality. The first is his construal of the relation between the feeling of 'satisfaction' (or 'uneasiness'), which is evoked in us by the contemplation of an action, or character, and our 'pronouncing' it virtuous (or vicious). In fact, Hume does not *always* identify the two. Certain of his remarks suggest that moral pronouncements – perhaps in implicit acknowledgement that they are in form at least assertions, capable of truth or falsity – are something over and above the feeling. But the question then arises just what, on Hume's view, this extra thing is. One remark in particular has been read[4] as implicitly committing him to the view that moral judgements are, after all, statements of belief, namely about the speaker's own feelings on contemplating the relevant action or character trait: 'So . . . when you pronounce any action or character to be vicious, you mean nothing, but that from the constitution of your nature you have a feeling or sentiment of blame from the contemplation of it' (3.1.1:26).

But this remark is an isolated one, and so we may not wish to put too much weight on it. Also it might be interpreted as implying, not that expressing a moral judgement is stating a belief about one's feelings,[5] but rather that it is (what we would call) a first person avowal of feeling. The latter interpretation may be preferred when it is recalled that 'feelings', as Hume uses the term, is more properly rendered by our 'sensations'. To speak of belief in this context therefore might be thought to foist on Hume a conceptually odd view: one which would also allow talk of a person doubting what their immediate sensations were, or even of trying to infer them, as a spectator might, on the basis of evidence.[6]

Other remarks have been cited[7] as taking more seriously, than is consonant with Hume's emphasis on inner feeling as the core of morality, the fact that our moral pronouncements ostensibly ascribe qualities, e.g. viciousness, to (in Hume's terminology) 'objects'. For instance, he speaks (3.1.2:2) of the 'impression *arising from* virtue' as 'agreeable', and that '*proceeding from* vice to be uneasy' (my italics). Again, he offers (E:289) the following 'definition' of virtue: 'Whatever mental action or quality gives to a spectator the pleasing sentiment of approbation'.

Hume could perhaps have expressed himself less misleadingly here. For instance, he could, when making the latter remark, have indicated that he was only talking about what we call 'virtue', as he does when, at *Treatise* 3.3.1:30, he claims that, 'Every quality of mind is *denominated* virtuous which gives pleasure by the mere survey' (my italics). Even so, there seems little justification for reading into either remark the idea that the distinctive feeling of pleasure associated with moral approbation is caused by virtue, where that in turn is construed as an objective quality of the action, or character trait, in view. Hume certainly thinks that the actions, or characters, from the contemplation of which 'we reap a pleasure' have, as a matter of fact, common properties, such as their usefulness to society. Moreover, he thinks that once it is clear which actions are thus approved, philosophers (as opposed to ordinary people engaged in making moral judgements) can set about trying to discover what these properties are. But the whole thrust of his analysis is to distinguish these objective properties from virtue. For though these properties are, as he points out at 3.3.1:30, the 'sources' from which our pleasure arises,[8] there is nothing special to e.g. usefulness to society, which could logically dictate that we feel this pleasure when contemplating socially useful actions. Indeed, we might have been so constituted that we did not feel it, and we might still cease to do so. The feeling of pleasure must therefore itself occupy morality's foreground.[9]

But couldn't Hume's stress on this feeling be preserved by suggesting[10] that, while admittedly we do not mean by virtue an independently identifiable quality (like usefulness), we do mean by it the quality whatever it is which causes the feeling? But if so, the judgement that an action was virtuous could only be verified by seeing whether the action really possessed a quality with the alleged causal powers. But Hume dismisses such a process of verification as in any way relevant to the ordinary business of making moral judgements. Thus, he expressly points out that, once we have felt the distinctive satisfaction which is our praise, 'We go no farther: nor do we enquire into the cause of the satisfaction' (3.1.2:3). He adds that we 'do not infer a character to be virtuous, because it pleases: But in feeling that it pleases after such a particular manner, we in effect feel that it is virtuous.' Virtue must, he therefore seems to imply, be the feeling of pleasure itself projected[11] on to the outside world. This is made still clearer in his famous remark (3.1.1:26) comparing vice and virtue to 'sounds, colours, heat and cold which, according to modern philosophy, are not qualities in objects, but perceptions in the mind'.[12]

The other area in which reason may seem to get a foothold[13] is Hume's attempt to distinguish moral feelings from other kinds of painful and pleasant feelings. For a feeling to count as moral, he stipulates, we must contemplate the action (or character trait), which arouses it, from a special point of view. This point of view must not only be disinterested, but also one in which we have compensated for the object's nearness, or remoteness, in time or place. In this way, Hume seeks to explain why, though the love that virtuous actions arouse in us is much greater when their author is a close friend than when she is a stranger, or a remote historical figure, our moral esteem does not similarly fluctuate. In order, however, to stabilize our viewpoint, we have according to Hume, to make certain inferences from what we have observed on past occasions (rather as when, seeing a tiny object on the horizon, we estimate it to be large). Moral feelings therefore (in so far as they are *actual* feelings) are, it would seem, arrived at by a process of inductive reasoning.

Our method of inquiry, however, has an advantage not shared by those commentators who allow it to remain equivocal whether Hume (in formulating his practicality argument) holds that reason is 'inert', or has a role – a necessary, if subordinate, one – in action. For, having disambiguated these two readings, we are presently concentrating unequivocally on the second, 'moderate', one. But we shall hardly be disconcerted[14] to find that Hume, in the detailed working out of his account of morality, accords to reason the very same motivating role anticipated by this 'moderate' reading. The question is only whether he goes beyond it, in allowing reason a role at least equal, if not superior, to that of feeling. But it is not immediately obvious which parts of the detailed working out would count as evidence of this. The mere fact that he does not always identify moral judgements with feelings is scarcely enough. But nor – on its own – is the implication of some of his claims that these judgements are part of a more complex moral 'process' involving beliefs and reasoning. One would have to show that he does not partition off, and has no way (even metaphorically) of partitioning off, this reasoning from the central core of feeling.[15]

But isn't the point, it will be retorted, this: since moral feelings are those we think we would experience if we adopted Hume's general point of view, they cannot be, for him, actual feelings at all, but are merely hypothetical? Since only actual feelings are really feelings, Hume has, by reintroducing reason here, effectively excised feelings altogether from morality. But who is to say that we might not, in some sense or other, even if only temporarily, actually adopt a disinterested and impartial point of view, and so actually experience the requisite feelings.

Perhaps the thought is[16] that these can't be actual feelings because they are arrived at by a process of reasoning, and Hume holds that reason, being 'inert' cannot itself engender feelings. But this is a view we have challenged: Hume, as we have seen, states on more than one occasion that reason can excite passion. Of course, he does also say, on other occasions, that reason is 'inert'. But again we must remember that we are assuming here the 'moderate' account of reason's role in motivation, having disentangled it from the 'extreme' one, and so these 'extreme' remarks need not detain us any longer.

I shall therefore take it that, though in the detailed working out, Hume represents morality as less insulated from reason than his initial characterizations in this constructive phase might have led us to expect, there is still here no firm basis for abandoning the stronger reading of the practicality argument's conclusion. This view, moreover, is supported by the literature. In fact, there are scarcely any commentators who, once they turn to Hume's constructive phase, do not acknowledge the unambiguous clarity of Hume's central contention concerning the sentimental nature of morality. Mackie, for instance, states (1980: 64) that, for Hume, 'the essential fact of the matter, when virtue is distinguished from vice, . . . is simply that people have different feelings or sentiments with regard to them'. Stroud (1977: 186) goes further, emphasising that, for Hume, 'the impotence of reason and the force of sentiment in morality is Hume's most important point'. Moreover, these commentators, though they suggest that Hume's detailed working out of his positive account of morality is not fully consistent with his initial characterizations of it as 'nothing but' feeling, reject the idea that he ever contemplated reintroducing reason in anything more than a subordinate role (see, particularly, Stroud, 1977: 192).

Suppose this is conceded, but that it is now suggested that the practicality argument, like Hume's other negative arguments, is only meant to get us part of the way to that fully negative conclusion – that morality has no basis in reason – which would entail the strong positive conclusion that it is just feeling. For instance, Hume only manages to refute the claim (3.1.1:26) that morality is not 'any matter of fact, which can be discover'd by the understanding', by offering an independent proof from introspection, that it is essentially a matter of desire or feeling.

But it is just not true that Hume looks upon his negative arguments as requiring to be supplemented by independent positive claims, as though they were not already authoritative in their own right. Quite the contrary: he explicitly states that no further argumentative step is required in order to reach his positive characterization of morality from his negative arguments. The findings concerning morality, yielded by his negative arguments, together with that fundamental axiom of his system according to which perceptions are either impressions or ideas, he tells us at 3.1.2:1, logically entail this positive characterization:

> Our decisions concerning moral rectitude and depravity are evidently perceptions; and as all perceptions are either impressions or ideas, the exclusion of the one is a convincing argument for the other. Morality therefore is more properly felt than judg'd of.

Nor is there any reason to suppose that Hume regarded the practicality argument as any less decisive in its own right than his other negative arguments. Moreover, to suggest otherwise would be to dramatically revise the order of importance in which his negative arguments have come to be viewed by today's cognitivists and non-cognitivists, whose interest and attention are exclusively focussed on the practicality argument.

(iii) 'Feeling' versus 'desire'

If this brief excursion into Hume's positive account suggests that we are right to state the practicality argument's conclusion in the 'stronger' form, does it not at the same time have the unexpected, and unsettling, consequence of undermining the identification, in the conclusion, of moral judgements with desires? For it surely cannot have escaped notice that in discussing this positive account, the word 'feeling', or 'sentiment', has everywhere replaced 'desire'.

It is perfectly true that, in his constructive phase, Hume speaks of morality as, and only as, a matter of feeling or sentiment. Nor is it merely that he does not speak of desires in this context, he does not speak either of passions. In fact, it is only such natural, non-moral, motives as benevolence which he describes in the latter way. Nevertheless I think we are justified in taking the aim of the practicality argument itself to be to show that moral judgements are, positively speaking, matters of desire. This is because, not only in the section where he formulates his practicality argument, but also when expounding his theory of motivation in Book 2 (to which he refers back in Book 3) what he expressly opposes to reason, or belief, is desire, preference or passion, not feeling or sentiment.

We should beware, however, of taking it for granted that when Hume comes to speak, in the constructive phase, of morality as feeling, this feeling must necessarily be desire, despite his earlier intention to forge a link between morality and desire. Certainly, for Hume all desires are feelings. However, not all feelings are desires. (We shall later see – a point of great significance for us – that he even sometimes speaks of belief as a feeling.) It is not even the case that, for Hume, all passions are desires since he distinguishes between 'direct' and 'indirect' passions, and only assigns desires to the former category. Moral sentiments, on the other hand, in so far as they are passions, seem to fall into the 'indirect' category. There is then a gap between the picture of morality that can be inferred from his negative arguments, and that which emerges in his constructive phase. We can do no more at this stage than simply register this disparity, while retaining 'desire' in the formulation of the practicality argument's conclusion.

With the 'stronger' reading of its conclusion decisively reinstated, we are now in a position to say with authority that a second requirement is needed if we are finally to secure the validity of the 'moderate' version.

(iv) A second requirement

To recap on what was said at the beginning of the chapter, requirement (i^1) stipulated that premiss 1 must assert a relation between moral judgements and action so close that it could still be denied of belief while leaving room for belief to have a necessary role. Now the second requirement arises in part out of the fulfilment of this first one, since belief's role in motivation can only be acknowledged, and accommodated, as the first specifies, provided this does not then compromise the identification of moral judgements with (or essentially with) *desires*. Adding this requirement – let us call it (ii) – to requirement (i^1), we have this compound requirement:

Whatever premiss 1 asserts of the relation between moral judgements and motivation, must:

(i^1) *not* be true of the relation between belief and motivation postulated by premiss 2, yet belief must still be necessary

but must:

(ii) *be true* of the relation between desire and motivation.

Unless (ii), as well as (i^1), is fulfilled, entailing a corresponding *a*symmetry between beliefs and desires in their relation to motivation, it will be difficult, as we suggested, to see why desires should be any more closely associated with moral judgements than beliefs. It follows that the 'moderate' version of the practicality argument must, if it is to be valid, have this general form:

> Premiss 1: Moral judgements have a specially close relation with motivation.
> Premiss 2: Beliefs are necessary, alongside desire, for motivation, *but only desires are related to motivation in the specially close way that moral judgements are.*
> Conclusion: Moral judgements are not beliefs but desires.[17]

3 'Sufficiency', 'intrinsicality' and the first premiss

(i) Reinterpreting the 'moderate' version

There are two major ways of restating premiss 1, with corresponding adjustments to premiss 2, which would enable the argument at least to meet requirement (i^1). These differ as to whether the relation asserted between moral judgements and action is merely causal or necessary (in the sense of non-contingent). For instance, on (what I shall call) the 'sufficiency' reinterpretation, which falls into the first category, the first premiss will entail that moral judgements are, or can be, causally *sufficient on their own* for motivation. Thus, on this reinterpretation, (to take a contemporary example) if I have made the judgement that I morally ought to give to famine relief, then this could be (causally) sufficient on its own to lead me, in appropriate circumstances, e.g. on seeing a famine relief box, to act, e.g. drop money in. But the second premiss can deny this of belief so ensuring the requisite contrast, without conflicting with the claim, entailed by the 'moderate' reading of premiss 2, that a belief is nevertheless required if action is to occur.

Turning to the second category, premiss 1 now asserts that the relation between moral judgements and action is necessary, in contrast to the merely contingent relation which, on these reinterpretations, holds between belief and action. The necessity in question can itself – at least in principle – be understood in two different senses. On (what I shall call) the 'intrinsicality' interpretation, premiss 1 builds motivation into the very idea of moral judgement. To say of someone that she judges that she ought to give to famine relief, now therefore logically entails that she behaves in the required way; if she neglects the opportunity to give to famine relief, it cannot truly be said of her that she has made this moral judgement. But premiss 2 can still deny that there is any such conceptual link between belief and motivation without putting at risk the merely factual link that is implicit in the 'moderate' reading of this premiss.[18]

On the 'mandatory'[19] reinterpretation, however, if I have made the judgement that I morally ought to give to famine relief, then this constrains me to, or makes me, act in the relevant way, whatever I may want to do. But for the second premiss to deny that a mere belief could exert any such distinctive peremptory force is once again not to deny that we have to have a relevant belief, as well as a desire, if we are to be moved to action.

Two questions now urgently arise. One is whether all these reinterpretations, or indeed any, enable the argument to meet the second requirement (concerning belief–desire asymmetry). Clearly unless they do, the argument's invalidity will not be repaired. The other concerns their coherence with Hume's intentions: can any of them really be advanced as plausible reinterpretations of Hume? It will not always be possible to keep the two issues separate. I begin by considering the 'sufficiency' reinterpretation.

(ii) 'Sufficiency': opening a loop-hole

Hume's first premiss, on the 'sufficiency' reinterpretation posits an ordinary causal relation between moral judgements and motivation, or action. But it is precisely such a relation – the only kind that, for Hume, holds between events in the natural world, or can be verified from ordinary experience – that he himself seems to have in mind when providing support for the first premiss. He points out, for instance, at 3.1.1:5, that if 'morality had *naturally* no influence on human passions and actions, 'twere in vain to take such pains to inculcate it: and nothing wou'd be more fruitless than that multitude of rules and precepts, with which all moralists abound' (my italics). Again he appeals to 'common experience' which he states 'informs us, that men are often govern'd by their duties, and are deter'd from some actions by the opinion of injustice, and impell'd to others by that of obligation'. To this extent then the 'sufficiency' reinterpretation seems to be closely in accord with Hume's intentions, but can anything more be said in favour of it? Is the argument, on this reinterpretation, even valid?

Consider a preliminary formulation:

Premiss 1: Moral judgements can be sufficient on their own for motivation. (cf. Stroud: '"the sense of morality or duty" is often enough in itself to lead people to act.'[20])
Premiss 2: Beliefs are necessary for motivation, but none can be sufficient on its own; a desire must also be present.
Conclusion: Moral judgements are not beliefs but desires.

But clearly the conclusion does not follow from the premisses as stated. It would only do so if desires, also, could be sufficient on their own, so meeting requirement (ii). Now it is all too easy to fall into the temptation of securing the argument's validity at the cost of temporarily converting one's 'moderate' reading of premiss 2 into an 'extreme' reading. An example is McNaughton (1988: 22), who characterizes 'the belief–desire theory' as 'tell[ing] us that a complete explanation of any action must mention a desire as well as some beliefs', but then identifies moral judgements with desires on grounds that (according to this theory) only desires are suitably 'motivational', and 'pure beliefs cannot motivate'. He thus seems to deny what he has just claimed: that beliefs do perform an explanatory function, and therefore that desires are only necessary, not sufficient, for motivation and action.[21]

In fact, of course, if moral judgements could be sufficient on their own for motivation, then since desires are only necessary, the most that could be concluded would be that moral judgements, rather than being purely beliefs, would be a combination of belief and desire, with each being equally essential. But this, we have seen, is a conclusion too weak to represent Hume's view.

But, it might now be objected, premiss 1 is misleadingly stated. It should only entail – as McNaughton and others surely mean it to – that moral judgements can be sufficient without an independent desire, not that relevant factual beliefs are not required. Obviously, I must see that there is a famine relief box on the counter before I can put money into it. But my desires, given relevant factual beliefs, can be similarly sufficient. Thus, given my belief that *Merci pour le Chocolat* is showing at my local cinema and at a suitable time, my desire to see it can fully account for my going there: I don't need to have an independent desire, such as that I like the interior of cinemas. But surely this restores the symmetry between desires and moral judgements in their relation to motivation, as well as ensuring the requisite asymmetry between desires and moral judgements, on the one hand, and beliefs, on the other. Let us then set out the argument a second time in order to take account of this objection:

> Premiss 1: Moral judgements, given relevant factual beliefs, can be sufficient for motivation *without an independent desire*.
> Premiss 2: Factual beliefs are necessary for motivation, but none can be sufficient without an independent desire.
> Conclusion: Moral judgements are not beliefs but desires.

But the most that has been asserted so far is that a factual belief has to be relevant either to an independent desire or to a moral judgement, if it is to move us to action. There is therefore no warrant yet for saying that moral judgements are not beliefs of any kind, but must be desires. Indeed, it is perfectly consistent with premiss 1, as now formulated, that my judgement that I morally ought to donate to famine relief should, given the relevant factual beliefs, move me to action by itself producing the requisite desire. Only if it were impossible for a moral judgement to be a belief, and yet itself produce the desire relevant to action, would the conclusion follow.

Now instrumentalists today typically not only rule out of court the possibility that a belief might give rise to a desire all by itself, but appeal in so doing to Hume. Indeed, when Smith (1994: Chapters 4 and 5) wants to allow that at least some beliefs (namely moral ones) can engender desires, he sees himself as deviating from what is otherwise a commitment to the Humean theory of motivation. It is hardly surprising then that those who reinterpret Hume's argument along 'sufficiency' lines do not think it necessary even to broach the objection that a moral judgement might be a belief, and yet itself produce the desire relevant for action. But, as we saw in the last chapter, it is just a myth that Hume repudiates as unthinkable the idea that a belief might causally engender a desire. Quite the contrary – and here he diverges strikingly from orthodox instrumentalism as it is understood today, and so, paradoxically, from so called 'Humeanism' – he gives examples of this occurring.

Nor will it help to point out that Hume denies that a belief can logically entail a desire. For even accepting this, the only relation between moral judgements and desire, with which premiss 1, on the 'sufficiency' reinterpretation, is consistent is an ordinary empirical one. It is correspondingly only such a connection that now has to be denied between belief and desire. But it is just this empirical connection which Hume endorses when he speaks of beliefs about the sources of pain and pleasure 'prompt[ing]' or 'excit[ing]' desire and passion. He therefore would seem to have little problem with the idea that beliefs – even certain factual ones – can sometimes move us to action without the assistance of an independent desire, where this is understood as consistent with the belief itself producing the desire.

Suppose now, however, in order to get around this qualification, it is suggested that what premiss 1 really means is something stronger, namely this:

> Once I have made the judgement, e.g. that I morally ought to donate to famine relief, and the relevant circumstances arise, I am straightaway motivated to act.

If so, the defender of the 'sufficiency' reinterpretation will go on, the claim denied by premiss 2 will be that a belief could likewise straightaway move us to action, without first producing a desire, and Hume surely denies that. But opponents might now cite the premiss as evidence for the existence of a different type of belief from a factual one, namely a moral judgement, that does not, like a factual one, require a desire, in order to motivate us. They could thus use premiss 1, on the new reading, to cast doubt on, or even overturn, premiss 2's insistence that desire is always necessary for action, provoking no less than a collapse of the motivational claims underlying the 'moderate' version itself.

To stave off such a collapse, it might hastily be replied that Hume could (and would) rule out of court the idea that anything that was a belief, even of the special kind that moral judgements are now being claimed to be, could be linked directly with action as cause to effect. The grounds would be that this could not be accommodated within his naturalistic framework. But once it is acknowledged that Hume links belief directly with desire, as cause and effect, this defence loses much of its traditional force. For it is no longer clear why a naturalism which allows Hume to do the one thing, could not allow him to do the other, and so in the special case of morality, link belief directly with action.

The 'Humean' idea that no belief can be linked directly with action, as cause to effect, has of course exercised considerable influence over contemporary minds. It has even constrained what contemporary naturalists have felt able to endorse when formulating their own version of the practicality argument, unconstrained by Hume's intentions. However, it has recently been challenged by writers (see particularly Scheffler, 1992: 91) attempting to make sense, within a purely naturalistic framework, of there being a direct link between moral judgements (construed as purely beliefs) and motivation – which bypasses desire altogether. Scheffler, for instance, takes premiss 1, on this strong 'sufficiency' reading, to accurately reflect the phenomena of moral experience. He then takes the truth of this premiss, understood in this way, together with what he regards as the common-sense conviction that moral judgements are nevertheless cognitive, to show that the corresponding premiss 2 must be false. (He draws on Freudian psychoanalytic theories to sketch a picture of the human personality and motivation that he maintains is sufficiently complex to account for morality's independent motivating force.)

Retreating to a weaker position, the defender of the 'sufficiency' reinterpretation, might now counter that, even if there is nothing in principle to stop a naturalist like Hume from relating beliefs directly with action, as cause to effect, he just does not do this. Although this reply, concessive as it is, somewhat shakily reinstates the motivational claims on which the 'moderate' version is based, it now invites the question whether it is even remotely plausible to suggest that, on Hume's view, moral judgements straightaway move us to action. I shall postpone dealing with this question until we have the benefit of the next section's detailed examination of the text.

In summary, the problem with the 'sufficiency' reinterpretation so far is that the first premiss – according to which, as originally stated, moral judgements can be causally sufficient on their own for motivation – has to be weakened in order to allow, without provoking a contradiction, the requisite identification with desire. (Desire, it will be recalled, only motivates together with a relevant belief.) But this opens up a loop-hole for it to be claimed that moral judgements are, after all, equally matters of belief and desire. Once Hume's remarks that reason can itself arouse desire are taken on board, only a tightening of the link between moral judgements and motivation which puts at risk the motivational theory underpinning the 'moderate' version, seems capable of averting this consequence. Bringing this theory back from the brink, however, still leaves the defender of the 'sufficiency' reinterpretation with an uphill struggle: will the text really support his new claim about the link between moral judgement and motivation? As we shall see, the 'intrinsicality' reinterpretation, to which we now turn, allows us to progress far more smoothly than the previous one, to this textual question concerning the first premiss. Indeed, it becomes the main focus of attention as we move from the initial straightforward conceptual reading to its variations.

(iii) 'Intrinsicality': not dragging in metaphysics

Consider a preliminary formulation of the practicality argument thus reinterpreted:

> Premiss 1: Moral judgements are intrinsically motivating. (cf. Stroud: Moral judgements are those 'in the very making of which one is moved to act'.[22])
> Premiss 2: Beliefs are as a matter of contingent fact required for motivation but none is intrinsically motivating.
> Conclusion: Moral judgements are not beliefs but desires.

But the conclusion again only follows provided it is tacitly understood that desires themselves, like moral judgements, and unlike beliefs, are intrinsically motivating. This suggests the following reformulation making this explicit:

> Premiss 1: Moral judgements are intrinsically motivating.
> Premiss 2: Beliefs are, as a matter of contingent fact, required for motivation, but none is intrinsically motivating, *as are desires*.
> Conclusion: Moral judgements are not beliefs but desires.

Given the earlier discussion of the 'sufficiency' reinterpretation, and its difficulties, the superficial attractions of this new reinterpretation will surely be evident. By making premiss 2 merely a denial that beliefs are intrinsically motivating it apparently improves in two crucial ways on the earlier reinterpretation. First, it secures, without more ado, the requisite desire-belief asymmetry while safeguarding, in accordance with the 'moderate' version of Hume's argument, a role for belief in motivation and action: beliefs are still, as a matter of contingent fact, required for action, though only desires are necessarily (or intrinsically) motivating. Second, once reinterpreted in this way, the argument no longer requires for its validity, as it does on the 'sufficiency' reinterpretation, that Hume deny what in fact he asserts: that there can be an empirical link between belief and desire. For the only link between these two mental states that, on the new reinterpretation, Hume must be shown to deny is merely a necessary one, and Hume's name is, after all, famously associated with the slogan 'any desire can go with any belief'.

As regards premiss 1, the new reinterpretation can meet the objection that to claim that Hume posits a necessary relation between moral judgements and motivation would drag him back into that metaphysical realm which, as a resolute naturalist, he has repudiated. For, on this reinterpretation, motivation is built into the very idea of moral judgement, betokening therefore not two independent psychological states between which a substantial, yet necessary, link is posited, but one psychological state, capable of description in two ways. To take our earlier example, to say of someone that she judges she ought to give to famine relief now logically entails that, given the relevant circumstances, she behaves in the required way. If, however, she neglects the opportunity to give to famine relief, it cannot truly be said of her that she has made this moral judgement. In this way, the disallowed metaphysical link between moral judgement and motivation is dissolved into a mere conceptual one, acceptable even to naturalists.

(iv) Is Hume's moral approval intrinsically motivating?

Naturalistically acceptable it may be to posit this sort of necessary link, it still, however, does not follow that Hume himself actually did so, nor even guarantee that his remarks can be read in such a way that it is not ruled out that he might have done. Were we, however, to rely on much recent literature,[23] we could certainly be forgiven for supposing that Hume does posit such a link, or some variation of it, and so that the 'intrinsicality' reinterpretation is not merely conjectural, but beyond dispute. I shall focus here again on Foot.

Speaking of Hume's invocation of sentiment or feeling, as the basis of morality, Foot (1966: 74–5) writes that, in this, 'Hume thought that he himself had hit on the perfect solution to the problem . . . at a blow he seemed to have put an end to the hunt for mysterious extra properties, and also to have shown the necessary connexion between morality and the will.' And again she writes: '"To know virtue is to love it." This, Hume might have said, is a logical truth.' Again, she speaks of Hume (in his practicality argument) as 'starting from his premise about the necessarily practical nature of morality' and she goes on to offer a corrective of the position she has imputed to Hume. She tells us, 'it is not that this [Humean position] is false but that one may easily insist on too close a connexion between moral judgement and the will.' Finally, chiding Hume for a certain disingenuousness, she writes that, though people are indeed influenced by considerations of morality, 'They are not *necessarily* influenced, as Hume must have known' (her italics).

For Hume, morality is in some sense practical. But is there any warrant for inserting the adverb 'necessarily', as Foot does? One crucial source of evidence is obviously Hume's formulations of the first premiss. Now he formulates the premiss seven times. The first and seventh, however, state only that moral judgements 'have an influence on' action. But this singularly loose claim is compatible, as we noted earlier, with them requiring an independent desire, if they are to lead to action. These formulations therefore would scarcely provide support even for a 'sufficiency' reading (construed as entailing that moral judgements can motivate us on their own without an independent desire).

Hume's second formulation of the premiss, though it claims more promisingly that 'Morals excite passions, and produce or prevent actions', is also of little help since, as we have seen, Hume speaks of reason itself as likewise both 'exciting', and 'prompting', passions. (We cannot of course deny that in the present context he intends, by speaking of morals in this way, to sharply contrast them with reason, but this is just further testimony to the contradiction. lying at the heart of his theory of motivation.) This leaves us with the third, fourth, fifth and sixth formulations. The third and sixth describe 'conscience or a sense of morals' as an 'active principle'. But the epithet 'active', as Hume uses it, is (as we saw in the previous chapter) notoriously vague; if it is meant to supplement the other formulations of the premiss, it is not clear in exactly what way. As for the intended contrast with reason's 'inertia', either this belongs to the 'extreme' reading, or 'inertia' must be understood in a way which makes it compatible, as the present 'moderate' reading requires, with reason having a role in action, and even being able itself to give rise to desire.

We are left then with the fourth and fifth formulations where Hume speaks of 'moral good and evil' as able to influence action 'by contradicting or approving of it', and again of 'the merit and demerit of actions frequently contradict[ing], and sometimes controul[ing] our natural propensities'. This might suggest that, for Hume, the sense of duty can, after all, have a direct and unmediated effect on action. This impression is bolstered when taken in conjunction with the evidence Hume adduces in support of his first premiss. For here, mentioning no intervening desire, he observes (3.1.1:5) that men are 'govern'd by their duties', and again 'deter'd . . . by the opinion of injustice' and 'impell'd . . . by that of obligation'.

The snag, however, for an 'intrinsicality' reading (as opposed to a 'sufficiency' one) is that it is to how men behave that Hume looks here for corroboration of his premiss, not to the concepts in terms of which we talk about that behaviour. But the only relation of which we shall ever find evidence in experience is, according to Hume, an ordinary causal one. Nor is it just that there is nothing in what he says here to suggest that he wishes to redirect our attention from actual conduct to (what we would now call) 'moral discourse'. It would sit oddly with his treatment of other feelings, such as love which, Hume claims, if it leads to motivation, only does so (see below) by causing a feeling of benevolence – or, in other words, a desire for the beloved's happiness. But this connection, he insists, can only be known about through observation and experience.[24]

(v) A pleasurable sentiment that inclines us to what arouses it

But Foot might now reply that the relation which Hume asserts between moral judgement and motivation is more complex than we have so far allowed. It is a two-part relation of which only the first – that between moral judgement and feeling – is strictly conceptual. Thus, Hume, according to Foot (1966: 74), takes 'propositions about virtue' to contain a reference to 'the special sentiment of approbation' which is pleasurable. But (and here comes the second part of the link) it is, for Hume, just a fact about human nature that this 'pleasurable sentiment 'incline[s]' us towards performing those actions whose contemplation gave rise to it.

Now, of course, there are remarks of Hume's which seem to identify moral approval with a distinctive feeling of pleasure. He writes, as we have noted, that 'the sense of virtue is nothing but to feel a satisfaction of a particular kind from the contemplation of a character', and again that 'the very feeling constitutes our praise or admiration'. However, as we also noted, other remarks suggest that to morally approve an action is something more than just to feel the relevant kind of pleasure.

Even overlooking this difficulty, the second factual component poses its own problems. At first sight it might seem that Foot takes this to be straightforwardly causal. But if the pleasurable feeling with which moral approval is here being identified has a mere causal role in inclining us to perform the relevant act, this outcome cannot be guaranteed, and the necessity of the link as a whole is undermined. Perhaps Foot's thought, then, is that, for Hume, there are not here two separate 'items' of experience, but just one: the pleasurable sentiment, to which the contemplation of, say, a generous action gives rise, is itself felt as an inclination to act generously. But what could be the evidence for attributing such a view to Hume?[25]

When, at 2.2.6:4–6, Hume raises a roughly similar question concerning love and the desire for the beloved's happiness (do they 'mixing together make only one passion' so that they are not only 'inseparable but the same', or is 'benevolence . . . [a] passion different from love'?) he sees these as two different 'hypotheses' between which a principled decision has to be made. (In fact, he argues that love and benevolence are different, and that being 'only conjoined . . . by the original constitution of the mind', there is nothing 'necessary' about 'this order of things'.) Foot is not, then, entitled, with moral sentiment and the inclination to act, simply to assume one of these hypotheses (that, for Hume, there is here a single feeling, or passion, rather than two distinct ones).

There are, however, two more direct pieces of evidence which also go against Foot's reading. The first is Hume's explanation of why moral judgement cannot be necessarily connected to motivation in the way his opponents, the moral rationalists, think. 'These two particulars', he writes (3.1.1:22), 'are evidently distinct. 'Tis one thing to know virtue, and another to conform the will to it.' Now if we take it, as seems plausible, that the rationalists' 'knowing virtue' would, for Hume, be the feeling of moral approval, and that 'conforming the will' involves having the relevant desire, we can then say that, for him, moral sentiment is likewise one 'particular', and being inclined to act 'another'.

The second piece of evidence is an example – the so-called 'self-hatred' example – situated close to the start of the section on whether justice is a natural or artificial virtue (3.2.1). It represents, moreover, Hume's only attempt to show *how* a moral sentiment might lead to action. To understand the example, it is necessary to sketch in the context which gives its point.

(vi) The 'self-hatred' example

Hume opens the section with the observation that, strictly speaking, our praise, and blame, attach only to the motive of action; the action itself functions merely as a 'sign' of a virtuous, or vicious, motive. Thus, when we applaud a generous action, we are really applauding the generosity of character that lies behind it. Hume concludes from this that 'To suppose . . . the mere regard to the virtue of the action, may be the first motive, which produc'd the action, and render'd it virtuous', is 'to reason in a circle'. His thought seems to be that, without an original natural motive – benevolence, paternal affection and such like – there would be no action towards which the sentiment of moral approval might be felt. But then the moral dimension of conduct would never have been revealed to us.[26]

Having stripped moral sentiment of any status it might have as a necessary condition of virtuous action, he now, however, seeks (3.2.1:8) to claw back, with the help of his 'self-hatred' example, at least a peripheral role, as a kind of stop-gap for natural motives:

But may not the sense of morality or duty produce an action, without any other motive? I answer, It may. But this is no objection to the present doctrine. When any virtuous motive or principle is common in human nature, a person, who feels his heart devoid of that principle, may hate himself upon that account, and may perform the action without the motive, from a certain sense of duty, in order to acquire by practice, that virtuous principle, or at least to disguise to himself, as much as possible, his want of it. A man that feels no gratitude in his temper, is still pleas'd to perform grateful actions, and thinks he has, by that means, fulfill'd his duty.

Now the example contained in this passage, while intended merely to illustrate moral sentiment's derivative role in motivation, is most obviously read as implying that, for Hume, the relevant link has to be mediated by a desire. A person becomes acutely aware of her cold heart and ungrateful nature. Desiring to relieve herself of the mental distress this causes her, she goes ahead, and performs, 'without the [natural] motive from a certain sense of duty', generous actions. She hopes thereby either to 'acquire by practice' the habit of gratitude, or to 'disguise' from herself the fact that she does not possess it.

This reading, according to which 'the sense of morality or duty' must be aided by a relevant desire if it is to lead to action, coheres with other remarks of Hume's. In the *Enquiry*, for instance, he advocates (E:282–3) the virtuous life on grounds that it is 'attended with a pleasing consciousness . . . keep[ing] us in humour with ourselves . . . while we retain the agreeable reflection of having done our part towards mankind and society', and again he speaks of it as affording us 'inward peace of mind', adding that all these are 'circumstances very requisite to happiness'. Nor does he leave merely implicit the idea that, where the natural non-moral motive is missing, these external inducements are required. He explicitly points out that a person, who is not fearful of being personally diminished, and losing her self-respect, as a result of doing bad things, has also 'lost a considerable motive to virtue'.

But the evidence for the reading is not restricted to the *Enquiry*. In the *Treatise* (3.3.1:3) Hume characterizes a person's moral disapproval of her own vicious motives, and actions, as a kind of humility; but the passion of humility (of which more will be said below) cannot, he tells us at 2.2.6:3, 'immediately excite us to action'.

(vii) Radcliffe's attempt to subvert the example

The 'self-hatred' example, reinforcing other remarks of Hume's, may thus seem to stand in the way of an 'intrinsicality' reinterpretation of premiss 1 of the practicality argument, even one based on Foot's suggestions. However, a recent defender of this reinterpretation, Radcliffe (2001: 363–87), does not just deny that the 'self-hatred' passage is a counter-example to the claim that Hume holds that moral sentiment is directly, or necessarily, linked with motivation, but asserts that it is positive evidence for this claim. Her laborious make-over of the example is of additional interest since it revives Foot's suggestion that the necessity of the link between moral sentiment and motivation is mediated by Hume's description of this sentiment as pleasurable.

It will also serve to illustrate the lengths writers will go to ensure that the practicality argument is valid when they assume that the 'moderate' reading of its second premiss is the only possible one. It thus raises an important question of principle: just how far is it legitimate to go in making a writer such as Hume mean what you want him to mean in order to save a key argument of his from invalidity? My answer will become clear: not as far as Radcliffe is prepared to go, especially when there is an alternative version of the argument on offer.[27]

Radcliffe first attempts to dissociate Hume's talk of the ungrateful person 'hating' himself from the Humean passion of hatred. She needs to do this because hatred, for Hume, being (like love) an indirect passion, only leads to motivation by way of a desire (that the hated person should suffer). Hume cannot, she argues, really mean 'hatred' since it would, in this example, have to be *self*-hatred but hatred, according to him, is never felt for ourselves, but only for others. Her conclusion is that the 'hatred' in question is really a kind of 'self-disapprobation or self-reproach', and that this, for Hume, is 'a feeling unique to the moral sense'. Having thus freed the moral feeling from its connection with hatred, she sees her way open to showing that it is, unlike hatred, directly motivating.

Now admittedly Hume cannot call self-disapproval a kind of hatred. But this is not because moral sentiment in general is, for him, a unique type of passion, unrelated to any specific indirect passions, but because hatred is the wrong indirect passion to link with self-disapproval. Hume writes at 3.3.1:3 that 'every quality *in ourselves* . . . that produces uneasiness excites *humility*' (my italics). But humility, Hume tells us, in the continuation of this passage, stands to an individual's disapproval of her own conduct as hatred stands to her disapproval of other people's conduct, and he later (at 3.3.5:1), describes this moral disapproval of others as 'nothing but a fainter and more imperceptible . . . hatred'. Self-disapproval therefore would seem to be, for Hume, a similarly calm form of humility. However, Hume regards humility as even more tenuously linked to motivation than hatred. Not only does he state (as was noted above) that humility does not 'immediately excite us to action', but he also characterizes it as 'pure sensation without any direction or tendency to action'.

Radcliffe is well aware that Hume links self-disapproval with humility, and she naturally wishes to limit the damage it could do to her position. She seems, however, to hope that we might suspend judgement about the remarks at 3.3.1:3 and 3.3.5:1 until she has expounded her argument for the direct motivating power of moral sentiment. Presumably, we will then see that Hume cannot really mean to identify self-disapproval with humility – a mere indirect passion. It should, however, from the outset, be stressed that the relevant remarks do not, considered in themselves, imply any hesitancy, or equivocation, on Hume's part about identifying self-disapproval with humility. They are not, therefore, as Radcliffe later claims, themselves consistent with Hume's having distinguished self-disapproval from humility, allowing merely that the latter might presuppose the former. Her argument for attributing to Hume the view that self-disapproval is directly motivating, and so cannot be a form of humility, will have then to be powerful enough to coun-teract the plain implication of these remarks that it is a form of humility.

Her argument is pieced together from two passages in Book 2. In the first (2.1.1:3), she reports Hume as stating that 'the senses of morality and beauty' are calm passions. In fact what Hume describes as a calm passion is 'the sense of beauty and deformity in action, composition, and external objects'. But it is not clear whether he means this phrase to include morality at all. For a little further on in 'On beauty and deformity' (2.1.8:2), he seems, when again applying these terms to action, to have in mind, not so much virtue and vice, but (among other things) gracefulness and ungainliness of movement, whether in humans or animals. He does, however, once during the section (at 2.1.8:3) refer to 'moral beauty', coupling it with 'natural' beauty. Elsewhere (3.3.1:23) he classes moral and aesthetic sentiment together as 'adhering to the general view of things' in contrast to passions which 'arise from our particular and momentary situation'. Moreover, we know from his remark at 3.3.5:1 that he regards moral sentiments as calm forms of the indirect passions of love, hatred, pride and humility. Let us therefore give Radcliffe the benefit of the doubt, and agree that moral sentiments are, for Hume, calm passions.

In the second passage, she cites (2.3.3:3:8), Hume lists a number of calm passions (in fact he calls them 'calm desires and tendencies'), including 'the general appetite to good and aversion to evil', and states that they are 'influencing motives of the will'. Putting these two passages together, she concludes that, for Hume, moral sentiment is directly, or intrinsically, motivating.

Now a valid argument from the claim (entailed by the first passage) that 'moral sentiments are calm passions', to the conclusion 'that moral sentiments are "influ-encing motives of the will"', would require an intermediary premiss entailing that anything that is a calm passion is an 'influencing motive of the will'. But the second passage contains no such claim. Nor indeed would we expect it to. After all, Hume makes it perfectly clear elsewhere that even indirect passions – those that, like love, hatred, pride and humility only motivate, if at all, in the presence of independent desires – have both violent and calm forms. Radcliffe's argument must therefore hang entirely on the plausibility of taking 'the general appetite for good, and aver-sion to evil' to refer to moral sentiment. But if this reading was uncontroversial, the first claim (that moral sentiments are calm passions) would be redundant. It would seem then that this otherwise redundant claim is meant somehow to persuade us of this reading.

In fact, there is scarcely any reason at all to accept the reading. As Radcliffe grants, there is a 'competing interpretation'. This is that the 'appetite' referred to is for ordinary pleasure and happiness – for pursuing 'our own good' – while the 'aver-sion' mentioned is to suffering pain and misfortune. This competing reading has two crucial advantages over hers. We get around having to attribute to Hume the strained, and improbable, idea that we have an appetite for morally approving, and an aversion to morally disapproving, actions. Also, when Hume refers to the 'good' again, just 16 lines further on at 2.3.3:10, there can be no doubt that he is using it in accordance with the 'competing interpretation'. He writes: 'Men often act know-ingly against their interest: For which reason the view of the greatest possible good does not always influence them'. But then being influenced by the 'good' must surely mean, for Hume, acting in pursuit of one's interests. The 'good', referring therefore to these interests, would seem to have nothing to do with specifically moral feelings or actions.

The only consideration Radcliffe musters in support of her reading is the claim, at 2.1.1:3, that the sense of 'beauty and deformity in action' is a calm passion. But it hardly follows from the fact that Hume, in the later passage, also describes 'the general appetite to good and aversion to evil' as a calm passion (actually a 'calm desire') that he is talking about the same passion, or hence that the sense of 'beauty and deformity in action' is likewise an 'influencing motive of the will'. Indeed, one might think that precisely because 'the general appetite to good' is 'an influencing motive of the will', it cannot be identified with the sense of 'beauty and deformity in action'. For in so far as this phrase does refer to moral sentiment, it is coupled with aesthetic sensibility. But aesthetic sensibility is often regarded as paradigmatically contemplative rather than active. As Hume later states (3.3.1:23):

> Sentiments must touch the heart, to make them controul our passions: But they need not extend beyond the imagination, to make them influence our taste. When a building seems clumsy and tottering to the eye, it is ugly and disagreeable; tho' we be fully assur'd of the solidity of the workmanship. 'Tis a kind of fear, which causes this sentiment of disapprobation; but the passion is not the same with that which we feel, when oblig'd to stand under a wall that we really think tottering and insecure.

Hume is perhaps implicitly acknowledging this contemplative aspect of the moral sentiments, which they share with aesthetic ones, when he goes on to raise doubts whether either is properly a 'passion' at all (let alone a desire).

Radcliffe may have been influenced by certain things Hume goes on to say in the second passage immediately after the remark (quoted above) about 'men knowingly act[ing] against their interests'. For here he describes as a 'virtue' the 'strength of mind' which allows a man who has conflicting calm and violent passions, to withstand the violent, and act on the calm, one. Radcliffe, quoting this passage, takes Hume to be here 'confirm[ing] that the moral sentiments are among the motivating passions'. But, in fact, what Hume depicts this man as doing is counter-acting a violent passion in the prosecution of his interests and designs. Again there is no mention either of specifically virtuous conduct, or of the sense of virtue, which is supposed to directly motivate it.

Radcliffe's argument, flimsy as it is, is hardly therefore likely to persuade us to reconstrue remarks implying an identity between self-disapproval and humility, on grounds that this identification would entail a lack of motivating force incompatible with the argument's conclusion. She has, however, another, and independent, tack. She tries to show that Hume's motivational psychology contains the materials out of which an explanation can be fashioned as to how moral sentiment directly motivates us. It is here that she revives, and fleshes out, Foot's suggestion that this motivating power springs, for Hume, from moral sentiment's being pleasurable.

As Radcliffe correctly observes, taking the view that moral sentiment is capable of directly motivating us because it is pleasurable (or painful), logically commits one to holding that pleasure (and pain) themselves directly motivate. But to motivate directly, she continues, is to do so without any pre-existing desire. But surely, she says, anticipating an immediate objection, everyone knows that, for Hume, it is the desire for pleasure (or aversion to pain) that is the source of motivation. If, therefore, she is to convince us that pleasure, or pain, motivates directly, she has to overturn this received view.

As, however, we saw in the last chapter, Hume's actual account of motivation, as expounded in 'Of the influencing motives of the will', does not, contrary to the received view, invoke any such pre-existing desire. Rather, the belief, or expectation, that an object will cause us pain, or bring us pleasure ('the prospect of pain or pleasure from any object'), produces 'a consequent emotion of aversion or propensity', so that we 'are carry'd to avoid or embrace what will give us this uneasiness or satisfaction'. It is not, however, this account which Radcliffe proposes to substitute for the purely desire-based one usually attributed to Hume. Rather it is one suggested to her by a remark of Locke's. According to Locke, as she presents him, we are galvanized into action in an attempt to relieve ourselves of the painful experience of not yet having in our possession the object which promises pleasure. On this 'Lockean' view, she argues, a prior desire for pleasure is not therefore required since 'to be in a painful state is [already] to be in a state one has a motive to be relieved of'.

Radcliffe, referring to the 'Lockean' view, asserts that 'Hume must have thought this as well'. But why must he? There is no direct evidence that he did: he does not, in expounding his theory of motivation, allude to feelings of frustration at not yet enjoying an anticipated pleasure. Radcliffe is again reliant on indirect evidence which she attempts to piece together from remarks made by Hume at different stages of the *Treatise*. These are first Hume's claim, right at the start of the work (1.1.2:1), that 'this idea of pleasure or pain ... produces the new impressions of desire and aversion'. (She is aware of course that this claim later forms part of Hume's exposition of his theory of motivation, but she does not see why Hume cannot propound this, together with her 'Lockean' one.) The second is a related claim, occurring at 2.1.1:4. Paraphrasing it as 'the passions arise, either directly or indirectly, from pleasure and pain', she adds in parenthesis that, for Hume, many of these passions are motives. It is difficult, though, to see how this second claim, even with her addendum, can be brought to bear on the first in such a way as to justify her conclusion that, for Hume, 'ideas of pleasures and pains become desires and aversions'.

Since it is unclear how the two claims cited by Radcliffe are meant to yield her conclusion, a diagnosis of her underlying confusion is perhaps in order. Hume does maintain (2.1.1:4) that the passions, both direct and indirect, 'arise from good or evil, from pain or pleasure'. Moreover, the direct ones – desire, aversion, grief, joy, fear etc. – are, he tells us, just those passions which do so 'immediately', whereas the indirect ones require 'the conjunction of other qualities'. It soon becomes clear (2.3.9:2) that the 'good or evil, pain or pleasure', which cause the direct passions, are merely those anticipated ones which feature so prominently in 2.3.3, the section where Hume expounds his theory of motivation Such pains or pleasures, being 'conceived merely in idea and consider'd to exist in [a] future period of time', do not themselves become the passions or desires which lead to action.

It is, in fact, to the indirect passions that we must look if we are to find the immediate impressions of pain (or pleasure) which Radcliffe requires for her 'Lockean' account of Hume. Consider, for instance, pride. Here, according to Hume, the thought of something belonging, or in some way related, to me – my beautiful vase, my svelte figure – arouses an immediate feeling of pleasure in me. This 'agreeable' impression produces pride, a similarly agreeable impression, which in turn directs my attention to myself. (Even here, however, the immediate impression of pleasure isn't actually converted into the passion; rather it produces it by association.) Most crucially, however, the indirect passions, as we have seen, are not, for Hume, motives: if they lead to action at all they only do so fortu-itously. It looks therefore as though Radcliffe has taken the immediate impressions of pain (and pleasure) associated with the indirect passions, and placed them within the motivational shell of the direct passions, presenting the amalgam as Hume's 'Lockean' theory of motivation. In so far as representing a position Hume actually holds, it is hard to regard it as anything more than pure fabrication.

But even if we could (as we obviously cannot) legitimately attribute to Hume Radcliffe's 'Lockean' account of motivation, her difficulties would not be over. According to her, Hume holds that moral approval, as well as disapproval, motivate directly. But moral approval, for him, is a pleasurable feeling whereas, according to the 'Lockean' view, it is only painful feelings which we seek to relieve through action. It would therefore seem that moral approval cannot provide a requisite motive. It is perhaps hardly surprising therefore that, after initially claiming that, for Hume, moral sentiment in general is directly motivating, she soon narrows her brief to showing this specifically for moral *dis*approval.

But could her 'Lockean' account be coherently applied even to *self*-disapproval as Hume's example requires? It would hardly seem so. For Hume, the moral senti-ments are calm passions. Indeed, this, as we saw, was a central plank of Radcliffe's original argument. But to a person experiencing them, calm passions are, Hume repeatedly states, scarcely perceptible at all. Speaking of moral sentiments in partic-ular, he tells us that they are nothing but 'fainter and more imperceptible' forms of the indirect passions, and of calm passions generally, he states that they are those which have 'become, in a manner, imperceptible' (2.1.1:3). He speaks of calm passions (2.3.3:8) as 'causing no disorder in the soul', and again as 'producing little emotion in the mind', and 'more known by their effects than by the immediate feeling or sensation'. Moreover, as a characterization of moral sentiment this accords with the stipulation that they are the feelings which arise when we contemplate an action from an impartial and disinterested perspective. It is particularly unfortunate, then, that she requires of moral self-disapproval that it cause so much mental discomfort and perturbation that a person feels impelled to take action in order to flee it.

(viii) An overview

This is an appropriate moment to pause, and draw together the different strands, as they have emerged in the foregoing sections, of Hume's view of moral sentiment in its relation to motivation. It will also allow us to pick up a thread left dangling at the end of the 'sufficiency' discussion, and answer the question posed there. This was whether it is at all plausible to attribute to Hume the view that my judgement that, e.g. I ought to donate to famine relief, could cause me on its own, without an intervening desire, to drop money into the charity box.

Now it is clear that moral sentiments, whether of approval or disapproval, are not, as the 'intrinsicality' reinterpretation would require, forms of direct passion. The direct passions are desires, or aversions, caused by the 'idea', or 'prospect' (Hume uses both terms), of pleasure or pain. Indeed, we have Hume's word for it that moral sentiments are calm forms of the indirect passions, of love and hatred, pride and humility. Not only this, but his analyses both of moral sentiment, and the indirect passions, supports these explicit identifications. Indirect passions, like moral sentiment, are themselves pleasurable, or painful, sensations, rather than being, like the direct passions, merely caused by the idea of pleasure or pain. Both moral sentiments and the indirect passions produce ideas either of the self or others. (We shall recall how, on Hume's account of pride, pleasure at the excellence of some achievement of mine brings the thought of myself to mind.) But these ideas, unlike the ideas of future pleasure or pain, have no particular connection with action.

Hume thinks that the indirect passions of love and hatred combine with desires to bring about action. (Desiring the loved person's happiness, for instance, we act to promote it.) But does Hume hold that these passions are capable themselves of producing the relevant desires, or are they dependent, if they are to lead to action, on an independent desire? Hume's position seems to be that we just happen to be so constituted naturally that the experience of love, or hatred, causes in us the relevant desire. So it is in this sense fortuitous that a person who loves someone desires her happiness, but not in the sense that the desire has a source extraneous to the passion. It is plausible to extrapolate from Hume's remarks about humility's even more tenuous connection with action than love, or hatred, that humility (and possibly pride) would be dependent on an extraneous desire.

The question arises how far we may take this further characterization of the indirect passions as a guide to Hume's view of the moral sentiments. It has been queried whether, despite Hume's remarks, he really means to class these sentiments with the indirect passions. If there is a justification, however, for excluding them from this category, it is not because they are more like the direct passions. It is because they are even less connected with action than most of the indirect passions. This is apparent from Hume's self-hatred example which suggests that 'the sense of morality' is dependent, if action is to ensue, on an extraneous desire. (We should not forget that this example is in any case only invoked in order to restore to 'the sense of morality' a peripheral role in motivation, virtuous actions usually having natural, non-moral motives.) Then there are the remarks, quoted earlier (p. 44) from the *Enquiry* which again suggest that 'the sense of morality' needs bolstering, if it is to lead to action, by the desire to feel good about oneself. Finally, and perhaps most crucially, there is Hume's stipulation that moral approval, or disapproval, is that distinctive pleasure, or pain, felt on contemplating an action from a disinterested and impartial standpoint. As Baillie (2000: 141) observes, 'this requires me to abstract away from' the person who has, say, harmed me, and who I would ordinarily feel hatred for, 'to consider the general practices involved' in doing harm. But this robs me of much of the immediate impetus to act that ordinary hatred would give me. It is this reference to the 'general view' which makes sense of Hume's coupling of moral sentiment with something so essentially contemplative as aesthetic sensibility.

What then of that restatement of the first premiss to which the defenders of the 'sufficiency' reinterpretation were driven in order to restore the argument's validity? It is true, as we saw earlier, that Hume observes (3.1.1:5), without mentioning any intervening desire, that men 'are govern'd by their duties', and 'deter'd by the opinion of injustice'. But he never explicitly denies that a desire is required. Even leaving aside the evidence cited above concerning moral sentiment in particular, it is doubtful that Hume ever contemplates any action coming about in the absence of desire altogether.

4 A defence through the second premiss must fail

(i) Belief and desire as 'distinct existences'

Let us suppose that, incautiously brushing aside this evidence from Hume's positive account of morality (and also from his analysis of the passions), and still clinging to the 'intrinsicality' reinterpretation of the argument's first premiss, a defender now demands that we cross-check our rejection of it by reference to its second premiss. After all, this defender will say, whatever influence Hume is denying to reason in the second premiss he must, if the practicality argument is to be valid, be attributing to morality in premiss 1. Consequently if it is clear that he is denying a necessary practical influence to reason, it must surely follow that he means (whatever he misleadingly says) to attribute exactly that same influence to morality. But the denial that reason can have a necessary influence over action is no less than one of the central planks of Humeanism, together with Hume's defence of this denial in terms of belief and desire being, in his famous phrase, 'distinct existences'. Moreover, so convincing is this defence, it will be added, that the term 'distinct existence' has taken on a life of its own, becoming common coinage in such discussions even outside the strictly Humean context.

So much is true. But it does not automatically license us simply to overlook what Hume actually says in formulating premiss 1. Rather, it shows that even to question whether, in premiss 2, he is denying to reason a necessary influence over action will involve prizing apart his premiss from the 'traditional' Humean defence in terms of 'distinct existences' in which it is embedded, and trying to discern what Hume's defence of premiss 2 actually *is*.

Turning then to this second premiss, a recent appeal to what I call the 'traditional' defence can be found in Smith (1994: 7) who states that:

According to the standard picture of human psychology – a picture we owe to Hume – there are two main kinds of psychological state . . . there are beliefs, states that purport to represent the way the world is. Since our beliefs purport to represent the world, they are assessable in terms of truth and falsehood . . . Desires are unlike beliefs in that they do not even purport to represent the way the world is. They are therefore not assessable in terms of truth and falsehood. Hume concludes that belief and desire are therefore distinct existences: that is, that we can always pull belief and desire apart, at least modally.

Assuming that to have a desire to act in a given way is, for Hume, tantamount to being motivated to act in that way, and also that, for Hume (as for Smith himself), morality's necessary practicality is, after all, an indisputable fact, Smith goes on to attribute to him the further conclusion that if moral judgements did express beliefs then: 'it [would] leave it entirely mysterious how or why having a moral view is supposed to have special links with what we are motivated to do' (ibid.: 11).

However, the 'traditional' defence of premiss 2, as contained in the first of these two quotations, differs from Hume's actual defence of the premiss, in reversing the direction of justification between the following two claims:

(i) Desires (or passions) lack the representative element of beliefs, and so are not assessable, as are beliefs in terms of truth and falsehood.

(ii) Desires (or passions) are logically distinct from beliefs.

Thus, as it functions in the 'traditional' defence, (ii) is primary, with (i) cited, as Smith cites it above, as the ground of (ii). In other words, according to the 'traditional' defence, it follows from the fact that desires or passions lack that representative element which enables beliefs to be assessed by reason as true or false that they must be logically distinct from those beliefs. Often (i) is further re-expressed as the claim that desire and belief are *distinctive* mental states, and (ii) as the claim that they are *distinct existences,* the adjectives 'distinctive' and 'distinct' being then more-or-less conflated despite their different meanings.[28]

In Hume's actual defence, however, (i) is primary, with (ii) invoked in order to save (i) from refutation in face of obvious counter-examples. Thus, admitting that e.g. a fear will dissolve when we realize we were mistaken in believing that the feared object was present, Hume nevertheless insists that such beliefs only 'accompany' our passions. He concludes from this that it is not, properly speaking, these passions that are unreasonable, and so give way in face of the truth, but only the beliefs, which though associated with, or even causing, them, are sharply distinct from them. Moreover, once Hume has met the objection to (i) by appeal to (ii), the latter, pivotal though it is to the 'traditional' defence, drops out of consideration altogether.

Hume's own defence, as we saw in the previous chapter (and here I merely summarize and recap), draws upon the implications, not just of the negative characterization of passions as lacking a representative dimension – as not being copies of 'original existences' – but also of their positive characterization as being themselves 'original existences'. The negative characterization is designed, as we saw, to ensure that passions are not directly amenable to reason, as merely a procedure for assessing truth or falsehood. But the positive characterization, planting them firmly in 'the world of realities' (to which causal interaction is evidently confined), 'totally remove[s]' them, from reason, as belonging to 'the world of ideas'.

In fact, therefore, that feature of passions, which Hume is now popularly thought to have cited in order to show that there is no necessary link between them and reason, but which yet affirms the possibility of a causal one, is the very same feature, which seen positively, seems to rule out even this causal connection. Once we emphasize the latter more radical view, however, Hume's thought seems to be this. If desire and passion are not susceptible of assessment as true or false, then since this is reason's only mode of operation, it can have no influence at all over desire, and action, even a causal one. But morality does have such an influence – an ordinary causal influence – and so morality cannot be a matter of reason. Of course, in formulating the practicality argument this way, we have already lost our grip upon the 'moderate' reading of premiss 2, as a separate reading, and are teetering on the edge of allowing it to merge with, or abandoning it for, the 'extreme' reading.

This last consideration ought, however, to make it apparent how mistaken it is to suppose, as proponents of the 'intrinsicality' reinterpretation do in appealing to the 'traditional' defence, that they can here simply substitute their 'belief' for Hume's 'reason'. For in assigning reason to the 'world of ideas' Hume has effectively cut it off from belief, in so far as belief is a 'distinct existence', just as irretrievably as from any other component of the 'world of realities'. But this has the consequence of aligning belief with those very desires and passions which Hume is here claiming are inaccessible to reason, and over which it therefore could have absolutely no influence.

This observation in fact puts a little more flesh on to a suggestion broached at the end of the last chapter as to how the contradiction that was the subject of the chapter might yet possibly be resolved. The suggestion was that it is reason of which Hume is speaking when he states that it *cannot* move us to action, but belief that he has in mind when he states that it can do so. As we recall, however, the suggestion – any assessment of which would involve extending our investigation back into Book 1 – was put on hold in the hope that it might be possible to secure the argument's validity just using a second premiss which states that reason can move us to action, but only with the help of desire. I propose to postpone a little longer entertaining the new suggestion as to how the contradiction might be resolved, until we are quite sure that the 'moderate' version cannot meet our requirements.

(ii) 'Distinct existences' taken out of context

Returning one final time to the 'intrinsicality' reinterpretation, might it not be salvaged by boldly dropping those elements of Hume's account that conflict and, holding on to those which cohere, with this reinterpretation, presenting the result as an improved, but still essentially 'Humean', rendering of the argument? Thus we could, for instance, simply dissociate Hume's claim that belief and desire are 'distinct existences' from the subsidiary role it actually plays in the *Treatise* passages. The claim, as still a distinctively Humean claim, could then be used to argue for the impossibility of belief's being anything more than causally related to desire, or hence to motivation, in contrast to morality, which is necessarily motivating. (Here it will be granted that Hume does not officially construe morality in this way, but it will be suggested that he ought to have done.)

But these adherents of the 'intrinsicality' reinterpretation, still aspiring to be Humeans, will now find themselves on the horns of a dilemma. Suppose they hold merely on Hume's authority that belief and desire are 'distinct existences', and so cannot be necessarily connected. In this case, they must surely also defer to Hume's authority as regards moral judgement and desire, or moral judgement and motivation. But Hume, as we have repeatedly seen, states that 'two particulars' so evidently distinct as 'knowing virtue' and 'conforming the will to it' *cannot* be necessarily connected. But this contradicts premiss 1, on the 'intrinsicality' reinterpretation, which entails that moral judgements are intrinsically related to motivation.

Suppose, on the other hand, that these defenders of the 'intrinsicality' reinterpretation do not consider themselves slavish followers of Hume: they want, after all, to improve on his account while preserving their basic allegiance to him. They thus attempt to save their construal of premiss 1 as entailing a necessary link between moral judgement and motivation by pointing out that, unlike Hume, they do not treat moral judgement and motivation as two distinct psychological states. Were they to do so, they will say, then of course, as good Humean naturalists, they could not possibly claim a necessary link between them; only the defenders of the metaphysical version of the 'mandatory' reinterpretation of the practicality argument would be foolish enough to attempt that. Their position, however, as we saw earlier, is that motivation is built into the concept of moral judgement, betokening, not two independent psychological states, but one capable of description in two ways.

But if it is not objectionable even to these Humean naturalists to disagree with Hume over whether moral judgement and motivation are 'distinct existences' – perhaps they will say this is just a harmless disagreement about detail not about substance – can it really be objectionable to them if someone should wish to extend this disagreement with Hume to the issue of whether belief and desire, or belief and motivation, are likewise logically distinct? This too, it might be said, is merely a disagreement about detail not about substance. If defenders of the 'intrinsicality' reinterpretation are to resist this move, without being charged with simply drawing an arbitrary line between moral judgement in its relation to motivation, and belief in its relation to motivation, then they surely will have to provide independent arguments in support of this differential treatment. But equally crucially, they will have to justify their differential treatment of belief and desire.

It is precisely at this point in fact that recent writers make their appeal to the different 'directions of fit' to the world of the two attitudes. This, however, would take us well beyond our present brief, which is to find a plausible reinterpretation of Hume's original formulation of the practicality argument, which, given a 'moderate' reading of premiss 2, is able to secure its validity. I turn then finally to the 'mandatory' reinterpretation.

5 Mandatoriness

(i) Mackie's Hume: surprisingly metaphysical

As with the 'sufficiency' and the 'intrinsicality' reinterpretations, we will try out some preliminary formulations, starting with the following:

> Premiss 1: Moral judgements constrain our actions. (cf. Mackie: 'Just seeing that this is right and that is wrong . . . tends to *make* someone do this or refrain from that.')[29]
> Premiss 2: Beliefs are required if we are to act, but none can constrain us to do so.
> Conclusion: Moral judgements are not beliefs but desires.

Now premiss 2, in denying to any belief the power to constrain our actions, which is ascribed by premiss 1 to moral judgements, ensures the fulfilment of requirement (i[1]). However, the conclusion will only follow provided it is also tacitly understood that desires, like moral judgements, and unlike beliefs, can also be said to constrain our actions, so meeting requirement (ii). Making this explicit, the following revised, valid, formulation might now be proposed:

> Premiss 1: Moral judgements constrain our actions.
> Premiss 2: Beliefs are required if we are to act, but none can constrain us to do so, *as desires can*.
> Conclusion: Moral judgements are not beliefs but desires.

But once premiss 1 is restated in this way, we cannot avoid the question whether any sense could be given on a Humean view (indeed, on any view) to talk of desires 'constraining' our actions. If we are to make any headway with this question we must first know how 'constrain' is being understood in premiss 1 where it is applied to moral judgements. Now two different ways of construing the term in this context are in principle possible: what we might call a 'metaphysical' and a 'moral phenomenological' construal.

The 'metaphysical' construal is chiefly associated with the Moral Rationalists – and so with some of Hume's most important opponents – for whom the claim that moral judgements constrain our actions has a basis in the so-called eternal 'fitness' of certain actions to certain situations. This 'fitness' is supposed both to be necessarily evident, as Clarke (see Mackie, 1980: 54) puts it, to 'all intelligent beings', and also to necessarily determine their wills accordingly, unless these were 'corrupted' by particular passions and affections. But it will surely seem that the idea of incorporating such a metaphysical view into the first premiss of any argument originating with Hume must be dismissed outright.

It may be suggested that we pass on immediately to the moral phenomenological construal on grounds that it possesses the advantages of the 'intrinsicality' reinterpretation without its attendant disadvantages. For, as we saw, on the latter reinterpretation, the metaphysical implications of positing a necessary link between moral judgements and motivation could only be avoided by maintaining that there was here only one psychological state, capable of two different descriptions. But this contradicted Hume's explicitly stated position. On the phenomenological construal, however, 'constraint' refers merely to a subjective feeling of constraint experienced by the moral agent, and so there is no need to explain it as an actual nexus of any kind, and so no need to conflate moral judgement and motivation, any more than Hume does.

Before, however, we take this advice, we should pause to note the somewhat surprising fact that Mackie (recently joined by other writers),[30] draws heavily on the metaphysical reading in attempting to refute those, like Harrison, who agree that a type of 'mandatory' reinterpretation secures the argument's formal validity,[31] but complain that its first premiss is (and would be taken by Hume to be) obviously false. Since Mackie, though sceptical as to whether it would ever be possible to find the 'correct interpretation of what Hume says', claims to be using Hume's 'materials' in his reconstruction of the argument, it is worthwhile considering this unexpected reconstruction further.

Mackie first rejects a linguistic reading of premiss 1 as claiming that our moral judgements constrain our actions. It would, he claims, be inadequate to 'moral characterization [as it] has been understood throughout the whole history of moral philosophy' were the premiss meant merely to draw attention to the *linguistic* oddity of using words like right and wrong without prescriptive force. He then expounds the alternative metaphysical reading of the premiss as one 'represented by the way in which . . . moral terms combine a descriptive logic with a prescriptive force, namely that there are objective requirements or categorical imperatives, in the nature of things' (1980: 55). He suggests that on this reading, premiss 1 not only reflects our traditional understanding of morality, but that indeed of the Moral Rationalists – Hume's opponents – themselves. Hence, he argues, to reject the premiss, as does Harrison, would find, even as a way of 'draw[ing] the teeth of Hume's argument' (ibid.: 54), little general favour, even among Hume's opponents.

Mackie seems to be suggesting that if the metaphysical reading is adopted, Hume's argument can be defended against critics, such as Harrison, who deny the premiss's truth on this interpretation. But it is difficult to see who among Hume's supporters would wish to avail themselves of this peculiarly self-defeating strategy. We are not surely to imagine Hume himself proposing such a traditional metaphysical reading. We have seen not only that he emphasizes (3.1.1:22) that 'knowing virtue' and 'conforming the will to it' are two distinct particulars precisely in order to demonstrate the absurdity of the implied necessary connection, but also that all the evidence he adduces for premiss 1 is from 'common experience'.

Nor, I think, would it help to point out that in two of his formulations of the practicality argument, Hume attributes to moral judgement, and denies to reason, the capacity to 'contradict or approve' a passion or action. As the text makes clear, he does not take himself to be talking (whether in denying it to reason, or attributing it to morality) of a special normative power – a power, that is, to 'require' us to relinquish vicious tendencies as it might be said reason can require us to relinquish false beliefs. Rather, his intention seems to be to establish that reason cannot conflict with passion as other passions and desires can. It cannot do this, moreover, because it is not the same kind of thing as a passion or desire, or because as Hume puts it: 'nothing can oppose or retard the impulse of passion but a contrary impulse'. There is thus no question here of any other influence being at stake than an ordinary causal one. (Of course, identifying this as the influence that Hume is here denying to reason in denying that it cannot generate the requisite impulse, we have again passed – almost imperceptibly – from the 'moderate' reading of premiss 2, which is our sole concern here, to the 'extreme' reading.)

We must then reject the suggestion that Hume himself could have endorsed premiss 1 on the metaphysical construal. The suggestion, however, is almost as incredible that he might have deliberately counted, for the success of his argument, on his first premiss being understood in such a way that it could have been consented to by his opponents, but not by himself. Perhaps Mackie's point is simply that the metaphysical reading is theoretically available to anyone trying to see what can be said for Hume's argument from a number of different angles. But even this can be challenged: if premiss 1 were really to encapsulate Mackie's traditional picture of morality as a set of objectively binding requirements to be discovered in 'the nature of things' it would already seem to entail that fusion of cognitive and volitional elements which would bring it into collision with premiss 2. For the latter premiss, if the argument's validity is to be secured, must at least deny, even on the 'moderate' version, that an exercise of reason, a belief or piece of knowledge (as Mackie refers to them) could thus logically implicate a practical response.

The situation could be eased if the scope of this denial were restricted, as Mackie notes, to ordinary exercises of reason, namely, demonstrative and means–end reasoning (the latter utilizing causal knowledge and factual information) which, as Mackie correctly observes, is in any case all Hume's evidence covers. But then the scope of the conclusion would have to be (as Mackie again points out) correspondingly restricted: it would thus no longer rule out those cognitivists, such as Clarke, who hold that the making of moral distinctions involves a special kind of reason. However, it would exclude all varieties of (cognitivist) naturalist. But this amendment of the second premiss only serves to increase the oddness of an account which would so construe the first premiss as to have Hume temporarily donning the colours of his anti-naturalist opponents in order to make his argument work. For now he is represented as having to do this merely in order to win a limited victory: that over a second type of cognitivist who, despite being a cognitivist, does at least share with Hume his naturalism.

No less problematic would be the attempt, which led us to consider the metaphysical account in the first place, to represent desire as constraining action in just the way moral judgements are represented on this account as doing. However, the source of the difficulty now is not the subsumption of alien Humean elements within an essentially metaphysical framework, but rather the character of the metaphysical account itself. For desire only enters the motivational picture on this account as an irrational and subversive force preventing the agent's rational apprehension of morality's demands from inexorably engendering the relevant actions. It would seem therefore to involve a serious misunderstanding of this view to ascribe to desire that very motivational function whose disruption is apparently desire's main effect.

(ii) Mandatoriness as a subjective feeling of constraint

We turn then to the second, and *prima facie* more promising construal of the claim that moral judgements constrain our actions: that in terms of ordinary moral phenomenology. Now it is sometimes pointed out (see, e.g. McNaughton, 1988: 48) that once we become aware of a moral requirement our choice of action seems to us, as moral agents, to be constrained by that recognition. Now this account of what it is like to be a moral agent fits best with the kind of naturalistic cognitivism that McNaughton (and others) have recently advocated. It is unclear, however, what could, within such a framework, be the precise force of their claim other than that we typically feel constrained by our moral judgements, or at least not in any conventional way attracted to the course of action they prescribe. To adapt our example to the two cases: I may be reluctant to donate to famine relief because it would mean going without some luxury. Therefore, I feel the judgement that I ought to as an unwelcome demand. Alternatively, I am not reluctant to donate money, and going without the luxury will be no hardship for me. In fact, alleviating the suffering caused by famine is an important concern of mine. However, this concern is not a form of 'attraction', as it would be were I to have some romantic idea of myself as a great philanthropist, rather it has a distinctive peremptory quality.

Now it is no accident that it is mainly those naturalists who hold that moral judgements are states of belief who typically espouse this construal of their relation with action, since it seems to get its plausibility at least partly, as we can see, from the contrast with desire, and what it feels like to be moved by desire.[32] It is another matter altogether therefore when we wish to import the moral phenomenological construal of the link between moral judgements and action into an argument purporting to demonstrate that moral judgements are themselves feelings or desires. For there is at the very least a *prima facie* oddness about taking a characterization which only seems in the first place to apply to moral judgements because of their possible conflict with desire, and applying it to desire itself.

In fact, the move would only be acceptable if we had a principled account of the difference between those desires which, like moral judgements on this interpretation, it makes sense to say that we feel constrained to fulfil – our desire, say, not to be the kind of person who would let down a friend, or who couldn't keep a secret, etc. – and those to which, by contrast, we easily yield, or even have to struggle not to succumb to, say our desire for cream cakes. But any such account would have to make it credible that obedience to morality, when properly understood, could turn out to be essentially a matter of fulfilling those of one's desires that fall into the former category, while at the same time not giving the impression that these 'desires' are really just thinly disguised moral judgements masquerading as desires.

(iii) Morality as natural and pleasurable, not constraining

We need not, however, pursue this particular line of inquiry further. The picture of agents who only act rightly because they feel compelled to do so by their sense of duty is, as we saw earlier, wholly alien to Hume's emphasis on natural, non-moral, motives as the genesis of virtuous action. In fact, Hume holds that our sense of morality always follows the common and natural course of the passions, rather than leading it. We drop money into the charity box as a pleasurable outflowing of our generous natures, only later recognizing that such generous actions arouse in a disinterested spectator a sentiment of moral approval. Admittedly there are exceptional circumstances, as illustrated by Hume's 'self-hatred' example, where a person, acutely conscious that she lacks the requisite natural motive, tries to escape this uncomfortable feeling by performing 'grateful' actions from 'a sense of duty'. But even here it is noteworthy that Hume speaks of the person as 'pleas'd' to perform grateful acts, and so banishes any impression of unwillingness or constraint.

But what of the situation which we described earlier as a clash of duty and desire? The nearest Hume comes to describing such a situation is at 3.3.1:23 where he observes that:

> My sympathy with another may give me the sentiment of pain and disapprobation, when any object is presented, that has a tendency to give him uneasiness; tho' I may not be willing to sacrifice any thing of my own interest, or cross any of my passions, for his satisfaction . . . [thus] a house may displease me by being ill-contriv'd for the convenience of the owner, and yet I may refuse to give a shilling toward the rebuilding of it.

The striking thing here is that, as Hume presents it, there is really no clash at all. My behaviour is just a fact about me, and so like any other, simply to be recorded rather than moralized about. It is perhaps conceivable that I may be naturally blessed with a benevolent disposition, and so will be moved to contribute out of my own pocket to the rebuilding of the miserable shack in which its owner presently finds shelter. Otherwise, as is far more likely, I will not be prepared to lift a finger. Even here, however, I will, on Hume's view, probably still experience that disagreeable feeling of moral disapproval at the thought of anyone having to live in such a mean and rundown dwelling. But whether I am gifted with a benevolent nature is ultimately, or so this passage implies, beyond my control. Consequently both the idea of deliberately submitting myself to the precept 'help others in distress', or of being racked with remorse at failing to do so, appears finally irrelevant, if not incoherent.

6 A radical proposal

It looks then as though the last of the three possible reinterpretations to be considered is no more, perhaps even less, feasible than the other two. Our project of seeing whether the argument's validity could be sustained by using just the 'moderate' reading of the second premiss is therefore more or less in tatters. Shouldn't we simply abandon this 'moderate' version of the argument, and wholeheartedly embrace the 'extreme' one which is valid just as it stands? But this would mean deliberately disregarding all those remarks of Hume's implying that reason does, with the help of desire, move us to action, and around which we have built the 'moderate' version. Moreover, no clear sense has yet been given to the second premiss of the 'extreme' version, according to which reason is 'perfectly inert'.

These difficulties prompt a radical proposal. Accepting (at least for the time being) the *prima facie* contradiction affirmed in the previous chapter, we shall treat the practicality argument *as if* there were, compressed within its apparently unitary structure, two arguments – one valid, one invalid – depending upon whether premiss 2 is taken to mean that reason moves us to action, but only with the help of desire, or that reason cannot move us to action. In the next two chapters, we shall consider what light this putative division might shed on Hume's underlying intentions. It will, of course, only qualify as a reconstruction of them if we can find a corresponding variation in the conceptions of reason, as it impinges on morality, propounded by Hume's different opponents. There would also have to be evidence that Hume himself recognized this variation, and fashioned his argument sometimes in one way, sometimes in the other, to take account of it. The apparent contradiction would then resolve itself into a systematic ambiguity in Hume's use of 'reason' across the different readings. The immediately following chapter, in making clear who, among his contemporaries, the 'extreme' version might be directed against, will at the very least have the merit of removing much of the obscurity presently surrounding that version.

3 Metaphysics and the 'Extreme' Version

The only opponents we can be certain that Hume is addressing in the whole of 3.1.1 are moral rationalists, such as Cudworth, Wollaston and Clarke – indeed, they have been called Hume's 'real opponents' (Mackie, 1980: 47). Our chapter begins by expounding their position in general, and their conception of reason in particular. This allows us to identify a difficulty, peculiar to this conception, which is bound to seem to anyone not sharing their metaphysical world view to rule out, as an absurdity, reason having *any* motivating influence. We thus have here at last a possible sense, and content, for Hume's claim that reason is 'perfectly inert'. It still does not follow that, in bringing his 'extreme' charge, Hume actually has this singular metaphysical difficulty in mind. In order therefore to establish that he does, we sift through all his various arguments against the moral rationalists (excepting the practicality argument itself), seeking to pick out at least one which explicitly draws attention to the very difficulty that we have isolated in expounding the moral rationalists' conception of reason. We also attempt to show that, among Hume's objections to moral rationalism, there are none which might suggest an alternative, less radical, interpretation of his dramatic metaphor.

It may be asked why we cannot go directly to the *Treatise,* but must approach the relevant passages gingerly already apprised of what we are looking for. Admittedly, Hume's criticisms lay open to view. However, our post-Humean distaste for metaphysics has tended to blind us to the metaphysical import of these criticisms. It has rendered them virtually indistinguishable from the more stock 'Humean' criticisms of ordinary naturalistic cognitivism. In this way, the 'extreme' reading of premiss 2 of the practicality argument collapses into the 'moderate' one.

It would, of course, be a result of some significance should it turn out that these philosophers – the only ones Hume is clearly, if implicitly, singling out for attack – propound a concept of reason which fits them to be targets of the 'extreme' version of the practicality argument, when it is generally the 'moderate' version (despite its invalidity) that is endorsed by today's writers. Nevertheless, in order to fully justify our proposal of treating the practicality argument as really containing two separate arguments, depending upon how the second premiss is read, it will also be necessary to identify a second type of opponent: one who might credibly represent the target of the 'moderate' version. But this will be left to Chapter 4, where we will maintain that it is quite implausible that it could be these same rationalists whom Hume has in mind when he goes on to deny (3.1.1:26) that moral distinctions can be *inferences from matters of fact*.

1 Cudworth and Clarke: reason mired

Since Hume mentions no opponent by name, how can we be so certain that he is addressing Cudworth, Clarke and Wollaston? With Clarke, it is a matter of Hume's various references to the claim 'that there are eternal fitnesses and unfitnesses of things' (see, for instance, 3.1.1:4,17). For this claim, couched in exactly this terminology, is characteristic of Clarke, in whose work, *A Discourse of Natural Religion*,[1] it is (as we shall shortly see) repeatedly found. On the other hand, Hume's discussion of the assertion that 'falshood is the foundation of all guilt and deformity' (3.1.1:15) is just as clearly a reference to Wollaston, who makes this distinctive assertion in his *The Religion of Nature Delineated*,[2] and who is the 'late author' mentioned in note 68 (3.1.1:15). Hume's talk of 'the immutable measures of right and wrong' suggests Cudworth whose work is entitled 'A *Treatise Concerning Eternal and Immutable Morality*'.[3] His reference (3.1.1:18) to 'an opinion very industriously propagated by certain philosophers, that morality is susceptible of demonstration . . . and may be brought to an equal certainty with geometry or algebra' suggests both Cudworth and Clarke. Most telling of all is perhaps his allusion (3.1.1:4) to the claim that 'the Deity himself', alongside 'every rational being that considers them', is obliged by these 'immutable measures of right and wrong'. For this extension of the scope of obligation to cover God is a peculiar feature of the moral rationalism of these two writers.

(i) The precaution of shutting the windows

Many recent commentators, discussing Hume's predecessors and opponents, do not mention Cudworth at all, while treating Clarke and Wollaston separately. It has been said indeed (Mackie, 1980: 20) that Wollaston marks an advance on Clarke since he provides a general account of the distinction between virtue and vice, whereas Clarke's list of moral and immoral actions remains essentially heterogeneous. Wollaston's account also satisfies, in the simplest and most direct way possible, Hume's requirement that if morality is to be a matter of reason, then since reason is 'the discovery of truth or falshood', morality must likewise be a matter of truth or falsehood. For, according to Wollaston, *actions*, and not only propositions, are true or false. Actions are true, he claims, when they 'express things as they are', and then they are virtuous. They are false when they deny this reality, and then they are vicious. If I fail to keep a promise I have made to you, my failure to do so is 'saying' that I never made that promise, and it is this falsehood that makes my conduct immoral. If I take your car keys, and drive off in your car, my action declares falsely that this is my car, and so again my action is wrong.

Hume (3.1.1:13–15) refutes this view in a number of different ways. First, in many instances, the falsehood that I supposedly express by my action is not something I myself am deceived about. Consequently, for my action, in these instances, to be immoral others must witness it, and be taken in by the falsehood it expresses. But then all that seems necessary if I am to avoid falling into immorality here is for me to conceal my action from others. Thus Hume sarcastically advises the adulterer who wants to escape blameworthiness that all he has to do is to 'use the precaution of shutting the windows' before 'indulging [himself] in those liberties with [his] neighbour's wife' (3.1.1:15, note 68).

Leaving this objection aside, examples such as this and others, concerning e.g. stealing, and promise keeping, seem, as Hume notes, to be reliant upon, rather than providing a foundation for, notions of property, rights and obligations. Consequently, once we divest ourselves of the relevant assumptions, and moral categories, the problem arises of why truth and falsehood (Hume's 'agreement and disagreement to reason') should be considered in themselves to mark the distinction between virtue and vice. Certainly, as Hume observes, there are many falsehoods which do not attract moral culpability. As he points out (3.1.1:12) 'errors' so far from being 'the source of all immorality . . . are commonly very innocent, and draw no manner of guilt upon the person who is so unfortunate as to fall into them'. Indeed, such a person is 'more to be lamented than blam'd'. Then, again, if it is being in error which in itself is immoral, the *content* of the error will not matter; it will not matter, that is to say, 'whether the question be concerning an apple or a kingdom, or whether the error is avoidable or unavoidable' (3.1.1:13). In fact, Wollaston himself admits that different falsehoods have different degrees of immorality attaching to them. But if not all falsehoods are immoral – or not immoral to the same extent – then a criterion is required for singling out those which are immoral from those which aren't – or for singling out those which are more, from those which are less, immoral.

I shall not pursue further this discussion of Wollaston since in order to provide such a criterion, he eventually moves away from simple 'truth-as-correspondence' (as Baillie, 2000: 119, aptly calls it) as determining why certain actions express, and others do not, culpable falsehoods. Virtuous actions, Wollaston now tells us (1969: 280), are true in the sense of being in agreement with the 'natures of the things themselves', whereas vicious actions are false in that they deny this reality, and so are 'unnatural' or 'wrong in nature'. Moreover, according to Wollaston (ibid.: 282), things are as God has ordained them, so that to deny their nature is at once to disobey God, and to go against 'truths eternal'. This appeal, however, to 'the natures of the things' reveals that Wollaston's position rests ultimately on the same metaphysical foundation as Clarke's. Hence, it seems feasible, for our purposes, to subsume Wollaston under Clarke, and to take the latter, together with his interesting predecessor, Cudworth, as exemplary moral rationalists.

(ii) Things: their necessary and eternal differences

At the heart of the moral rationalist position is the claim that 'things are what they are by nature' (Cudworth, [1731] 1969: 122) or, expressed less gnomically, that each thing has an 'essence', which is responsible for its being what it is, and not another thing. As Clarke puts it ([1728] 1969: 226), extending Cudworth's point to cover relations: 'there are differences of things; and different relations, respects or proportions, of some things towards others.' Now the 'things' referred to include not only actions, situations, inanimate objects, abstract values, mathematical and geometrical figures, but also human beings and even God. The qualitative and relational characteristics that are responsible for their differences are similarly heterogeneous. Cudworth tells us that 'things are white by whiteness, and black by blackness, triangular by triangularity, and round by rotundity, like by likeness, and equal by equality, that is by such certain natures of their own', and again he writes, 'If there is to be anything good or evil, just or unjust, there must be something naturally good and just.'

Bound up with this central contention is the idea that whatever a thing is *by nature* it is so *necessarily,* or that, as Cudworth puts it ([1731] 1969: 120–1), 'when things exist, they are what they are, this or that, ... by the necessity of their own nature.' Hence, according to him, to deny that things have the nature they have is to incur a contradiction. He dismisses what he calls an 'arbitrarious essence' as an absurdity. Evidently conflating the ideas of a thing's having to have *some* essence rather than *none*, and of its having to have *this* particular essence rather than *that*, he argues that 'a being without a nature [is] ... a non-entity', and that to assert the existence of a non-entity is clearly contradictory. Indeed, even God, according to Cudworth, must respect a thing's nature, or else incur a contradiction. He writes, 'Omnipotence itself [cannot] make a thing white or black without whiteness or blackness', nor (in the case of 'geometrical figures') can 'it ... make a body triangular without having the nature and properties of a triangle in it ... nor circular without the nature of a circle'. Again, in respect of relational properties, he writes, '[Even an] omnipotent will cannot make things like or equal one to another, without the natures of likeness and equality.' 'The reason whereof', he goes on, 'is plain': it is 'because all these things imply a manifest contradiction ... and contradictories cannot be true; for otherwise, nothing would be certainly true or false'.

For Clarke, that there are 'differences of things' is 'as evident and undeniable, as that one magnitude or number, is greater, equal to, or smaller than another'. Of morality in particular, he writes ([1728] 1969: 229) 'Right and wrong are in themselves totally and essentially different, even altogether as much as white and black, light and darkness.' Consequently it would be, he observes (ibid.: 232), echoing Cudworth's charge of contradictoriness, as much an 'insolence and absurdity' for a person to try to 'pervert right', or 'to make light darkness, and darkness light; or to call sweet bitter and bitter sweet' as 'to pretend to alter the certain proportions of numbers, to take away the demonstrable relations and properties of mathematical figures'.

Since, however, as Cudworth puts it, 'a thing cannot be made any thing by mere will without a being or nature' it follows that 'every thing must [not only] be necessarily [but also] *immutably* determined by its own nature.' He speaks ([1731] 1969: 133) of the 'eternal and immutable essences and natures of things ... and their unchangeable relations to one another'. Clarke likewise ([1728] 1969: 225) speaks of the 'real difference, originally, necessarily and absolutely in the nature of things', and of 'the necessary and eternal different relations, that different things bear to one another'. These descriptions apply, for the moral rationalists, as much to morality as to all other areas. For Clark, therefore (ibid.: 227, 234, 249), there is an 'eternal difference' between 'good and evil', and again 'a natural unalterable difference' between 'right and wrong', while Cudworth's Treatise, as we observed earlier, is itself entitled *Eternal and Immutable Morality.*

Things being necessarily, immutably and eternally what they are, moral rationalists hold that their existence is *independent* of our (finite) minds. Thus Clarke speaks of 'the existence of the things themselves', and Cudworth ([1731] 1969: 133) of 'the truth and reality of things' and of 'that which really and absolutely is'. Earlier (ibid.: 122), confining his attention to morality, he had affirmed unequivocally that 'The natures of good or evil, just or unjust, really exist[s] in the world.'

(iii) Things: their intelligible nature

With this metaphysical backdrop in place, we can now go on to see how reason, as Cudworth and Clarke understand it, mediates our relation to this real world of essences and, thereby comes to play that pre-eminent role in moral judgement and motivation, decried by Hume. Cudworth does not, despite sometimes seeming to fall into this incoherence, evidently wish to attribute necessity *directly* to things, or their natures – to what Hume would call 'real existences'. He recognizes that we can only describe as thus necessary *relations between ideas* which, in turn, must be ([1731] 1969: 133) 'objects of the mind'. It is perhaps justifiable therefore to interpret Cudworth, thus far, as claiming no more than that *knowledge* of essences is expressed in *propositions* which are necessary truths. Since – and here Cudworth and the moral rationalists plunge back into metaphysics – a thing's nature, or essence, is *eternal*, it can only be 'the object' of a similarly 'eternal mind or intellect', namely God's. But Cudworth also claims that this 'eternal intellect' is that from which 'all [our] particular intellects are derived', and in which (ibid.: 133, 128) they 'participat[e]'. Hence in so far as these eternal and immutable things are intelligible to us (and both Cudworth and Clarke hold that they are), it would seem only to be because their intelligibility is already part of their natures, as objects of God's eternal mind. But then from our finite point of view their intelligibility will seem to be a feature of the world itself. It is hardly surprising therefore to find Cudworth ([1731] 1969: 134) speaking of 'the intelligible natures and essences of things', and again of 'the nature and reason of the world', and Clarke ([1728] 1969: 231) of 'the reason of things', or (ibid.: 233, 242, 245) of 'the same eternal reason of things'.

For the moral rationalists then, reason inheres, both in our individual minds and in the world. It seems indeed that, for them, our comprehension of the eternal and immutable truths posited is made possible precisely because the reason of the world finds this echo in our minds. As Cudworth ([1731] 1969: 135) puts it: things have '[an] interior analogy . . . to a certain inward determination in the soul itself', and again (ibid.: 132) 'to know or understand a thing is nothing else but by some inward anticipation of the mind,[4] that is native and domestic, and so familiar to it, to take acquaintance with it.' As we should expect, their view entails a sharp distinction between reason and mere 'sense'. Cudworth, for instance, echoing Boethius, contrasts the rational mind which 'as it were looks down . . . upon the individuals below it', and so 'views . . . and understands . . . them', with 'sense' which 'lies flat and grovelling in the individuals . . . stupidly fixed in the material form . . . not able to rise up or ascend to an abstract universal notion'. It is, he goes on, developing the metaphor, like 'an eye which is placed in a level with the sea, and touch[ing] the surface of it, cannot take [as can reason] any large prospect on the sea'.

(iv) Clarke's 'fitnesses' and 'unfitnesses' and moral obligation

But moral judgements, as the rationalists acknowledge, are primarily about what we ought, or ought not, to *do*. How then do such obligations, and our acknowledgement of them, fit into the largely theoretical picture so far expounded? Clarke here ([1728] 1969: 225) introduces a crucial notion – one indeed that was taken over by his rationalist successors, and used well into the twentieth century: that of the 'fitnesses' and 'unfitnesses' of things. Having made his opening claim concerning the necessary and eternal relations that different things bear to each other, he develops, and extends, this claim in three ways. First, he tells us (ibid.: 226) that 'from these different relations of different things, there necessarily arises an agreement or disagreement of some things with others, or a fitness or unfitness of the application of different things or different relations one to another.' His illustration is that it follows from God's necessary, eternal and immutable nature as infinitely superior to men that it is fitting that they 'should honour and worship, obey and imitate God, rather than . . . endeavour to dishonour and disobey Him'.

Second, he asserts that 'there is a fitness or suitableness of certain circumstances to certain persons, and an unsuitableness of others', which he tells us are 'founded in the nature of things and the qualifications of persons, antecedent to all positive appointments whatsoever'. He illustrates this claim, again theologically, as follows:

> it is a thing absolutely and necessarily fitter in itself, that the supreme author and creator of the universe, should govern, order, and direct all things to certain constant and regular ends; than that every thing should be permitted to go on at adventures, and produce uncertain effects merely by chance and in the utmost confusion, without any determinate view or design at all.

Finally, turning to conduct between people, he states that it is 'from the different relations of one person to another' that 'there necessarily arises a fitness or unfitness of certain manners of behaviour of some persons towards others.' Illustrating, he writes:

> in men's dealing and conversing one with another, it is undeniably more fit, absolutely and in the nature of the thing itself, that all men should endeavour to promote the universal good and welfare of all; than that all men should be continually contriving the ruin and destruction of all.

Though Cudworth, unlike Clarke, does not invoke this idea of 'fitnesses'and 'unfitnesses' in elucidating obligation, his underlying position is similar. For Clarke's 'fitnesses' and 'unfitnesses' are, as we have seen, ultimately founded in the eternal nature of things, to which Cudworth also constantly points as the source of obligation. Indeed, for him, any obligatoriness that 'positive laws and commands' possess is entirely due ([1731] 1969: 122) to 'the natures of good and evil, just and unjust, really existing in the world'. It is, he tells us, this 'moral nature of things' (ibid.: 123), which obliges us to obey lawful authority and keep oaths and covenants. No mere enactment of a law, could Cudworth declares, conjure 'a new moral entity' out of nothing: our obligations hold not only 'immediately', but also 'absolutely and perpetually'. Indeed, even 'the bare will of God himself could not beget an obligation upon any to do what he willed and commanded, because the natures of things do not depend upon will, being not things that are arbitrarily made, but things that are' (ibid.: 122, and Clarke, [1728] 1969: 231).

(v) Self-evidence of obligation

As we have seen, Clarke's 'fitnesses' and 'unfitnesses' of behaviour, and so our obligation to perform particular actions in particular situations, arise *necessarily* out of the different eternal relations of different things to each other. That they do so is therefore, Clarke argues, as 'plain as that there is any such thing as proportion, or disproportion, in geometry and arithmetic, or uniformity or difformity in comparing together the respective figures of bodies', and again, as 'manifest' as that 'the properties which flow from the essences of different mathematical figures, have different congruities or incongruities between themselves'. In order then to discover our obligations in different situations, we have only to *read them off* from these 'different eternal relations of different things to each other', as we would the properties of different mathematical figures, by reflection upon the figures themselves, and their interrelations. Moreover, the knowledge we thereby gain is similarly *indubitable*. As Clarke puts it:

> what these eternal and unalterable relations, respects, and proportions of things, with their consequent agreements or disagreements, fitnesses and unfitnesses . . . *are* in themselves that also they *appear to be* to the *understandings* of all intelligent beings, except those only who understand things to be what they are not, that is whose understanding are either very imperfect, or very much depraved.
>
> ([1728] 1969: 230, his italics)

Cudworth goes further in stating ([1731] 1969: 126) that it is only because we are rational that we have obligations at all. 'Natural justice', he writes, is partly a matter of the moral nature of things really existing in the world, and partly of our own nature as intellectual beings.

In short, we are bound, according to these writers, by obligations which, flowing necessarily from the eternal, immutable nature and reason of things, as well as from our own rational natures, are not only self-evident, so that we *must* assent to them, but hold *logically prior* to any such assent.

(vi) Clarke's 'fitnesses' and 'unfitnesses' and moral motivation

But the moral rationalists recognize that our obligations are practical, not merely in having actions as their *objects*, but also in actually *leading* to action. As Clarke puts it ([1728] 1969: 230): 'By [their] understanding or knowledge of the natural and necessary relations, fitnesses and proportions of things, the *wills* likewise of all intelligent beings are constantly directed, and must needs be determined to act accordingly.' The only exception he makes indeed is for 'those only, who will things to be what they are not and cannot be: that is whose wills are corrupted by particular interest or affection; or swayed by some unreasonable and prevailing passion'.

We saw just above that, for these writers, our moral obligations, ultimately derived as they are from the eternal, immutable nature of things, hold prior to, and independently of, any recognition by us of them. We can now also see that, though of course we can scarcely obey obligations that we are unaware of, it is nevertheless, for these writers, no mere subjective psychological state of ours, cognitive or otherwise, which is the immediate determinant of our will. It is, as Clarke puts it (ibid.: 231): '[that] same eternal reason of things' which God is pleased to allow to determine his own will. He goes on to insist that:

> originally and in reality it is as natural and (morally speaking) necessary, that the will should be determined in every action by the reason of the thing . . . as it is natural and (absolutely speaking) necessary, that the understanding should submit to a demonstrated truth.
>
> (ibid.: 232)

Clarke also admits here that there is a difference between *rationally assenting* to the necessary truth that we are obliged, say, to keep our promises, and actually *keeping*, or choosing to keep, them. He writes, 'assent to a plain speculative truth is not in a man's power to withhold; but to act according to the plain right and reason of things this he may by the natural liberty of his will, forbear.' This is not, however, as might have been expected, a prelude to a consideration of how, in this case, our wills can possibly be said to be accessible to reason at all. Rather, he simply affirms that they *are* so. A person who breaches his obligations is, he tells us, 'guilty of as great an absurdity *in practice*, and of as plainly contradicting the right reason of his own mind, as he who in a *dispute* is reduced to a necessity of asserting something inconsistent with itself' (1728] 1969: 257, Clarke's italics).

There is a point (Cudworth, [1731] 1969: 127–8) where Cudworth seems similarly poised to raise doubts about the will's tractability to reason, going so far as to describe it as 'not only a blind and dark thing . . . but also indefinite and indeterminate', and contrasting it with 'wisdom . . . a most determinate and inflexible thing'. But again these doubts, if there at all, do not materialize. In fact, he holds up the will's inchoateness as evidence of its being perfectly fitted by nature to be controlled by 'wisdom' or 'knowledge'. The will, he states 'has [thus] the nature of a thing regulable and measurable' unlike wisdom, which 'in itself hath the nature of a rule and measure'.

(vii) Reason's inertia and causal laws

The difficulty that looks as if it might surface in these remarks, but never does, concerns how we can bring *our* reason (the 'reason of the soul', as Clarke and Cudworth would call it), whose sphere of operation is solely ideas, to bear on anything so apparently rationally opaque as the will. There is, however, another difficulty which cannot be fully disentangled from the first, and on top of which the first has, in so far as the moral rationalists are nowadays discussed at all, become largely superimposed. The first difficulty can still today be formulated without incoherence whereas, such is our conceptual distance from the moral rationalists, it is not clear that the second can be. It concerns how (to use Clarke's phrase) 'the bare reason *of the world*' – the reason inhering in things, and their relations, as they 'really exist' outside us – can impinge *directly* on our wills, and so lead to action.

In fact, this difficulty breaks down into two separate ones. The first concerns how 'the different relations that different things bear to one another', and the entailed 'fitnesses' and 'unfitnesses' of different actions to different situations, can be characterized as *rational,* despite apparently *really existing* outside our minds. But even supposing this problem could be eased by invoking (as we did earlier) the theological background, there would still remain a second one. For the rationalists, the immediate and sole precursor of moral action – that which affords a complete explanation of the action – is not any subjective, psychological state of the agent. It is not, that is to say, his personally coming to believe, where he did not before, that there is out there a certain 'fitness' or 'unfitness' of actions to situations; nor is it his personally coming to accept, where he did not before, that a certain kind of conduct is obligatory on him. This would introduce into the outcome an element of contingency, of individual variation, and uncertainty which, for the rationalists, only characterizes *immoral* conduct. Rather, it is the objective 'fitnesses', or 'unfitnesses' themselves, laid bare to his understanding, even as they are to God's, which provides his motive for action. But how, it will be asked, can any human action occur otherwise than through the usual psychological channels, no matter whether these are characterized cognitively or conatively?

Behind this question there looms an even more far-reaching one. How can there occur any change from one state of affairs, B (my not being motivated to P) to another, C (my being motivated to P), without there having first occurred a change in some other, relevantly related, state of affairs, A? To suppose, as do the rationalists, that the change from B to C is brought about by 'relations' and 'fitnesses' which, being fixed and eternal, cannot themselves suffer any change is, it will be complained, to contemplate an absurdity: the abrogation of ordinary causal laws.

(viii) The meaning of 'inert'

Lying somewhere near the centre of this tangled skein of difficulties concerning Clarke's and Cudworth's claim that reason, construed as an objective system of relations, or essences, can be a motive for actions, is one particular feature: reason's immutability. Our question now is: could Hume be referring to this feature when he dismisses reason as 'inert'? Consider first the terms 'inert', 'inertia' and 'inertness'.

The *OED* offers two main meanings for the adjective, 'inert', depending on whether it is predicated of 'matter and material things' or of 'persons'. Confining ourselves to the first category (the second adds little of relevance for our inquiry), we find again two meanings either (i) 'having no inherent powers of action, motion or resistance; inactive, inanimate; having the property of inertia', or (ii) 'without active chemical, physiological, or other properties'. (i) is illustrated by, among other quotations, Herschel's remark (1830) that 'to say that matter is inert is only to say that the cause is expended in producing its effect.' Examples given of the figurative use of 'inert' in sense (i) include Hazlitt, writing (1820) of 'the inert mass of accumulated prejudices'. 'Inert' in sense (ii) is illustrated by reference to H. Spencer's assertion (1864) that 'carbon is totally inert at ordinary heats', and also by the claim in *Cassell's Technical Education Manual* (1879) that 'the collodian film is inert and plays no actual part in the production of a picture.'

Turning next to 'inertia', this term, introduced into physics by Keppler, is defined as 'That property of matter by virtue of which it continues in its existing state, whether of rest or uniform motion in a straight line, unless that state is altered by an external force'. The illustrations offered of its use include Phillips' (1706) definition of *'vis inertiae'* as 'That bare power of resistance only, by which every body endeavours to continue in the state in which it is either of rest or motion', and J. Woods' (1803) as 'That quality by which [a body] resists . . . change'. The figurative use of 'inertia' in this sense is illustrated by J. Martineau's reference (1843) to 'the inertia of a massive civilization'. Finally, 'inertness' is defined as 'inactivity', and yet again as 'an inactive, or inoperative, condition'.

Now it is striking that, though the core idea conveyed by all three terms, in all their various usages, is of inactivity, what is thereby denied of, say, x, may be either its ability to affect something else, or to be affected itself. For instance, to say that a chemical substance is 'inert' typically entails that it cannot interact with other chemicals so as to affect its environment. Likewise, if we speak of the 'inertness' of something, meaning that it is in 'an inoperative condition', we are suggesting that it is not 'taking effect' in whatever way it usually does. But the idea that to call something 'inert' is to deny that it is thus, in some sense or other, an agent of change is most clear in the Cassell quotation, where it is just another way of saying that it 'plays no actual part' in producing an outcome.

By contrast, to draw attention to x's 'inertia' typically indicates that x cannot itself be moved, or changed, or affected, or at least only with great difficulty. Thus, Martineau, by speaking of the 'inertia of a massive civilization' conveys the idea of stagnation, of something into which it is almost impossible to introduce change. But this leeway in the use of 'inert' and 'inertia', as to whether we are talking about something from the point of view of its being an *agent*, or a *subject*, of change, should not really surprise us since, as we saw earlier, the ability of one thing to bring about a change in another, and its own ability to undergo change are, certainly for us, intimately linked. In fact, Herschel's remark even contributes a kind of intuitive explanation for this: something, all of whose force is used up just in its remaining still, inactive, unchanging, has no surplus force to expend on changing something else.

In applying these findings to Hume's use of the epithet 'inert', we must bear in mind that, on whatever meaning we settle, we shall of course be speaking figuratively. Now if we assume unreflectively that Hume must be thinking of reason from the point of view of its being an agent of change, then for us his calling it 'inert' will be just another way of denying that it can have the requisite effect on the will. That is, to say that reason is inert will be to state what is here the conclusion, rather than to point to the grounds of this conclusion in the more fundamental inability of reason, as construed by Clarke and Cudworth, to undergo change itself. But we are in the fortunate position of having noted that 'inert' can be used either to point to something's inability to affect something else, or to point to its inability to be itself affected. What is to stop us then taking Hume's use of the epithet to indicate why reason, as construed here, cannot influence the will, rather than merely that it cannot, namely because of its imperviousness to change? Of course, the *vis inertiae*, even employed figuratively, merely signifies, as we saw, the property of resistance to change, not that of rendering change inconceivable. But surely it would have to signify the latter if applied to Clarke and Cudworth's 'eternal reason of the world'? However, in transposing a term from a scientific, or everyday, context, to a metaphysical one some slippage seems unavoidable, and can, I think, be tolerated. In any case, may we not plausibly read into the fact that Hume says, not just that reason is 'inert', but that it is *'perfectly* inert', an implicit acknowledgement of this more profound changelessness?

Looking ahead, and also backward to our earlier analysis of the practicality argument, we can see that this way of giving sense and content to Hume's description would, if acceptable, advance our inquiry several steps. For it would effectively seal off the 'extreme' reading of premiss 2 (with which we have associated Hume's talk of reason's perfect inertia), from the 'moderate' reading, according to which, though reason cannot on its own move us to action, it can do so with the help of desire. It would seem a hopeless enterprise for anyone, rejecting the claim that 'the eternal reason of the world' could (given the break in causal laws it would entail) impinge on the will, to try to salvage for this *same* conception of reason any motivating role at all, even a minor one alongside desire. The two accounts of motivation – one which flouts, and one, which respects causal laws – like the two different conceptions of reason involved, belong, it must surely be apparent, to incompatible systems of thought. It is hard to see how any attempt to graft part of one of these systems on to the other without falling into incoherence could succeed. Consequently, the objection (familiar from the 'moderate' reading of the practicality argument) that reason cannot on its own bring about action, but needs desire must, if it is to have any relevance at all, be directed at a wholly different position from that of the moral rationalists.

But all this, it will be countered, is premature. In dismissing reason as 'inert', Hume *might*, given the range of meanings of this term, be pointing to the absurdity of claiming that anything as *immutable* as Clarke's eternal 'fitnesses' and unfitnesses' could, bypassing the ordinary psychological channels, affect the will. In order conclusively to establish this interpretation, however, it would be necessary to show that, among Hume's objections to moral rationalism, there are none which might suggest an alternative, but equally plausible, interpretation. Then, we must clinch our interpretation by citing other passages, aside from Hume's characterization of reason as 'inert', which, primed as we now are, we plainly see can *only* be references to the cluster of difficulties, of which the charge of abrogating causal laws is at the heart.

2 The forbidden transition from 'is' to 'ought'

(i) Moral rationalists not necessarily Hume's sole targets

So far, we have proceeded in the sure knowledge that, at the very least, Hume has among his targets in 3.1.1, moral rationalists, such as Clarke and Cudworth. This is the background to our detailed exposition of the Clarke–Cudworth position. It is also the background to our attempt to show how their conception of reason, as inhering in 'the eternal nature of things' might, when claimed to be motivational, plausibly draw from Hume the sarcastic retort but '[your] reason is perfectly inert.' In considering, however, whether, among his arguments against the moral rationalists (leaving aside the practicality argument), there is not one which might suggest a less 'metaphysical' interpretation of Hume's metaphor, a question arises: but which of Hume's arguments *are* directed at the moral rationalists?

This question might at first seem otiose. Don't all Hume's arguments have as their target the claim that moral distinctions are discovered by reason, and haven't we just said that the moral rationalists are the only philosophers that we can be sure Hume is here addressing? So much is true. However, it does not follow – though most commentators give this impression – that *all* Hume's arguments are directed against the moral rationalists. This would only follow if we could be certain that, when Hume mentions those for whom 'moral distinctions are . . . deriv'd from reason', he is referring solely to the moral rationalists. But, out of the three passages bearing on this issue, only one, the first actually suggests this.

Hume 'opens up his inquiry' (3.1.1:3) by asking '*whether 'tis by means of our* ideas *or* impressions *we* distinguish *betwixt vice and virtue, and pronounce an action blameable or praise-worthy*' (his italics). He goes on:

> Those who affirm that virtue is nothing but a conformity to reason; that there are eternal fitnesses and unfitnesses of things, which are the same to every rational being that considers them; that the immutable measures of right and wrong impose an obligation, not only on human creatures, but also on the Deity himself: All these systems concur in the opinion, that morality, like truth, is discern'd merely by ideas, and by their juxta-position and comparison.
>
> (3.1.1:4)

Now it must surely seem that Hume intends us to take the statements with which this passage begins and ends as equivalent. In other words, to 'affirm that virtue is nothing but a conformity to reason' is evidently to hold 'that morality, like truth, is discern'd merely by ideas, and by their juxtaposition and comparison'. But this in turn suggests that when, in 3, he spoke of 'distinguish [ing] betwixt vice and virtue' by means of our ideas, he meant more particularly, by means of their juxtaposition and comparison. It is natural therefore to conclude that Hume is going to be solely concerned in 3.1.1 with *one* view, that namely of the moral rationalists. This impression is reinforced by his sandwiching between the initial and final statements of the passage what are, pretty definitively, descriptions of Clarke's and Cudworth's positions.

Both passages which, by contrast, suggest that the moral rationalists are *not* Hume's only targets, come after the practicality argument has been stated in its various forms. Thus, having announced (3.1.1:17) that he is going 'to be more particular, and to show that those eternal immutable fitnesses and unfitnesses of things cannot be defended by sound philosophy', he suddenly and unexpectedly broadens the terms of his inquiry. It is now to include not only philosophers (such as the moral rationalists) who hold that moral distinctions involve a 'compar[ison] of ideas', but also others for whom they involve 'infer[ences] of matter of fact'. Re-invoking the division of reasoning into two kinds originally drawn in 2.3.3, he writes:

> If the thought and understanding were alone capable of fixing the boundaries of right and wrong, the character of virtuous and vicious either must lie in some relations of objects or must be a matter of fact, which is discover'd by our reasoning. This consequence is evident. As the operations of human understanding divide themselves into two kinds, the comparing of ideas, and the inferring of matter of fact; were virtue discover'd by the understanding; it must be an object of one of these operations, nor is there any third operation of the understanding, which can discover it.

It appears therefore that those who hold that morality is 'deriv'd from reason' may propound either of two views, only one of which is that of moral rationalists, such as Clarke and Cudworth. Hume goes on indeed to characterize the latter view still more narrowly as one according to which 'morality is susceptible of demonstration', and in which ''tis taken for granted, that this science may be brought to an equal certainty with geometry or algebra'.

The other passage which suggests that he has more than just the moral rationalists in mind is to be found (3.1.1:26) at the close of a sustained attempt to refute these philosophers. Here he states that the 'reasoning' which he has just employed in proving that morality 'consists not in any relations, that are the objects of science', can also be used to 'prove with equal certainty' that 'morality consists not in *any matter of fact*, which can be discover'd by the understanding.' Moreover, he describes this further application of his 'reasoning' as 'the *second* part of [an] argument', in which he aims to prove that 'morality is not an object of reason' (his italics).

It is not just, however, that Hume, in rejecting the claim that morality is 'deriv'd from reason', gives conflicting messages as to whether he is addressing a single type or two different types of opponent. The distinction itself, especially in light of what he has already said in Book 2 (3.3) is somewhat confusing. For instance, he contrasts

(3.1.1:18) those – presumably the moral rationalists – who regard morality as lying in *'some relations of objects'* with those for whom morality concerns *'matter of fact'*. That he wishes to link the talk of relations exclusively with demonstrative reasoning, and not with inferences to matters of fact is again apparent from the following remark: 'Upon this supposition, vice and virtue must consist *in some relations*; since 'tis allow'd on all hands, that no matter of fact is capable of being demonstrated' (my italics). However, in Book 2 (3.3:3) he allowed that there could be 'relations of objects *of which experience gives us information*' (my italics), writing: 'The understanding exerts itself after two ways, as it judges from demonstration or probability; as it regards the abstract relations of our ideas or those relations of objects of which experience only gives us information.'

There is certainly a puzzle here. The fact that only one out of the three cited passages suggests that Hume's sole target is the moral rationalists makes it doubtful that they are so. On the other hand, we must wonder why, if Hume has other opponents in view, he waits until halfway through the section to announce it. Did he perhaps change his mind mid-stream? Or did he, from the beginning, have two targets, but think that by and large the same arguments would demolish both? Or was it that he never completely distinguished them from each other in the first place?

It is interesting that virtually all commentators are silent on these questions. Perhaps they have chosen not to broach them because they would then be required to speculate as to the identity of Hume's 'second category' of opponents (as we might call them), when there are no obvious candidates. It is common practice, after all, to divide Hume's predecessors and contemporaries into, on the one hand, moral rationalists, comprising writers like Clarke, Cudworth and Wollaston and, on the other, sentimentalists, such as Lord Shaftesbury and Hutcheson. But it is taken for granted that these sentimentalists are, like Hume himself, subjectivists, not objectivists. Hence the possibility that they might be ranged alongside the moral rationalists, even as naturalistic, as opposed to metaphysical, opponents of Hume's, is never entertained. Indeed, the popular picture is of Hume having inherited the subjectivist mantle *from* Hutcheson. These assumptions can, however, be queried as we shall see in the next chapter.

(ii) The is–ought passage not necessarily directed at moral rationalists

While remaining aware of these puzzles and unclarities, let us take it that Hume, in 3.1.1, is concerned with two types of opponent, and not just with the moral rationalists. A further question now arises: just *which* arguments (again excluding the practicality argument) are directed specifically against the moral rationalists?

There can be no doubt that the group of arguments, occupying paragraphs 12–15, about the inappropriateness of error as a 'source of immorality', are aimed at Wollaston. They develop almost seamlessly out of Hume's treatment of a possible objection to his claim that reason cannot contradict passions, or actions, and so are technically a digression from his exposition of the practicality argument. Despite this, they have patently nothing to do with the question of reason's motivating power, and hence are irrelevant to us here.

In paragraph 17, however, Hume announces that he will now show that 'those eternal immutable fitnesses and unfitnesses of things cannot be defended by sound philosophy.' He further describes the position he intends to refute as one according to which 'vice and virtue consists in relations susceptible of certainty and demonstration.' It is clear then that the argument, with its two illustrations, extending from paragraph 19 to 25, is directed against Clarke and Cudworth. As we shall later see, it is precisely here that we shall seek confirmation of our original proposal as to the meaning of Hume's remark about reason's perfect 'inert[ia]'. Since, however, we must first rule out the possibility that any of Hume's remaining arguments in 3.1.1 can provide a rival interpretation, I simply flag these particular paragraphs for future attention.

The next argument is to be found in paragraph 26, and is the only one which is expressly and exclusively addressed to those philosophers (whoever they are) who hold that 'vice and virtue are . . . matters of fact whose existence we can infer by reason'. Moreover, he gives clear examples of these 'matters of fact': the 'passions, motives, volitions and thoughts' characteristic of wilful murder. Since therefore this argument has no relevance to the moral rationalists, we can put it aside also.

This leaves us with, apart from the practicality argument itself, just one other argument – the argument expounded in 3.1.1:27, and bringing the whole section to a close. It concerns the transition from 'is' to 'ought' and has been claimed (see, e.g., Stroud, 1977: 186–8) to concern reason's impotence in morality. Since it is going to require a detailed analysis, it will be helpful to have it before us:

> I cannot forbear adding to these reasonings an observation, which may, perhaps, be found of some importance. In every system of morality, which I have hitherto met with, I have always remark'd, that the author proceeds for sometime in the ordinary way of reasoning, and establishes the being of a God, or makes observations concerning human affairs; when of a sudden I am surpriz'd to find, that instead of the usual copulations of propositions, *is* and *is not*, I meet with no proposition that is not connected with an *ought*, or an *ought not*. This change is imperceptible; but is, however, of the last consequence. For as this *ought*, or *ought not*, expresses some new relation or affirmation, 'tis necessary that it shou'd be observ'd and explain'd; and at the same time that a reason shou'd be given, for what seems altogether inconceivable, how this new relation can be a deduction from others, which are entirely different from it. But as authors do not commonly use this precaution, I shall presume to recommend it to the reader; and am perswaded, that this small attention wou'd subvert all the vulgar systems of morality, and let us see, that the distinction of vice and virtue is not founded merely on the relations of objects, nor is perceiv'd by reason.

There are two preliminary and general points to make about this 'puckish'[5] passage. The first is that its meaning, let alone its target, is notoriously hard to pin down. Second, it has exerted a fascination over the contemporary philosophical mind only eclipsed by the practicality argument itself. In fact, the pre-eminence of the practicality argument is a comparatively recent phenomenon, much more being written,

during the twentieth century, about the is–ought passage. Today (see the first interpretation below) the latter passage is often read in conjunction with the practicality
argument: thus the claim that it also has to do with reason's impotence, and the
consequences for morality.

Baillie (2000: 137) – one of the few commentators who raises the issue – believes
that, despite its famed elusiveness, contextual considerations alone are sufficient to
establish the passage's target. Hume, he suggests, obviously means us to take the
'systems of morality', which he hopes to 'subvert', as holding that 'the distinction
between vice and virtue is . . . founded merely on the relation of objects, . . . [and]
perceived by reason.' But Baillie takes this latter description as an allusion to the
moral rationalists. We have seen, however, that Hume's talk of 'relations of objects' is
not a reliable indication that he is referring to these particular writers. On the
contrary, sometimes he qualifies this phrase in such a way that it can cover naturalists.
We shall recall how he writes, in 2.3.3, of 'relations of objects *of which experience gives
us information*'. Moreover, those who see morality as consisting in 'matters of fact' still,
according to Hume, hold that moral distinctions are 'perceived by reason'. Baillie, I
suspect, is here making the error, I alluded to above, of identifying *all* those for whom
morality is 'deriv'd from reason' with a mere subgroup of these: the so-called moral
rationalists. It is further noteworthy that there is no specific reference, in the passage,
to the 'eternal immutable fitnesses and unfitnesses of things' of paragraph 18.

Baillie also points to the 'precise location' of the is–ought passage as a consideration in favour of the moral rationalists being its targets. It comes, he writes, 'at the
end of a chapter devoted to a sustained critique of moral rationalism'. But again if
'moral rationalism' is to be acceptable as a *general* description of Hume's targets in
3.1.1, it cannot be tied down merely to the view of those actually called moral rationalists. Moreover, the argument which is expounded just before the is–ought passage
is explicitly addressed by Hume to philosophers who hold that morality consists in a
'matter of fact'. Considerations of location therefore might seem to point to the is–
ought passage having a naturalist target, rather than moral rationalists such as
Clarke and Cudworth, for whom moral relations are analogous to mathematical or
geometrical relations.

Contextual considerations of this kind are hardly therefore conclusive.
Consequently, we must first come up with a feasible interpretation of the is–ought
passage before we can decide whether it concerns the moral rationalists, and so
whether it has any chance of undermining our earlier proposal as to Hume's meaning
when he describes reason as 'perfectly inert'.

(iii) A rerun of the practicality argument

A quick way of dismissing the is–ought passage as relevant to Hume's metaphor
might seem to be this. The metaphor is integral to his discussion of how moral
judgements, given that they lead to motivation and action, could be rationally
grounded. But the present passage seems to have nothing to do with the transition
from moral judgement *to* motivation; it concerns only the transition *to* a moral judgement from what is evidently a factual belief (to an 'ought' from an 'is').

Certain recent readings of the passage, such as those by Stroud (1977: 186–7) and Baillie (2000: 138) suggest, however, a possible way round this difficulty. Though it is the transition from a factual belief to a moral judgement on which Hume explicitly focuses, he assumes, and relies upon for the success of his argument, a view about the link from moral judgement to *motivation*. His point (it will be said) is that, precisely because moral judgements *entail* motivation – precisely because therefore a person's motivation can be deduced from her moral judgement – it is *im*possible to deduce a moral judgement from a factual belief or set of such beliefs. For a moral judgement would then be reducible to a set of non-moral, or factual beliefs: but for Hume no such set could entail *motivation*.

The trouble with this reading is that it takes for granted that Hume holds that moral judgements *do* entail motivation. But we have argued that this is not so. On the contrary, despite its being so frequently and unthinkingly affirmed, the claim that he does is at bottom just a desperate way of salvaging the practicality argument's validity, when its second premiss is read 'moderately'. Our evidence has suggested that, for Hume, moral judgements are related to motivation and action merely in the way that any other pair of distinct items is linked in experience, namely causally.

It might be thought that the general thrust of the reading could be preserved by recasting Hume's point in terms of *desire* or *feeling*. Hume holds that since a desire, or feeling, is indispensable for motivation, and since moral judgements do typically lead to motivation, these judgements must be, or involve, a desire or feeling. But one cannot get from a factual belief to a desire or feeling. Hence a moral judgement cannot be reduced to a factual belief, and one cannot deduce an 'ought' from an 'is'. The trouble here is that, as we have repeatedly seen, even factual beliefs can sometimes, according to Hume, 'excite' desire or feeling. Anyone therefore who, like Stroud, or Baillie, acknowledges this, but wishes to uphold the reading, must deal with the question why such beliefs do not therefore count as 'reasons' for the feelings they produce, and the actions, moral or otherwise, to which these feelings lead.

Stroud's and Baillie's solution is to say that, though indeed the belief that e.g. a given action is socially useful typically arouses in us a feeling of pleasure, this, according to Hume, is because, and only because, we are so naturally constituted as to be caused to feel pleasure on the contemplation of such an action. Since, however, we might have been constituted differently, or may come to be constituted differently at some time in the future, it is impossible logically to infer the occurrence of this feeling of pleasure from the relevant belief.

At this point, however, the privileged status of feeling over belief as the chief constituent of moral judgement is threatened. This is because ordinary factual belief – a belief for instance about where pleasure can be had, or whether an action is socially useful – is now being recognized, just as much as feeling, as a causal factor in the process leading to action. Only, as we saw earlier, if the relation between moral judgement and motivation is declared to be altogether closer than a merely causal one, and only if this closeness can be said to be a consequence of moral judgement being essentially a matter of feeling, will the latter's privileged status be restored. The temptation, for those favouring this reading, is thus almost irresistibly to stress again (as Stroud does more than once) the '"active" power of moral judgement[s]'. But it is difficult to give any sense to an 'active', as distinct from an ordinary causal, power without re-invoking the idea of some kind of entailment.

From our point of view then the amended interpretation is no better than the unamended one. The ultimate reliance of both on the claim that moral judgement entails motivation should have alerted us to the fact that they are integrally linked with a 'moderate' reading of the practicality argument. Thus they confront us once more with the problems about its validity which dog any version of the argument which takes 'reason', as it occurs in the second premiss, as ordinary causal belief. But if Hume really were, in the passage, assuming this conception of reason, we should have to abandon any hope of relating it to the 'extreme' reading of premiss 2, and so to the depiction, with which we have connected this reading, of reason as 'perfectly inert'. It goes without saying that it could hardly have any relevance, either, for the eternal and unalterable 'fitnesses' and 'unfitnesses' with which a moral rationalist such as Clarke identifies reason.

(iv) An anticipation of Moore's naturalistic fallacy

I turn then to a second interpretation. Hume, it will be said, is charging those who attempt to deduce an 'ought' from an 'is' with a fallacy akin to that which Moore ([1903] 1966) was later to deploy against Mill, of which it is a striking anticipation. This interpretation, though presently unfashionable has a distinguished pedigree. Searle ([1964] 1967: 101–14) cites Hume's passage as the source of the argument aiming to show that this derivation is illegitimate, and identifies the derivation itself as what 'in more contemporary terms' is called 'commit[ting] . . . the naturalistic fallacy'. Frankena ([1939] 1967: 50–63) refers to philosophers who 'have thought it appropriate to chastise as the naturalistic fallacy the attempt to derive the Ought from the Is', and states that this 'bifurcation' was originally affirmed by Hume in the *Treatise* passage. Nowell-Smith (1954: 36) describes Moore's fallacy as 'a crushing argument . . . derived from Hume'.

Since this interpretation is not directly dependent on the claim that moral judgements *entail* motivation, it does not share the difficulty of the first interpretation. On the other hand, it may be that the passage, thus interpreted, will turn out to have nothing at all to do with motivation, or therefore with reason's role in it. Then it will be straightforwardly irrelevant to Hume's metaphor concerning reason's inertia. This, however, cannot be determined until a crucial ambiguity in Moore's argument is ironed out. For only then will we know precisely what is being attributed to Hume, when it is claimed that he anticipates, in his is–ought passage, this later philosopher. We may not, however, at this stage, cavalierly rule out the possibility of the passage on such an interpretation being relevant to the moral rationalists on the ground that what is in question is a naturalistic fallacy and they are non-naturalists. For though Moore originally directs his criticism against naturalists he proceeds, as we shall see, to expand it to cover any attempt, natural or non-natural, to derive moral conclusions from non-moral premisses.

(a) The fallacy as identifying moral values with natural properties

Mill ([1861] 1966: 288) as is well known, claims that, just as we can deduce a thing's visibility from its being seen, and a sound's audibility from its being heard, so we can deduce a thing's desirability, and therefore its goodness, from the fact that 'people do actually desire it'. Moore retorts ([1903] 1966: 66–7) that 'desirable' means '*ought* to be desired' not '*is* desired', and so comes to accuse Mill of 'as naive and artless a use of the naturalistic fallacy as anybody could desire'. But in what exactly, according to Moore, does Mill's commission of the naturalistic fallacy lie? Does he commit it merely by identifying a natural property of an object, such as its being desired, or pleasant, with (what Moore holds to be) another quite distinct type of property of that object, its being good? Or does he only commit it when he takes an *additional* step, to which Moore also draws attention (see below), which is not merely logically independent of the first step, but inconsistent with it? Only if the fallacy is committed as soon as 'good' is identified with the given natural quality, will it be, as the epithet 'naturalistic' suggests, a fallacy which, allegedly, every naturalist necessarily commits. Otherwise, Moore's charge will have as its target only *inconsistent* naturalists. As we shall now see, however, only with this narrowed scope of application, will Moore's charge not provoke the sceptical question: but what precisely is fallacious about *that*?

It is not that Moore fails to adduce considerations against defining 'good' in terms of a natural quality, such as 'desired'. If 'desired', or 'pleasant' *meant* 'good' (or 'ought to be desired'), then, Moore argues, in stating that a given object of desire was good, we would have uttered something as vacuous as if we had said pleasure is pleasant, or goodness is good. Likewise, it would be just as self-contradictory to speak of bad desires as to speak of what is desired not being desired. But surely Moore objects, 'is it merely a tautology when the Prayer Book talks of good desires?', and aren't 'bad desires possible'?

But if this identification of goodness with a natural property (such as being desired, or pleasant) *is* the fallacy, then while certain common ways of speaking will, if Moore is right, be rendered logically absurd thereby, it cannot *itself* be a logical fallacy. The naturalist could, after all, retort that he has pointed to the identity of 'good' and 'pleasant' precisely in order to deflate (in Hobbes' memorable phrase) the 'puffed up' sound of moral epithets. It is this inflated rhetoric, he will go on, which has misled people into supposing that terms like 'good' and 'ought' stand for a distinctive quality, independent of ordinary natural properties. He will add that, once people understand their real meaning, they will stop treating statements in which they occur, such as 'pleasure is good' as ethically significant. They will see them for what they are, as empty truisms that do no more than redirect our attention to the proper subject of ethical investigation: natural facts.

Whatever else one may say about this reply, it can hardly be faulted on formal grounds. Moreover many would hold it inappropriate even to talk about an 'error' here, however misguided they might believe the naturalists to be. Frankena ([1939] 1967: 61) for instance, suggests that Moore's charge is at bottom one of moral blindness, to which the naturalists might reply that their detractors themselves are

'suffering a moral hallucination'. This is not to say that the counter-intuitive implications of identifying good with a natural property to which Moore draws attention
should be disregarded. Broad (Frankena, [1939] 1967: 52) observed that the 'fallacy'
of conflating 'desirable' and 'desired' was 'something we all learn about at our
mother's knees'. Nevertheless one may wonder whether Moore's stricture on identifying the two has not been misdescribed as an 'argument', let alone a 'crushing' one.

(b) The fallacy as a logical impropriety

But Moore ([1903] 1966: 67) has a further objection up his sleeve. He claims that
Mill holds that what is desired, what is pleasant, is '*ipso facto* the good', and *yet at the
same time* singles out some objects of desire as 'better and nobler' than others.
Wanting it both ways, he contradicts himself, Moore argues, over whether desires
can, or cannot, be ranked in terms of their goodness. If Moore is right, Mill is not a
consistent naturalist. He is therefore not of the militant type we have just described,
who enthusiastically accepts the reduction of moral terms to natural ones, and is
even ready to campaign for the reformation of our ordinary ways of speaking. Quite
contrarily, by way of his very definitional strategy, and despite its reductive implications for moral terms, Mill is surreptitiously attempting to *elevate* the natural to the
moral. He has, as Moore more vividly puts it, 'smuggled in, under cover of the word
"desirable", the very notion about which he ought to be quite clear', namely what 'it
is good to desire', or again even more pithily ([1903] 1966: 73) has 'arrived at an
ethical conclusion, by denying that any ethical conclusion is possible'.

Moore maintains that if Mill *were* clear about these issues, he would face, given
only that the conclusion of a deductive argument can contain nothing not already in
the premises, a stark dilemma. Either he must give up talking of some desires as
being better than others, or he must give up the identification of 'desired' with
'good', in which case his 'proof of Hedonism [will be] absolutely worthless'.
Construed therefore as an attempt to embrace elements of mutually exclusive views,
the naturalistic fallacy is now indeed a *logical* fallacy, though with a much narrower
scope of application than on the first account.

One consideration in favour of taking the naturalistic fallacy in the first way is
that, immediately after Moore has explained how Mill identifies 'good' *via* 'desirable'
with 'desired', he alleges that Mill commits the fallacy. But a consideration against
this reading is that the naturalistic fallacy is then, as we have seen, not a *fallacy* in
the strict sense of implying logical confusion, nor even a straightforward error. A
consideration in favour of the other 'formal' reading is the fact that Moore includes
Mill's inconsistent attitude to ranking desires in terms of their goodness among what
he calls '[the] specimens of the contradictions which, as I have tried to shew, must
always follow from the use of the naturalistic fallacy'. For this inclusion makes it
sound as if Mill's inconsistency here is not logically independent of, but integral to,
the fallacy. A further consideration in favour of the formal reading is that the naturalistic fallacy now becomes a *bona fide* logical fallacy. On the other hand, it may now
seem a misnomer to call the fallacy 'naturalistic' when, far from its being endemic to
naturalism, only confused, careless or disingenuous naturalists make it. Whichever

reading we opt for, Frankena's comment ([1939] 1967: 62) that the nomenclature 'naturalistic fallacy' is 'somewhat loose in its habits' will remain apt.

(c) The is–ought passage not about identifying moral values with natural properties

With this indication of the roughly equally balanced pros and cons of these two construals of the naturalistic fallacy, I now ask how well each in turn would sit with Hume's is–ought passage. Could Hume really be objecting to the identification *itself* of a moral 'relation', such as is expressed (as he puts it) by an 'ought', or an 'ought not', with a natural one (that expressed by an 'is', or an 'is not')? On the face of it, it would be very odd if a thoroughgoing naturalist, such as Hume, were to be the source of an argument later seized upon by non-naturalists, and deployed *against* naturalists. However, it might be suggested that what he is objecting to is the reduction of any claim couched in moral terms, irrespective of whether it is made by a naturalist or a rationalist opponent, to a non-moral one. But Hume, much to the consternation of some commentators (e.g. Hunter, 1962) on the is–ought passage, sometimes appears himself to identify moral claims with certain non-moral ones concerning our psychological reactions. For instance, as we shall recall, he writes: 'when you pronounce any action or character to be vicious, you mean nothing, but that from the constitution of your nature you have a feeling or sentiment of blame from the contemplation of it.'

Even leaving aside this difficulty, there is no explicit attempt by Hume in the is–ought passage to point (as Moore does) to how the identification of 'is' and 'ought' would lead to ethically significant propositions becoming tautological, or alternatively, self-contradictory. Still less is there any indication why this might be unacceptable. Is it, for instance, as Moore suggests, that it is counter-intuitive, conflicting with our common understanding of such claims? An answer could be supplied from later sections in Book 3. For there Hume is at pains, as we have seen, to point out that our contemplation of socially useful actions causes us to experience that distinctive pleasure associated with moral approval. But since the link is only causal, it might have been the case that we did not approve such socially useful actions. Hence, for Hume, there can be no entailment from the belief that 'an action is socially useful' to the judgement that 'it ought to be performed.' It follows that, for him, there is nothing tautological about the assertion that socially useful actions ought to be performed, nor self-contradictory about its denial.

Were Hume to draw attention to this aspect of moral discourse, as he views it, it would, however, not be because he objected to the attempt to render moral judgements *naturalistically*. Rather, his objection would be to the *particular* kind of naturalistic rendering involved, namely the idea that what our moral judgements reduce to is *objective* statements about the external world. For Hume of course maintains that morality is essentially a matter of subjective feeling. But then Hume's target would be merely those naturalists, who take moral statements to be statements about the objective world, not those naturalists who take them to be statements about our subjective feelings on viewing actions or characters. Moore, by contrast, has no quarrel with his opponents for treating moral judgements as objective; his criticism of them is, on this first reading, on grounds of their naturalism. It hardly seems then that Hume's is–ought passage could plausibly be described as anticipating Moore's argument, given this first account of the naturalistic fallacy.

(d) The passage as pointing out a logical impropriety

Suppose, turning to the second account, we were to interpret the naturalistic fallacy purely formally, would this make it any more plausible to suggest that Hume, in his is–ought passage anticipates Moore? Those who commit the fallacy use the identification of moral terms with natural ones as a covert opportunity for *investing* these natural terms with the very ethical significance which they have, by this identification, just denied to the moral terms. Clearly therefore, as a fallacy committed only by inconsistent naturalists, it would not impugn Hume's own professed naturalism for him to draw attention to it. Moreover, in denying the legitimacy of the transition from 'is' to 'ought' on grounds that a 'new relation' cannot be deduced from 'others ... entirely different from it', Hume appears to be pointing to a *logical* impropriety. It is also possible to read into Hume's complaint that 'this change is imperceptible' a criticism akin to Moore's when he writes of Mill that he has 'smuggled in under cover of the word "desirable" the very notion about which he ought to be quite clear'.

On the other hand, Hume does not in this passage explicitly place before his opponents Moore's bald choice between the valid, but tautological, option and the invalid, but morally significant, one. Hume himself admittedly asserts that 'ought' implies a 'new relation'. But this is not the same as alleging that his opponents, having reduced the relation expressed by an 'ought' to the kind of relations expressed by an 'is', use the 'ought' to covertly reintroduce the eliminated relation. It seems, however, despite the missing components, to be just about possible to discern in Hume's is–ought passage an anticipation of Moore's argument, where that is understood in purely formal terms. The next question is whether it is plausible to suppose that Hume could have as his target, in bringing this Moore-like argument, moral rationalists, such as Clarke and Cudworth.

(e) Clarke and Cudworth do not commit the non-naturalistic fallacy

For Clarke and Cudworth, the moral is part *of* the natural. Indeed, according to them, as we saw, not only white and black, but also good and evil, are what they are *by nature*. It would, however, be a grotesque misunderstanding of their use of the term 'natural' to confound it with 'naturalistic', as Moore uses it in his critique of Mill, and as we have used it above. For the latter term has there roughly the sense of 'susceptible of explanation by ordinary scientific methods' (Moore, [1903] 1966: 40).[6] As such the natural(istic) realm contrasts sharply with the non-natural realm of values. But the moral rationalists' 'nature', far from having the characteristics that would fit it for such empirical investigation, is 'eternal', 'necessary' and 'unalterable', and so is itself non-natural in Moore's sense. Indeed it is only that with which the rationalists contrast their 'nature', namely convention, which as fleeting, arbitrary, and contingent, is a suitable subject for empirical investigation.[7] Consequently, the conventional stands to the moral rationalists' 'natural', as Moore's 'natural' stands to the 'non-natural'.

Shortly we shall look at how the naturalistic fallacy, despite its name, may be extended to cover certain kinds of *non*-naturalism. First, however, it is worth noting an irony. We have just identified a stumbling block to any definitive interpretation of Hume's is–ought passage as an anticipation of Moore, even on the formal reading of the naturalistic fallacy. This is that Hume does not explicitly confront his opponents with Moore's 'valid but tautological/morally significant but invalid' dilemma. Nor does he indicate how they inconsistently seek to combine the validity, only afforded by the first option, with the moral significance, only afforded by the second. But Clarke and Cudworth *themselves* confront Hobbes with just such a Moorean-type dilemma.

Clarke, for instance, ([1728] 1969: 228, 256–7) observes that Hobbes, holding that there is 'no such thing as good and evil in the nature of things, antecedent to all laws', goes on to define 'good' (or 'obligatory') as 'whatever the chief magistrate commands to be accounted good', and 'evil' as 'whatever he forbids'. It follows, Clarke argues, that for a conventionalist such as Hobbes,

> [no] law [can] be better than another; nor any one thing whatever be more justly established and enforced by laws than the contrary: nor can any reason be given, why any laws should ever be made at all; but all laws equally, will be either arbitrary and tyrannical, or frivolous and needless.

However, Clarke writes, Hobbes is not prepared to be hemmed in by these logical implications of his conventionalism. He wishes to invest his political proposals, despite his professed moral scepticism, with an air of moral legitimacy. Consequently when appraising certain arrangements, he slips in tell-tale extra adverbs stating, for instance, that these arrangements are '*wisely* enforced by the authority of laws', as though it were not, on his own terms, just self-contradictory to deny this. Likewise, he recommends such precepts as that 'compacts ought to be faithfully performed' and that 'obedience' ought to be 'duly paid to civil powers', as though these were ethically significant propositions, and not empty tautologies. Clarke pronounces him in consequence 'guilty of the grossest absurdity and inconsistency there can be'. It is surely therefore Clarke, much more than Hume, who may seem to anticipate Moore.

It does not follow that a writer may not also commit – in some form or other – a fallacy which he justifiably attributes to someone else.[8] It is still open to us therefore to explore the possibility that Hume, in the is–ought passage, is turning the tables on the moral rationalists. But how could Clarke or Cudworth, as *non*-naturalists, be accused of committing what is effectively a *naturalistic* fallacy? Moore tells us, however ([1903] 1966: 39), that the fallacy, though 'I give it but one name, the naturalistic fallacy' is also found in certain types of metaphysical ethics. Like the naturalists, these metaphysicians (Moore, ibid.: 114) seek to infer from their identification of good with a given property, y, that some particular thing, x, which has property, y, is non-tautologically good. They differ from the naturalists only in that the property, with which they identify good, rather than being natural, belongs to what Moore calls a 'supersensible' reality.[9] In both cases an ethical notion is reduced to a non-ethical one, and then the non-ethical one is implicitly, and spuriously, invested with that very significance of which the ethical notion has just been deprived. Could the moral rationalists be guilty of a similar inconsistency? Do they define 'obligatory' as 'standing in a certain supersensible relation to a situation', and then appeal to this *definition* in order to ground the *non-tautological* claim that a particular action, x, standing in this relation, is obligatory? If so, then the claim that x ought to be performed will seem, by the fact that it is masquerading as a morally significant proposition, to have conjured out of thin air Hume's 'new relation'. The moral rationalists will, in Moore's words (ibid.: 73), have 'arrived at an ethical conclusion . . . by denying that any ethical conclusion is possible'.

Cudworth's system of essences, like Clarke's 'relations and dependencies of things', is certainly, as we saw, a network of necessary truths. For Cudworth, for instance – and here I recap – the nature of a thing is what makes that thing itself, and not another thing. It is also what makes it something rather than nothing; for a being without a nature, Cudworth tells us, is a 'nonentity'. Each thing is therefore 'necessarily and indubitably' determined by its own nature. Since moreover a thing is good, or just, because it is what it is, neither Hobbes, nor even God, can *make* a good thing bad, or a just thing unjust by commanding that it be so. Nor can they make an indifferent thing good or just. This would be as absurd as to decree that triangles would henceforth be circular. For just as things are triangular *by triangularity*, and circular *by circularity* so, according to Cudworth, they are just *by justice*, and good *by goodness*. Since for him therefore a thing's goodness does not – could not – consist in its being *something else*, but only in its being *itself*, namely good, he would surely object to Mill's attempt to define 'good' in terms of something else, pleasure. Indeed the *reduction* of goodness to some other non-ethical feature of reality, even a supersensible one, would for him be just another example of Hobbes' absurd attempt to prise apart a thing – goodness, obligatoriness – from its nature. But it is difficult to see how, if the moral rationalists rule out in the first place such a reduction, they could coherently be censured for appealing to it to ground substantial ethical claims.

It might be thought, however, that, whatever these rationalists officially profess, there is evidence in their texts of their treating their system of 'different things and relations' (in Clarke's words) as the non-ethical foundation of their ethical precepts. Moore's account of metaphysical ethics in which ([1903] 1966: 114) 'Knowledge of super-sensible reality is necessary *as a premise* for correct conclusions about what ought to exist', could therefore fit their position, as well as those of which he gives explicit examples.

One main reason for this gross misrepresentation of the rationalists' view is, I suggest, that writers have been overly impressed by the abundance of mathematical and geometrical examples in their work. Take Mackie, for instance. Having cited (1980: 62) a series of different usages where an 'ought' really does seem deducible from an 'is', he offers what he takes to be the 'defensible form of Hume's law':

An ought statement which expresses a categorical imperative cannot be validly derived by ordinary, general logic – by deductively valid reasoning – from any set of premises each of which is either a logical or mathematical truth or an ordinary empirical . . . statement

He states that, construed in this way, 'Hume's law' subverts Clarke's claim that morality is demonstrable. Since statements about 'the eternal different relations between different things' are clearly not ordinary empirical ones, the implication is that Clarke seeks to deduce a purely ethical conclusion from logical, or mathematical, premises. But Clarke, like Cudworth, could scarcely make it clearer that he is merely *drawing an analogy* between ethical and mathematical, or geometrical, truths, and then only in terms of their indubitability. To give one instance, Clarke states:

> *in like manner as* no-one, who is instructed in mathematics, can forbear giving his assent to every geometrical demonstration . . . *so* no man who . . . has the means of being taught and instructed. . . . concerning the necessary relations and dependencies of things; can avoid giving his assent to the fitness and reasonableness of his governing all his actions by . . . the [moral] law.
>
> ([1728] 1969: 233, my italics)

It is noteworthy that Clarke does not say that someone instructed in *mathematics* cannot forbear giving assent to *moral* propositions, only that he cannot so forbear where *mathematical* propositions are concerned. That his mathematical, and geometrical, analogies have no pre-eminent status is apparent from the way he introduces alongside them, in order to convey the indubitability of moral truths, other types of analogy. He writes, for instance that to deny moral truths is the very same thing

> as if a man that has the use of his sight, should at the same time that he beholds the sun, deny that there is any such thing as light in the world, *or* as if a man that understands geometry or arithmetic should deny the most obvious and known proportions of lines or numbers, and perversely contend that the whole is not equal to all its parts, or that a square is not double to a triangle of equal base and height.
>
> (ibid.: 227, my italics)

A second reason for this misrepresentation is taking Clarke's references to 'foundations', 'proof' and 'deduction' out of context. Clarke states (both at ibid.; 226, and at 229), that the 'fitnesses' or 'suitablenesses' of certain actions to certain circumstances are 'founded in the nature of things'. However, the contrast that soon emerges is not between a non-ethical base and an ethical superstructure. On the contrary, it is between a morality that is objective and 'unchang[ing]' *because* it subsists in 'the nature of things', and one, such as Hobbes', which, depending on 'positive appointment', or 'positive constitutions', is as shifting and various as human decrees and commands.

Again, when Clarke speaks of 'proof' (see, for instance, ibid.: 227, and also 243), he is not referring to the deduction of ethical propositions from non-ethical premises. Rather, he is referring to his various philosophical arguments aiming to show that good and evil exists 'in the nature of things, antecedent to all laws', or that there is 'a natural and necessary difference between good and evil', and so to refute the Hobbesian view that 'there is no such thing as just and unjust, right and wrong originally in the nature of things.' Some of his arguments, however, are directed, not at the reduction, propounded by Hobbes, of moral propositions to statements concerning what the ruler has commanded, but at their reduction to statements about 'public utility'. Clarke attempts, for instance, ([1728] 1969: 251) to show that 'fidelity and truth', as irreducible moral values cannot, unlike 'public utility', considered as a criterion for right action, be twisted to favour particular interest groups. On the contrary, these values are, he writes, 'necessarily one and the same to every man's understanding; just as light is the same, to every man's eyes'.

Finally, what he calls 'deduction' is really an attempt to derive from morality's first principles precepts that have enough content intelligibly to guide individuals in their daily life. For instance, he takes (ibid.: 243) the axiom, 'that which is good is fit and reasonable . . . to be done', and shows how it yields, by way of simple considerations of proportionality, and the invocation of the part–whole, and means–end, relations, the precept 'constantly endeavour to promote in general to the utmost of [your] power, the welfare and happiness of all men'. The stages involved are worth detailing since they show that there is no attempt to derive this precept from anything which is not already moral. If 'what is good is fit . . . to be done', then the 'greatest good is always the most fit to be chosen'; but since God does the most good 'extending [his goodness] universally over all his works through the whole creation, by doing always what is absolutely best in the whole', this is the most fit to be chosen; therefore God's creatures, as parts of that whole, should do what they can, given their own 'sphere and station . . . faculties and powers', to further these Divine works. But 'the most direct, certain and effectual means [to this end]' is, Clarke claims, universal love and benevolence.

It is perhaps, however, 'deductions' of this kind which account for the widespread failure to take on board Clarke's repeated insistence that moral truths are, as he puts it (ibid.: 226–7) 'notoriously plain and self-evident', or his comparison of their indubitability with that of the simplest propositions of arithmetic and geometry, such as that 'twice two equals four', or that 'infinity is larger than a point.' Perhaps it seems puzzling how a proposition can be self-evident if it has to be deduced from others. But even if one hesitates to follow Clarke in calling such propositions self-evident, this still does not license the suggestion that he is therefore reducing them to propositions of other kinds. Reid[10] who, though writing after Hume, adopts a position close to Clarke's on these issues, explicitly resists any such reduction as follows:

> The first principles of morals are not deductions. They are self-evident; and their truth, like that of other axioms, is perceived without reasoning or deduction. And moral truths, that are not self-evident, are deduced, not from relations quite different from them, but from the first principles of morals.

A convincing case can, however, be made for extending 'self-evident' to cover not merely, as above, propositions whose evidence, or proof, lies in themselves, (let us call these 'simple' propositions) but *also* those which can be logically deduced from these 'simple' ones. Some remarks by Moore are helpful here:

> The expression 'self-evident' means properly that the proposition so called is evident or true *by itself* alone; that it is not an inference from some proposition other than *itself*. The expression does *not* mean that the proposition is true, because it is evident to you or me or all mankind, because in other words, it appears to us to be true ... By saying that a proposition is self-evident, we mean emphatically that its appearing so to us, is *not* the reason why it is true for we mean that it has absolutely no reason. It would not be a self-evident proposition, if we could say of it: I cannot think otherwise and therefore it is true.
>
> ([1903] 1966: 143)

Now Moore wishes, like Reid, to drive a wedge between 'simple' propositions and those that are reached only by inference from other propositions. However, he also defends the use of what we might call a 'logical', as opposed to a 'psychological', criterion for determining whether a proposition is self-evident. This self-evidence, he claims, is never a function of a person's mere psychological conviction concerning the proposition's truth: that is just what it emphatically is *not*. Indeed, if it were, it would *not* be self-evident. He goes further: observing that we can make errors, on occasion, even with arithmetical propositions, such as that 6 + 7 = 13, he – rightly – denies that this in any way impugns their self-evidence. However, if a person's failure to get the right answer does not impugn self-evidence in these 'simple' cases, there is surely no ground for stipulating that it must do so, even where long and complicated chains of deductive reasoning are concerned. Why, in other words, should the logical criterion suddenly, and apparently arbitrarily, switch to a psychological one? On the view here proposed, and which accords with Clarke's usage, to say that a self-evident proposition is one which is transparent to reason is not to say that it is necessarily transparent to our limited and fallible intellect. It is only to say that it would be so to an infinitely powerful intellect, such as God's.

There is then a crucial difference between the metaphysicians whom Moore charges with the naturalistic fallacy and moral rationalists like Clarke or Cudworth. The latter would admittedly agree that the validity of ethical propositions cannot be established except by a discussion of the rational universe. However, they would only do so because *their* rational universe, unlike that of these other metaphysicians, is *already* a moral universe. In so far therefore as Hume's stricture on deriving an 'ought' from an 'is' anticipates either version of Moore's argument so far expounded, it would be misplaced as an attack on the moral rationalists. However, there seems to be no positive evidence to support the claim that Hume – unlike more recent writers – misconstrued the rationalist position in a way which would lead him to mount such an attack, or suppose it either coherent or justified.

If Wollaston is contrasted with Clarke and Cudworth as seeking, unlike them, to provide a non-moral foundation for morality in the idea that vice is the expression (or communication) through action of a falsehood it is plausible to suggest that he could be a target of the is–ought passage on this second interpretation. This would, however, involve making the passage dependent on Hume's earlier and much more explicit critique of Wollaston in paragraph 15, particularly in the note. For there Hume argues that falsely claiming that something is one's rightful possession can only validly be considered 'the source of the immorality of injustice' in so far as property rights are already presupposed. But then a circularity is involved. In terms of the present passage, unless the 'new' relation – that expressed by the 'ought'-conclusion – is not a new relation at all but already contained in a disguised form in the 'is'-premiss, the transition will be invalid. But if this is how the passage is to be read it clearly has nothing directly to do with reason's motivational impotence, and so cannot be the source of an alternative interpretation to the one we canvassed earlier of Hume's claim that reason is inert.

(v) The passage indicates the gap between descriptive and practical discourse

If moral rationalists such as Clarke and Cudworth derive propositions 'connected' (in Hume's words) 'with an ought or an ought not' from any propositions at all, it is, as we have seen, from other similar propositions, and not from those connected with 'an is or an is not'. Couldn't we then safely exonerate them from attempting to derive moral judgements from any kind of statement of fact even when this notion is stretched so as to be able to refer to the rational universe or some other super-sensible reality? Not quite: consider the following proposal for a third interpretation of the is–ought passage.

Proposal: the moral rationalists do not, it is true, derive moral judgements from *non-moral* facts, but their 'eternal fitnesses and unfitnesses', belonging as they do to a supersensible reality, are facts none-the-less: *moral* facts. On their account, moral judgements *describe* these moral, non-natural facts, just as on the naturalist account, moral judgements describe non-moral, natural facts. But if we are to make sense of morality's link with *motivation*, it is not enough for moral judgements to be merely descriptions. Descriptions do not just reflect how things are, *they leave them as they are*. Moral judgements must therefore have a form more appropriate to their function of exciting action; they must be (in Hare's famous words) prescriptive rather than descriptive. So a sort of Moorean 'gap' does after all open up in the moral rationalists' position between 'is' and 'ought', where these indicate, respectively, a descriptive and a prescriptive construal of moral judgement. It is this 'gap' between descriptive and prescriptive, or commendatory, in the moral rationalists' position, which Hume, in his is–ought passage, is drawing attention to.

This third interpretation has in a sense come full circle. For just like the first interpretation, it is concerned with the is–ought divide as one between what we might call 'static' facts and dynamic judgements, though now modified in light of Moore's factual/evaluative dichotomy. It may therefore seem to have the advantage of reviving the possibility – non-existent with the second interpretation – of finding an alternative, and less radical, content to that canvassed earlier for Hume's claim that 'reason is perfectly inert.'

But let us be under no misapprehension. This new interpretation of Hume's passage cannot be said just to 'restate' Moore's argument as for instance Hare (1952: 84)[11] takes it to. Nor can it be considered an attempt merely to extend the scope of Moore's argument. It seems actually to subvert his argument. For it now has to be accepted that writers can commit the naturalistic fallacy – or contravene Hume's Law – *even though* they have an impeccably moral 'ought' on both sides of what the second interpretation treated as the factual/evaluative divide. This factual/evaluative division has been replaced by a distinction between what we might call a 'descriptive' 'ought' and a 'practical', or 'prescriptive', one. Moreover the moral status of the 'ought', which has been taken for granted in both previous interpretations, now becomes secondary. The 'practical-prescriptive' 'oughts', on the right side of the divide, include non-moral 'oughts', such as prudential ones, while the 'descriptive' 'oughts', on the left side, include impeccably moral ones. It is merely that, as their new epithet suggests, these moral 'oughts' are now components of a wholly descriptive discourse.

Why should it be supposed that Hume (or anyone else) would wish to maintain that, if a descriptive account were offered of moral judgements, their link with action would be severed? Even if he were to hold such a view, why would he think it bore in any way on the moral rationalists? The answer to the first question is composed of three strands. Once scrutinized, they fall apart, revealing their individual flimsiness.

The first strand is just a recycling of the claim which underpinned the first interpretation. This is that, for Hume, factual beliefs, reflecting how things are, do not entail motivation. Consequently, they cannot function as moral judgements, which *do* entail motivation. Mackie evidently has this in mind when he warns (1980: 69) of the difficulty involved in both acknowledging that, for Hume, moral statements are 'action-guiding', and yet assigning to them 'a dispositionally descriptive meaning'. He explains:

> any purely descriptivist account of the meanings of moral statements seems open to this criticism: no purely descriptive statement can be action-guiding in itself . . . My belief that an impartial spectator . . . would condemn a possible action which I am contemplating will prevent me from performing it only if I also [independently] want to fit in with the spectator's system of approbation.

But Hume does *not*, we have argued, hold that moral judgements are action-guiding in the strong sense of entailing – as opposed to merely causing – motivation. Moreover he *does* hold that factual beliefs can, by *themselves,* excite desires, and so lead to action; there is thus no need for Mackie's independent desire.

The second strand (like the second interpretation) takes the is–ought passage to be an anticipation of Moore. Hume, it is said, is censuring as fallacious the reduction of one function of language to another – prescription to description – rather as Moore later censures the reduction of moral to other types of property. But this would, apart from anything else, involve crediting Hume, anachronistically, with a sensitivity to grammatical form that only came to preoccupy moral philosophers much later. Moreover, the is–ought passage lacks too many features of Moore's argument against the reduction of moral, to non-moral, properties (e.g. the appeal to the non-tautological nature of moral judgements) to be plausibly seen as even analogous to it. Of course, if Moore really *did* intend his naturalistic fallacy to apply to this reduction *itself,* it could hardly count as a genuine fallacy. That, as we saw, would require an attempt to re-invest the resultant non-moral property with moral value.

When the two strands are combined, it is suggested that Moore's *own* underlying reason for resisting the reduction of moral, to non-moral, properties is that the latter, but not the former, are linked to motivation. '*Practical* discourse, *of which moral discourse is a part*, cannot', says Nowell-Smith (1954: 36) citing Moore, 'be identified with, or reduced to any other kind of discourse . . . psychological, or metaphysical, or theological' (my italics). He then goes on to suggest that Hume, in his is–ought passage, anticipates Moore by drawing a similarly sharp distinction between 'judgements of value *or commands*' and 'statements of fact. . . . contain[ing] no moral words' (my italics). More famously, Hare (1952: 29–30) formulates what he calls a 'logical rule' to the effect that 'if to say something is good is to guide action, then it cannot be merely to state a fact about the world.' He claims that it is 'the basis of Hume's celebrated observation on the impossibility of deducing an "ought"-proposition from a series of "is"-propositions', and also 'the point behind Professor G. E. Moore's celebrated "refutation of naturalism"'. Later he attempts (Hare, 1952: 84–5) to restate Moore's argument in order that it might explicitly yield the conclusion that defining 'good' in naturalistic terms disables it from fulfilling its commendatory, or prescriptive, function.

I have already, in interpretation (i) and elsewhere, argued against attributing to Hume a strong view about the link between moral judgements and motivation. I cannot see how associating the is–ought passage with Moore's argument, even when the latter is restated, makes it any more likely that Hume's passage is really about the so-called descriptive–prescriptive gap. But it should also be said that Hare's restatement is not one that Moore would have been likely to endorse. There is no evidence that Moore would have acknowledged Hare's 'logical rule'. The idea that there is a special link between morality and action is nowhere to be found, either explicitly or implicitly, in Moore's remarks. On the contrary, one of Moore's main objections to Mill's identification of 'desired' with 'desirable', is that then there *would* be, *ipso facto*, a motive for bringing about the good, or what 'ought to be'. However, Moore states ([1903] 1966: 67) that Mill himself acknowledges that moral language carries with it no such motive. He refers, apparently uncritically, to Mill's distinguishing between 'the rule of action', which *is* given by morality, and the 'motive' which is *not*.

The first two strands then depend on flawed readings of Hume (in particular the first premise of the practicality argument) and of Moore. Once disentangled from these, the third strand can plainly be seen to be implausible as an elucidation of the is–ought passage. The idea is that the 'unbridgeable gap' between descriptive, and practical, discourse is so intuitively obvious that Hume, allegedly encountering it in the work of the moral rationalists, used his is–ought argument to draw attention to it. The following quotation from Nowell-Smith (1954: 41) gives a flavour of the appeal that is made here to our ordinary intuitions. Suppose, he says, being confronted with a moral judgement were like being 'confronted with a new set of data or phenomena or characteristics', and goes on:

> from statements to the effect that these exist no conclusions follow about what I *ought to do*. A new world is revealed for our inspection; it contains such and such objects, phenomena, and characteristics . . . no doubt it is all very inter-esting. If I happen to have a thirst for knowledge, I shall read on to satisfy my curiosity, . . . learning about 'values' or 'duties', might well be as exciting as learning about spiral nebulae or waterspouts. But what if I am not interested? Why should I do anything about these newly-revealed objects? Some things I have now learnt, are right and others wrong; but why should I *do* what is right and eschew what is wrong?

Let us overlook as far as we can the apparently nonsensical nature – admitted[12] by the author himself – of the last question. It just does not seem intuitively obvious, unless one begs the question, that a curiosity about facts – about how things are – must necessarily, in the way Nowell-Smith suggests, lack practical consequences. But even were we to concede this 'unbridgeable gulf' between descriptive and prescriptive discourses, to then attempt to superimpose it upon moral rationalism would be to sorely misunderstand that position. For Nowell-Smith, 'the unbridge-able gap' is between, on the one side, *our believing*, or *being convinced*, that we have such-and-such an obligation and, on the other, a motivational state leading to the appropriate action. But for the moral rationalists, it is not our personally believing or being convinced of anything at all that moves us to moral action. Our motive is, as we saw earlier, the objective 'fitness' itself, laid bare to our understanding. Moreover, far from Hume taking the rationalists to task for allowing the supposed gap to develop at the heart of their account of morality, he censures them, quite contrarily, for propounding 'a *connexion*' here. In fact, as we shall now see, of all the various aspects of moral rationalism, there is one which arouses in Hume more scorn than any other. This is their attempt to locate the moral motive outside agents, in the 'eternal, immutable reason of things', so that the agent's subjective psycholog-ical states are altogether bypassed in the production of action. The relevant passages are those – particularly T 3.1.1:22 – which we flagged for later attention. It is in these passages that we shall find, despite its strong metaphysical connotations, confirmation of our original suggestion, as to Hume's meaning when he describes reason as 'perfectly inert'.

3 'The relation and the will': reason's inertia again

In his preliminary exposition (3.1.1:4), Hume characterizes moral rationalism in terms of two by now familiar claims. The first is that 'the essence of [virtue and] vice' consists in certain 'eternal immutable fitnesses and unfitnesses of things', which are self-evident to rational agents. The second is that these 'fitnesses and unfitnesses' make certain actions obligatory for these agents. In his detailed criticisms of his opponents' position (3.1.1:19–25), Hume deals with the two claims in turn. Thus, in the more frequently discussed first prong of his attack (3.1.1:19–21), he casts doubt on the very idea that there could exist these 'fitnesses' and 'unfitnesses' of certain actions to certain situations. In the second prong, however, he argues (3.1.1:22) that, even were these relations to exist, even were they self-evident to every rational agent who contemplated the relevant actions in the relevant circumstances, 'it [would] be still more difficult to fulfil [a] second condition, requisite to justify this system.' He goes on:

> According to the principles of those who maintain an abstract rational difference betwixt moral good and evil, and a natural fitness and unfitness of things, 'tis not only suppos'd, that these relations, being eternal and immutable, are the same, when consider'd by every rational creature, but their *effects* are also suppos'd to be necessarily the same; and 'tis concluded they have no less, or rather a greater, influence in directing the will of the deity, than in governing the rational and virtuous of our own species. These two particulars are evidently distinct. 'Tis one thing to know virtue, and another to conform the will to it. In order therefore, to prove, that the measures of right and wrong are eternal laws, *obligatory* on every rational mind, 'tis not sufficient to show the relations on which they are founded: We must also point out the connexion betwixt the relation and the will, and must prove that this connexion is so necessary that in every well-disposed mind, it must take place and have its influence, though the difference betwixt these minds be in other respects immense and infinite.

Hume's concern here, then, is with the moral rationalists' second claim, that it is obligatory for rational agents to respect in their conduct the 'fitness', or 'unfitness', of certain actions to certain situations. Hume maintains that, in order to defend this claim, his opponents must 'point out the connexion betwixt the *relation* and the will' (my italics). He does *not* say that they must point out the connexion between the agent's *recognition* of the relation and the will (though of course it is only when the relation is recognized that it can have its effects). However, for the moral rationalists, as we have seen, these 'fitnesses' and 'unfitnesses' are objective. They exist outside the agent in, as Clarke puts it, 'the reason and nature of things'. Hume even intimates why this must be so. Unless the source of motivation is placed beyond the vagaries of individual circumstances, and temperament, in an objective relation of some kind, its 'effects' cannot be, as the moral rationalists claim, the same 'in every well-disposed mind', including God's. For the 'difference betwixt these minds' is, as Hume puts it, 'in other respects immense and infinite'.

It should now be apparent why Hume finds the very idea of this 'connexion' so implausible. It does not hold, after all, between two *subjective psychological states:* one cognitive and the other conative. Rather, it holds directly between the *objective relation* itself – that 'fitness' of an action to its circumstances whose existence guarantees the truth of the corresponding moral judgement – and a *subjective state* of the agent, namely, a determination of the agent's will. Besides this, these 'fitnesses' and 'unfitnesses' are part of a metaphysical system of relations. Hence the supposed 'connexion' would have, so to speak, one foot in this metaphysical world, and the other in the ordinary empirical one.

It is worth pausing for a moment to say something about how – and why – commentators have blunted the sharp edge of Hume's critique here, and allowed its metaphysical significance to drain away. Penelhum is the only one of the commentators we have discussed who seems to have noticed that Hume's objection to the moral rationalists here is to their assertion that the objective relation *itself* influences the will. However, he dismisses the objection on grounds that it is based on a misunderstanding of his opponents' position. 'For surely', writes Penelhum (1975: 136), 'what is supposed to influence the will is not a relation one discerns but one's discernment of it.' But it would seem, if we are right, that it is Penelhum who misunderstands the moral rationalist position.

Other commentators ignore what Hume actually says altogether and take him to be criticizing the position that, according to Penelhum, he *ought* to be criticizing but does not actually criticize. Thus, Harrison (1976: 54) takes him to be criticizing the view that 'the apprehension of the presence of a relation . . . necessarily moves us to action', or can 'move us to action without the co-operation of a passion'. Baillie writes (2000: 113): '[Hume's] knock down argument is to say that even if such necessary and eternal relations existed, mere recognition of them would be insufficient to motivate action. For that we would need some *desire*, moral or otherwise.'[13] But Baillie (like Harrison), rather than telling us what Hume actually says, seems to be stating what he would expect Hume to say were this criticism meant to reflect the practicality argument's second premiss on (our) '*moderate*' reading. For Baillie makes it appear as though all that is wrong, on Hume's view, with the moral rationalists' position is that a desire is missing from the motivational process. Once this desire is reinstated, alongside the relevant belief (already supposedly supplied by the moral rationalists), the sufficient antecedent conditions for action will be present. But as we saw earlier, the profound nature of the moral rationalists' error, as Hume looks upon it, cannot be redeemed by a bit of tinkering. From Hume's perspective, it is a hopeless enterprise to attempt to salvage for a conception of reason, as residing outside the agent, in 'the eternal and immutable nature of things', any motivational role at all; it is to attempt to graft on to one picture of motivation – which Hume wishes wholeheartedly and unequivocally to reject – elements belonging to another, and wholly incompatible, picture.

But is there anything in the passage itself that could have encouraged Baillie to read it in this way? Half-way through, Hume makes a famous assertion to the effect that 'knowing virtue' and 'conforming the will to it' are 'two particulars evidently distinct'. Baillie seems to have taken this as a refutation of a claim to the effect that recognizing an action's fitness, and being moved to perform it, are bound together necessarily. How could this be, Hume would then be asking, when – and here we would supply the missing 'moderate' premiss of the practicality argument – their distinctness precludes anything other than a causal or contingent link?

The trouble with this reading is that it forces us to ignore Hume's clear indication that it is the relation of fitness *itself* that must be connected with the will, *not* the agent's recognition that this relation exists. Likewise, we are forced to ignore the fact that Hume speaks of the 'effects' of this relation, *not* of the effects of the agent's recognition of it. If we are to respect the text, the famous remark must be read in a different way. It really re-emphasizes the *independence* from each other of the two claims that Hume mentions at the outset as constituting moral rationalism. We can imagine him addressing his opponents in the following way: suppose you had proved the first claim – that these fitnesses and unfitnesses exist, and are self-evident to rational beings – you wouldn't *ipso facto* have proved the second. To have shown that rational agents can 'know virtue' is not at all the same thing as to have shown that they can 'conform their wills to it'. It will take therefore a quite different argument to prove this second claim: an argument that seems quite impossible.

There is no reason therefore to suppose that Hume means suddenly to collapse the relation of 'fitness', as that which has to be connected to the will, into the agent's recognition of this 'fitness'.

Our original suggestion as to how Hume's claim that 'reason is perfectly inert' might plausibly be understood was prompted by our formulation of an objection to Clarke's and Cudworth's position. At the heart of this objection was contemporary incredulity at how their 'fitnesses and unfitnesses of things' could possibly be agents of change, when they themselves remained unchanged. To contemplate such a possibility, we explained, was to contemplate what to post-Humeans must seem like an absurdity: the abrogation of ordinary causal laws. We have now come close to identifying this very objection in Hume's own detailed criticisms of the moral rationalist position. Twice in 3.1.1:22 he refers to the 'eternal' nature of these rational fitnesses and unfitnesses, and also refers to their 'immutability'. He even offers an explanation of why they must themselves be in this way changeless. It is that, in the case of 'every well disposed mind' including the Deity's, 'the effects [of these fitnesses and unfitnesses] are . . . suppos'd to be necessarily the same.' But how can the effects be the same if their causes are different? We can say then that his opponents' concept of reason – that rational system of 'eternal, immutable, fitnesses and unfitnesses of things' – is not only, in his view, 'perfectly inert' – in the sense of being profoundly impervious to motion or change – but must necessarily be so.

We have completed the task set out at the beginning of the chapter. We have expounded the moral rationalists' position, formulated an objection to it which might illuminate Hume's metaphor concerning reason's inertia, and sifted through Hume's criticisms to find confirmation for this construal. This, in turn, has enabled us to give point, and content, to the second premiss of the practicality argument, on the 'extreme' reading. It can therefore no longer be an adequate justification for holding back from endorsing the formally valid, 'extreme' version of the argument to complain about the obscurity of the corresponding second premiss. In fact a paraphrase of the argument would now go something like this. Premiss 1 would state that moral judgements are linked in the ordinary causal way with motivation. Premiss 2 would state that reason, as the moral rationalists construe it, could not on pain of absurdity – indeed it would require the abrogation of ordinary causal laws –

play any part in motivation. The conclusion would now be that morality cannot be a matter of reason (or rather of their 'eternal immutable fitnesses and unfitnesses of things').

This paraphrase is, however, likely to provoke a disappointed and indignant retort. Admittedly, if Hume were to hold unequivocally to the 'extreme' reading, the argument would be formally valid. However, it would have become much narrower in scope, indeed historically bounded. But surely the argument is still immensely relevant today, even though the moral rationalists have themselves become mere academic fossils? The 'extreme' reading leaves it entirely open that moral judgements could be beliefs about ordinary matters of fact, yet surely this cannot be right. Did not Hume fashion his argument to rule out this very possibility? Isn't that why he needs the 'moderate' version despite its invalidity?

It is impossible not to feel the competing pull of these two readings. In the next chapter, we pick up a loose end left by our attempt above to pin down the individual targets of Hume's various other arguments in 3.1.1, and so we investigate the mystery surrounding his *naturalistic* opponents. These are the opponents who we would expect to be the targets of the 'moderate' version of the practicality argument, were this properly detached from the 'extreme' version. On the immediate horizon we can already glimpse a further question: whether in giving his *sentimental* account of morality, Hume really means to rule out the possibility that moral judgements are beliefs, even *about our own feelings*. In the second part of the book we shall produce evidence to suggest that what was offered above as an incontestable fact – that the kind of position represented in the eighteenth century by the moral rationalists no longer exerts an influence on our thinking today – is wholly false.

4   Sentimentalists, Secondary Qualities and Sensations

This chapter is largely taken up by Hutcheson's moral sense theory. Since it may seem a digression from the main lines of our inquiry I will, before launching upon it, recap on why it is necessary from the point of view of my overall strategy. At the close of Chapter 1, we decided to look for a reinterpretation of the 'moderate' version of the practicality argument, which was both consistent with Hume's larger views in Book 2, and would secure the argument's validity. We resolved, if this was successful, simply to drop all reference to the obscure 'extreme' version. With the failure, however, of Chapter 2 to produce any such satisfactory reinterpretation, the 'extreme' version, being already valid, naturally came back into play. Would it not be better, we asked, rather than ignoring either version, to treat both as somehow contained within the apparently unitary structure of the practicality argument? Each version would then be directed at a different position, depending on how its proponents construed the reason which they saw as informing, or underpinning morality. With the 'extreme' version, Hume's charge would be that, in giving morality the rational basis envisaged, his opponents had made it absolutely inconceivable that it could motivate us. With the 'moderate' version, his charge would be that reason, as now construed, could have a role alongside desire in moral motivation, but not the substantial one claimed. It would seem crucial in defending our proposal that we are able to point to a corresponding variation in the concepts of reason propounded by Hume's different opponents in formulating their moral theories. We must also aim to provide evidence that Hume recognized this variation, and fashioned other arguments in 3.1.1 to take account of it.

Chapter 3 concentrated on the 'extreme' version. We pointed to aspects of Clarke's and Cudworth's concept of reason which, we claimed, would lead anyone, not sharing their metaphysical world-view, to rule out, as absurd, any motivating influence for their rationally based morality. In fact, as we saw, to allow such an influence would be to countenance an abrogation of ordinary causal laws. We also provided evidence that Hume had in mind precisely this metaphysical difficulty in at least one of his other arguments in 3.1.1. It was not open, we suggested, to introduce desire unobtrusively into an account of moral motivation, such as Clarke's, in order to salvage a role for reason as a subordinate partner. For this would be to try to incorporate naturalistic elements into a metaphysical system with which they were wholly incompatible. The effect, in short, of acknowledging moral rationalism, as here expounded, as the target of the 'extreme' version was to seal it off irrevocably from the 'moderate' one.

If, however, the proposal to treat the practicality argument as somehow combining both 'extreme' and 'moderate' versions was really to form the basis of an acceptable reconstruction of Hume's underlying intentions, more would have to be done. It would be necessary to point to naturalistic opponents of Hume's who, like the metaphysicians, held that moral properties existed independently of the moral spectator's thoughts, attitudes or responses. We could then say that, for these philosophers also, judging actions virtuous would mean becoming aware of their objective properties, and so would fall on the 'belief', rather than the 'desire' side of Hume's dichotomy. We would at the same time have to show why Hume might have thought that, despite allowing a motivating role to desire, these naturalists did not give it a sufficiently large one compared with belief or reason. This would bring these naturalistic objectivists within the scope of the 'moderate' version.

The problem is, however, that it is not immediately clear who these naturalist opponents could be. Just like Hume's rationalist opponents we would expect them to be significant philosophical figures. But Hume's most notable naturalistic predecessors – those who must certainly have left their imprint on the *Treatise* – are the moral sense theorists, particularly Hutcheson. These philosophers, however, as their other name – 'sentimentalists' – reminds us, have standardly been taken as subjectivist allies of Hume. Indeed, Hutcheson has not just been thought of as a subjectivist, but as a sufficiently clear and convincing one to have influenced Hume to adopt a similar position. Nevertheless in recent times the subjectivist interpretation has been challenged, most notably by David Fate Norton (1982: 55–83). Below, despite the virulence of the response to Norton by writers such as Winkler (1985: 79–94) and Stafford (1985: 133–51) defending the traditional picture, we again try to loosen the grip of that interpretation. Here, however, it is in order that the question whether Hutcheson could be a target of the 'moderate' version can be seriously entertained.

I begin by claiming that his extended comparison of the moral sense with sense perception (in his most famous work, *An Inquiry Concerning Moral Good and Evil*)[1] suggests a relatively uncomplicated, if somewhat imperilled objectivism. I then tackle the passage (from his later work *Illustrations upon the Moral Sense*)[2] most often cited by those maintaining that Hutcheson was a thorough-going subjectivist. Here Hutcheson, drawing on Locke's famous distinction, compares moral perceptions with our ideas of secondary qualities, such as colour. Commentators, such as Mackie (1980), I will suggest, have reached their subjectivist reading by assuming without justification that Hutcheson's secondary qualities are logically on a par with bodily sensations. On another construal – more tenable both as regards Locke and Hutcheson – secondary qualities, though having an ineradicable subjective element, are justifiably said to be 'in the object'.

Returning to the *Treatise*, I then ask how far this 'tempered' objectivism could be said to be under attack in Hume's 'wilful murder' passage, where we know he has naturalist opponents in mind. I argue that it surely can be, even though Hume himself, in this very passage, compares moral perceptions, as Hutcheson does, with secondary qualities. I finally consider whether Hume could have regarded this diluted objectivism, which we have attributed to Hutcheson, as undermining the link between morality and motivation. But this is just to seek an answer to the question whether Hutcheson is a credible target of the 'moderate' version of the practicality argument.

1   Hutcheson's moral objectivism

(i) The analogy with sense perception

One of the strongest *prima facie* considerations in favour of an objectivist interpretation of Hutcheson – though one which is surprisingly often overlooked – is the crucial role that the comparison of the moral sense with sense perception plays in his theory. For to speak of perceiving an object ordinarily entails that we take it really to exist outside us. As Harrison (1976: 115) puts it more generally: 'There is an important difference between sense and sentiment . . . my senses give me information about the things I see or hear or feel'.[3] It might seem therefore that Hutcheson is here indicating that there also exists a *moral* reality independent of the observer who apprehends and appraises it.[4]

But it is not just that, in expounding the moral sense, Hutcheson gestures vaguely in the direction of sense-perception. On the contrary, he works out the analogy in some detail. The moral sense, though not an 'external' sense ([1738]1969: 307, 309, 348, 356), and lacking any corresponding bodily organ, is to be defined, just as sense-perception is, as 'a determination of the mind, to receive any idea from the presence of an object which occurs to us independent on our will' (ibid.: 307). However, its object – 'moral good' – differs sharply from the object of sense perception, namely 'natural good'. Whereas (ibid.: 304) the latter is roughly anything that contributes to, or enhances, our (or anyone else's) welfare, the former – moral good – is manifest only in the unself-regarding motives of rational agents, for instance, in their benevolence and generosity. But natural and moral good differ still more importantly, for Hutcheson, in terms of the type of response they arouse in the spectator. Thus, natural good 'raises only desire of possession toward the good object' (ibid.: 307), and frequently 'procure[s] [for the possessor] envy and hatred' (ibid.: 303). Moral good, by contrast, raises in the observer only 'approbation and good will toward those we apprehend possessed of it'. Neither kind of good can be revealed to us through the alternative sense, each being accessible (ibid.: 307, 340) only from a single perspective. The 'sense of good' is, according to Hutcheson (ibid.: 307), 'distinct from the advantage or interest arising from the external senses'. It is 'a power of receiving perceptions' other than 'those of advantage'. Again, he writes (ibid.: 309) 'those senses by which we perceive pleasure in natural objects, whence they are constituted advantageous . . . could [n]ever make us approve an action merely because of its promoting the happiness of others'.

Paying attention to the analogy with sense perception is salutary. It can help to counter the suggestion – often unthinkingly put forward in combatting the objectivist interpretation – that Hutcheson is not really interested in the subjectivism–

objectivism debate at all, being only concerned to show that people sometimes act out of genuine altruism. For once we have clearly before us the fact that Hutcheson's moral sense theory is exclusively formulated from the viewpoint of an observer, not of an agent seeking inducements to act, a claim such as Selby-Bigge's (cited by Stafford, 1985: 136), that it is 'essentially a theory of motive' will cease to seem plausible.[5]

But stressing the analogy is also a corrective to those who, agreeing that Hutcheson's is primarily a meta-ethical theory, think they can nevertheless establish his subjectivism simply by declaring that he, like Hume, means by 'sense 'sentiment or feeling'. It would moreover set up a false contrast between the moral sense and sense perception, as Hutcheson understands them, were it to be added in favour of this subjectivist reading that the deliverances of the moral sense are 'attended with pleasure'. For Hutcheson also holds that ordinary sense perception is accompanied by pleasure. The only way to drive a wedge between the moral sense and sense perception would be to argue that, for Hutcheson, the perceptions associated with 'the sense of good', unlike those of the ordinary external senses, were *nothing but* feelings of pleasure. However, Hutcheson frequently goes out of his way precisely to caution us against so construing them, reminding us yet again of the parallels with sense perception. Thus, he writes ([1738]1969: 314): 'The perception of the approver, tho' attended with pleasure, plainly represents something quite distinct from this pleasure; even as the perception of external forms is attended with pleasure, and yet represents something distinct from this pleasure.'

There are nevertheless more cogent reasons than those so far advanced for playing down the analogy with sense perception. Few contemporary philosophers will long contemplate the picture painted here of a relatively uncomplicated naturalistic objectivism without becoming aware of cracks in its surface. Hutcheson, they will say, evidently wishes to distinguish moral and natural good in wholly naturalistic terms – in terms that is of 'their relation to [the] selfish advantage [of the spectator]'. Why, then, they will ask, are two separate senses required? If on the other hand becoming aware of moral good really does require a distinct sense, as Hutcheson repeatedly stresses, isn't he covertly admitting that it is not identical with any natural quality, and so must inhere in these qualities non-naturally? They may conclude that Hutcheson's only option, as a rigorous naturalist, confronted with the possibility of having to admit a supra-sensible realm of moral facts, is to embrace subjectivism.[6]

Mackie, for instance (1980: 32–3), suggests that, for Hutcheson, the quality of an action which procures approbation is simply benevolence which we become aware of in the ordinary way: by observation and inference. What makes us call this natural quality virtuous, however, is purely our subjective response to it. The moral sense then is required, not as our bodily senses are, to inform us about the world around us, but to 'attach approval and love for the agent to an action already observed to be benevolent'.

But how is this interpretation of Hutcheson's moral sense to be integrated with his distinction between moral and natural good? Consider the claim that before the moral sense can approve it, an action has first to be shown to be benevolent. As we noted, according to Mackie, this involves a combination of ordinary sense perception and inference from the observations thereby made. But is this quality of benevolence then first a *natural* good? After all, according to Hutcheson, anything which is the object of the external senses, and gives pleasure, is a natural good. Does it only become morally good when it is approved of? But for Hutcheson the categories of natural and moral good are mutually exclusive. It does not seem possible therefore for a natural good to be converted to a moral one. Indeed, how can the benevolence in question be even in the first place a natural good since Hutcheson characterizes such a good as necessarily perceived from the viewpoint of 'selfish advantage'? Here, however, deciding that the action is benevolent is *ex hypothesi* a stage on the road to morally approving it. Is its benevolence then first a 'neutral' good, only becoming a natural good if it arouses the selfish interest of a spectator, or a moral good if it evokes his disinterested concern? But according to Hutcheson not just any good can become natural or moral depending on whether we bring selfish or disinterested concerns to bear upon it. He holds that our approving, or disapproving, only the motives of rational agents, and not their material possessions – in which natural good consists – is a matter of God's strict ordinance.

Despite this conceptual independence of moral and natural good, Hutcheson compounds the problems of the proponents of the subjectivist interpretation by representing these goods as in practice inextricably interwoven. As we have seen, the perceptions of the moral sense, as well as those of the ordinary senses afford pleasure. It is precisely because moral approbation is thus itself a source of 'immediate natural good' that Hutcheson thinks it necessary to point out that one cannot call it up at will in order to gain the attendant pleasure. Likewise, he is careful to exclude from the category of virtuous actions those undertaken in order subsequently to enjoy ([1738]1969: 305) that 'secret sense of pleasure arising from reflection upon such of our own actions as we call virtuous, even when we expect no other advantage from them'. The difficulty of unravelling these connections, in order to place moral, but not natural, good, in the mind rather than in the world, is further aggravated by the fact that, for Hutcheson, both are in part characterized in terms of the spectator's subjective responses.

These objections, however, already presuppose something which is itself highly questionable: that Hutcheson would have judged the threat from non-naturalism to be so great as to compel him to retreat to subjectivism. Admittedly, moral good is not for him reducible to natural good. However, it does not follow that he would therefore have felt himself obliged to construe it as non-natural. When he applies the adjective 'natural' to 'good', it has a different, and much narrower, meaning than when he applies it to, say, 'quality', where it is interchangeable with 'naturalistic'. As we have seen, 'natural good' is just that good which provokes a purely selfish desire for possession. Therefore to state, or to deny, that something is 'natural' in this sense has nothing to do with its inclusion or exclusion from the natural world. Again, he may have accepted that moral qualities, being by his own account accessible only through a distinct moral sense, could not be identical with any particular natural qualities that could be known about in ordinary ways. But this still leaves room for them to be a unique type of natural quality, irreducible to any others.

Although Hutcheson himself twice concedes (1969: 348) that a critic may well accuse him of introducing 'the occult quality of a moral sense', he betrays none of the faint-heartedness at the idea of the 'occult' which might lead contemporary naturalists to embrace subjectivism. He simply stands his ground. He boldly demands to know if 'it is any more mysterious, that the idea of an action should raise esteem . . . than [for instance] that . . . the act of volition should move flesh and bones?' It is perhaps passages such as these that Norton (1985: 417) has in mind when he writes that, for Hutcheson, 'nature itself is normatively structured', and which lead him to categorize Hutcheson as 'both a naturalist and a moral realist'. It may be these also that Darwall (1995: 211) is thinking of when he writes that 'Morality has [for Hutcheson] a distinctive, irreducible place in nature.'

(ii) The analogy with secondary qualities

There is one passage – frequently the only one cited by proponents of the subjectivist interpretation – which may seem to undercut these conclusions. It comes not from Hutcheson's most famous work *An Inquiry Concerning Moral Good and Evil*, on which we have so far concentrated, but from the later work *Illustrations upon the Moral Sense*. He writes:

> Just so in our ideas of actions. These three things are to be distinguished, 1. The idea of the external motion, known first by sense, and its tendency to the happiness or misery of some sensitive nature, often inferred by argument or reason . . . 2. Apprehension or opinion of the affections in the agent, inferred by our reason: so far the idea of an action represents something external to the observer, really existing whether he had perceived it or not, and having a real tendency to certain ends. 3. The perception of approbation or disapprobation arising in the observer, according as the affections of the agent are apprehended kind in their just degree, or deficient or malicious. This approbation cannot be supposed an image of anything external, more than the pleasures of harmony, of taste or of smell.
>
> ([1742] 1969: 371)

This passage evidently marks an evolution in, perhaps even a break with, his prior thinking in two ways. First, the tight link between 'the external senses' and 'perceptions of advantage' has been relaxed. He is able now therefore, without running up against the difficulties just mentioned, to divide an action into three separate elements, with only the moral component not discoverable in the ordinary way through observation and inference. Second, he now compares our ideas of moral qualities with those of, what Locke called, secondary qualities, such as colour, sounds, tastes which, evidently following Locke, he denies ([1742] 1969: 371) are 'images of any like external quality'. But even this passage seems hardly to provide the irrefutable evidence of that unequivocal and thorough going subjectivism that Mackie (and others) attributes quite generally to Hutcheson, and which would make him an ally, not an opponent, of Hume.

Mackie (1980: 32–3) represents Hutcheson in this passage as contrasting the unassailable objectivity of such features of an action as its 'external motion', motive and consequences, with the irremediable subjectivity of our moral response to it. He thinks that it is Hutcheson's intention thereby to show that moral perceptions are like experiences of pain rather than like perceptions of Lockean primary qualities. But, as Mackie points out, whereas our ideas of primary qualities are held to resemble these qualities as they really are in the object, pain 'does not inform me about anything like pain-as-I-feel-it in the object'. It therefore cannot coherently be said to correctly or incorrectly represent anything. He ignores, however, Hutcheson's explicit comparison (in the previous paragraph) of our moral perceptions with ideas of secondary qualities. But it is to this comparison that Hutcheson's claim that approval 'cannot be supposed an image of anything external' refers back. Mackie therefore fails to consider the possibility that, for Hutcheson, moral perceptions might occupy, as ideas of secondary qualities, an intermediate position on the scale of objectivity between pain, with its incorrigible subjectivity, and ideas of primary qualities as simulacra of real existents.

In fact, the surrounding context makes clear that the passage, far from denying as Mackie claims the possibility of there being, in Hutcheson's words ([1742] 1969: 371), 'a right or wrong state of our moral sense', is precisely premised *on* this possibility. Hutcheson, as a moral sense theorist, committed to the exclusion of reason from any fundamental role in morality, is attempting to deal with an apparently contradictory implication of his comparison of the ideas of moral qualities with those of secondary qualities – his 'purely sensible ideas'. He imagines an objector getting the moral sense theorist to agree that just as 'a vitiated sight [can] misrepresent colours' so there may be 'a right or wrong state of our moral sense'. He then has the objector argue that in this case we must surely 'know antecedently what is morally good or evil by our reason'. Hutcheson's retort is that while reason can correct our senses, it cannot usurp their fundamental role either in the perception of primary or secondary qualities. His argument trades on a similarity between our ideas of secondary and primary qualities (his 'pure sensible ideas' and his 'concomitant ideas of sensation'). He writes:

> As to the purely sensible ideas, we know they are altered by any disorder in our organs, and made different from what arise in us from the same objects at other times. We do not denominate objects from our perceptions during the disorder, but according to our ordinary perceptions, or those of others in good health: yet no body imagines that therefore colours, sounds, tastes, are not sensible ideas. In like manner many circumstances diversify the concomitant ideas: but we denominate objects from the appearances they make to us in an uniform medium, when our organs are in no disorder, and the object not very distant from them. But none therefore imagines that it is reason, and not sense which discovers these concomitant ideas, or primary qualities.
>
> (ibid.: 371)

When Hutcheson introduces the next paragraph (the one quoted on p. 101) with the words 'just so in our idea of action' he is in fact extending the above argument from primary and secondary qualities to cover moral qualities. Certainly he denies that our ideas of secondary qualities, unlike those of primary ones (such as are involved in our perception of 'external motion') are 'image[s] of anything external'. However, he evidently does not take this restriction to affect their ability to be, in some non-pictorial sense, correct or incorrect representations of objects. Otherwise there would be no need for his argument showing that reason is not implicated in our perception of secondary qualities, and that the criteria for veridicality are internal to the senses. He is less clear as to how reason might correct the moral sense. Nevertheless he offers two suggestions as to what such a correction might look like. He then reaffirms his claim that even if such a correction were made, it would not prove 'the ideas of vice and virtue to be previous to a sense more than a like correction of the ideas of colour in a person under the jaundice proves that colours are perceived by reason previously to a sense.'[7]

(iii) Lockean secondary qualities are not sensations

To see why writers have been led to ignore Hutcheson's comparison of moral qualities with (Lockean) secondary qualities, and so misleadingly to suggest that they are just, for Hutcheson, subjective feelings, on grounds that the only alternative is for them to be, absurdly, primary qualities, it is necessary to point to an ambiguity surrounding Locke's original denial that secondary qualities, unlike primary ones, are 'in the object'. It is to be found in Book 2, Chapter 8 of his *Essay Concerning Human Understanding* (Locke, [1690] 1961: 102–11).

Now at one extreme this denial has been taken to mean that, though these qualities *are* in objects, the ideas we have of them, unlike those of primary qualities, do not resemble them. As Locke puts it in a remark which may appear to support this interpretation: 'There is nothing *like* our ideas [of secondary qualities] existing in the bodies themselves' (my italics). Whereas, on this interpretation, primary qualities are sensible macroscopic qualities, producing resembling ideas in the mind, secondary qualities are (ibid.: 105–6) 'bodies . . . so small that we cannot by any of our senses discover either their bulk, figure or motion' yet which 'produce in us those different sensations which we have from the colours and smells of bodies . . . with which they have no similitude'.

If this view of secondary qualities were correct, then of course we would habitually misrepresent them in supposing that an object really is as it looks and feels to us. This is not, however, to say – in fact it would be to go to the opposite extreme – that secondary qualities are *just* sensations of ours, having no more existence outside our minds than pains. Locke does, however, occasionally speak (ibid.: 107) in this extreme vein, as when he tries to get us to acknowledge that 'light, heat, whiteness or coldness, are no more really in [fire and snow] than sickness or pain is in manna'. If this were Locke's considered view, in so far as we do think of whiteness or coldness as being 'in' snow, we would not just (as on the first interpretation) be misrepresenting something that really is there, though in another form. Rather we would be making an altogether more fundamental error of 'projection'. We would be erroneously attributing to objects in the world qualities whose only existence is in our minds. It would be as absurd, on this construal, to speak of patches of colour on the wall opposite, as to speak of patches of pain out there. On this view, we wouldn't *see* colour at all; if anything were coloured it would be our mental experiences, not external objects.

If the first interpretation locates secondary qualities more resolutely 'in the object' than Locke's text as a whole warrants, the second view, due originally to Berkeley,[8] has Locke, implausibly and systematically collapsing secondary qualities into our ideas of them. However, Locke, as a proponent of the representative theory of perception, holds that there are both ideas of secondary qualities and secondary qualities, just as there are in the case of primary qualities.

On the third interpretation – and the one which we will see in a moment is most relevant to Hutcheson – Locke regards secondary qualities as being neither wholly 'in objects' nor wholly in the mind, but as somehow between them. They are essentially 'powers', or dispositions, to produce certain mental effects.[9] Thus he writes that they are 'nothing in the objects *themselves* but powers to produce various sensations in us by their primary qualities' (my italics).

This 'intermediate' interpretation forms the basis of one of the most attractive recent accounts[10] of secondary qualities, according to which colour (for instance) is a relation between the object and a normally sighted person. Colours are 'in the object' in the sense that it is the object that has the disposition to cause in us the relevant sensory experience. However, they are now defined by reference to their sensory effects rather than their causes. It thus becomes legitimate to talk of a ball (say) really being red, and even of redness as a perceptible feature of the external world. It no longer makes sense to speak of the viewer as being here deceived into taking 'red' as a primary quality of the ball when it is not. On the contrary, there is room on this account, as there is not on the other two, for a genuine distinction between veridical and non-veridical perceptions. For instance, if what you see as red would not look red to a standard perceiver, your perception is non-veridical.

Writers like Mackie, I suspect, have not so much ignored Hutcheson's comparison of vice and virtue with secondary qualities as simply assumed a Berkeleyian reduction of these qualities to sensations. But this as regards Hutcheson is unjustified. His denial ([1742] 1969: 371) that our ideas of secondary qualities (our 'purely sensible ideas') are '*images* of anything external' (my italics) leaves it open at least that they may be non-resembling ideas of something really in the object which they represent. But as we have just seen if this were Hutcheson's view, my claim that the ball is red, though not involving an error of projection, would be at least misleading in so far as it implies that the ball really is as it looks. This hardly coheres with Hutcheson's acknowledgement of the possibility of both correct and erroneous representations by the senses of secondary qualities. This acknowledgment suggests the 'tempered' objectivity of the third interpretation, particularly as developed in recent accounts of secondary qualities.

It may well appear then that, whereas the earlier Hutcheson was a somewhat imperilled, if relatively straightforward, naturalistic objectivist, his later work suggests an account of moral experience which, as it were, intrudes the subjective mode of perception into what is 'objectively' perceived. But one might want to go further and say that he was already, even in the earlier work, aiming for a picture of moral perceptions as bearing in this way indelible marks of the mode of perception. For there he attempts to bind both the moral sense and ordinary sense perception so tightly to their respective objects – moral and natural good – that these are inaccessible except from the single viewpoint. The difference, however, is perhaps that earlier he sought to achieve his end by distinguishing between the moral sense and sense-perception. Later he distinguishes within sense perception between secondary-like moral qualities and primary qualities. Our question now is whether this 'tempered' objectivism is enough to make him a possible target of Hume's practicality argument (in the 'moderate' version).

2 Hutcheson and Hume's 'wilful murder'

(i) But both deny that morality is a matter of fact inferred by reason

As we saw in the last chapter, only with regard to one of his arguments in 3.1.1 does Hume make it clear that his target is specifically naturalistic objectivism. This is the argument from 'wilful murder' expounded in paragraph 26. Here he announces that he is turning, in this 'second part of our argument', from those philosophers for whom 'morality consists . . . in relations' to those for whom it concerns 'matters of fact'. But we may safely assume that any philosophers for whom morality concerns such 'matters of fact' must be naturalists. That they can still be said to treat morality as 'an object of reason' indicates that they locate these matters of fact in the world rather than in the mind of the spectator.

We would do well, then, rather than going directly to the practicality argument, where Hume makes no such explicit reference to naturalistic opponents, to see first what case can be made out for Hutcheson's being a target of the later argument. If we could show that this was plausible, it would be an important step on the way to showing that he might also be a target of the practicality argument (in the 'moderate' version). It will not, however, take us all the way to this conclusion. For the argument in paragraph 26 is only about the objectivity of moral distinctions, which Hume wants to replace with a subjectivist account; it is not about the bearing of that on questions of moral *motivation*.

It will be helpful to have before us Hume's argument at 3.1.1:26:

> Nor does this reasoning only prove, that morality consists not in any relations, that are the objects of science; but if examin'd, will prove with equal certainty, that [morality] consists not in any matter of fact, which can be discover'd by the understanding. This is the second part of our argument; and if it can be made evident, we may conclude, that morality is not an object of reason. But can there be any difficulty in proving, that vice and virtue are not matters of fact, whose existence we can infer by reason? Take any action allow'd to be vicious: Wilful murder, for instance. Examine it in all lights, and see if you can find that matter of fact, or real existence, which you call vice. In which-ever way you take it, you find only certain passions, motives, volitions, and

thoughts. There is no other matter of fact in the case. The vice entirely escapes you, as long as you consider the object. You never can find it, till you turn your reflection into your breast, and find a sentiment of disapprobation, which arises in you, towards this action. Here is a matter of fact; but 'tis the object of feeling, not of reason. It lies in yourself, not in the object. So that when you pronounce any action or character to be vicious, you mean nothing, but that from the constitution of your nature you have a feeling or sentiment of blame from the contemplation of it. Vice and virtue, therefore, may be compar'd to sounds, colours, heat and cold, which, according to modern philosophy are not qualities in objects, but perceptions in the mind.

It will immediately be observed that Hume intends his argument to prove that 'vice and virtue are not matters of fact *whose existence we can infer by reason*' (my italics). But surely, it will be objected, this qualification already rules out Hutcheson as a target of the argument. For Hutcheson also sets out to refute, not just the view that morality can be demonstrated, but also that it is a matter of fact inferred by reason.

Consider, for instance, the section 'Concerning the character of virtue, agreeable to truth or reason' in *Illustrations* ([1742] 1969: 360–6). Here he is evidently criticizing both metaphysical and naturalistic attempts to show how reason provides 'a [moral] standard antecedent... to any sense'. In discussing the naturalistic attempt, he agrees that we may legitimately give reasons for our disapproval of 'luxury', explaining that 'it evidences a selfish base temper'. Nevertheless, he claims, we do not infer our disapproval of luxury from such psychological observations: rather our disapproval, even if its object is ultimately the underlying temperament of the luxury lover, is immediate and unreasoned. As he elsewhere (ibid.: 306) writes – this time with regard to virtue rather than vice: 'some actions have to men an immediate goodness'. Again, he tells us (ibid.: 313) that 'we are not to imagine that this moral sense, more than the other senses, supposes any... knowledge'. Finally in the passage, discussed earlier, Hutcheson states that the motive and consequences of an action are 'often inferred by reason'. However, he distinguishes our reaching these conclusions as to the empirical nature of the action from our approval or disapproval of it. Must we not conclude that, even if Hutcheson is a naturalist and an objectivist (of some kind), it is not of a kind that Hume sets out to refute in this passage?

But this is too swift. It ignores the fact that, inexplicably, Hume's statement of intention diverges from what he subsequently attempts to prove. For whereas he indeed says that he is going to prove that 'vice and virtue are not matters of fact whose existence we can infer by reason', what he offers a proof of is that they are not (objective) matters of fact *simpliciter*. His argument takes the form of a thought-experiment. He asks his readers to consider an action – 'wilful murder' – together with its circumstances and surroundings and see if they can 'find [there] that matter of fact, or real existence, which you call vice'.

This disparity has embarrassed commentators, who remain divided as to whether to acknowledge it or, if they do, what to say about it. Mackie, for instance, (1980:

58) does not even mention Hume's stated aim with its reference to 'inference' but proceeds, in quoting from 3.1.1:26, straight to the thought-experiment.[11] He then takes Hume to be concerned negatively to show only that '[the] moral judgement that a certain action is wicked is not a description of any empirical features of the object . . . about which it is made'. But this gives the impression again that Hume's opponent holds that virtue and vice are to be observed directly either in the agent's 'passions, motives, volitions or thoughts' or in some *sui generis* quality of his action, rather than being an inference *from* any observation.

Stroud, by contrast (1977: 176–7), declares from the outset that the argument at 3.1.1:26 is concerned with morality as involving an 'inference to some matter of fact'. Though, however, he admits that this argument is both 'confusing and obscure' he does not allude to the ostensible gap between what Hume says he will do and what he actually attempts to do. He just treats the argument (or thought-experiment) as intended to show *both* that 'an action or character's being vicious is not something that can be observed "in" the action or character in question', and also that it is not 'something we can reasonably infer to obtain on the basis of something we do observe'.

Harrison (1976: 60–2) is the only one of these important commentators to allude to the disparity just described, or hint at the quandaries of interpretation it raises. Hume, he says, announces that he is going to prove that 'moral distinctions . . . are not established by a process of probable inference'. However, what he actually attempts to show, he goes on, is that 'moral distinctions do not consist in any matters of fact'. He observes that, were Hume to have shown, as he says he is going to, that virtue and vice are not matters of fact established by a process of inference, he would not thereby have shown that they could not be matters of fact observed directly in the action. Consequently he would have left an important kind of objectivism unrefuted.

There are, I suggest, two possible solutions. The first relies on the observation that if morality is a matter of fact whose existence is inferred by reason, it would have to be inferred from another matter of fact – one which we observe directly. For in light of this, it would make sense for Hume to begin by showing that morality does not consist in this immediately observed matter of fact: thus his thought-experiment. The puzzle, though, is why in this case he does not go on, after the thought-experiment, to deal with the inferential claim. The other – and better one – relies on the observation that, though the way Hume talks makes it seem that the 'motives' and 'thoughts' mentioned are directly observable, this is not how he (any more than Hutcheson) would have regarded them. Rather, he would have seen them as themselves inferences from the more outward manifestations of the action, together with e.g. what the agent says about it, etc. Now if it is assumed that moral qualities pertain to the motive of which the action is a mere 'sign', as Hume later calls it, then inference will be involved in reaching a moral judgement. However, it will not be an inference from the directly observable features of the action to its moral qualities, but from these features to its motive, in which the objectivist would then hold that the – perhaps *sui generis* – moral quality resides. But this objectivism may well be thought to be Hutcheson's.

(ii) But both liken moral perceptions to secondary qualities

This is all very well, the objector will say, now coming at the issue from a new angle, if we really are entitled to interpret Hutcheson as holding in a more wholehearted way than Hume that moral qualities are 'in the object'. But are we so entitled? After all we are relying here, especially in so far as Hutcheson's *Illustrations* view is concerned, on his comparison of moral qualities with secondary ones. But Hume himself in 3.1.1:26 compares virtue and vice to secondary qualities.

One thing should be clear from our earlier discussion of secondary qualities: merely to point out that both Hume and Hutcheson invoke such qualities in their accounts of morality does not establish that these philosophers are as one over the objectivist/subjectivist distinction. Still less may we assume, as many writers have done, that this fact settles the matter in favour of Hutcheson's being, as Hume is taken to be, a subjectivist. There is nevertheless a challenge to be met. We have perhaps established that Hutcheson, given the way he construes secondary qualities, is a 'tempered' objectivist (as we have defined the term). But can we be sure that Hume, given the way he construes secondary qualities, isn't one also? In other words, we might simply and futilely have exchanged one kind of terminology for its opposite without its representing any clear difference between the two philosophers. But if this is so, we might as well have called them both 'tempered' subjectivists.

But there are crucial differences between the way the two philosophers describe secondary qualities in comparing moral qualities with them. Hume, speaking of secondary qualities, directly offers only two alternatives as to their status: either they are 'qualities in objects [or] perceptions in the mind'. He unequivocally denies that they are the first, and just as unequivocally asserts that they are the second. But Hutcheson, since he is only talking about our *ideas* of secondary qualities, not the qualities themselves, does not need to deny that they are 'qualities in objects': that much is obvious. Moreover in telling us that these ideas are 'only perceptions in our minds' he crucially qualifies his meaning by adding: 'they are not images of any like external quality'. Likewise, he writes that approbation 'cannot be supposed an image of anything external'. But Hutcheson makes these remarks in a context in which he is also discussing primary qualities. He may seem therefore only to be contrasting two ways – a non-resembling and a resembling one – in which ideas can represent qualities, rather than, like Hume, drastically collapsing secondary qualities into mere sensations.

Again, as we saw earlier, Hutcheson acknowledges a difficulty which his comparison of moral perceptions with our ideas of secondary qualities poses for anyone who like himself wishes to exclude reason from playing a fundamental role in morality. This is that our ideas of secondary qualities are (like those of primary qualities) capable of correctly and incorrectly representing these qualities. But no similar suggestion as to the possibility of testing our ideas of secondary qualities for their veridicality is discussed by Hume in his comparison of vice and virtue with these qualities.

It seems legitimate to maintain that Hutcheson's position is sufficiently distinct from Hume's, even where they both invoke the comparison with secondary qualities, to allow us to talk of Hutcheson as a 'tempered' objectivist, whilst reserving the term 'subjectivist' exclusively for Hume. I propose therefore to treat the 'wilful murder' passage as a criticism, if a veiled one, of Hutcheson. Hume is attempting to push (with the help of a Berkeleyan reading of Locke's seminal discussion) Hutcheson's comparison of moral perceptions with secondary qualities to its logical conclusion, and so over the edge into moral subjectivism.

3 Hutcheson, motivation and the practicality argument

(i) The practicality argument

At the start of his discussion of *Treatise* 3.1.1, Mackie (1980: 51–2) observes, with particular reference to the practicality argument, that it is unclear for what meaning of 'reason' Hume is saying that moral distinctions are not derived from reason. He goes on to explain how the more comprehensive the view of reason that is being ruled out, the more compromised becomes the moral objectivism that can survive Hume's strictures. If Hume wished only to deny that moral distinctions could be demonstrated, he would leave standing (and could consistently espouse) the view that they are derivable from 'true beliefs'. If, more ambitiously, he included under 'reason' any true belief, so ruling out the view that drawing moral distinctions is a matter of having such beliefs, his former allies in this view would now be opponents. He could still maintain, positively, that in making a moral judgement about an action we attribute a relevant moral quality to the action itself. However, he would be compelled, Mackie maintains, to say that, in doing so, we are mistaken, and that in fact we are really just projecting onto the action our own feelings. Hume may wish, however, to defend the still more sweeping claim that moral judgements are not beliefs of any kind, even false ones: he may wish to deny that they even have the form of beliefs. The only position then open to him, according to Mackie, would be that a person making a moral judgement no more even mistakenly attributes the given moral quality to actions, than she does her own pain to something outside her. Morality is finally just a matter of subjective feeling.

Now Mackie (1980: 51) interestingly explicitly closes off the possibility that Hutcheson might be a target of Hume's practicality argument on any of these interpretations of 'reason'. He does so by assuming, as he had done earlier, that if Hutcheson were a moral objectivist, it would be one who robustly maintains that moral distinctions are derived from true beliefs. For Mackie, moreover, this is tantamount to treating moral qualities as akin to Lockean primary qualities. Mackie correctly maintains that this is *not* Hutcheson's position. But just as before he does not allude to Hutcheson's explicit comparison of moral perceptions with ideas of secondary qualities. He does not therefore consider whether Hutcheson might have occupied an intermediate position between the robust moral objectivism, which is not his, and thorough-going subjectivism. This omission is even more puzzling than it was in his earlier discussion of Hutcheson. For there Mackie did not mention secondary qualities at all, but here he does. He suggests – without alluding to Hutcheson – that to compare moral qualities with secondary qualities is precisely to espouse an intermediate position between a more robust objectivism and subjectivism. In other words, he does not here, as he appeared – at least implicitly – to do earlier, simply collapse secondary qualities into sensations.

Even if, however, Mackie were to, as he does not, attribute this intermediate position to Hutcheson it would still be different from the position we have attributed to him. For the only construal of secondary qualities that Mackie entertains is one according to which they are taken for primary qualities of the objects to which they are attributed. All attributions of secondary qualities are therefore necessarily mistaken.[12] Just as the belief that e.g. 'the ball is red' is, on this view, always false, so also are attributions of vice and virtue to actions and motives. On our interpretation of Hutcheson, however, he would hold that both the judgement that 'the ball is red', and the judgement that 'benevolence is virtuous' can, despite their ineliminable subjective component, express in some sense true beliefs.

Could Hutcheson, then, on our interpretation, be a target of the 'moderate' version of the practicality argument? A preliminary question would seem to be this: might Hume have held that the perceptual-like belief, associated by Hutcheson with moral approval, would have compromised the power of morality to motivate us? Clearly such a belief is wholly different from the rational apprehension with which Cudworth and Clarke identify moral judgement. Indeed, Hutcheson, as an empirical naturalist, rejects the moral rationalism of these metaphysicians in the same outright fashion as Hume. With Hutcheson therefore there is no possibility of pointing, as there was with Clarke and Cudworth, to that rupture of the natural order which, I argued, may well lie behind Hume's 'extreme' charge that reason is 'perfectly inert'.

Beyond these observations we enter murky waters. As we shall recall, the main reason for undertaking this whole inquiry was that the practicality argument, in its better known 'moderate' version, is as it stands obviously invalid. This raised questions about Hume's real intentions, and whether the premises ought to be – or could be – recast in order to secure the requisite validity. We concluded that the first premiss would have to posit a specially close link between moral judgement and motivation. The second would have to claim a motivational asymmetry between belief and desire, with only desire related to motivation in the same close way as moral judgement. Belief would lead to action but only conditionally upon the presence of an independent desire which would have the pre-eminent motivating role.

But we failed to find confirmation in the surrounding passages that these revamped premises represented, any better than his original formulations, Hume's considered views. On the contrary, several remarks appeared to conflict with the reformulated second premiss. To take one example, Hume sometimes suggests that reason, in the form of an ordinary perceptual belief, i.e. my seeing that there is a tasty fruit before me, can lead to action by itself exciting the requisite desire. Nor were we any better off with regard to the revised first premiss, according to which moral judgement is now directly, or even necessarily, linked with motivation. For no evidence was found either in the original formulations, or in the surrounding context, to support this revision. Worse still, when Hume much later gives an example of motivation specifically by moral sentiment, the latter has, as we saw, a merely peripheral role compared with benevolence. But benevolence turns out to be a species of spontaneous *pre*-moral motivation.

It is thus unclear what we ought to take as Hume's official view on the relevant matters in order to assess how far Hutcheson might plausibly be thought to have fallen short of Hume's stipulations and expectations. Should we be content with Hume's own formulations of the practicality argument's premises, and disregard the fact that they do not entail his conclusion? Alternatively, should we recast the premises along the above lines, disregarding the fact that, as an interpretation of Hume, they are ill-supported by the text, and sometimes contradict it?

In the last few pages of the chapter, I propose to cut through these difficulties and uncertainties, and look in broad terms at two pertinent questions concerning Hutcheson. First, could his moral sense motivate action? Second, does Hutcheson's conception of motivation in general give more of a role to reason than Hume would have wished to countenance? I shall do little more than gesture towards answers.

(ii) Could Hutcheson's moral sense move us to action?

In the *Inquiry*, Hutcheson at least twice suggests that the moral sense either includes, or can give rise to, a motive – a specifically disinterested one. Thus, he speaks ([1738] 1969: 346) of disinterested obligation as 'a determination, without regard to our own interest, to approve actions, and to perform them'. Again, he states (ibid.: 313) that, 'The Author of nature . . . has given us a moral sense to direct our actions.' But these are the exception rather than the rule. Moreover, as Darwall (1995: 223–32) convincingly argues,[13] the view even in these passages is not quite what it appears. Nor is it a view that he retains in his later work. In fact, it would be impossible for him consistently to hold it, given other elements in his theory.

First, the idea that the moral sense can motivate us sits oddly with a theory which is formulated, as was observed earlier, from the viewpoint of a spectator, not of an agent. Second, what the moral sense approves is the motive with which an action is performed, not the action itself. Hence the moral sense would have to be a 'determination' to act from this motive, namely, benevolence. But Hutcheson repeatedly emphasizes ([1738] 1969: 321–2) that the 'desire of the good of others', like any other instinct or affection, cannot 'be voluntarily raised'. At best then the moral sense (as Darwall puts it) could 'second' motives that the moral spectator, as agent, happens already to possess. But, thirdly, it would seem that there could not even, on Hutcheson's account, be a frustrated desire to act out of such 'kindly' motives. For an action motivated by kindness would be a moral good, and desire, for Hutcheson, exclusively aims at natural good. Benevolence, Hutcheson writes ([1738] 1969: 351) is a 'desire of the public natural happiness of rational agents'. One might perhaps coherently desire 'the secret pleasure' (ibid.: 305) that comes of knowing that one has acted out of a benevolent motive since that pleasure – like every pleasure – is, according to Hutcheson, an 'immediate natural good'. But the lack of disinterestedness would immediately rule it out as of moral value.

This last feature – even more than the other two which have some parallel in Hume's *Treatise* – entails an underlying radical discontinuity between moral approval and motivation. It is hard not to conclude that this would have dissatisfied the Hume of 3.1.1 who attempts to link morality and action in premiss 1 of his practicality argument. But still we have not established Hutcheson as a possible target of that argument. There is a further requirement: the explanation of why Hutcheson's moral sense fails to engage the will would have to implicate reason or belief. More specifically, Hutcheson would have to grant a more important role to it than Hume, by premiss 2, would have found compatible with motivation.

But earlier we suggested that Hutchesonian moral approval involved (on the spectator's part) the belief that an agent's motive was virtuous, where this quality was truly thought of as being (like secondary qualities on one plausible construal) 'in the object'. Would not this alone, even in the absence of the other factors, have been seen by Hume as compromising any link between the moral sense and action, should Hutcheson have chosen to postulate one? This question is tantamount to asking whether Hutcheson, in his account of ordinary motivation, gives a role to reason, or belief that Hume would have felt necessarily to undermine that account. Hutcheson himself (again a point I owe to Darwall, 1995: 223) distinguishes in the *Essay* between those things which can be motives – 'desires' and 'affections' – and those which cannot – 'the pleasurable or disagreeable ideas of an object' ([1738] 1969: 313) – received through the senses. But this leaves it open whether, nevertheless, a perceptual or other belief might, for him, be capable of giving rise to a desire, and hence of leading indirectly to action.

(iii) Does Hutcheson give reason more of a crucial role than Hume?

At first sight even entertaining such an idea will seem puzzling. In the *Illustrations*, for instance, Hutcheson apparently allots to reason the merely subsidiary role of discovering the means to ends already given by instinct, affection and desire. He tells us ([1742] 1969: 362) that 'no end can be intended or desired previously to some . . . affection' and that no end can be previous to . . . all [affections]' so that 'there can . . . be no exciting reason previous to affection'. However, as Darwall (1995: 225) points out, Hutcheson seems here to be overstating his case. Darwall suggests in fact that the *Illustrations* view should be set against the *Essay* distinction between motivational states. 'Desire' and 'affection', Hutcheson suggests ([1742] 1969: 357), are aimed at (natural) good whereas 'the particular passions' and 'appetites', felt 'towards objects immediately presented to some sense', may not be aimed at any good at all. In fact the 'violent bodily motion' and 'confused sensations' with which our passions and appetites are attended stultify 'all deliberative reasoning about our conduct'. Hutcheson goes on to counsel us 'to abstract from them, and consider in what manner we should act upon the several occasions which now excite our passions, if we have none of these sensations whence our desires become passionate'.[14] Moreover he defines 'the calm desire of good, and aversion to evil, either selfish or public' (ibid.: 357) as precisely that desire and aversion which arise from such extended rational reflection. He also suggests that once calm reason has its sway, we shall find ourselves desiring to perform actions in proportion to the magnitude and extent of the happiness they promise. If we are acting out of rational self-love, then the relevant happiness will concern just ourselves; if, however, we are acting out of 'calm universal benevolence' the projected recipients of the happiness will be everyone.

Let us accept that Hutcheson – though he will not allow, as the *Illustrations* makes clear, a truth just because it is a truth to motivate action – will allow the expectation of pleasure to prompt desire. But this will surely not distinguish him from Hume. For Hume, to go by certain of his remarks, countenances such a possibility himself. However, as can be seen from the above, Hutcheson goes further. For whereas Hume's 'calm desires and tendencies' are merely 'confounded with reason', Hutcheson's have, it would seem, a genuine rational component. Consequently, though one cannot (as the *Illustrations* makes clear) choose rationally between such ultimate ends as rational self-love and universal calm benevolence, one can rationally assess either a self-interested, or a benevolent, desire on its own terms. One can ask, for instance, how far it is rational to have a given self-regarding desire in light of the amount of happiness the desired action promises us. But Hume sometimes goes out of his way to contradict such a view. In 2.3.3:6, for instance, he famously declares that 'tis as little contrary to reason to prefer even my own acknowledg'd lesser good to my greater, and have a more ardent affection for the former than the latter'.

The answer to the first question that we posed – 'could Hutcheson's moral sense move us to action?' – is 'no'. The answer to the second – 'does Hutcheson give reason more of a role in motivation than Hume could allow?' is, on this brief examination, 'yes'. Suppose we take the second premiss on the 'moderate' version of the practicality argument to entail that reason, or belief, has a minor role alongside an independent desire in producing action: that of showing how the desire can be satisfied. It would follow that the belief – being only about means – could not on its own explain the action. It would be essential to point to a desire which the agent experienced quite independently of the belief, and which indeed she then sought means to satisfy. On Hutcheson's account, the belief that a given action will produce the greatest possible happiness for all concerned necessarily engenders the relevant benevolent desire. Hence it is to this belief that we would primarily refer in seeking an explanation of the benevolent action which results.

Suppose, however, the second premiss of the 'moderate' version is construed in such a way as to be consistent with Hume's remarks to the effect that though reason, or belief, can only lead to action through the mediation of desire, it can itself sometimes cause the requisite desire. Hume will still differ from Hutcheson in declaring that any desire can go with any belief. He writes after all (2.3.3:6) that "Tis not contrary to reason to prefer the destruction of the whole world to the scratching of my finger.' For Hutcheson, as we have just seen, the belief that a particular action will increase the well-being of others will necessarily engender the corresponding desire.

There are therefore grounds in Hutcheson's theory of the moral sense and, independently, in his theory of agency for Humean dissatisfaction. Whether Hume did ever feel this dissatisfaction we cannot be certain. Even if he did feel it, the question whether the two separate sources of dissatisfaction could be drawn together in such a way as to make Hutcheson a plausible target of the 'moderate' version of the practicality argument would still have to be settled. It will no longer be possible, however, just to rule out his being one of Hume's targets by unthinkingly assuming that he was a subjectivist, or one who gave no greater role to reason in moral motivation than Hume himself. (Of course I mean here by 'moral motivation' action performed out of benevolent motives, not from a sense of morality.)

We have perhaps done enough by now to partially vindicate the claim that, though they do not correspond to distinct intentions on Hume's part, there are effectively two separate arguments contained within the formal unity of the practicality argument. The more tenable 'extreme' version is, we sought to make clear in Chapter 3, addressed to the moral rationalists, and bears, to a perhaps surprising degree, the marks of these metaphysical predecessors of Hume. Perhaps the 'moderate' version also, if it is ever to have a valid form, and yet cohere with other things Hume says, will have to be interpreted in a much more philosophically, and historically, specific way. This would be the case were Hutcheson to be decisively confirmed as its target.

In so far as all this is correct, the apparent contradiction we pointed to in Chapter 1 will resolve itself into an ambiguity in Hume's notion of reason across the different contexts. In the next chapter we attempt to trace this ambiguity back to his original exposition, in Book 1, of this, and related, notions. There, as we observed earlier, Hume includes under 'reason' both what we would think of as reason proper, namely, logical demonstration, and what we would think of as belief, described by Hume as part of our sensitive natures, like passion or desire. Whether any such neat division into 'reason' and 'belief' – the former pertaining to the 'extreme' version and the latter to the 'moderate' one – will survive scrutiny, allowing us to talk here of a *systematic* ambiguity, remains to be seen. We will also consider whether perhaps Hume stopped short of resolving such ambiguities because he preferred a teasing instability to remain even at the heart of such a key argument as that from morality's practicality: now one of the most famous in all moral philosophy.

5 The Inconsolable Sceptic

I will now say more about the different notions of reason appropriate to the different readings of premiss 2, as these notions first make their appearance in Book 1. As we shall see, there are three, rather than two to be considered: reason as giving us access to a metaphysical realm (or as itself a metaphysical entity), demonstrative reasoning and probabilistic reasoning or beliefs about 'matters of fact'. Hume rejects metaphysical reasoning as unintelligible, while placing demonstrative and probabilistic reasoning in our 'cogitative' and 'sensitive' natures, respectively (1.4.1:8). Only the former yields knowledge but only probabilistic reasoning and belief are linked to passions and action, their relevance for 'the conduct of life' (Abstract 10) being continually stressed.

This threefold division is nevertheless not as tidy as it looks. Metaphysical reasoning is, as we saw in an earlier chapter, demonstrative in form. Moreover by becoming entangled with metaphysics, demonstration, according to Hume, forfeits its normal legitimacy as a mental operation on a par with probabilistic reasoning. In his section 'Of scepticism with regard to reason' (1.4.1), however, Hume suggests that ultimately knowledge 'runs insensibly' or 'degenerates' into 'probability'. As to probabilistic reasoning itself, he is never, as we shall see, entirely happy with his characterization of it as a feeling or sentiment. But only in Books 2 and 3 does he actually reverse the order of assimilation in 1.4.1 and place it with demonstrative reasoning in the 'world of ideas', rather than of 'realities'. In thus cutting it off from feeling and the will, he compromises its earlier relation to action.

1 Reason: the three-fold division

(i) Hume's attack on metaphysical reason[1]

At the very same time as he announces his resolve to follow the 'experimental method' Hume also makes it clear that metaphysical reason, or the subjects it pretends to give us knowledge of, falls outside the scope of legitimate inquiry. He writes (Intro. 8–9):

> For to me it seems evident, that the essence of mind being equally unknown to us with that of external bodies, it must be equally impossible to form any

notion of its powers and qualities otherwise than from careful and exact experiments, and the observation of those particular effects, which result from its different circumstances and situations. And tho' we must endeavour to render all our principles as universal as possible, by tracing up our experiments to the utmost, and explaining all effects from the simplest and fewest causes, 'tis still certain that we cannot go beyond experience; and any hypothesis that pretends to discover the ultimate original qualities of human nature, ought at first to be rejected as presumptious and chimerical . . . When we see that we have arriv'd at the utmost extent of human reason, we sit down contented; tho' we be perfectly satisfy'd in the main of our ignorance, and perceive that we can give no reason for our most general and most refin'd principles, beside our experience of their reality; which is the reason of the mere vulgar.

But what exactly does all this mean in terms of Hume's theory of ideas? How precisely, for instance, does 'go[ing] beyond experience',[2] or attempting to penetrate 'the essence of mind', contravene the theory's tenets? Why in short is metaphysical reasoning 'chimerical'? In fact, it offends against Hume's theory in two related ways. A crucial tenet of this theory is the *priority* of impressions over ideas. Thus, for Hume, not only is 'nothing . . . ever really present with the mind but its perceptions or impressions and ideas, (1.2.6:7) but ideas are merely 'the faint images of [impressions] in thinking and reasoning' (1.1.1:1). It follows that an idea which cannot be traced to an impression is meaningless. But ideas, such as those of causal power, or of physical or mental substance, propounded (among others) by the metaphysicians, are not, Hume maintains, copied from impressions. 'There is', he writes, 'no impression convey'd by our senses which can give rise to the idea of [for instance] causal power' and again (1.3.14:11) that 'we never have any impression that contains any power or efficacy'. These ideas must therefore be meaningless.

But metaphysicians are not like those naïve empiricists whom Hume also criticizes for failing to cite impressions to match such crucial ideas as that of causal necessity. They do not, like the empiricists, point to *fictitious* impressions. They do not point to impressions at all. On the contrary, they hold that there can be ideas without corresponding impressions: abstract or general ideas. But this contravenes a second vital tenet of Hume's theory, according to which 'We know nothing but particular qualities and perceptions' (Abstract: 28). Bringing this stricture against Descartes's account of the soul, he writes: 'Descartes maintained that thought was the essence of the mind; not this thought or that thought, but thought in general. This seems to be absolutely unintelligible since everything, that exists, is particular.'

Since experience, according to Hume's theory, is composed of distinct particulars, no logically necessary relations can hold between them.[3] But metaphysicians, as we saw with the moral rationalists, commonly postulate such an objective network of rational relations. In Book 1 Hume is especially exercised, as we have noted, with the metaphysical treatment of issues such as causality. These philosophers, Hume tells us, attempt to penetrate behind 'the multiplicity of resembling instances' (1.3.14:16) to expose that 'power or operating principle' of causes', which 'makes them be follow'd by their effects' (1.3.14:3). But he rejects any such attempt. 'We cannot', he writes (1.3.6:15), 'penetrate into the reason of the conjunction [between cause and effect].' 'Objects', as we are acquainted with them, cannot imply the existence of one another (1.3.6:1), and 'never point out any other event which may result from them'.

Reason understood either as giving us access to a metaphysical realm, or as itself a metaphysical entity, is therefore for Hume nonsensical. In Book 3 he is nevertheless obliged to countenance the moral rationalists' version of this 'fiction' simply in order to refute their claim that it could be a source of action. It is in this context that we find his arguments against the possibility that something which is not part of the natural order, and so not itself subject to change, could influence that order, let alone necessarily. In fact his remarks in Book 1 suggest that as a critique of the moral rationalists the practicality argument's second premiss should if anything be read in an even more extreme fashion than we have so far proposed. This premiss ought, it would now seem, to be recast as: 'Reason, *if it were imaginable at all*, could not possibly move us to action'. The gap therefore between the premiss on this reading and on the 'moderate' reading becomes even wider.

(ii) The two legitimate kinds of reasoning distinguished[4]

Probabilistic reasoning is, in Book 1, sharply contrasted with metaphysical reasoning in being, like demonstration (when not pressed beyond its proper limits), a legitimate mental operation. However, it is also contrasted with metaphysical reasoning in leading (and here there is no suggestion of a similarity with legitimate demonstrative reasoning) to passion and action. As we indicated, probabilistic reasoning (and the belief about matters of fact in which it culminates) owes this connection to its status as a feeling which demonstrative reasoning does not share. Before, however, we can explain just how being a sensation links probabilistic reasoning and belief with the practicalities of life, and distances them from demonstrative reasoning, we need to see why Hume thinks they not only are but must be sensations. This requires us to say more about the problem he encounters in distinguishing belief from mere 'idle fancy': a problem which is not posed by demonstrated conclusions.

Hume draws an important distinction at 1.1.5 between what he calls 'natural' and 'philosophical' relations. In the previous section he had defined a 'natural relation' as holding between two ideas, one of which, by a 'uniting principle of ideas', or an 'associating principle of thought' (1.3.9:2) conveys the mind automatically and irresistibly to the other. He lists the three natural relations as 'resemblance, contiguity in time or place and cause and effect'. Consider merely the last: we have countless times experienced heat on lighting a flame. Now the sight (even the thought) of a flame brings heat to mind. Here then events are originally experienced in a fixed order which is reflected in the subsequent association of ideas in our minds. Pears (1990: 68), puts Hume's view thus: 'the human mind is attuned to three of the many relations holding between things in the world'.

Philosophical relations, on the other hand, involve our deliberately comparing ideas which we have either voluntarily called up, or which have entered our mind arbitrarily. Since we can deliberately call up ideas of cause and effect, and other naturally related ideas as well as ideas that are not naturally related, the category of philosophical relations includes, though is not co-extensive with, natural ones.

Turning now to the more inclusive category, Hume lists (1.3.1) seven types of philosophical relation. The first four are those of resemblance, contrariety, degrees in quality, and of proportion and quantity in number. Depending wholly on the ideas compared, these relations are said to be the only objects of knowledge or certainty because 'they remain invariable as long as our idea remains the same'. Since, for instance, 8 is included in the very idea of 5 and 3, one knows that $5 + 3 = 8$, directly one grasps the ideas involved. Such an arithmetical proposition could only conceivably be wrong if the meaning of either 5 or 3, on the one hand, or 8 on the other was changed. The other three relations – identity, situation in time and place and causation – for evidence of which we must consult experience – can, however, be changed without a change in the ideas. Take again the claim that flame produces heat: it could be disconfirmed by new observations, though our ideas of flame and heat remain unaltered.

Hume further sub-divides each of these types of philosophical relation. Relations depending wholly upon the ideas compared are either matters of 'intuition', and so of certainty, or matters of 'demonstration', which are necessary truths. The former somewhat surprisingly for a modern reader includes such patent matters of fact as one shade of a colour being darker or lighter than another (Hume's 'degrees in quality discoverable at first sight').[5] The latter include mathematical proofs, and involve at least one inferential step. Relations which depend on further empirical input and so are only ever objects of belief are again either matters of immediate perception or involve inferential steps. Here, however, the difference depends on whether, when we make the comparison, both objects are, or are not, 'present to the senses along with the relation' (1.3.2:2). The relation of contiguity is an instance of the former (we directly perceive that the table is near the chair), causation of the latter (we only infer from the sight of the flame that heat will be produced). Given the fact that we have on countless past occasions experienced this conjunction an associative principle now carries our mind beyond what is immediately present to the senses 'to inform . . . us of existences and objects which we do not see or feel'.[6]

(iii) Belief: the role of sensation in making up the deficit in reason

'Wherein' asks Hume (1.3.7:3–4) 'consists the difference betwixt believing and disbelieving any proposition?' The answer, he tells us, is easy with those propositions proved by intuition or demonstrated (where in fact it is more appropriate to speak of 'knowledge'). Since the idea of a triangle includes the idea of its angles adding up to two right angles, it is simply inconceivable to anyone who grasps both ideas that the angles of a triangle should not add up to two right angles. A proof is precisely that which leaves us no option but to assent to its conclusion: dissent is absurd and 'whatever is absurd is unintelligible'. The matter is, Hume observes, entirely different where causal reasoning and belief about matters of fact are concerned. There is nothing inconceivable about the contradictory of an empirical proposition. For instance, it is perfectly easy to imagine flames not producing heat or, to take Hume's example, Caesar not having died in bed. 'The imagination', he writes, 'is free to conceive both sides of the question.' Indeed, if it were not, we could not understand someone who took the opposite view from us, and so dissent from their view. But what then is the principle, Hume asks again 'which fixes one of these different situations?' for until it is so fixed 'we have in reality no opinion'.

He immediately observes that having an idea of an object is not all that is meant when we say that we believe that there is such an object. He then considers, and rejects, three possibilities as to what the extra feature could be. Observing that causal inferences terminate in the affirmation of 'the existence of objects or of qualities', he asks whether belief might consist in the idea of existence being added to that of the object or quality. The second possibility is that belief involves a change in the content of the original idea. The third is that belief is an impression 'distinguishable from the conception' and 'only annex'd' (Appendix: 4) to it 'after the same manner that will and desire are annex'd to particular conceptions of good and pleasure'.

Taking the first possibility, he argues (1.3.7:2) that there just is no separate idea of existence. To think of an object is already to think of it as existing (though not of course to think that it does actually exist). He goes further: believing that an object exists adds no new ideas to those of the object itself. The point is this: given that there is no separate idea of existence, there is no idea which could be added to the original idea to turn it into a belief. But if there were such an idea, a new difficulty would in any case arise. Since we can, according to Hume, call up at will any idea and unite it with any other in our imagination, we would now, absurdly, simply by annexing the idea of existence to that of the relevant object, be able to make ourselves believe anything.

As far as the second possibility is concerned, Hume argues that if the content of the idea changed, it would no longer be the same idea. But then I could not be said to be dissenting from my companion's view that Caesar died in his bed – a view which I entertain before finally rejecting.

Third, Hume rejects (Appendix: 4), the claim that belief is a separate impression, distinct from, and merely annexed to, 'the simple conception' on the ground that this is directly contrary to experience. I cite here just one of his supporting examples:

> . . . when I recollect the several incidents of a journey, or the events of any history. Every particular fact is there the object of belief. Its idea is modify'd differently from the loose reveries of a castle-builder: But no distinct impression attends every distinct idea, or conception of matter of fact. This is the subject of plain experience.

None of these options is then, according to Hume tenable. He concludes (1.3.7:3–8) that belief can only vary 'the manner of conception of our precedent ideas' or, more fully, that it is 'nothing but an idea that is different from a fiction not in the nature, or the order of its parts, but in the manner of its being conceived'. But since, for Hume, an idea can only be varied by a variation in its force or vivacity, a belief must just *be* a more lively idea. To believe that Caesar died in his bed, as opposed merely to entertaining this possibility, is therefore to experience the relevant cluster of ideas in a more vivacious and lively form. But vivacity is a matter of feeling. Hume writes: 'An idea assented to *feels* different from a fictitious idea, that the fancy alone presents to us: And this different feeling I endeavour to explain by calling it a superior *force*, or *vivacity* or *solidity* or *firmness* or *steadiness*' (his italics). He repeats the claim that belief is a feeling no less than five times in paragraph 7, and once more in paragraph 8. Moreover he extends this characterization to the process of probable inference. He writes (1.3.8:12): 'All probable reasoning is nothing but a species of sensation', adding provocatively 'When I give the preference to one set of arguments above another, I do nothing but decide from my feeling concerning the superiority of their influence.'

But how exactly does an idea become enlivened and so turn into a belief? Hume's reply is that it is its proximity to a (sense) impression. He defines belief (1.3.7:6) as 'a lively idea produc'd by a relation to a present impression' and again writes (1.3.8:1): 'When any impression becomes present to us, it not only transports the mind to such ideas as are related to it, but likewise communicates to them a share of its force and vivacity.'

We should note that the requisite impression need not be the one which corresponds to the idea which is to become a belief. With causal reasoning indeed it cannot be. For here the mind is conveyed beyond a present impression (such as that of the flame) to an idea of something else (heat) which we do not yet (but believe we shall) feel. Of course for the idea of heat to be meaningful at all there must be a matching impression from which it was originally derived: the impression of heat. Moreover, if the impression of flame is now to bring to mind the idea of heat, we must in the past have many times experienced this impression being followed by the actual sensation of heat, so that a customary association has been set up between the two ideas. However, for the idea of heat to be so enlivened that it becomes the belief that we will shortly feel heat, the idea's proximity to the impression of *flame* is enough. In this way a mixture of impressions and ideas is, Hume tells us, guaranteed without which our causal conclusions would be 'chimerical' (1.3.6:6).

(iv) Beliefs, impressions and the will

For Hume, the idea of an orange differs from the impression of one only in being less forceful or vivacious. By stating that beliefs are more forceful or vivacious ideas, he is therefore indicating, not just that they arise when ideas are brought into contact with relevant impressions, but that they become themselves in a certain sense impressions. Thus he tells us (1.3.10:3) that beliefs 'raise up' these ideas to an equality with impressions, supplying the place of impressions. But this, as we shall now see, is how they get linked with passions and action.

Hume announces (1.3.10:2) that 'The chief spring and moving principle of all ... action' is the perception of pleasure and pain. But this perception may be either an impression (I see a juicy pear before me or feel a burning sensation on touching a hot surface) or an idea (I imagine a juicy pear, or think of what it would be like to get burnt). Now, according to him, impressions, but not ideas, have a powerful and immediate motivating force. The difference, he explains (1.3.7:7), is due to the fact that impressions 'render realities more present to us than fictions' so that they weigh more with us and have more influence on our passions and imagination. But since beliefs (1.3.10:3) occupy the place of impressions, they likewise can influence our will and passions. In fact, Hume points to his account of belief as showing how causal reasoning comes to have the powerful motivational effects it does.

But he goes further. He now suggests (1.3.10) that beliefs are even better suited than pure impressions to fulfil a motivational role. To be influenced by impressions alone, he argues, would leave a person constantly vulnerable to calamity. For though she would see these calamities approaching she would lack 'any principle of action' that might 'impel [her] to avoid them'. On the other hand were every *idea* of pain or pleasure to move us to action, things would be just as practically disastrous, for we would be moved hither and thither by every stray thought. Only reasoning about cause and effect, with its mixture of impressions and ideas can, Hume claims, ensure that our actions are appropriate and effective responses to the situation in hand. It is no wonder therefore that he describes causal inference as 'all our reasonings in the conduct of life (Abstract: 10) and applauds (Abstract: 4) Leibniz who called for a more detailed treatment of the probabilities on which life and action depend.

(v) The three notions of reason and the practicality argument

Probable reasoning and belief, as described by Hume in Book 1, are therefore not only necessary for action (and its regulation) but can arouse that other requirement for action: a relevant passion. If 'reason' in this sense were therefore the subject of the second premiss of the practicality argument, the 'moderate' reading would be the only appropriate one. What, however, of demonstrative reasoning, where this has not been pushed beyond its legitimate limits? Does Book 1 provide any grounds for supposing that Hume might regard even this legitimate form as (in the language of Book 3) 'perfectly inert', or can it, like probable reasoning, in some way impinge on the will? As we have seen, he makes it absolutely clear (Abstract: 16, 25) that demonstration has no place in our reaching causal conclusions. ''Tis custom alone', he writes (Abstract: 25), 'not reason, which determines us to make it the standard of our future judgements.' But this is not yet to deny that demonstration can have an influence on passion and action. Of course, causal inference, and the beliefs which result from it are, for Hume, 'a species of sensation', and sensations are also, for him, crucially linked with passion and action. But he does not go on here to draw any explicit conclusions concerning a difference between causal inference and demonstration as regards their practical influence.

May we not, however, draw these conclusions for him and say that, for him, demonstration, unlike causal inference and belief – which are sensations – can have no influence on the will, and so place it with the metaphysical variety as the 'reason' of the 'extreme' version? I do not think this is warranted on the basis of Hume's remarks here. This is not to say that he wishes to assert that demonstration has, or could have, a practical influence. On the contrary, his silence on a question, which he is so keen to discuss in the case of probable reasoning and belief, suggests that he does not see it as worth raising. Perhaps his thought is that demonstration is only a logical tool or procedure, a method for (as we might put it now) manipulating data, which people may or may not avail themselves of as they choose. It does not make sense therefore either to attribute or deny to it an influence on passion or action. It is not, as causal reasoning and belief are, a (subjective) experience of the agent's and so one which just happens to her. It does not, like the impressions which initiate the process of causal inference and then enliven the associated ideas so as to transform them into beliefs, 'enter the mind through the common channels of sensation and reflection'. Moreover, he leaves us in no doubt of either the extent or importance of this link between probable reasoning and experience – a link from which demonstrative reasoning is decisively excluded. For instance, in the Abstract where he sums up what he has said in the *Treatise*, he writes (paragraph 27): 'Almost all reasoning is there [i.e. in the *Treatise*] reduced to experience and the belief which attends experience is explained to be nothing but a peculiar sentiment, or lively conception produced by habit.'

If our only evidence, then, were to come from Book 1, and assuming our interpretation is correct, it would seem that the 'reason' which, in the 'extreme' version, *is* denied any role in action – cannot be demonstration, understood as a legitimate method of argument. It must be that distortion of demonstration to be found in the work of the metaphysicians. Even as regards this distorted notion, it is only by dint of temporarily adopting the moral rationalists' viewpoint, and so with, so to speak, one foot in metaphysics, that Hume is able meaningfully to declare its perfect 'inert[ia]'. There is no similar way of giving even temporary sense to claims about the inertia or otherwise of ordinary demonstrative reasoning.

But surely, it will be objected, Hume does, in Book 2, raise the question whether demonstration can have an influence on action. Moreover, he replies negatively, maintaining that 'the world of ideas' which is its 'proper province' is 'totally remov'd' from that 'of realities' in which 'the will always places us'. But it would be rash to let these later remarks affect our interpretation of his position in Book 1. We might just as well, looking back from Book 3 to the remarks in Book 2, suggest that they are not really about ordinary demonstrative reasoning at all. They are rather precursors of his discussion, and rejection, of the moral rationalists' claim that obligatoriness is a demonstrable truth which logically compels action. But there are quite other grounds for resisting revision. Hume goes on, in the passage from Book 2, to give the impression at least intermittently that causal, as well as demonstrative, reasoning can have no influence on action. Moreover, both kinds of reasoning are evidently run together in Book 3 (1.1:5) where he states that 'philosophy is commonly divided into speculative and practical: and as morality is always comprehended under the latter division, 'tis supposed to influence our passions and actions, and to go beyond the calm and indolent judgements of the understanding'. But it is difficult to conceive of any more categorical assertions of the influence on passion and action of causal reasoning and belief than those to be found in Book 1. Why then should we – rightly – refuse to modify the findings of Book 1 concerning causal reasoning in order to bring them into line with the later remarks, and yet be prepared to do so in the case of demonstrative reasoning?

It is vital to recall here that we only in the first place turned to Book 1 in the hope of finding distinctions there between types or notions of reason which would allow us to replace, with talk of a systematic ambiguity across its different formulations, the contradictions inherent in the practicality argument. Certainly these developments of Book 3 suggest that Hume has either lost or, perhaps better, deliberately loosened, without actually relinquishing, his grip on the distinctions of Book 1. Why he should have done so, and done so in that irresolute way which allows them to creep back, constantly breaking through the latterly imposed unitariness, is the question to which we finally turn. In answer we point to Hume's quandary, already apparent in Book 1, about belief, and also to the extraordinarily dynamic nature of the scepticism he there expresses.

2 Belief, scepticism and the subversion of reason

As we have seen, Hume repeatedly rejects all attempts (e.g. 1.3.6:8) to provide causal inferences with 'a just foundation', to base them in 'solid reasoning', to 'prove' them. 'However easy [the] step may seem [to suppose the future conformable with the past], he writes (Abstract: 16), 'reason would never, to all eternity, be able to make it'; reason must therefore (1.3.6:11) always fail us. However, as a further glance at the text shows, he is at the same time maintaining something apparently quite different. Comparing causality with resemblance and contiguity, he writes (1.3.6:7) that it 'is the only [relation], on which we can found a *just inference* from one object to another' (my italics). Again he claims (1.3.2:2) that only causal reasoning can 'go beyond what is immediately present to the senses . . . to give us *assurance* from the existence . . . of one object, that 'twas follow'd or preced'd by [another]' (my italics again). Accordingly, he contrasts beliefs resulting from causal reasoning, where our ideas are vivified 'justly' and 'naturally' (1.4.4:1), with those resulting from our being manipulated, or from our own emotional suggestibility, where the vivification is inappropriate. As far as arguments from causation are concerned, he claims that sometimes (1.3.11:2) the 'assurance' afforded is so 'full' as to 'exceed probability', and amount to 'proof'.

Despite this conflicting evidence, there is a strong tendency among philosophers (Winters, 1995, is discussed below) to take Hume's sentimentalist account of causal inference and belief in general as decisively cutting them off from reason, logically committing him to the view that no belief can be rationally justified. His account, it is frequently said, in laying bare the psychological mechanisms by which beliefs are inexorably formed, can leave no doubt that we place our trust in them at our peril. It is at the same time assumed that Hume himself not only grasps these sceptical implications, but wholeheartedly accepts them. He is, for these writers, a willing, even an eager, sceptic. Yes, it is admitted, in ranking different methods of belief acquisition he may be reflecting, even deferring to, common usage. But it does not follow, it is argued, that just because these same rankings are commonly defended by appeal to whether the resultant beliefs are true, this must be *his* criterion also. Textual evidence is then sought of Hume's having adopted quite different criteria, and criteria which precisely reconcile common usage with the most uncompromising scepticism.

Even those writers (for instance, Owen, 1999) who acknowledge that Hume is not consistently sceptical in Book 1 tend to see any falling away as due to his having not (at the relevant stage) fully grasped the implications of his own account of belief. Once he has done this, they maintain, he unequivocally embraces these implications, and so scepticism. In so far as he continues to talk of the truth or falsity of beliefs, they argue, he is merely detachedly describing our normative practices, not himself endorsing them. Now I do not propose to ally myself with the odd heretical voice (Ferreira, 1995) claiming that, for Hume, not only are the beliefs resulting from causal inference reliable and warranted, but that they can attain a certainty (and not merely a psychological one) equal to that of demonstration.[7] I will argue, however, that, though Hume perfectly well understands all through Book 1 the sceptical implications of his account of belief, he is by no means always ready to embrace them.[8] This unwillingness causes him, I shall suggest, at the very same time as almost triumphantly putting forward certain problematical examples of the vivification of ideas as further corroboration of his account of belief, to draw back and ask, as if under his breath, but is it really *belief* that I am talking about here?

I will argue that though he is not prepared in light of such examples to give up his account, he never fully reconciles himself to, for him, its alarming sceptical implications. In the conclusion of Book 1, he finds an ingenious way of accommodating his conflicting attitudes. He depicts himself as having by turn two different *persona*. One is that of 'the [sceptical] philosopher in his study'. The other is that of one of those 'honest gentlemen who being employ'd in their domestic affairs . . . have carry'd their thoughts very little beyond those objects, which are every day expos'd to their senses', and who ridicule scepticism. But even then, as we shall see, Nature has the last word over Reason.

(i) Why Hume is not a thoroughgoing sceptic

We first look at three passages which might be thought to help those who take Hume to be an unequivocal sceptic. They, we shall recall, admit that he ranks beliefs as we ordinarily do, but claim that he substitutes criteria of his own for ours, exchanging e.g. universality, stability and agreeableness for our truth. Each passage (two of which are often cited by defenders of the 'sceptical' interpretation) suggests something different from the others, but none supports the 'sceptical' interpretation. The first (1.3.11–12) suggests that Hume is fully engaged, at least where causal beliefs are concerned, on the side of the common view. This is that some causal beliefs are so incontrovertible that anyone who doubted them would be derided. The second (1.3.9–10) suggests that he falters in his account of belief as vivification when he tries to extend it from central cases, such as beliefs resulting from causal inference, to those evidently produced, given the vivification of ideas involved, by education, poetry and passion. In the third (1.4.4), Hume distinguishes the 'just' and 'natural' reasoning of the healthy mind from the spurious reasoning of the unhealthy one. However, it proves impossible to impose this single distinction upon the heterogeneity of examples with which Hume deals in the second passage, 1.3.9–10.

(a) Hume on the side of the ordinary non-sceptic

It would help defenders of the 'sceptical' interpretation if they could cite passages where Hume explicitly acknowledges, and then attempts to mitigate, a perceived disparity between his sceptical position and the distinctions commonly drawn between beliefs in terms of their reliability as indicators of truth. The only place where this might possibly seem to occur is in sections 1.3.11 and 12. Hume observes here that 'common discourse' according to which 'many arguments from causation exceed probability, and may be receiv'd as a superior kind of evidence' is at variance with his earlier claim that only demonstration yields certainty, whereas causal inference merely yields probability. Evidently referring to the counter-intuitive implications of his claim, he writes 'One wou'd appear ridiculous, who wou'd say, that 'tis only probable the sun will rise tomorrow, or that all men must dye.' He then attempts 'to preserve the common signification of words' by 'mark[ing] the several degrees of evidence to distinguish human reason into three kinds, viz. that from knowledge, from proofs and from probabilities'. He goes on to define as 'proofs' 'those arguments which are deriv'd from the relation of cause and effect, and which are entirely free from doubt and uncertainty'.

Now it is noteworthy how much he has already, in these passages, blunted the force of his earlier sceptical remarks. He does not ask, as we might have expected, given these earlier remarks, how we can speak of 'assurance' at all in the context of causal inference. On the contrary, he speaks in this very vein himself. The issue seems only to concern the different degrees, or gradations, of assurance: 'common discourse' recognizes three, he only two. Nevertheless, the question arises whether, in so far as he here embraces our common ways of talking, he can retain even a vestige of his earlier scepticism. For this would seem at least to require him to intro-duce a new terminology to mark that higher level of assurance which, he now admits, selected causal arguments can yield, but which is still not the certainty of demonstration. However, he now applies to these causal arguments themselves the same epithets which he had earlier reserved for the outcome of demonstrative reasoning, and adamantly refused to apply to *any* causal argument. Thus, as we have seen, he now declares them to be 'certain' and to yield 'proofs'.

A few writers suggest, not just that Hume here jettisons an earlier scepticism about causal inference in order to bring it into line with 'common discourse', but that he never was sceptical about it in the first place. Bringing remarks in the *Enquiry* to bear on Hume's claim that causal judgements can be 'free from doubt', Ferreira (1995: 274), for instance, does not interpret him as meaning that we are merely, as a matter of psychological fact, incapable of doubting such judgements. This would leave it open whether doubt might nevertheless be justified and appro-priate, even though *we* could never feel it. Rather, he takes Hume to mean, much more strongly, that 'there is no room for doubt', that doubt is unintelligible, and therefore that the certainty of causal judgements is on a par with, though different from, that of demonstration. But it is surely far-fetched to suggest that Hume consistently repudiates scepticism (any more than that he consistently affirms it). Nevertheless it is difficult to read these sections without gaining the strong impression that he is here at any rate fully engaged on the side of common practice, and not just describing it detachedly. There is for instance no attempt, as in other parts of Book 1, to distance himself from the views he is discussing by attributing them to 'the vulgar' or the 'weak-minded' or the 'unphilosophical'.

(b) Hume vacillating over vivification

I turn next to two sections actually cited by defenders of the sceptical interpretation. Hume begins section 10 by reminding us that 'education', whose 'maxims' he has just stated (1.3.9:19) are 'frequently contrary to reason', is dismissed by philosophers as a 'fallacious ground of assent to any opinion'. Nor is this surprising since Hume depicts it, as we shall see in a moment, as a kind of brainwashing. The rest of the section is taken up with a discussion of what seem to be other such 'fallacious grounds of assent': various types of manipulation by others, and our own emotional suggestibility or instability. Isn't Hume here, at least implicitly, attempting to persuade us that beliefs thus induced are undesirable in other ways than as indicators of truth, so that even a sceptic could sensibly reject them in favour of more 'genuinely' grounded ones? In fact, Hume's attitude to these so-called 'fallacious grounds of assent' is complicated, equivocal and confusing.

His stated intention is to provide, in this section, further corroboration of his account of belief as 'nothing but a more forcible and vivid conception of an idea' by extending it from causal beliefs to those produced in other ways, such as by education. The latter, he suggests, is 'built almost on the same foundation of custom and repetition' (1.3.9:19) as the former. Obviously, as he sees it, the greater the number of superficially disparate psychological phenomena he can bring under this single explanatory umbrella, the more powerful a tool he will have at his disposal. But then it must seem that the proposed interpretation should be rejected out of hand since it is the basic similarity between 'genuine' and (what 'philosophers' call) 'fallacious' grounds of assent that evidently interests him here, not their differences, as the interpretation requires.

Some writers would go further in rejecting this kind of interpretation. For Owen (1999: 208–9), Hume, in advertising as a strength of his account of belief that it can explain, not only causal beliefs, but the effects of education, and the liar's belief in his lies, reveals just how little he has yet grasped of its sceptical import. He has not, in other words, got to the point of asking why, if the indoctrination that here goes under the name of 'education', or habitual lying, produces the very same assent as causal inference, we – or the philosophers – should prefer the latter to the other two. Plainly, if Owen were right, Hume could hardly be said to be already, as the proposed interpretation requires, seeking to avoid a collision between these sceptical implications – which he is not yet aware of – and ordinary discourse.

But this is not the whole story. For there runs alongside Hume's attempt here to corroborate his account of belief by extending it from causal inference to further instances of vivification, a subversive subtext of doubt: is it belief in these new instances? Moreover, even where the vivified idea apparently retains its status as a belief its doing so is put down to some kind of mental weakness on the part of the believer. But this suggests another explanation for why Hume does not raise Owen's question than that he has not yet grasped the sceptical implications of his account of belief. It suggests, on the contrary, that he has done so, but neither wishes to abandon his account, so admitting that belief is something more than vivification, nor on the other hand to wholeheartedly accept these sceptical implications.

Let us look first at how Hume ostensibly seeks to 'extract' from these 'several new instances' 'a proof of the present doctrine', and afterwards at what I have called 'the subtext of doubt'.

(c) Vivification of ideas in education, poetry, passion

There are, we remember, two factors crucial to the production of a causal belief through the invigoration of an idea. The first is the presence of a *sense-impression*. But this impression, let us call it A, must in our past experience have been invariably followed by another impression, B, so that now A inexorably evokes in our minds the idea of B. The second factor is therefore Hume's 'custom or repetition'. The idea of B is subsequently invigorated by its proximity to A (an impression), and transformed into the relevant belief. But this 'invigoration', Hume now suggests (1.3.9:16), can occur in the absence of one or other of these factors, and even occasionally (as in 'madness or folly') of both: thus the various 'fallacious' grounds of assent.

With resemblance and contiguity, for instance (which Hume has discussed in 1.3.9), a sense-impression is present but custom or repetition is lacking. Nevertheless we may feign the idea of an object resembling, or contiguous to, that of an object of which we are presently having an impression. The idea of the resembling (or contiguous) object is then invigorated by proximity to the original sense-impression, its influence thereby being increased. With education, and habitual lying, it is the other way round: there is custom and repetition but no sense-impression. Thus, an idea, which has been strongly imprinted on the mind by frequent repetition of relevant words or phrases, 'by degree[s] acquires [that] facility and force' which, Hume emphasizes, does not just produce the belief but *is* the belief. The vividness of the idea and the belief are, he declares, 'individually the same.'

The passions are also, Hume goes on to claim (1.3.10:4), very favourable to belief. Here, however, the passion itself (having been excited by an 'affecting object') invigorates, without the help of custom and repetition, the idea of the object. This is how the fearful person – the coward – comes so 'readily [to] assent to every account of danger', and why the person of 'sorrowful and melancholy disposition' is 'very credulous of everything that nourishes his prevailing passion'. 'Quacks and projectors', writes Hume, exploit the same psychological mechanism when they deliberately make extravagant claims. The initial awe and astonishment aroused by their ostentatious claims, Hume explains, 'spreads itself over the whole soul, and so vivifies and enlivens the idea, that it resembles the inferences we draw from experience'. Yet again (1.3.10:8) the poet's powerful imagination is, Hume writes, 'of all talents the most proper to procure belief and authority'. This is because 'tis difficult for us to withhold our assent from what is painted out to us in all the colours of eloquence; the vivacity produc'd by the fancy [being] in many cases greater than that which arises from custom and experience'.

(d) A subversive subtext

I will now point out how, having thus asserted, or strongly implied, that the vivified idea is in all these instances a belief, Hume goes on either to throw this claim into doubt or to qualify it. Where he merely qualifies the claim, the vivified idea survives as a belief, but only as the product of weak and credulous minds. To take resemblance first, the main example that Hume cites in illustration is of an idea's being vivified precisely without becoming a belief. The poet (1.3.9:5) who visits a beautiful meadow or garden in order to be able to better describe the Elysian Fields obviously never believes that this mythical place is actually before him, nor that it ever did or will exist. Indeed, Hume speaks of him as merely attempting to stimulate his imagination with the real scene, and observes that: 'the relation of cause and effect is requisite to perswade us of any real existence'. Moreover, he explains why this is so. Custom and repetition make the passage from the impression to the idea not only unavoidable, but feel so to us. But we feel it is optional whether or not, where an object merely resembles another that is before us, we allow our minds to stray to the idea of the resembling object, with its consequent enlivening by the original impression.

With contiguity, it appears that Hume is in any case going to be satisfied with a less ambitious claim than that invigoration produces belief – merely that it is capable of ' augment[ing] opinion' or 'increas[ing] a belief' that we already hold. The Mohammedan who has seen Mecca, and the Christian who has seen the Holy Land, and so have memories of these places are, Hume maintains, more zealous believers than those who have not. 'The lively idea of the places', he writes, 'passes by an easy transition to the facts, which are suppos'd to have been related to them by contiguity, and encreases the belief by encreasing the vivacity of the conception.' Though Hume ends by suggesting that the remembrance of such places can act 'like a new argument', he confines this effect to the vulgar whose (presumed) weakness of mind somewhat mitigates the force of the claim.

With education, Hume is, as we have seen, keen not only to emphasize that it produces belief, but a belief so deep-rooted that it is virtually ineradicable by reason and experience, and can hold its own even with conflicting causal beliefs. Yet even here he cites 'parallel instances', which seem to undermine his claim that the vivified idea is a belief, in that in these instances it precisely is *not* a belief. Thus, Hume describes how someone, unacquainted with a celebrated person, will nevertheless remark: 'I have never seen such a one but almost fancy I have; so often have I heard talk of him.' But the person who says this kind of thing, as Hume would surely admit, does not expect us to suppose that she is ever actually misled, or taken in, by her doubtless curious state of mind.

As far as his treatment of the passions goes, Hume as we have just seen first suggests, rather as he does with education, that we are all naturally prone to having our ideas vivified in the relevant way, with the result that we come to form the associated belief. However, the examples he cites are either of individuals who are pathologically dominated by a single emotion – the coward, the melancholic – or who are weak-minded: it is only the vulgar, Hume suggests, who are actually fooled by quacks.

(e) The baffling case of literary depiction

Given that Hume's professed aim is to provide further confirmation of how our ideas of objects can be so vivified as to turn into the belief that these objects either exist or will exist, possibly the most baffling instance discussed is that of literary depiction. Poets, Hume observes, do not only rely on their eloquence to procure 'belief and authority'. They also make use of 'artifices' such as mixing truth and falshood (1.3.10:7). For instance, they 'borrow . . . the names of their persons, and the chief events of their poems, from history'. The fact that some incidents are objects of belief, maintains Hume, 'bestows a force and vivacity on the others, which are related to it'. He writes:

> The several incidents of the piece acquire a kind of relation by being united into one poem or representation and if any of these incidents be an object of belief, it bestows a force and vivacity on the others which are related to it. The vividness of the first conception diffuses itself along the relations, and is convey'd as by so many pipes or canals to every idea that has any communication with the primary one.

Our bafflement at all this is likely to be twofold. First, when we think of our responses to plays, novels and poems, however much our imagination takes fire, we have not the slightest inclination to say that we believe that the characters are actually before us, or ever did or will live, or that the incidents portrayed are taking place, or ever did take place. We may speak of a fiction's 'truth to life' but this is notoriously not to say that we assent to it as true. In short, Hume would appear here to be citing an instance of the vivification of an idea which is in obvious and immediate conflict with the claim that he is seeking to prove, namely that it is a belief.

But, second, Hume's attitude to this concern is unexpected and disconcerting. Far from trying to quiet it, he encourages it, assuring us that he is not suggesting that we are, or should, be taken in by such fictions. On the contrary, the poet does not use these various devices, he tells us, 'in order to deceive the spectators'. Moreover the claim to be corroborated has by now been considerably weakened. Hume's intention is apparently only to show (1.3.10:7) that 'absolute belief and assurance' are not requisite for producing the *effects* of belief. In other words, the invigoration of the spectators' ideas only mimics such full belief, being produced by 'other principles beside truth and reality'. This is evidently enough to 'procure a more easy reception into the imagination for those extraordinary events, which the [fiction] represent[s]', and thus to give 'an equal entertainment to the imagination', which is the poet's concern.

But Hume now retreats still further from the claim that a belief is nothing but the vivification of an idea. For he goes on to state that 'how great soever the pitch may be' to which this vivification attains, it will always feel different 'from when we reason, tho' even upon the lowest species of probability'. In fact, he declares the vivified idea to be 'a mere phantom of belief or perswasion', and a 'counterfeit belief'. Not only this but he now proceeds to undercut even his claim that it produces the same effects as belief and reality. He writes:

> A passion which is disagreeable in real life, may afford the highest entertainment in a tragedy or epic poem. In the latter case it lies not with that weight upon us . . . And has no other than the agreeable effect of exciting the spirits and rouzing the attention.

Perhaps he is thinking of the fact that members of the audience do not rush on stage to prevent one protagonist 'murdering' another.

Our examination, then, of Hume's treatment of these 'several new instances' in which an idea is vivified suggests that he is in fact equivocal as to whether he has shown, or even sets out to show, that the vivified idea is a belief. It can therefore give little comfort to those propounding the view that he not only unquestionably maintains that these are beliefs, but that he stipulates criteria which will enable us to rank them (and their grounds), without appealing to their truth or falsity.

(f) Health, torment and scepticism

The third and last passage to be considered is 1.4.4:1–2. Winters (1995) is one defender of the sceptical interpretation who makes extensive use of this passage in attempting to show how Hume might have reconciled his view that (on her reading) 'all beliefs [about matters of fact] are equally unjustified no matter how they are acquired' with his ranking of different methods of belief acquisition. For Hume, she claims, the beliefs arrived at by causal reasoning are 'strong, stable and long-lasting' which in turn makes them (ibid.: 269) 'more natural and agreeable to the mind than others'. But the sceptical claim by Winters remains intact. She suggests that, though the source of superiority of causal beliefs over other kinds is already implicit in 1.3.9–10 – from which she, like us, quotes – it can be made explicit by bringing the later passage to bear on these earlier sections. She correctly points out that Hume in this later passage is ostensibly addressing the objection that, in propounding his system, he places a reliance on the imagination for which he had rebuked the ancient philosophers. He replies:

> In order to justify myself, I must distinguish in the imagination betwixt the principles which are permanent, irresistible, and universal; such as the

customary transition from causes to effects, and from effects to causes: And the principles, which are changeable, weak and irregular . . . The former are the foundation of all our thoughts and actions, so that upon their removal human nature must immediately perish and go to ruin. The latter are neither unavoidable to mankind, nor necessary, or so much as useful in the conduct of life; but on the contrary are observ'd only to take place in weak minds, and being opposite to the other principles of custom and reasoning, may easily be subverted by a due contrast and opposition. For this reason the former are received by philosophy, and the latter rejected. One who concludes somebody to be near him, when he hears an articulate voice in the dark, reasons justly and naturally; tho' the conclusion be deriv'd from nothing but custom, which infixes and enlivens the idea of a human creature, on account of his usual conjunction with the present impression. But one, who is tormented he knows not why, with the apprehension of spectres in the dark, may, perhaps, be said to reason, and to reason naturally too: But then it must be in the same sense, that a malady is said to be natural; as arising from natural causes, tho' it be contrary to health, the most agreeable and most natural situation of man . . . The opinions of the antient philosophers . . . are like the spectres in the dark, and are deriv'd from principles, which however common, are neither universal nor unavoidable in human nature. The *modern philosophy* pretends to be entirely free from this defect, and to arise only from the solid, permanent, and consistent principles of the imagination.

Hume is certainly acknowledging here that his system is built on the imagination, and therefore implicitly that, for him, all beliefs, no matter how they are formed, are products of the imagination. Moreover, he relates this position to the distinction between beliefs that are the outcome of normal causal reasoning and those that result from a pathology. No doubt this is a distinction which Hume would acknowledge that we ordinarily make. But it is not clear that he is thinking of it here primarily as an expression of our common ways of talking with which he must reconcile his position. It may be that he is merely appealing to the predicament of the person 'tormented with the apprehension of spectres in the dark' as a vivid and effective way of bringing home to us, by analogy, what is wrong with the views of the ancient philosophers. For their 'opinions', he writes, are '*like* the spectres in the dark' (my italics).

But let us set aside doubts arising out of the specialized context and pursue Winter's argument further. She cites Hume's striking remark that were we to cease reasoning causally 'human nature must immediately perish and go to ruin'. She rejects Ardal's (1976) suggestion that it indicates Hume's wish to single out causal beliefs from others in terms of their usefulness: they show us how to attain our ends, and so are indispensable even to our physical survival. According to Winters, Ardal's interpretation entails attributing to Hume a view which he forcibly rejects: that we are rationally entitled to rely on the future resembling the past. For her, the remark, and the passage in general, consolidate claims and distinctions made, or implicit, elsewhere particularly in 1.3.9–10. Causal beliefs, she states, are for Hume the

result of 'the operation of natural instinct'. But natural instinct, as she further characterizes his view, is 'an essential property of human beings', or again 'an essential
part of our [human] nature', which 'makes us what we are'. Its 'principles' are
'permanent' – (or in her gloss on Hume) 'they must continue to operate' – and
'universal' – (in her gloss) 'they affect all humans'. Unlike 'the diseased principles',
they produce 'immediately', 'easily' and 'irresistibly' beliefs which are 'strong, stable
and long-lasting' and 'may [not] easily be subverted by a due contrast and opposition'. Since, moreover, according to Hume 'what is most natural to us is best and
most agreeable', causal reasoning and its culmination in belief, being an operation of
natural instinct, are also pleasurable.

It might seem that when she describes natural instinct and its workings as
'making us what we are' Winters is attributing to Hume a view of causal reasoning
as an essentially human activity in the sense of setting us apart from lesser creatures.
But this is not borne out by the passage to which she refers us (1.3.16:9) when she
uses the phrase 'natural instinct'. In fact Hume does not use this phrase. She seems
to have arrived at it, despite putting it in inverted commas, by running together a
number of separate remarks, the closest of which is: 'habit is nothing but one of the
principles of nature'. In any case, Hume's whole point here is to show that this
'wonderful and unintelligible instinct in our souls which carries us along a certain
train of ideas, and endows them with particular qualities, according to their particular situations and relations' belongs as much to animals as ourselves. The section
from which this famous remark comes is entitled 'Of the reason of animals'. But
once it is ruled out that Hume regards causal reasoning as a specially human accomplishment, it becomes much less clear what exactly is the significance of Winters'
attribution (1995: 266) to him of the view that it is 'an essential part of our nature'
as human beings.

With this somewhat negative clarification, I now turn to two major difficulties.
Winters, it would appear, is seeking to include as products of 'the diseased principles' not only the apprehensions of a tormented mind which Hume actually
mentions in this passage but all those other instances of the vivification of ideas
mentioned in 1.3.9–10. She presumably hopes thus to provide a rationale for
Hume's larger distinction between causal beliefs on the one hand and beliefs formed
in these 'inferior' ways on the other. But the sheer heterogeneity of the instances of
vivification discussed in the earlier sections (let alone the doubt whether Hume looks
upon all of them as beliefs) fatally undermines any such project.

Consider, for instance, the criterion of 'universality' (1995: 266). Winters is
presumably here attributing to Hume the view that whereas natural instinct oper-
ates in the normal healthy mind to produce causal beliefs, other diseased principles
are at work in abnormal minds producing these other types of belief. However, it is
clearly not Hume's intention to suggest that it is only in abnormal minds that, for
instance, education or passion or poetry can vivify ideas in such a way as to produce
belief or pseudo-belief. Consider next the criterion of 'stability' or 'long-lastingness'.
Hume stresses, as we saw, that the beliefs resulting from education are so tenacious
that they can persist even in the face of conflicting causal beliefs. Consider finally the
criterion of 'agreeableness'. In fact, Hume suggests that a belief, however formed,

gives pleasure to the believer. He writes, for instance (1.3.10:5), without stipulating that the assent be the result of causal inference: 'Tis certain we cannot take pleasure in any discourse, where our judgement gives no assent to those images which are presented to our fancy.' Indeed, he goes on to claim that poets attempt to produce belief, or a semblance of it, in the spectators precisely in order to increase enjoyment of their fictions. Nor, incidentally, is it the case that only causal beliefs meet all these criteria, for also, it would seem, do beliefs that result from education.

Suppose that it could be shown (as I have argued it cannot) that Hume does think, say, that their stability and long-lastingness mark out beliefs resulting from causal inference from those produced in these other ways. It would still have to be established that he aimed to substitute these new terms of appraisal for those ordinarily employed in assessing beliefs, namely, 'true', 'correspondent with the facts', and such like. But not only does Hume never propose such a substitution, he continues to rely on the original terms of appraisal in making the relevant distinctions. He states (1.3.10:5) that a mere idea of the 'fancy' and a belief differ in their relations to 'truth and reality'. He also speaks (1.3.10:6) of the vivification of ideas that occurs when we respond to poetry as proceeding from 'other principles beside truth or reality'. Again, he claims (1.3.10:9) that a person who is mad has 'no means of distinguishing betwixt truth and falshood', and he couples (causal) belief with reality in distinguishing it from those counterfeits produced in us by poetry, which he states are connected 'with nothing that is real'.

Winters acknowledges (1995: 264) that remarks like these seem to undermine the claim that Hume is a consistent sceptic. She writes: 'Such claims might appear to involve him in an inconsistency. The implication, especially of the remark about truth and falsity, might seem to be that natural instinct, in contrast, yields justified beliefs.' However, she dismisses this implication: 'But his sceptical result precludes such a claim.' She then resumes her search in the text for a set of criteria which might replace truth or correspondence in assessing beliefs. But it is surely unacceptable to discount this evidence of Hume's falling away from scepticism by simply asserting that he *is* a sceptic, with the implication that he just cannot mean what he says in these passages.

Another way of dealing with Hume's references to truth, falsehood, and reality, is to construe them as elements of a wholly descriptive enterprise. According to Owen (1999: 206, 223), for instance, Hume is primarily concerned to explain how we come to assent to things as true, or hold them to be true. Rather like an anthropologist dealing with other cultures, he is not himself endorsing these normative practices. The reason which Hume sees at work in causal inference, and to which he holds the products of education to be contrary is not, Owen writes (ibid.: 223), 'the arbiter of truths; it is their means of production'. This approach may seem to be supported by Hume's refraining from referring directly to e.g. reality, and speaking instead of what we call 'reality'. Thus, at 1.3.9:3, he states that we join our present impressions with the impressions or ideas of memory to form a coherent system which 'we *are pleas'd to call* a reality' (my italics), and that we form a second system which is the object of our causal judgements, and which we likewise '*dignify with the title*' of realities' (my italics). Again it might seem that he is stepping back from directly endorsing the claim that belief is the vivification of an idea, when he says (1.3.13:19) this 'force and vivacity' of perception is *'what we call* the belief in the existence of any object' (my italics). But just as often, in fact more often, as we have seen, he drops the precaution of referring to these 'realities' at one remove and talks directly, apparently in his own name of truth, falsehood, reality and belief.

My claim is a relatively weak one. I do not wish to assert against those who maintain that Hume is unequivocally a sceptic that he is not a sceptic at all. Nor do I wish to assert against those who maintain that he is not a sceptic, that he is unequivocally one. I claim only that in the way I have suggested, he has one foot in scepticism and one foot out of it. That is not, however, to suggest that there is any smooth progression from Hume's not grasping the sceptical implications of his account of belief to his grasping them. Owen (1999: 209) maintains that it is only when Hume comes to discuss external existence in 1.4.2 that it is suddenly brought home to him how manifestly false can be such universal beliefs as our belief in bodies. This makes him reflect again on his account of causal inference, becoming at length aware of its starkly sceptical implications. But it is not the case that 1.4.2 is the first time that Hume acknowledges the sheer falsity of a pervasive belief of this kind. He has earlier (1.3.14: 24–6), dismissed our belief that causes must produce their effects as an 'inveterate prejudice of mankind', 'a bias' which 'is so riveted in the mind' that it impedes our recognizing that this necessity does not exist outside us.[9]

(ii) Scepticism and oscillation

Hume explicitly confronts the question whether his account of belief entails scepticism in 1.4.7 – the conclusion of Book 1. I will shortly suggest that it is the empiricist presuppositions underpinning the *Treatise* that put him into a quandary over belief. Here I want to show how, independently of that quandary, leaving the matter unresolved introduces a dynamism into his treatment of the topic which is highly congenial to his temperament. It also allows him to offer, through his own person, a dramatic re-enactment of the triumph of nature over reason.

It is, in fact, 1.4.1, not 1.4.7, which is entitled 'Of scepticism with regard to reason'. But the earlier section is merely a preamble to the headlong confrontation of scepticism of the later section. Ostensibly it concerns our proneness to make errors in reaching conclusions on the basis of evidence or via long chains of argument, and how in trying to guard against these errors, we ultimately undermine the conclusions themselves. But this is a problem as much of practical life, on which Hume concentrates here, as of philosophy. Nevertheless the section will repay scrutiny for it contains two claims which, applied to philosophical doubt, prefigure the dramatic fluctuations in Hume's state of mind of which the later section is largely a record.

Our mental fallibility is, of course, as much a problem with demonstrations, where Hume allows that there is nothing 'inherent in the subject' to impede our arriving at certainty, as with probable reasoning, and he begins with an example of the former. Even an expert algebraist or mathematician, he observes, will given his past experience feel some doubt as to whether he has got a lengthy and complex calculation right. Many considerations will serve to increase his confidence – the number of times he has run through the proof, others' confidence in him, his high professional standing, and so on. But each of these factors, Hume points out, is 'just the addition of new probabilities', and so can never amount to certainty. Indeed, he goes further, these factors themselves pose new questions for our expert algebraist: for instance, has he properly assessed their bearing on his reliability? But the new questions, and the new checks they necessitate give rise to still further questions requiring further checks, and so on *ad infinitum*. Hume's conclusion is twofold. 'Knowledge', he writes, 'resolves itself into probability', so that we may henceforth confine our attention exclusively to the latter. Secondly – and this is the first of the two claims which will become pivotal to 1.4.7 – any probabilistic belief, subjected to such repeated examinations, will finally suffer 'total extinction'. At the same time he points to the fact that such beliefs do survive as yet further confirmation of his account of belief. He argues that were belief 'a simple act of the thought . . . without the addition of a force and vivacity it must infallibly destroy itself, and in every case terminate in a total suspence of judgement'. It is precisely then because beliefs are sensations that they cannot, according to Hume, be destroyed by mere reflection.

He introduces the second claim which, as I have indicated, is to become so crucial in 1.4.7 by way of taking issue with his own last point. Surely, he says, even if beliefs are sensations, this will not prevent them from being eventually weakened by the exhaustive checks described. For 'the new probabilities', he goes on, 'which by their repetition perpetually diminish the original evidence, are founded on the very same principles whether of thought or sensation as the primary judgement'. He is led therefore to pose his question anew: 'How [does] it happen [then], that even after all we retain a degree of belief, which is sufficient for our purpose either in philosophy or common life?' It is at this point that he introduces the second claim: extended and abstruse arguments, he declares, just cannot as a matter of psychological fact hold our attention for long: 'After the first and second decision', he writes, 'the action of the mind becomes forc'd and unnatural, and the ideas faint and obscure'. Moreover, he is keen to show how the ordinary canons of rationality are overridden: 'tho' the principles of judgement, and the ballancing of opposite causes be the same as at the very beginning; yet their influence on the imagination, and the vigour they add to, or diminish from the thought, is by no means equal'. Thus 'nature', he declares, 'breaks the force of all sceptical arguments in time', and our original beliefs reassert themselves.

(a) The rebellious sceptic (1.4.7:1–5)

The later section – 1.4.7 – to which we now turn is, as I have already hinted, more an autobiographical record of Hume's shifting states of mind as he faces up to philosophical scepticism in all its facets than a series of structured arguments. The two claims made earlier in a theoretical context are moreover, as I also indicated, the key to these fluctuations, which occurring as and when they do, effectively bear out the claims in practice. Let us then follow – for this is all we can do – Hume's changing moods as they come and go through the section.

At the start, he presents all the appearance of a thorough-going philosophical sceptic: one who has taken on board the full implications of an account of belief such as his own. Confusingly, however, he rails against these implications with the vehemence of a resolute non-sceptic. How, he complains, can I possibly have any confidence in conclusions for which I can cite no reason, and where I can only point to a strong inclination on my part to view things in the way I do? He protests that the account of belief he has expounded has left him without a criterion of truth. He hints that seeking such a criterion has itself become an incoherent enterprise, asking how after all he would recognize the truth if he should come upon it by chance. He is dismayed that beliefs which we all take for granted such as that objects exist independently of us evidently depend on so trivial a quality of the imagination – a quality 'so little founded on reason' – as liveliness. He is equally troubled that without this trivial quality 'the lively images, with which our memory presents us [could not] be ever receiv'd as true pictures of past perceptions'. He deplores the fact that mankind's ardent desire for insight into ultimate causes must not only go unfulfilled but, since the idea of a cause as a hidden power is meaningless, cannot even be made sense of. It is noteworthy, however, that he does not take the further step of questioning, as the non-sceptic surely would, how given such implications, his account of belief could possibly be right or how, put differently, it could be an account of belief. On the contrary, he seems almost perversely to hold to it the more firmly.

(b) In the shoes of the honest gentleman (1.4.7:6–7)

At this problematic juncture he introduces a new distinction whose significance gradually becomes clearer as the section progresses. It is between 'the philosopher in his study', racked with sceptical doubt, resolved even 'to perish on [its] barren rock' rather than continue with an investigation so mired in confusion, and people in 'common life'. Later he (1.4.7:14) gives a fuller description of the latter: ' honest gentlemen, who being always employ'd in their domestic affairs, or amusing themselves in common recreations, have carry'd their thoughts very little beyond those objects, which are every day expos'd to their senses'. These people, he says, are unaware (unlike him) that their belief, for instance, in objective causal power is just an illusion of the imagination. In this way he begins, or so it might seem, to make a sceptical inroad into the common view of things from the relatively more enlightened standpoint of the philosopher.

We should not, however, rely on his remaining very long in that viewpoint. In fact, almost immediately he poses a question 'How far we ought to yield to these illusions?', which puts his position in doubt. For though he seems to be asking the question on behalf of those whose ignorance prevents them from asking it themselves, his use of the first person plural signals that he is also to be included among them. More evidence that he has now adopted the viewpoint of common life is provided by the fact that the distinction he appeals to in trying to answer his question is available from within common life. It is that between following every 'trivial suggestion of the fancy' and adhering to 'the general and more establish'd properties of the imagination'. We find him almost immediately dismissing the distinction as providing an answer. He does not see how, on the one hand, following one's every fancy can be contemplated by a reasonable person when it leads 'into such errors, absurdities, and obscurities, that we must at last become asham'd of our credulity'. On the other, to adhere to the general and more established properties of the imagination involves, he points out, that intensive scrutiny of beliefs which in the earlier section he had shown caused their force and vigour to dwindle, and reason to subvert itself.

He now, however, places alongside this last claim that other important one from the earlier section: that the more involved and complex an argument becomes, the less it will have power to influence us. He now proposes for consideration the maxim that no 'refin'd or elaborate reasoning is ever to be receiv'd'. But he immediately rejects it. For it is itself, he remarks, arrived at by the very same refin'd and abstruse reasoning that it seeks to proscribe, and so contains an internal contradiction. We thus seem, he concludes, metaphorically throwing his hands up, to have an impossible choice before us: that 'betwixt a false reason and none at all'. But if such an internally incoherent maxim cannot be recommended to our reason, is it not the case, he immediately goes on, that we *will* act – that we just cannot help acting – in the way it prescribes? And does not this entail that our sceptical reasonings themselves will come to nothing, broken, as he had put it earlier when considering doubt in ordinary life, by nature itself?

(c) The philosopher fiercely reasserts his scepticism (1.4.7:8)

Like someone who, fearing that he may be lulled to sleep, vigorously shakes himself awake, Hume now pulls sharply back from his own last suggestion, and with it from the intellectual oblivion into which, according to him, the common man is sunk. He protests that, after all, the refined and abstruse reasoning that he has engaged in *can* have an influence. Look at me, he seems to be saying, am I not living proof of its power? He then immediately launches into another passionate depiction, darker and more agonized even than the last, of his own dire predicament as a philosophical sceptic:

> The *intense* view of these manifold contradictions and imperfections in human reason has so wrought upon me, and heated my brain, that I am ready to reject all belief and reasoning, and can look upon no opinion even as more probable or likely than another. Where am I, or what? From what causes do I derive my existence, and to what condition shall I return? . . . What beings surround me? . . . I am confounded with all these questions, and begin to fancy myself in the most deplorable condition imaginable, inviron'd with the deepest darkness, and utterly depriv'd of the use of every member and faculty.

(d) The philosopher becomes the honest gentleman (1.4.7:9–15)

But just at this moment something unaccountable happens. Hume's mood suddenly lifts, and in the place of the sceptical philosopher in his study, there stands before us the honest gentleman who dines, plays backgammon, amuses himself with his friends and ridicules sceptical speculation. Recalling in so far as in this 'splenetic humour' he can the painful and dreary solitude of his study, he vows to 'throw all my books and papers into the fire and . . . never more renounce the pleasures of life for the sake of reasoning and philosophy'. Yet even now a philosophical muscle twitches sufficiently for him to observe that 'in this blind submission I show most perfectly my sceptical disposition and principles'.

But in a further twist to the story the 'reason' that has stirred briefly in order to place its imprimatur upon the proceedings is yet again crushed. For, Hume tells us, he cannot even rely on his love of intellectual argument to draw him back to his studies. He must helplessly wait for his splenetic and indolent mood to leave him, and for that other part of his nature to reassert itself as (he is certain) it inevitably must. 'Nature' after all, he told us in 1.4.1, has 'by an absolute and uncontroulable necessity . . . determin'd us to judge as well as to breathe and feel'. Even when his intellectual interest does reassert itself, it will be as much because he is fired by aspirations that find favour with his other *persona* – the honest gentleman – such as the desire to make a name for himself, as because of the interest itself. Indeed, from the viewpoint of common life the sceptical attitude to which his philosophical reflection has led him appears as little more than the unhealthy emanation of a melancholic and depressive temperament rather than as a legitimate and reasoned response to a genuine predicament that ought to be encouraged.

Hume has managed things, it would seem, so that, as before, he can have one foot in scepticism and one out of it. Now, however, the sceptical and non-sceptical stances, rather than being held to simultaneously in an implicit or intermittent way, are aspects of two larger mutually exclusive viewpoints which Hume occupies successively. It is true that he is able momentarily to resist this oscillation, and to acknowledge (and applaud) the fact that each viewpoint comes with its own set of assurances even though these last only as long as one continues in that viewpoint:

> Nor is it only proper we shou'd in general indulge our inclination in the most elaborate philosophical researches, notwithstanding our sceptical principles, but also that we shou'd yield to that propensity, which inclines us to be positive and certain in *particular points*, according to the light in which we survey them in any *particular instant*. 'Tis easier to forebear all examination and enquiry, than to check ourselves in so natural a propensity, and guard against that assurance which always arises from an exact and full survey of an object. On such an occasion we are not only apt to forget our scepticism, but even our modesty too; and make use of such terms as these: *'tis evident, 'tis certain, 'tis undeniable* . . . I may have fallen into this fault . . . but I here enter a caveat against any objections, which may be offer'd on that head, and declare that such expressions were extorted from me by the present view of the object, and imply no dogmatical spirit, nor conceited idea of my own judgement, which are sentiments that I am sensible can become nobody, and a sceptic less than any other.

(iii) Hume's quandary over belief

Someone may object thus: doubtless it admirably suits Hume's agnostic spirit to end Book 1 poised in this arresting way between philosopher and honest gentleman, and so between embracing and rejecting scepticism, but the plain fact is that he is in a quandary about belief. From this point of view, section 1.4.7 can only appear as an evasion. With this objection in mind, let us now try to diagnose the quandary.

Hume's project is one of analysis: he takes our various concepts and attempts to break them down into elementary units of experience, which are logically independent of each other. But belief has a complexity which is not obviously amenable to such a reduction. A belief is a belief *that* something is the case and so lacks the simplicity of e.g. pain which is not *about* anything. Hume approaches its analysis, as we have seen, with two questions: how am I to distinguish believing something from merely entertaining the idea of, or imagining, it? What determines me to believe P rather than not P when reason does not bar me (as it does where demonstration is concerned) from entertaining both possibilities? As we also saw, he decides that it is the occurrence of a feeling or sensation that distinguishes a belief from a mere idea, and it is this feeling which explains our believing P rather than not P when we can entertain both possibilities. He writes (in Appendix 2), 'When we express our incredulity concerning any fact, we mean, that the arguments for the fact produce not the feeling.'

But a question arises concerning the relation of the original idea to this feeling. Hume talks at one point as though the feeling is separate from the idea, and so presumably merely tacked on to it. He writes: 'Belief is nothing but a peculiar feeling different from the simple conception.' But this leads to an absurdity: that one might have the belief without the simple conception. It would be, as he himself puts it (Appendix 4) dismissing the view, 'only annex'd to it, after the same manner that *will* and *desire* are annex'd to particular conceptions of the good and pleasure'. Thus we find him moderating this description of belief with a second kind of description of it as merely 'a manner of conception' or 'a particular manner of forming an idea', distinguishable from 'fancy' only by its 'vivacity'(1.3.7:4, 6, 7).

Now it might be thought that, by retaining the idea element, he could restore to his notion of belief that representative function which links our ordinary notion with truth and justification. However, the 'vivacity' to which he at the same time appeals in order to distinguish a belief from an idea is precisely what, for him, distinguishes an impression from an idea. (We shall recall that an idea is merely a 'faint copy' of an impression.) It is not surprising then that Hume identifies a belief as an idea which approximates to, or imitates, an impression.

Not only, however, do ideas and impressions have, on Hume's account, wholly different relations to truth, but neither individually has that of ordinary beliefs. For instance, thinking of Humean belief as an idea, we can certainly attempt to find the impression from which it is supposedly derived, and of which therefore it is supposed to be a copy. The trouble is that even if we succeed, this will not yield a truth. It will only establish that the idea in question has meaning. On the other hand, in so far as the belief is thought of as an impression, not even this procedure of comparison has any place or makes any sense. For impressions are not copies of anything, and so cannot be assessed as true (or false). They are in the terminology which became so familiar to us in Books 2 and 3 those 'original existences', or 'original facts and realities', which being 'compleat in themselves' are themselves items to be *copied*.

But it is not just that if an impression is copied we get, on Hume's account, an idea not a belief, it would be redundant even to appeal to the idea where a perceptual belief is concerned. There is just no need on Hume's account to check the impression before us against our idea of it to ensure that we have identified it correctly. For Hume insists that impressions are self-authenticating and hence that all possibility of mistake is excluded. He writes (1.4.2:7): 'Since all actions and sensations of the mind are known to us by consciousness, they must necessarily appear in every particular what they are, and be what they appear'. But it would seem to be essential to belief that it is not self-authenticating. (It is for instance precisely because mistake makes no sense with first person expressions of pain that we do not normally say of a person in pain that she only *believes* she is in pain.) We could put it this way: Humean beliefs by striking upon us with the force of impressions stand in the way of their own truth. They have become opaque when they needed to retain the transparency of ideas.

My suggestion is that Hume, faced with the complex propositional attitude which is belief, never entirely loses hope of doing justice to the representative element which would restore its link with truth and justification. Thus, his frequent insistence that it is a 'peculiar manner of *conception*' (my italics). On the other hand, two imperatives spur him on to stress that it is a feeling or sensation, so alienating it from the notions of truth and justification: his conviction that causal inference cannot be grounded in reason and his need to establish that the beliefs which are its outcome are linked with passion and action. But it is hard to say which of these comes first.

3 Seeds of the later contradiction

In the final part of Book 1 we saw Hume closing the gap between demonstrative and inductive reasoning and belief, as he gradually downgraded the former to the status of the latter. He sought first to show that certainty even of the demonstrative kind was never practically possible for human beings. He later maintained that even philosophical reflection must wait upon nature to influence our moods so as to make us want to engage in it again. If, however, we now go forward to Books 2 and 3, we shall see that something new and significant has happened: the earlier trend has been reversed. Hume has swung the other way and, taking (at least intermittently) probabilistic reasoning and belief out of the 'world of realities', placed them, together with demonstrative reasoning, in 'the world of ideas'. But this would require him to lift belief or judgement from the category of 'real existences' which its status as a feeling or sensation gave it, and make it purely representative so that it can be 'contradictory to truth and reason' as 'real existences' cannot.

But this is just what he has done. He writes (3.1.1:9): 'Reason is the discovery of truth or falshood. Truth or falshood consists in an agreement or disagreement *either* to the real relations of ideas, *or to real existence and matter of fact*' (my italics). But 'real existence and matters of fact' were, in Book 1, what ordinary beliefs were about, and beliefs there, as we have seen, being primarily feelings or impressions, were neither arrived at by, nor correctable in terms of, reason.

With probabilistic reasoning, in such later passages, virtually removed, together with demonstrative reasoning, from the experiential world – something which he

had resolutely resisted in Book 1 where 'almost all reasoning is . . . reduced to experience' (Abstract: 27) – it is not surprising that both types of reason might, when he
thinks of their relation to action, become confused in his mind with that metaphysical variety which he declares 'perfectly inert'. Perhaps he is tempted to run together
the three notions of reason because it then becomes less obvious that, really, in order
to make this 'extreme' claim he has had to countenance ideas which he regards as
nonsensical, so himself having, as we put it earlier, 'one foot in metaphysics'. In
addition, denying to reason in general any motivating force is patently more
impressive than denying it to reason merely as construed by one group of his opponents: the moral rationalists. But we have argued that he is not entitled to
generalize in this way. His denial may be a powerful one; indeed, it is. Moreover, the
'extreme' version of the practicality argument, of which it is the second premiss,
owes its power to this denial. Nevertheless neither the argument, nor its second
premiss, can be detached from their metaphysical target, and still retain that power.

None of this is to say, as I have already indicated, that Book 1's account of probabilistic reasoning and belief as a feeling or sensation, and so part of the 'world of
realities', has been wiped out altogether and replaced by a reason which belongs
wholly to the 'world of ideas'. On the contrary – and this is largely the problem –
despite conflicting with it, the earlier account of belief lingers disconcertingly alongside this more rarified notion of reason. It is, as we saw in earlier chapters, still
needed to make sense of many of Hume's remarks in the later books. These are the
remarks which assert a causal connection between reason, passion and action (whether
reason is then claimed itself to 'excite' the passion or merely to help an independently
generated passion to produce action). It is also the 'reason' needed to make sense of
the 'moderate', as opposed to the 'extreme' version of the practicality argument. For
the second premiss of this 'moderate' – and invalid – version claims only that reason
alone cannot influence action, not that reason has no motivating role.

It is, I have suggested, to Hume's unappeasable scepticism in Book 1 that we
must finally look if we are to discover the source of that contradiction in the second
premiss of Book 3's practicality argument, which has been the focus of our attention
so far. I turn now, in Part II, to the argument as it has come to dominate recent
meta-ethics, and to the legacy of contradiction that Hume has bequeathed us.

Part II

The Practicality Argument Today

6 Morality's Dynamism

1 'Moderate' and 'extreme' versions today

The key controversy in meta-ethics today is between cognitivists holding that moral judgements are beliefs, and non-cognitivists holding that they are desires or feelings. Pivotal to this dispute is the practicality argument, currently regarded as the most serious obstacle to any coherent cognitivism.[1] Even cognitivists tend to assume that the argument – which they typically describe as 'Humean', or as an argument of 'Humeans' or of 'Humean non-cognitivists' – is formally valid.[2] Hence they frequently take it that all they can do in defending their position is to try to refute one of its premisses. It might be thought therefore that, whatever the difficulties and uncertainties surrounding Hume's original exposition of the argument, a standard or agreed formulation must by now have been arrived at. Certainly many of the participants in the debate talk as though this is so. But it is not: contemporary formulations diverge markedly both from Hume's original ones and from each other. Thus we find a range of reinterpretations of the first premiss which are best explained as different solutions to the attempt to ensure that the argument is valid when the second premiss is read 'moderately'. But we also find independent appeals to the second premiss, relying on the 'extreme' reading.

With regard to the first group of formulations, it would seem that writers have, unlike Hume, gone ahead, and clarified the second premiss as implying that reason or belief influences action, but only with the help of an independent desire. But this, as we showed when we tried to impose an unambiguously 'moderate' reading on Hume's own exposition of the argument, constrains how they may then construe the first premiss, if the conclusion, that moral judgements are not beliefs but desires, is to follow. Such a premiss must now make it clear that moral judgements do not, any more than desires, require the help that reason needs in order to motivate action. Consequently, these writers are now obliged to substitute for Hume's looser connection between morality and action (e.g. 'Morals . . . have an influence on the actions and affections') a much stronger ('internalist'[3]) claim.

There are three chief suggestions to be found in the literature as to what the first premiss must assert of moral judgement and the second deny of reason or belief. These are that (a) it is sufficient on its own for motivation (Dancy,[4] 1993: 3; McNaughton, 1988: 23, 46–7; Parfit, 1997: 107), (b) it is necessarily, or intrinsically, motivating, or entails motivation (McNaughton, 1988: 22, 113; Parfit, 1997: 106; Brink, 1997: 6), and (c) it can on its own 'make' us act in the required way (Mackie, 1980: 54; Smith, 1994: 10). Nor are these just different verbal formulations of the same basic type of claim. For those favouring the first formulation treat the premisses by and large as (1) empirical (Harrison, 1976: 9–10, Scheffler, 1992: 86–91). Those favouring the second treat it as (2) conceptual (Brink, Svavarsdottir, 1999: 163)[5]. Writers favouring the third have in mind (3) claims which are, in some sense both substantial and necessary (Mackie, Smith). Thus, the connection between moral judgement and motivation is, according to (1a), or what earlier we called the 'sufficiency' account, just a matter of observed fact. According to (2b), or the 'intrinsicality' account, it is an entailment: if someone judges it right to act in a certain way then, logically, she is motivated to act in that way. With (3c), or the 'mandatory'[6] account, the first premiss posits a relation such that moral judgements, though logically distinct from motivation, can somehow compel or mandate the relevant action. In each case, of course, the second premiss is held to deny that the corresponding relation exists between reason, or belief, and motivation.

The correspondence between the three verbal formulations and three types of claim is not, it must be said, completely reliable. Thus, some writers (McNaughton), though clearly holding that the conceptual version of the premisses is required for the argument's validity, use formulations (a) and (b) interchangeably. Others (Parfit,[7] Dancy) discriminate between these formulations in terms of the relative strength of the claims thereby made, but regard even the weaker formulation, (a), as enough for the argument's validity. Still others (Smith, Mackie) use formulations (b) and (c) interchangeably, while sometimes endorsing the conceptual version of the premisses, and sometimes representing them as attributing to morality, and denying to belief, the distinctive mandatory force alluded to in (3).

Despite these differences the interpretation of the second premiss on all these accounts remains similar at least in two basic respects. First, the premiss now denies that there holds between belief and motivation only that specific type of relation which, by the first premiss, is said to hold between moral judgement and motivation. It does not deny that any relation holds at all. On the 'sufficiency' account, the premiss denies only that belief is sufficient for motivation (whether directly or by producing the requisite desires), not that it isn't necessary. Indeed, the implication is that it is necessary. Again on the 'intrinsicality' account, the premiss denies only that belief is intrinsically linked with motivation (or with the desires deemed crucial to it), not that there is no extrinsic link. Indeed, the implication is that there is such a link. Finally, on the 'mandatory' account, the premiss denies only that a change in desire, or motivation, can actually be mandated by reason, not that beliefs cannot have an equivalent non-rational impact on our desires and conduct, as e.g. when the mere realization that there is a spider nearby arouses in us a panicky desire to flee.

The second basic respect in which the construal of the second premiss remains, on all three accounts, similar is that the *contradictory* of the premiss is held to be coherent. On the 'sufficiency' account, for instance, the premiss is taken as a statement of fact. Hence even its defenders would, according to this account, admit that its contradictory (namely, that belief *is* sufficient, directly or indirectly, for motivation) is only contingently false, and hence might conceivably have been true. Indeed, the premiss has been challenged by citing Hume's own examples in which reason is claimed itself to 'excite', or 'prompt', the desires that lead to motivation. With the 'intrinsicality' account, the premiss, as we saw, is taken as a claim about our concepts of belief and motivation, and so its defenders, also, would be expected to regard it as potentially corrigible – though now by reference to our linguistic practices. Finally, attempts to spell out the content of certain beliefs in such a way as to make plausible their having a rational impact upon desire and motivation, clearly assume that one can challenge the premiss, even on the 'mandatory' account, without falling into incoherence

A notable example, however, of the second type of writer who, invoking the second premiss of the 'extreme' reading, shares neither of these assumptions, is B. Williams (1981). Citing (ibid.: 108) the premiss in isolation from the argument as a whole, he takes it to deliver an unqualifiedly 'negative answer' to the question whether 'reason can give rise to a motivation'. There is, it would seem, both for Williams and for Hume on Williams' view, a complete absence of any link here. Indeed, Williams takes the premiss to indite the very idea of such a link as so metaphysically absurd as to be virtually unstateable.

It is worth observing that Williams treats the 'extreme' reading of premiss 2 as just as uncontroversial, just as given, as the first group treat their 'moderate' reading. Indeed neither seems aware of the alternative reading. Thus, we can see how *both* of the contradictory strands in Hume's thinking about reason in relation to motivation and action, which find expression in his divergent formulations of the second premiss, have passed side by side, their discrepancy almost unnoticed, into contemporary literature.

Our question is whether the practicality argument on at least one of the two versions, 'moderate' and 'extreme', to be found in recent literature deserves its current reputation as a major obstacle to cognitivism. With the 'moderate' version, the problem concerning its validity, now that the reinterpretation of its premisses does not have to cohere with Hume's original text, largely disappears. We shall simply therefore ask whether the reinterpreted premisses are true. Moreover, we shall for simplicity's sake focus mainly on what I have called the 'intrinsicality' reinterpretation, being by far the most favoured among recent writers.

With the 'extreme' version however, in the fragmentary form in which it appears in contemporary literature, its second premiss is just as obscure as it was – at least initially – when considered in the original *Treatise* setting. In other words, Williams' claim that reason cannot conceivably give rise to a motivation is at first sight just as unclear as was Hume's declaration that 'reason is perfectly inert'. We were of course eventually able to shed light on this latter pronouncement by relating it to a position actually held by some of Hume's predecessors – that of the moral rationalists – whom he mentions explicitly when expounding other arguments in 3.1.1. But the moral rationalists were metaphysicians. Who, it will be asked, among recent cognitivists could possibly be the object of Williams' attack? Would anyone in today's naturalistic climate be so rash as to posit, as did the moral rationalists, the existence of moral facts which, merely by our rational appreciation of them, and unmediated by our particular psychologies, necessarily influence our conduct?

Just as in earlier chapters, we shall postpone dealing with this question in the hope that the 'moderate' version will be found on its own to justify the argument's reputation as, in Dancy's words (1993: 3) 'driv[ing] us in this [non-cognitivist] direction'. For with the 'moderate' version there is no difficulty in identifying whom amongst recent writers it is aimed at. Often the very (naturalistic) cognitivists who are its targets come forward and identify themselves. Thus, McNaughton, Dancy, Smith and Brink, having taken care to expound the argument in what they take to be a valid form, go on, as cognitivists, to try and resist its non-cognitivist conclusion by attacking one or other of its premises. If, of course, we find their defence convincing we shall have to conclude that the argument does not in the 'moderate' version live up to its reputation. Then, but only then, will it be necessary to seek the source of its much vaunted power elsewhere, namely in the the 'extreme' version, and so finally confront the mystery surrounding Williams' hypothetical opponents.

2 The 'moderate' version: premiss 1

There are two broad types of cognitivism which the 'moderate' version might be expected to refute depending on which of its premises is contravened. One type – we shall call those who espouse it accidentalists – contravene the first premiss. This contravention is a logical consequence of their endorsing (along with the non-cognitivists) the argument's *second* premiss, namely, that a belief cannot motivate unless an independent desire happens to be present, while nevertheless maintaining that moral judgements are beliefs. It follows that, for them, moral judgements can only be contingently or accidentally linked with motivation, and not necessarily as premiss 1 maintains. The other type of cognitivist – the necessitarians – contravene the second but not the first premiss, and their dispute with the non-cognitivists will be the subject of the next chapter. Here we concentrate on the first premiss, and the attempt by both non-cognitivists and cognitivist necessitarians to defend it against, among others, the accidentalists.

First, I assess the threat posed to premiss 1 by the apparently well-attested fact that people, in particular the morally weak, are not always motivated to do what they believe they ought. To hold (as on one variant of premiss 1) that 'The attitude of accepting that an action is right is itself identical with the state of being motivated' is not just to ignore this phenomenon but to turn it into a logical absurdity.

(i) Explaining away moral weakness

The failure to do what one believes to be morally right may either be a manifestation of moral weakness or what I shall call 'amoralism'. Moral weakness is a special case of 'weak will'. Here we fail to do x, which we believe to be right, because we succumb to a conflicting desire to do y: colloquially speaking 'we give in to temptation'. Our failure is typically attended by feelings of guilt and remorse. Amoralism (at least as I shall define it) differs from moral weakness in that it does not involve capitulation to a repudiated desire. Two of its forms are not even characterized by feelings of guilt.

Thus (what I shall call) the 'defiant' amoralist admits that she knows that what she is doing is wrong, but deliberately – even perhaps triumphantly – does it all the same. The 'cautious' amoralist, on the other hand, assesses the deleterious consequences for her of doing what is morally required, and decides not to do it on grounds that it would be irrational. (Some philosophers, though, have sought to expound a sense of 'moral' and of 'rational' which, if accepted, would make such a conflict unintelligible.) Finally, the 'reluctant' amoralist is afflicted, like the morally weak individual, with feelings of guilt and remorse for failing to do what she believes she ought to have done. Typically (and here I am reliant on Stocker, 1979: 744), she has, through depression, become too apathetic, too lethargic, to be any longer motivated to pursue ends which she nevertheless still believes in, and is convinced she ought to pursue. Indeed, the poignancy of her case is, in Stocker's words, that she still 'sees all the good to be won or saved'.

Though the varieties of amoralism present interesting challenges for the proponents of premiss 1, I shall here concentrate on moral weakness. If it holds up as a counter-example to the premiss we shall have to look no further. Perhaps the most notable attempt by a non-cognitivist to diffuse the problem posed for it by moral weakness is Hare's (chiefly 1963, but also 1952 and 1992). He seeks to show that any behaviour we may care to cite as exemplifying moral weakness will turn out, upon further examination, to have been misdescribed. Either the agent will not have properly assented to the given moral judgement or she will be incapable of being moved to act in accordance with it. There is no third possibility. His strategy is to present a series of examples which he suggests might superficially be confused with moral weakness but which he develops in ways that belie such an identification. It is helpful to situate his examples along a spectrum.

At one end we find examples where individuals do not act in accordance with the moral precepts they enunciate for the good reason that it was never their intention to do so. They were simply pointing out, rather perhaps as an anthropologist or social scientist might, the moral standards governing our society; it may be that they personally do not subscribe to these standards at all. Hare (1952: 164, 167; 1963: 52, 75) calls this an 'inverted commas' use of moral language. He describes the use as 'ironic' when an individual is drawing attention to these standards in order to ridicule them, and 'conventional' when she hypocritically pays lip service to them. (Perhaps she thinks it to her advantage that others should abide by them.) More readily confused with moral weakness as we ordinarily understand it are the examples which Hare goes on to cite (1963: 82–3) of the 'back-sliders' whose assent, though they may be too self-deceived to realize it, is simply not whole-hearted enough to properly count as motivating.

At the other end of the spectrum, we find examples of individuals who, though their assent to a moral judgement is now genuine, are incapable for some reason of being moved to act in accordance with it. For Hare, who discusses moral weakness in terms of the relation between assent and action rather than between assent and motivation, there is no difficulty in establishing this inability in given circumstances. Someone whose hands are tied behind her cannot, however convinced she is that she ought to help the person on the ground before her, give this help, if it requires her hands to be free. It is obviously far less easy to verify a motivational incapacity. However, there is scientific evidence (Damascio, 1994: Chapters 1–4, cited by Brink, 1997: 17) to suggest that patients who have sustained damage to specific parts of the brain, such as the pre-frontal lobes, though continuing to make the same practical judgements as before the injury, are no longer motivated by them.

Closer to what we might ordinarily be inclined to class as moral weakness are the examples which Hare cites (1963: 82; 1992: 1306) of psychological compulsion – a description which can be applied to behaviour without hard evidence of underlying neuro-physiological abnormalities. Here people are said to be compelled by their desires to contravene moral judgements that they have genuinely assented to. A kleptomaniac is precisely defined as someone who, however convinced that it is morally wrong to steal, cannot help doing so because her desire to steal is compulsive. Closer still to our common notion of moral weakness is Hare's example of a type of behaviour which is not compulsive, but involves even on his understanding giving into temptation. He still, however, refuses to recognize it as moral weakness on grounds that giving into temptation may not be pathological but can still be an inability. Thus, he writes (1992: 1306): 'All inability is not compulsion in the pathological sense.'

These examples exhaust, Hare suggests, all the possibilities. Moral weakness is therefore, if he is right, squeezed out of the picture. Clearly, if we are to re-instate it we shall have to reclaim some of the middle ground between the two extremes. In fact, the examples at both ends of the spectrum can be discounted since they are hardly in the first place realistic candidates for confusion with moral weakness. The individuals who use 'ought' in an 'inverted commas', or an 'ironic', or a 'conventional' (i.e. hypocritical) sense do not subscribe even in a compromised way to the moral precepts they enunciate. They make no moral judgements at all. Not only this but that hallmark of moral weakness – a repudiated desire to which the agent succumbs – is absent. Nor is anyone likely to describe as morally weak a person with a brain lesion which is known to interfere with the process leading from moral judgement to motivation.

We are left then, in one half of the spectrum, with the self-deceivers and backsliders. Now their behaviour, were it to be construed as morally weak would threaten the claim that moral judgements are necessarily motivating. But Hare, by showing how such individuals' unsteady and vacillating moral convictions leave them with a let-out should they succumb to their desires, succeeds in refuting this construal.

But it does not automatically follow that his method can be used to dissolve all purported cases of moral weakness, where the ability to act (or to be motivated to act) is not in question. On the contrary, the very idea that the weak-willed person did not sincerely mean what he said when he said he ought to do a given thing, flies in the face of the authentic feelings of regret, remorse and guilt, and the sense of defeat, that so often accompany weakly capitulating to a repudiated desire. Moreover these feelings are very different in kind from those accompanying the revelation that one has been deceiving oneself. Hare maintains (1963: 84) that a moral judgement, if we are really to mean it as an evaluation, must have motivational elements already built into it. But we should refuse to be steam-rollered into allowing all moral judgements that do not lead to motivation to be assimilated to his 'off-colour' uses (ibid.: 68, 83).

It is worth observing that were we to go along with Hare, strong-willed, as well as weak-willed, behaviour would seem to be ruled out. We would no longer be able to talk, for instance, of our 'resolve [being] stiffened by duty' (as does the eponymous heroine of Mme de Lafayette's *The Princesse de Cleves*). For according to the above account, to acknowledge one's duty is already to be fully resolved to act upon it. If I have an opportunity to exert my will it can only lie in my coming to acknowledge my duty in the first place. For this acknowledgement is now itself a resolution to act. Hare himself (1963: 72) points to this consequence of his position when he writes that the real difficulty of the moral life, contrary to the way 'some moral philosophers speak', is 'to make up one's mind what one ought to do'. But this seems to get things the wrong way round. Admittedly there are rare people who have to steel themselves to recognize their duty because they know, once they do, they will straightaway act. But many others have to be steeled *by* their duty to act in face of temptation. Meister Eckhart, the thirteenth-century German mystic, explains why he places *this* struggle, between a duty that one already recognizes and temptation, at the heart of the moral life thus:

> If someone who is in the right state of mind had the power to make the temptation . . . go away then they would not exercise that power, for without temptation we would be untried in all things and in all that we do, unaware of the dangers of things, and without the honour of battle, victory and reward.

Turning now to the other half of the spectrum, there remain (once we have excluded motivational deficiencies due to brain lesions and the like) psychological compulsion and giving into temptation where this is, though not a pathology, apparently still an 'inability'. By upholding this distinction Hare admits that not all putative cases of moral weakness can be assimilated to psychological compulsion. Hence it would be enough to contest merely his claim that supposedly weak behaviour which does not involve psychological compulsion is really the result of a non-pathological inability. It is worth, however, first noting difficulties with the claim that *some* putative cases of moral weakness are really cases of psychological compulsion.

Not everyone, for instance, would accept that there is such a thing as psychological compulsion: it rests for its coherence, it might be said, on an analogy with physical compulsion. However, this requires the idea of a force impinging on the agent's body from outside. But we can nevertheless talk of one person compelling another even in the absence of physical force. But it still does not follow that it also makes sense to talk of a person being compelled by her *own* desires. This notion would have to be placed within a theoretical setting which would give it a sense. A famous attempt to provide such a setting is to be found in Frankfurt (1971). There a 'person' (as distinct from a 'wanton') is said to identify herself with those – 'second order' – desires which she endorses while distancing herself from those – 'first order' – desires which she repudiates. These latter desires can thus justifiably be described as 'alien' to her. It would take us too far afield to evaluate Frankfurt's attempt here. But even supposing the idea of psychological compulsion is coherent, it is surely implausible to assimilate ordinary weakness to those clinical disorders such as kleptomania and anorexia which would be its paradigmatic examples.

Hare's conceptual net, however, may seem to have been cast widely enough to encompass even this ordinary so called weak willed person, as well as the compulsive neurotic. Hare will simply state that such a person, unlike the compulsive neurotic, suffers from a *non*-pathological inability to be motivated in accordance with her moral judgement.

But what is the evidence of this non-pathological inability except that the person is *not* in fact motivated in accordance with the moral judgement which she has sincerely assented to? Perhaps it will be suggested that she will herself testify to this inability. But weak-willed individuals are not always of the opinion that they could not help yielding to temptation. Just as often – perhaps more often – they express a bewildered dismay at having been free to act in the way they knew was right, and yet having succumbed to a repudiated desire: thus their frequently acute feelings of guilt. When they do plead helplessness we might well be sceptical if we have only their word for it. Dorothy Wordsworth observed (Holmes 1998: 193–6) of the notoriously weak-willed Coleridge that he was always ready with 'an excuse for all his failures in duty to himself and others'. Even weak-willed individuals who do seek to excuse themselves often reveal through their morally charged language that they at the same time feel responsible for these failures. Thus, Coleridge again, confessing to his friend Tom Paine his habit of procrastination writes: 'I have sunk under such a strange cowardice of pain that I have not infrequently kept letters from persons dear to me for weeks together unopened' (Holmes: 98). His use of the phrase a 'strange cowardice of pain' suggests how inextricably entangled in the psyche of a weak-willed person can be self-accusation and the desire to be exculpated.

But, it will be retorted, feelings of guilt and remorse are not incompatible with a person's feeling that she was, and indeed with her actually having been, unable to do otherwise than she did. Hare (1963: 52, 80) points to the plight of Jocasta in Sophocles' *Oedipus Rex* who unknowingly marries, and has sexual relations with, her son. When she finally finds this out she hangs herself. However, she is perfectly aware, as are those who condemn her for committing incest, that she lacked the information that could have enabled her to avoid this terrible fate. But the example is flawed. It is true, as Kierkegaard ([1843] 1959: 137–62) observed, that the protagonists of Greek tragedy are fated to commit their evil deeds (either the gods have decreed it or the sins of the fathers must be visited on the children), and yet that they feel justly punished for them. But precisely for this reason[8] Kierkegaard coined a special term 'tragic guilt' to distinguish the 'guilt' of the protagonists of Greek tragedy, which does not require personal responsibility, from ours which does.

Hare (1963: 78) also cites St Paul's famous remark: 'The good which I want to do, I fail to do; but what I do is the wrong which is against my will; and if what I do is against my will, clearly it is no longer I who am agent but sin that has its lodging in me.' This has often been interpreted as an admission of moral weakness: St Paul is chastising himself for failing to resist temptation when he is capable of doing so. For Hare, however, he is (and believes himself to be) a helpless sinner who nevertheless 'gives plenty of evidence of remorse'. Even without choosing between these interpretations, there are good reasons why it would be rash to rip the remark out of the Christian religious context in which it is embedded and use it to make a point concerning ordinary secular behaviour. In other words, we cannot turn ordinary moral weakness into a non-pathological inability by importing from the Pauline context notions of sin and grace which are largely alien to us now.

(ii) Why non-cognitivists need moral judgements to be intrinsically motivating

It would seem, then, that it is not just possible to imagine, but also to provide examples of, the link between moral judgements and motivation being broken. But if this link is not even *de facto* exceptionless, why do non-cognitivists and even some cognitivists continue to assert that it is necessary? Typically, they also support their claim by pointing to common facts of everyday life. There is the 'puzzlement' (Smith, 1994: 6) that we would feel were anyone to say that they accepted that they ought to tell the truth but then denied that this gave them any reason to act accordingly. There is our tendency to dismiss a person's claim to have a moral conviction if it is clear to us that they never act upon it. As Hare (1952: 142), adopting the point of view of the agent, puts it: 'If I admit that the life of St Francis was morally better than mine . . . there is nothing for it but to try to be more like St Francis.' There is our practice of explaining moral actions by mentioning merely the relevant moral judgement and not an independent desire (challenged by Brink, 1997: 13–15).

Now such everyday facts may warrant our holding that, as Hare (1952: 143) puts it, 'Moral judgements always have a possible bearing on our own conduct.'[9] They hardly, however, warrant his more extreme, analytic, claim that (169) 'Everyone always does what he thinks he ought'. Nor do they warrant this variant (171–2): if a person does not assent to some imperative sentence derivable from it, this is 'knock down evidence that he hasn't assented to the moral judgement in an evaluative sense'. Likewise they do not warrant M. Smith's claim (1994: 10) that 'To have a moral opinion simply is to find ourselves with a corresponding motivation to act.'[10]

We saw in previous chapters something of the pressure that non-cognitivists are under to reinterpret the first premiss of the 'moderate' version of the practicality argument. Unless this premiss states that moral judgements motivate us necessarily, and not merely contingently upon an independent desire, there is no chance of securing the argument's validity or the requisite non-cognitivist conclusion. We also noted their tendency to read back without any real textual justification this reinterpretation into Hume's original formulations. They even sometimes cite Hume's authority as independent support for the claim itself that moral judgements are necessarily motivating. It would certainly be convenient for them if this claim were true. One could go further and say that they *need* it to be true. That the stakes are so high is a measure of the pre-eminence of the practicality argument today. It is no longer just a matter of those already committed for *other* reasons to non-cognitivism inviting us to see their resolution of the tension between morality's supposed objectivity and necessary practicality as a *further* advantage of their position. Rather, the resolution of this tension has come to be seen as itself driving non-cognitivism. Could it be then that the non-cognitivists' championing of the claim that moral judgements guarantee motivation is a kind of wishful thinking?

But why, it will be objected, if this is so, do cognitivists who have no such ulterior motive also endorse the claim? Surely they would not wish to give so much away to the non-cognitivists so to speak 'on a plate'. Why do even cognitivists who do not endorse the claim go so far as to acknowledge its evident appeal? For instance, Brink (1997: 12) – an accidentalist – writes almost apologetically of his own position: 'The externalist solution may . . . seem to be a solution of last resort because it may seem to deny the platitude that moral judgements are motivationally efficacious.' Moreover, he is initially prompted to 'Look seriously at rationalist theories of moral motivation, because they promise to represent moral judgements as intrinsically motivational.' Doesn't this suggest that the claim that moral judgements necessarily motivate has some plausibility in its own right? Either this, we may say, or the non-cognitivists have been so successful in setting in advance the terms of the practicality debate that their highly disputable claim has for many, including their opponents, slipped imperceptibly into the background of unquestioned dogma.

Before turning to assess a second possible defence of the reinterpreted first premiss – this time by appeal to morality's special authority – I offer an example of how the non-cognitivist agenda can inform a debate concerning the practicality argument, even when it takes place between two cognitivists, one of whom is an accidentalist. I cite Brink's critique (1997) of Smith's *The Moral Problem*. Smith (1994: 11) takes as his starting point a problem – thus the title of his book – which he sees as no less than 'the central organizing problem of meta-ethics'. It soon turns out, however, to be the very problem posed for cognitivists by the 'moderate' version of the practicality argument, only now recast in the form of the following triad of (allegedly) inconsistent propositions:

1   Moral judgements of the form 'It is right that I φ' express a subject's beliefs about an objective matter of fact, a fact about what it is right for her to do.
2   If someone judges that it is right that she φ's then, *ceteris paribus*, she is motivated to φ.
3   An agent is motivated to act in a certain way just in case she has an appropriate desire and a means–end belief, where belief and desire are, in Hume's terms, distinct existences.

(1994: 12)

Smith's first proposition is the contradictory of the practicality argument's conclusion. His third proposition is a variant on the argument's second premiss. His second proposition takes the place of the argument's first premiss. Smith adds, however, a *ceteris paribus* clause. He does so because he wishes to acknowledge, at least as a deviation from the rational norm, that the link between moral judgement and motivation can be broken (as in such cases as weak will or amoralism). He hopes nevertheless to preserve (what he calls) a necessity 'of sorts' here by stipulating that the link primarily holds between the moral judgements and motivation of perfectly rational agents, where any break is logically excluded. He then appeals to the aspiration of irrational, or imperfectly rational, agents to be fully rational in order to provide them with a reason, if not always a motivating one, for conforming their actions to their moral judgements.

Brink objects (1997: 7–8) that this slight but significant amendment means that moral judgements no longer entail, but merely accompany, motivation. This in turn, Brink charges, means that the three propositions are no longer genuinely inconsistent, and so a choice is no longer forced between them. In other words, Smith has suppressed the very 'problem' of his title by changing one of the elements on which it depended, rather than accepting it as originally given, and trying to resolve it. Relating this to the original (practicality) argument from which Smith's 'puzzle' is, as Brink recognizes, derived, it is as if a cognitivist had replaced premiss 1 with a looser formulation of the link between moral judgement and motivation than the non-cognitivists have stipulated, and then announced to them: your conclusion that moral judgements cannot be beliefs, but must be desires, does not follow from your premises, and so your argument is invalid. So Brink tries to hold Smith to the first premiss of the practicality argument as typically propounded by non-cognitivists.

But why, we might ask, should Brink bother to hold Smith to account in this way seemingly on behalf of the non-cognitivist proponents of the practicality argument? Is it because he thinks that their (reinterpreted) first premiss is actually true? Hardly. Brink (1997: 13), far from holding it acceptable to claim that moral judgements necessarily motivate, maintains robustly 'It is arguable that the motivation of all intentional action, including moral motivation, requires the existence of independent conative states or pro-attitudes'. However, he volunteers (ibid.: 8) this explanation of his puzzling move:

> Our interpretations should be guided at least in part by what central figures in the debate have claimed . . . First, I think that many parties to debates about moral motivation have in fact accepted and relied on my stronger formulation of internalism. This certainly seems true of the noncognitivists. Second only the stronger version of internalism makes the puzzle genuinely inconsistent . . . One consequence of [Smith's formulation] is that it requires us to interpret the familiar arguments for rejecting one element of the puzzle on the strength of the others as invalid. This gives us some reason to interpret the elements of the puzzle so as to make them jointly inconsistent
> . . .

It could be said perhaps that Brink, in insisting on a particular construal of the premiss, though he does not think it true on that construal, and though this gives an advantage to the non-cognitivists, is simply going along with the theoretical framework adopted by Smith in order to better engage with him in debate. Alternatively, it might be said that both of them do well to tackle the non-cognitivists' argument in its strongest form in order the more convincingly to refute it. But the explanation Brink himself gives is rather different. He insists on this construal, he says, because the 'central figures in the debate' have construed the premiss in this way, and that, unless it is so construed, the important argument of which it is a constitutive element will become invalid. But should one perpetuate an argument just because and for no other reason than that it has for so long dominated the meta-ethical landscape?

(iii) Appeal to morality's special authority

If the well-attested examples of evidently genuine moral weakness tell against the claim that moral judgements are necessarily motivating, and so against premiss 1 surely, it will be urged, the special authority that nevertheless attaches to these judgements tells in favour of the premiss. How, after all, it will be asked, can moral judgements possibly be said to have the requisite 'grip' on us, or 'bind' our conduct, unless motivation is guaranteed to follow?

Morality's authority, however, is generally taken to entail that we must conform to its precepts *whether or not we desire to*. This crucial qualification has two implications. First it rules out the idea that moral judgements can only motivate with the help of an independent desire. Not only do they not require this help, but it would no longer be moral motivation if they did. Moral judgements therefore do, and must, motivate us directly. This may give some initial succour to the proponents of the reinterpreted first premiss in their battle with the accidentalists, but it is still not to say that the relation between these judgements and motivation is the conceptually necessary one which they favour.

But consider now the second implication of the qualification. This is that moral judgements necessarily present themselves as *demands* upon us. Nor is this surprising when we recall the reluctance with which people frequently contemplate their moral duties.[11] For these typically involve at least an element of personal sacrifice and run counter to their inclinations, even some which may not be purely self-regarding. The Princesse de Cleves, for instance, laments the fact that 'the heart itself must be reconciled to duty'. But then it is not just accidentalism's *independent* desires that have no place in moral motivation; *no* desire at all can have such a place, not even desires which might be held to be constitutive of moral judgement itself. A normative gap or 'distance', as we might call it, thus opens up between moral judgements and motivation. The less a person desires to do what is morally required, or the more attractive to her is the prohibited behaviour, the wider is this gap, and the more proof she gives if she overcomes it of the binding force of her moral judgement. This again is perfectly illustrated in Madame de LaFayette's novel where the Princesse de Cleves is described as learning that duty put reasons 'between herself and her happiness [which] she found to her sorrow . . . were very powerful'. It must seem incautious then, indeed self-defeating, for non-cognitivists to appeal to morality's authority in order to back up a premiss which is supposed, in conjunction with the belief–desire theory to entail precisely the conclusion that moral judgements are themselves desires.

But, as we saw, it is not only non-cognitivists who hold that moral judgements are necessarily motivating, so do certain cognitivists. Surely the claim will fare better in their hands? They, after all, point to morality's special authority, understood in just the way we have understood it, in order to refute the non-cognitivists. McNaughton, for instance (1988: 48), asks how if 'a moral demand is experienced as something to which we must conform' it can 'itself depend on our wants and desires for its authority'.

We must remember here that cognitivists, such as McNaughton, reject the second premiss of the 'moderate' version of the practicality argument. They maintain therefore that beliefs do not require the help of desires in order to motivate us but motivate us necessarily. (It is of course from this claim, together with their claim that moral judgements motivate necessarily, that they deduce that these judgements can be beliefs.) Now they defend their claim by attempting to show that beliefs can on their own provide reasons for, and so explain actions: jobs which the non-cognitivists allot primarily to desire. Nevertheless it soon becomes clear that they have much the same idea of explanation as the non-cognitivists. For they also hold that an action has only been explained when it has been shown to be appealing or attractive from the point of view of the agent. In fact, McNaughton suggests (ibid.: 111) that beliefs fulfil this explanatory, or reason-giving function better than desires as ordinarily understood. Citing an action – seeking to have gratuitous pain inflicted upon oneself by being flogged or whipped – where our puzzlement is not diminished by learning that it was desired by the agent, he writes:

> The difficulty is that we have no insight into why being in the desired state should bring satisfaction. We cannot see the light in which the agent finds that state of affairs attractive . . . What is missing . . . is an account of the way the agent conceives of the desired state of affairs . . . when we have supplied that will we have a complete explanation of why the agent acted . . . the only way to come to understand how someone can desire . . . an activity which holds no attractions for you is to come to appreciate how he sees things . . . We need to appreciate the masochist's view of the whipping, to discover the light in which it can be seen as attractive. . . . We may, for example, point out that some things that are normally experienced as mildly painful can be enjoyable when we are sexually excited, or that punishment can have the pleasurable effect of relieving guilt.
>
> (ibid.: 111–12)

McNaughton, though repudiating the 'Humean' view of desire as an 'independent element in action explanation' (ibid.: 112), or 'a non-cognitive urge' (ibid.: 127, 128), does not wish to banish all reference to it, suitably reconstrued, from his account of motivation. On the contrary, according to him, to say of someone that she was motivated to act by her conception of the situation is just to say that she desired to do that thing. Moreover, this seems appropriate. For not only does he state (ibid.: 113) that 'a way of seeing a situation may itself be a way of caring or feeling' but, as we have noted, he draws attention to an agent's conception of her situation in order to bring out the attractiveness of her action from her viewpoint, so explaining it.

At first it might be thought that McNaughton is concerned only with ordinary non-moral motivation, but in fact he applies the same account to moral motivation. It must seem then that to point to a person's moral judgement as her reason for doing something is (just as it would be with any belief cited in explaining an action) to point to that conception of her situation under which the action appears attractive to her. Moreover much of what McNaughton says suggests this. For instance, he considers the state of affairs in which a person is torn between two courses of action – let us say keeping a promise by performing an irksome chore, and enjoying her idleness – but at last reluctantly decides that she must do the moral thing. He describes (ibid.: 115–16) this state of affairs not only as one in which the person 'sees more reason to do what is right [than what is wrong] but as one in which she is 'more attracted to the good [than to the bad]'. Again he speaks of the competing attractions of the conflicting courses of action both here and in his discussion of moral weakness. Thus, he suggests (ibid.: 130–1) that such weakness occurs when a person's 'global' perspective – in which competing conceptions are so organized that all 'the various considerations find their proper place' – is usurped by a more limited one which gives a partial and distorted view of these considerations. As a result, an action which has just been judged the morally right one suddenly looks 'less attractive' than it did, and the repudiated course 'more attractive'. (Incidentally moral weakness thus resolves itself unsatisfactorily into the error to which Plato, *Protagoras* 355 e2–3, refers of 'taking fewer good things at the cost of greater evils'.)

McNaughton (1988: 114) states that 'moral requirements are thought of as being independent of desire, in that neither their existence, nor their claim to provide us with reason to act, depends on what the agent happens to desire but, rather, on his conception of the situation'. But his position as we have so far expounded it does not seem able to accommodate such a sharp contrast between a person's desire to act a certain way and that 'conception of the situation' on which apparently moral requirements depend. This is because, as we have seen, to refer to how a person conceives of her situation in explaining her action is precisely to present this action as attractive from her point of view. It is difficult not to see McNaughton therefore, despite such statements, as effectively closing, as surely as the non-cognitivists, that crucial normative gap between moral judgement and motivation, and so destroying the peremptory character of morality in which its authority resides. It seems indeed that 'authority' could be claimed for whatever conception of the situation wins out in presenting the entailed course of action as most attractive compared with other courses.

But it would be unfair to give the impression that McNaughton sees no problem here at all. On the contrary, he warns (1988: 114) that it is not enough 'that the recognition of a moral requirement provides the agent with some reason to act in accordance with it, for that would be compatible with his finding more reason to act in some other way'. Moral requirements are authoritative, he maintains, in the following further sense: 'they are thought of as providing a reason to act which outweighs or overrides any reasons the agent may have to act in some other way', or again (ibid.: 115) 'have a claim on our obedience that is not conditional on there being nothing else which we want more'. Thus, 'Once an agent has formed a conception of the situation in which he takes it that morality requires an action, then the thought that there might be some other action which he has more reason to do is no longer available to him.'

Now while this is an admirable statement of the kind of authority morality is generally acknowledged to possess, it is by no means clear that McNaughton has the materials at his disposal to account for it. According to him, for a person to judge in the first place that it would be morally right to act in a given way is to see the action, or have it presented to her, in a favourable or attractive light. Otherwise – or so the underlying thought seems to be – her moral judgement will not provide her with reasons for action, and motivation in these circumstances will be inexplicable. Of course 'attractive' need not mean anything as crude as personally advantageous. Even an action that is personally costly, even damaging, to the agent could have features which redeem it from her standpoint. Perhaps it will reveal the true extent of her courage, or of her love for another person, or perhaps it is the repayment of a debt of gratitude, or the furthering of a cause about which she cares deeply. Nevertheless given that she has reached her decision as to the morally right action by considering the various courses in light of such reasons, it must seem wholly arbitrary for her then to declare herself henceforth deaf to the claims of other possible courses to give her better reasons. It is rather as if the stable door had been slammed after the horse had bolted. It may be practically sound to stick to a deci- sion once it has been made. If, however, the suggestion is that it is because the decision is a moral one, we must reply that we are not clear what the force of 'moral' is here. Perhaps it is being stipulated that we treat certain kinds of judgement as overriding and that this is to be indicated by calling them 'moral'.

We have argued that the claim entailed by premiss 1 of the 'moderate' version of the practicality argument, namely that moral judgements necessarily motivate us, flies in the face of common experience which testifies to the existence of genuine moral weakness. We have also tried to show how the attempt by both non- cognitivist and cognitivist proponents of this claim to support it by appeal to morality's special authority can be turned against them. One thing, however, that has emerged from our discussion is the important kernel of truth behind their appeal to morality's authority. The question must now be raised: if neither non- cognitivists nor cognitivist necessitarians can do justice to this authority, who is left? The accidentalists can of course account – one might almost say too easily – for moral weakness. This is because they make the ability of moral judgements to moti- vate us reliant on an independent desire, which conceivably may not be present. However, by this very token they might be considered – and indeed were earlier considered – the first and most obvious casualties of the appeal to morality's authority. For that, as we saw, entails that we must do what is morally required of us *whether or not we desire to.* Surely therefore it would be utterly in vain for them to try to establish a kind of reliable link between moral judgement and motivation (whether by saying that we are so naturally constituted as to care about the ends that morality promotes, or by saying that early conditioning has developed in us a desire to act morally) as a means of underpinning this authority? It is nevertheless true that if they could make sense of morality's authority within their own terms, while repudiating its supposed necessary practicality, this would clinch the case against premiss 1. Now certain sophisticated accidentalists have attempted to do this. Their strategy is to ascribe to desire such a roundabout and indirect role in the genesis of moral action that they are able to present at least the semblance of a direct and unmediated link between moral judgements and motivation. We turn finally to look at this attempt.

3 Accidentalists embed morality in a social framework

(i) Prior acceptance of morality's authority

Cognitivist necessitarians such as McNaughton, we have argued, take it that a moral action (like any other intentional action) can only be explained by showing it to be reasonable for the particular agent to perform it. Thus they consider it crucial to exhibit the action in a favourable or attractive light from her individual viewpoint. Such an explanation is therefore 'subjective'. It is an explanation of her action, as McNaughton (1988: 123) explicitly puts it, 'from the inside'. But when it is stressed that moral requirements are those which we must fulfil whatever our personal desires or feelings, the aim is precisely to lift them above the contingencies of any particular individual's psychology or circumstances. Thus morality is often said to be authoritative in the sense of 'necessarily giv[ing] reasons to any man' (Foot, 1972: 161). If accidentalists are to respect this distinctive categoricity and universal relevance of moral judgements, it would seem that they will have to go beyond the discrete acts of decision-making of isolated individuals on which McNaughton and others focus.

In fact, sophisticated accidentalists have sought to embed moral judgement and action, either within a social framework or, relying on Freudian ideas, as does Scheffler,[12] within internal psychical structures. Since the same difficulties arise with both psychical and social embedding, we shall concentrate on two examples of the latter: those of Foot (1977) and Hart (1961).

According to Foot, morality presupposes a wholly contingent set of social facts. In particular it presupposes that there happens to be a tradition or custom of taking certain matters – in our society, killing, stealing and lying – as of concern to the whole community, and not just to the individuals immediately involved. Thus, all members of the community have in principle a say in these actions: these actions are, as Foot puts it (1977: 203), '"passed" or "not passed"'. Those who perform actions which are not 'passed' will typically be ostracized. These actions thus become the subject of social regulation, children are taught the relevant rules, and a characteristic type of discourse – so-called moral discourse – with its familiar 'oughts' and obligations grows up around them.

It follows that certain types of conduct may be said to be required or prohibited in given situations, independently of an individual's occurrent desires or interests. Thus what we earlier called the 'distance' requirement might at first sight seem to be fulfilled, moral action being directly determined by, or rationally grounded in, judgements about what ought to be done. But as we saw the categoricity of morality requires something more. That is to say, it is not enough for morality to be capable of giving individuals reason to act independently of their momentary personal desires or interests, or of being in this sense a source of non-hypothetical imperatives. It must also be capable of giving people reason to act irrespective of whether or not they have in the first place chosen to accept its authority. If this were not so, as we saw, its bindingness would seem to depend upon an unacknowledged condition, namely a prior desire leading to the prior acceptance of its authority, and could hardly be said to 'necessarily give reasons to any man'.

Now the evident dependence of moral norms, as understood by Foot, upon specific social settings 'which we might not have had, and perhaps will not always have' (ibid.: 203) would seem to entail that their authority could not extend beyond the given community, or even to individuals within the community who have not accepted them. Thus not just outsiders, but even members of the community, who have not responded to training or social pressure, and now refuse to adopt moral norms as their own, could legitimately deny that they give rise to duties or obligations binding on them. Such norms, they will say, pointing to their overtly local nature, only speak to the like-minded; they do not apply to, and bind, the unlike-minded as well as the like-minded.

They could go further and say that by only applying to the like-minded, they even fail to apply to them in a categorical form. For they are not in themselves rationally sufficient grounds for action. They count as grounds only for those who have accepted them in the first place – in other words only for those who have an underlying motive for subscribing to the practice.

Despite these obvious implications, Foot apparently envisages people who have accepted moral norms taking them to apply alike to others in the community, who have not accepted them, and even to outsiders. Nor is there any suggestion of incoherence in their morally disapproving of those who have not accepted these norms, even when they are members of a far flung 'tribe' (ibid.: 205), who do not care how these foreigners regard them. Indeed this preparedness to 'bring the pressure and authority of society' against anyone who does not conform to its norms, irrespective of their personal acceptance of its authority, is held up by Foot as 'an important fact about the phenomenon we call "morality"'.

Thus, the impression is created, surreptitiously if not overtly, that the scope of moral norms, in some sense, however vague, transcends – or at least may legitimately be taken to transcend – their parochial origins in a particular community or society, and their acceptance by individuals in that society. This impression is further strengthened by Foot's rejection (ibid.: 204) of the view that, despite morality's dependence on such contingent and particular social facts, anyone who speaks up for its norms can only be speaking with the voice of the community or society. This view, she suggests, would undermine the important activities of moral criticism and reform. But surely it is incoherent for those who accept the norms on the one hand to morally disapprove of those who, refusing to acknowledge their authority, flout them, and yet on the other to admit that these norms can really only bind those who do accept them?

Perhaps it will be queried at this point whether people who do accept the given norms must necessarily *themselves* acknowledge their lack of application to individuals who have not accepted them. But there is nothing to indicate in the account so far given that the dependence of morality upon a determinate social setting is in any way hidden from those seriously and genuinely engaged in moral discourse and practice. There would seem to be revealed therefore at the heart of this naturalist account an unsatisfactory prevarication over how far moral norms, when embedded in a social framework, can be claimed by those who accept them to be categorical. This very prevarication, however, suggests a potential solution. Thus, it might be used to identify two viewpoints which it might seem essential to seal off from each other if incoherencies are not to arise, when these norms are declared to be categorical.

The first of these viewpoints is that of the participants: those who, in allowing their conduct to be governed by moral norms, automatically take them to transcend any local conditions which might have been used to explain their origin. The second is the 'outsiders'' viewpoint: that of those who merely record the activities of the community, and analyse its practices, perhaps tracing their pre-moral roots in those specific facts, features and activities which, as Foot believes, make morality possible.

Now it will be urged that it is only when the 'outsiders'' viewpoint is not properly distinguished from that of the 'participants', that a foothold is provided for the damaging scepticism just voiced. It is for instance only from such a standpoint that a deflationary distinction could be drawn between members of the community merely *feeling* bound by the given norms, and actually being so, or again between the community's merely dressing up its demands in a categorical form and their actually having such a form.

Let us now consider an account of morality which attempts to seal off a 'participants'' viewpoint from that of outsiders', and do so by adapting Hart's (1961) analysis of the distinctive normative structure of the law.

(ii) Isolating participants and outsiders

The difference in Hart's view between being a participant in a practice and merely an outsider is that the participant typically 'manifests' her acceptance of its ultimate criteria of justification (1961: 99, 102), rather than 'stating' that she accepts them. Now 'manifesting' one's acceptance of such criteria is just a matter of spontaneously applying them to the situation at hand, and is characteristic of what Hart calls 'the internal point of view'.

Participants might directly apply them in identifying which are moral rules. Thus, for example, adherents of a Judaeo-Christian morality might appeal to the Decalogue when there is doubt as to the provenance of a particular rule. Another example would be the use of Kant's test to determine which maxims are moral. These ultimate criteria might also be indirectly applied as, for instance, in deriving particular judgements from recognized rules. Thus, for example, participants might declare that X is duty bound to take a friend to hospital because she promised to do so, and because it is wrong to break promises. An outsider, however, (ibid.: 99) is someone who 'states', without herself accepting them, that certain criteria of justification are accepted as authoritative by the participants, or, as Hart puts it, 'are accepted [by them] from an internal point of view'.

Having thus loosely characterized a participants' and an outsiders' viewpoint, we must next ask whether these viewpoints are sealed off from each other in the required way. At first sight it is difficult to see how they could be. For what could possibly stop participants from being sufficiently reflective to be able to state, as an outsider might, that they just happen to have accepted given criteria of justification? Of course, the day-to-day application of these criteria in identifying particular moral rules might typically leave much unstated that would be likely to be stated by an outsider. However, these omissions might be thought to be, given the background of shared acceptance, just a matter of practical convenience.

But then the present view does not seem to represent any real advance on the previous one. That an individual, together with a significant number of other individuals, has as a matter of contingent fact accepted as authoritative certain criteria of justification is a presupposition of moral practice as accessible in principle to participants as to outsiders. But in this case, any claim by participants that their moral norms, are categorical, that is to say that they apply equally to those who have not accepted them, looks doomed.

To avoid this difficulty, statements setting out the antecedent conditions for the coming into being and continued existence of moral practice, would have to be disqualified from counting as 'internal' statements of the practice itself. But this would seem to require that it be impossible from within moral practice to raise the question 'Why are those particular criteria of justification accepted as authoritative?' or 'What justifies them?' For this is just the question which would give sceptics the opportunity of drawing attention to the dependence of this authoritativeness on contingent circumstances. It is hardly convincing, for instance, to allow, as Foot does (1977: 206), that a question can intelligibly be raised as to 'why [we] go in for the approvals and disapprovals we call moral', and then to reassure us that 'no doubt is thrown on the [moral] attitude itself' even when we are told that there is no answer, and that we just happen to be motivated that way.

But how can this question be shown to be senseless? Hart's suggestion (1961: 104, 106), speaking of the law, is that the very idea of (legal) validity only comes into being with the relevant practice, and has a precisely delimited usage relative to it. Thus questions can be raised about the validity of what he calls 'primary' rules, the supreme criteria being used to test their validity. However, since the system provides for no further rule assessing the validity of the supreme criteria themselves, no similar question can be raised about *its* validity.

Applying this to morality, we might say that the relevant notion of justification is likewise internal to the practice. That is to say, it is the practice itself which gives the notion of moral justification its sense, and sets the limits of its application. Thus it makes no sense to seek assurances that the practice itself can be morally justified. Yet it is just the lack of these assurances which forces the admission that moral norms only bind those who accept them, and thus have no true categoricity.

A new difficulty, however, now confronts us. This way of isolating the viewpoint internal to a practice from that of the outsiders' is applicable to *any* system of rules, how ever trivial or inconsequential, and even to chess and draughts. Each now appears within its own narrow ambit, to be autonomous and self-authenticating.

But we would then have no way of accounting for the characteristic subordination of these other systems of rules to morality. Of course, we can say that *from within moral practice* these otherwise self-contained normative structures are open to moral assessment. Thus a law can be declared immoral. But the law, exerting so to speak its own centrifugal pull, seems to demand that we adopt a standpoint at least equidistant between it and morality. Thus we seem to have insulated legal and moral judgements from each other in mutually exclusive normative systems. The application of moral standards to those who reject them, and choose to be governed by other systems of rules, would seem once more to be a matter of contingent fact, and could not receive any special legitimation.

4 Conclusion

Our main concern in this chapter has been to assess the claim entailed by the first premiss of the 'moderate' version of the practicality argument. We concentrated on the most favoured of the three 'internalist' reinterpretations, namely that moral judgements are intrinsically, or necessarily, motivating. Its proponents, it seemed, were incapable of dealing satisfactorily with the problem posed for them by moral weakness. Their appeal to morality's special authority, far from supporting their claim, seemed to undermine it. Moreover, it appeared to undermine the claim whether propounded by non-cognitivists or cognitivist necessitarians. Turning to the accidentalists to see if we could clinch the case against the reinterpreted premiss 1, we asked whether perhaps, despite the initial lack of promise, they could do more justice to the notion of morality's special authority than the others. Despite their ingenious strategies however, even sophisticated accidentalists had difficulty in making sense of requirements that 'necessarily give reasons to any man'.

It is striking nevertheless how hard many of these writers struggle to give some sense to the notion of morality's authority within naturalistic accounts which are in many ways inimical to it. They clearly do not think it should be dismissed as in Kant's famous phrase ([1755] 1958: 60) a 'high-flown fantasticality'. Later we shall touch again on non-naturalistic treatments (which take us beyond the confines of the 'moderate' version of the practicality argument). But we shall also consider a Wittgensteinian response which would resist a naturalistic reduction, while at the same time blocking any automatic metaphysical implications. This, however, takes us beyond both 'moderate' and 'extreme' versions of Hume's argument.

For the moment we put this larger discussion to one side, and return to the 'moderate' version of the practicality argument, this time to its second premiss on the 'intrinsicality' reinterpretation.

7 Desires, Beliefs and 'Direction of Fit'

1 Premiss 2 and desire–belief asymmetry

Even today, despite the pioneering work of Nagel (1970) and others, it is still largely a commonplace of philosophy that desires are more closely linked than beliefs to motivation. That there should be this motivational asymmetry between desire and belief happens of course to be vital to non-cognitivists. For as we saw unless the second premiss of the 'moderate' version of the practicality argument is reinterpreted so as to entail such an asymmetry, the conclusion that moral judgements are desires will not follow. The point is this: the 'moderate' version accords to belief a necessary role in motivation, though only alongside desire. If therefore moral judgements are to be identified with desires, the latter will have to be as closely linked to motivation as moral judgements themselves, and more closely linked to it than any belief. Thus, premiss 2 must entail that desires, unlike beliefs, but like moral judgements (according to premiss 1) are essentially, or intrinsically, motivating.

We argued in Chapter 2 that, once cut adrift from its supposed moorings in the *Treatise,* the 'traditional' defence of desire–belief asymmetry by appeal to Humean 'distinct existences' falls to pieces. We mentioned the possibility that the claim might nevertheless be salvaged by appeal to the so-called difference in 'direction of fit' to the world of desire and belief. We flagged this further defence for consideration when Hume's intentions were no longer our primary concern.

The appeal to their difference in direction of fit to the world involves the recognition (only halting and intermittent in the *Treatise*) that desires as well as beliefs are complex propositional attitudes. Thus, just as I believe that my child is being bullied, so I desire that this bullying be stopped. Nevertheless the appeal to direction of fit exploits – and in so doing has been claimed to crystallize something Hume was groping towards – an important difference between them. Whereas beliefs purport to represent the world, and so are determined as true or false by reference to it, desires being merely about how the world might be, have no truth value and can only be satisfied or unsatisfied. Platts (1979), whose account of how this apparently purely logical difference between belief and desire leads to a difference in their so-called direction of fit to the world has become almost seminal, writes:

Beliefs aim at the true, and their being true is their fitting the world; falsity is a decisive failing in a belief, and false beliefs should be discarded; beliefs should be changed to fit with the world, not vice versa. Desires [however] aim at realisation, and their realisation is the world fitting with them; the fact that the indicative content of a desire is not realised in the world is not yet a failing *in the desire*, and not yet any reason to discard the desire; the world, crudely, should be changed to fit with our desires not vice versa.

(ibid.: 256–7)

Platts refers to an earlier presentation of what he takes to be the same idea in Anscombe (1957). He claims that she there draws a distinction between 'two *kinds* of mental state, factual belief being the prime exemplar of one kind and desire a prime exemplar of the other'. I will argue below that, though it has become customary if not compulsory for anyone writing about 'direction of fit' to cite Anscombe, or the now well-known example that she gives in the passage to which Platts refers, she cannot be enlisted in support of this supposed difference between beliefs and desires.

2 Platts' normative account of direction of fit

Let us begin, however, by setting out Platts' suggestive but highly metaphorical passage more formally:

P. I: When a desire is *realized*, a 'fit' exists between it and the world just as a 'fit' exists between a belief and the world, when the belief is *true*, but

P. II: When a belief is *false*, and there is no fit with the world, the failing is in *the belief*, which should be discarded, whereas when a desire is *unrealized*, and there is no fit with the world, the failing is *not* in *the desire*, and there is no reason to discard it.

P. III: When a desire is unrealized the consequent lack of fit with the world is a failing in *the world*.

Conclusion: Whereas (false) beliefs should be changed to fit with the world, the *world* should be changed to fit with our (unrealized) desires.

Once, however, it is set out in this way, each premiss can be seen to be implausible as we shall now attempt to show.

With P.I, one might wonder how two propositional attitudes which are held to differ so sharply that only one – belief – has a truth value, the other merely being 'satisfied' or 'unsatisfied', can nevertheless both be said, in the same sense of 'fit', to fit (or not fit) the world. Platts himself offers no explicit guidance on how this claim might be supported. Others, however, point in its defence to a logical similarity which according to them subsists at the heart of the difference between the two attitudes. Thus, Humberstone (1992: 71) writes:

From a logical point of view, the relation of a belief to its propositional object, which has to obtain for the belief to be true, is the same as the relation a desire must bear to its propositional object for the desire to be satisfied: if the object (or 'content') is the proposition that *p* then, in either case, for the attitude to have the property in question is for it to be the case that *p*.

But can it be confidently asserted that when p's being the case both satisfies a given desire, and makes a given belief true, the desire and the belief have the same propositional content, namely, *that* p? Suppose, for instance, that for p to be the case is *for the bullying to have been stopped*. That this state of affairs has already occurred certainly guarantees the truth of the belief that p, since this is just the belief that the bullying has been stopped. But it is difficult to identify a corresponding desire, viz. one which being satisfied by this same state of affairs having occurred has the same propositional content as the belief that p. For this desire – the desire that p – would be the desire that the bullying has been stopped, which is not clearly intelligible. I might of course wish that the bullying had been stopped, but the use of the verb 'wish', together with the subjunctive, implies that I believe that it has *not* been stopped – perhaps that I regard it as scarcely any longer feasible that it should be stopped – not that it *has* been stopped.

But someone might respond: of course we cannot desire an event to occur which we know would already be in the past. But this only means that for p to be the case must be for something *to* occur, rather than to have occurred, and thus, in our example, for the bullying to be stopped, rather than to have already been stopped. The relevant belief – the belief that p – is then, it will be said, the belief that the bullying will be stopped, just as the relevant desire – the desire that p – is the desire that it will be stopped.[1]

But the identity of propositional content is now secured at a cost: that of turning the expression of desire (like orders, on a similar analysis) into, if not a prediction, at least something like an expression of expectation, when it is surely nothing of the sort, not least because it lacks any content that could be discovered to be true or false. The content of a desire, one is inclined to say, is not (as Platts describes it) indicative at all but *subjunctive*: I desire that the bullying *should* be stopped. Thus though the fact that the bullying is stopped satisfies this desire, it does not do so by coinciding with the desire's propositional content. To suppose that it did would be to illicitly conflate what it is for a desire to be satisfied with what it is for a belief, or a prediction, or an expectation, to be correct.

An attempt might, however, now be made to identify a propositional core common both to the belief and the desire which is nevertheless 'non-assertorial'.[2] On this view the propositional content of the belief that the bullying has been stopped/is being stopped/will be stopped, and also of the desire that it should be stopped, is 'the bullying's being stopped'. But while the (non-assertorial) thought of the bullying being stopped provides the desire with a suitably non-truth bearing content, it seems simultaneously to deprive the belief of its truth-bearing content. In any case to treat propositions non-assertorially is highly controversial not least because it seems to deprive them of the role for which they were introduced: to be the bearers of truth (and falsity).

One way out of these difficulties[3] would be to extend to desire, or the expression of desire ('would that' . . . 'let it be that'), a method tentatively proposed for handling imperatives. Here an analogue of truth is defined which is applicable to them as non-truth bearing items, and which is represented symbolically by a shriek, or exclamation mark (!). Thus "'shut the door!' is satisfied iff "the door is shut" is true' is now rendered as "'p!" iff "p" is true'. "'I desire that the bullying should be stopped" is satisfied iff "the bullying is stopped" is true' could then be rendered in a similar way. But whereas p's being the case still *makes true* my belief that p, it now satisfies, not my desire that p, but my desire that p!, and hence there is no longer the required identity of propositional content between the belief and the desire. But it is hard to see how without this coincidence there is any real justification for talk of the two attitudes fitting, or not fitting, the world, where 'fit' is understood in exactly the same sense.

P.I, as we have seen, seeks to maintain that belief and desire are, despite the important difference between them, in a certain respect logically similar. P.II, consisting in the two halves of a contrast, focuses exclusively upon the difference which however, despite having seemed to be purely logical, is now interpreted normatively. Thus first, that a belief is false – that it does not fit with the world – is evaluated as a failing in the belief. Now it might be suggested that this otherwise abrupt transition to the normative level is prepared for in Platts' original passage by the claim (omitted from our schema) that beliefs aim at truth. For surely, it will be said, relative to that aim falsity is a failing. But we are surely entitled to ask what this talk of beliefs aiming at truth is supposed to mean. There seem only three possibilities. The claim may be just a metaphorical way of expressing the original logical point that beliefs have a truth value – how after all could beliefs 'aim' at anything except metaphorically? Alternatively it might be an unsupported assertion that truth is a norm for beliefs. Finally it could be a tacit directive to believers to believe only what is true. At least on the third interpretation we would not have to countenance (as on the second) the existence of a dubious kind of 'semantic' norm, according to which the terms 'successful' or 'failed' are predicated directly of beliefs, as opposed to those who have the beliefs. Nevertheless we would surely still be justified in demanding an explanation of what otherwise looks entirely puzzling: how we might set about following such a directive.

The puzzlement is engendered even more acutely in relation to the directive to discard false beliefs which is actually expressed in the premiss. For this directive, addressed presumably to a person with false beliefs, is surely incoherent. Consider, for instance, a parent who having believed that the bullying (of her child) had been stopped now realizes that this is false. It is not as if some deliberate adjustment of her original belief was still called for that she might intelligibly refuse to make, and against the background of which, the directive 'false beliefs should be discarded' might come into force. On the contrary, she just cannot, logically, be said any longer to have such a belief at all. Of course she could describe herself (or be described) as having made a mistake in believing what she had believed, but it is not clear what this would add to her acknowledgment that her belief was false. Perhaps what is really meant by the directive is that one should be constantly overhauling all one's beliefs in order to ensure that the evidence on which they are based remains sound, so that one can at least vouch for their truth. But this new directive, though certainly no longer incoherent, is both impractical (Humberstone, 1992: 67–8) and in so far as it rests on the psychological observation that people are better off without any false beliefs highly contestable.

Turning now to the second half of the contrast, the normative reinterpretation of the claim that desires, being merely about how the world *might* be, have no truth value, parallels (in negative form) the reinterpretation of the first half. Since the fact that a desire's propositional content is unrealized does not entail the desire's falsity – desires, unlike beliefs, can be neither true nor false – this fact, it is asserted, does *not* constitute a failing in, and is *not* a reason to discard, the desire.

Now even aside from the dubiety of once again interpreting an apparently purely conceptual point normatively, this denial itself must strike us as odd. For it seems to imply that a question can coherently be raised as to whether it *is* a failing in a desire to be for something which is not presently the case. But this suggests that reassurance is needed that (to quote one of Platts' followers) 'there is nothing *ipso facto* wrong with desiring that p when not-p is the case' (Zangwill, 1996: 177). But how could we need reassurance that it is not a failing in the desire-that-p that not-p is the case when it is precisely the desirer's belief that not-p that makes his desire understandable and intelligible? The normative re-expression of this second part of the contrast thus seems to entail a singular distortion of our ordinary way of thinking about desire.

It is perhaps unsurprising that the involvement of desire with elements of belief should be downplayed in the present context since it threatens the whole idea that the two attitudes can be sufficiently held apart to have ascribed to them mutually exclusive directions of fit. However, even writers who, acknowledging the conceptual reliance of desires on beliefs, reformulate the original distinction and make this reformulation the cornerstone of their own dispositional rendering of direction of fit, only become further mired in Platts' distortion. Smith (1994: 115), for instance, also assuming the requisite identity of propositional content, writes: 'a belief that p tends to *go out of existence* in the presence of a perception with the content that *not* p, whereas a desire that p tends *to endure,* disposing [us] . . . to bring it about that p' (my italics). But this makes the discovery that not p sound like a test which both the belief that p, and the corresponding desire, might have to face, but which only the desire will (tend to) survive. However, far from my only desiring that the bullying of my child be stopped so to speak *provisionally* upon the desire's tending to 'persist on my acquisition' of the belief that the bullying has not yet been stopped, my desire is firmly founded upon this negative belief.

The difficulty to which we next turn concerning the translation into normative terms of what is apparently merely a logical feature of desire affects both the second half of P. II and also P.III. For both evidently presuppose that there should be – that it is a good thing for there to be – a fit between desire and the world. (Humberstone, 1992: 72, puts it thus: 'we have a sense of things going right' when there is this fit.) We may already observe that whatever P.III is supposed to mean,[4] it is not something that could be refuted by pointing to examples where, the circumstances being entirely propitious, it is a person's own laziness, or lack of initiative, that is responsible for her failure to implement her desires. Even here apparently we would still have to be able to talk about the 'fault lying in the world'. Otherwise we would apparently not be able to explain why she acted to implement her desires even when, being neither lazy nor timid, she *did* so act.

Why then should anyone assume that it is a good thing for there to be a fit between desire and the world in any, let alone, in every instance of desire? We have already had a taste of the difficulties involved in establishing the parallel claim for belief, but there at least we were dealing with *truth*, which is often claimed to be of value, even if it is difficult to pin down in what way. Indeed, one writer (Zangwill, 1996: 175), who canvasses the idea that truth is a semantic norm, introduces it by stating that 'the truth value of a belief really is its truth *value*' (Zangwill's italics). But no such play on the word 'value' is available with desires since we do not customarily speak of the 'satisfaction value' of a desire. Perhaps those who endorse, for whatever reason, the claim that it is a good thing for there to be a fit between beliefs and the world — for beliefs to be true — think that they can extrapolate from this to the conclusion that it is also a good thing for there to be a fit between desires and the world — for desires to be satisfied. But if their defence is that when a belief that e.g. p is true, and when the corresponding desire is satisfied, the *same relation* holds between the propositional content of the two attitudes and the world, then this as we have seen is highly dubious.

Is the thought perhaps that it is a good thing for there to be a fit between desires and the world because then they are 'satisfied', and satisfaction is in itself a good thing? But though feeling satisfied is doubtless a good and pleasant state to be in, having one's desires satisfied is neither sufficient nor necessary for such a feeling. Thus, on the one hand, one may never know that one's desire has been satisfied, either because one never comes to hear about it, or because it happens after one's death, as with the desire of Marcel Proust's mother that her son should achieve literary renown. On the other hand, one may feel satisfied though one's desire has not been satisfied. It is further noteworthy that with attitudes like fear, their realization is likely to be learnt about, not with a feeling of satisfaction, but with dismay. This leaves two other possibilities: that it is supposed to be a good thing either *morally* or psychologically to have our desires satisfied. But it would be absurd to maintain that, morally, even wicked desires ought to be satisfied, while that people are better off without any unsatisfied desires is no more convincing than the parallel claim that people are better off without any false beliefs.

3 Anscombe and the shopping errand

It will perhaps be suggested that we could avoid some of the foregoing difficulties and infelicities by refraining from reading into Platts' original remarks the idea of its being 'a good thing' for there to be a fit between the two attitudes and the world. Anscombe's example, it might now be suggested, will help us to focus on the important claim being made by Platts: that different locations are involved in remedying, respectively, a false belief and an unrealized desire. In the first case, it is the belief itself, in the second, the world.

Anscombe (1957: 56) invites us to consider a man buying items from a shopping list made by his wife, and a detective following the husband around, and recording what he buys. Now, as she observes, if the man buys the wrong items – suppose he buys pears instead of the apples on the shopping list – he cannot put the mistake right when he gets home by simply amending his wife's shopping list. It would be a weird and irritating kind of joke were he to say: 'Oh, look, these are pears, so we'd better substitute the word "pears" for "apples" on your list.' He can only put things right by going out again and making sure he buys apples this time. But it is entirely different with the detective. Suppose he has noted down 'peaches' when what the man actually buys is pears. When he realizes the disparity between what he's written down and the items bought, he must correct his record; it would be absurd, and wholly self-defeating, given the purposes we may imagine him to have been hired for, for him to ask the man to go out and shop all over again, only this time, in order to conform with the detective's record, to exchange the pears for peaches.

Let us now try to relate the phrase 'difference in direction of fit to the world' to Anscombe's example, noting, however, that she herself never uses the expression. With keeping a record, as does the detective, the direction of fit is, we might say, from world (the actual event, or action, that is to be recorded) to record. The world – the man buying the pears in her example – dictates what shall be written down, since the whole purpose of the record is to represent the world; that is, its whole purpose is to represent what the man does. Consequently, when there is a lack of fit, it is the record that is at fault, and must be rectified. But with an order, or request or indeed expression of intention, the direction of fit is the other way round: it is from order, or request, to world. It is, in other words, the order or request – the shopping list in the example – that dictates what should be done. Consequently when there is lack of fit, it's the world – what is done – what the man actually buys – that is at fault, and must be rectified.

But, as we shall now argue, Anscombe's example though seeming initially amenable to Platts' purposes is not really so. For one thing, her Wittgensteinian sensitivity to conceptual complexity makes it highly unlikely that she would construe desire and belief in the required Humean way as conceptually distinct mental states. For another, she actually states her purpose in giving her example, and it has nothing whatsoever to do with the belief–desire distinction. But third, and most importantly, even ignoring the larger context, her example itself resists interpretation along Platts' lines.

Anscombe's purpose in giving her shopping example could hardly have been, as Platts claims, to explain the difference between belief and desire as 'two kinds of mental state' since she never sees them as conceptually distinct in the simple way envisaged. However, they have to be seen in this way if they are to be claimed to have the different relations to motivation and action specified.

For instance, though she states (1957: 68) that 'The primitive sign of wanting is *trying to get*' (Anscombe's italics), she carefully prefaces this claim by saying: 'The wanting *that interests us* . . . cannot be said to exist in a man who does nothing towards getting what he wants (my italics)'. In fact, she is contrasting desire, in this dynamic sense, not with *belief* at all, but with other notions of desire, for instance idle wishing of which, she says, the chief mark is that 'a man does nothing'. She is also contrasting this dynamical desire with desire, as it occurs in the expression the 'feeling of desire', which, she says, is also 'compatible with one's doing nothing at all towards getting' the object. Indeed, this mere feeling of desire is she suggests just as likely, perhaps more likely to evaporate than to lead to action when its object is envisaged as a likelihood.

Far from distinguishing desire and belief, she incorporates a relevant belief as part of the conditions of ascription of desire in the dynamic sense. Thus, she writes (ibid.: 68): 'There are two features present in wanting; movement towards a thing and knowledge (or at least opinion) that the thing is there', and again '[Wanting] is not mere movement or stretching out towards something, but this on the part of a creature that can be said to know the thing.'

But even if it is not feasible to suppose that Anscombe herself could be using her example to point up the required distinction between desire and belief, may not the example be used anyway to illustrate the idea of difference in direction of fit? The wife's order 'Buy apples', it might be urged, is meant to stand to the carrying out of this order as the *desire* that apples should be bought stands to its realization: apples being bought. Likewise the detective's record which states that peaches were bought stands to what actually was bought as a belief stands to the state of affairs it purports to represent.

Now it is Anscombe's contrast between two kinds of mistake, and their different locations, in the case of the wife's order (the shopping list) and the detective's record which makes talk of two different directions of fit to the world seem appropriate here. It is this which we would have to be able to carry into the desire–belief context. Moreover we can certainly talk of a mistaken belief just in the way we talk of an incorrect record (which is therefore what has to be corrected). But it is quite unclear how we could apply the talk of a mistake in carrying out an order – perfectly natural as it is – to the case where a desire is unrealized (a mistake here which the world has to make good). Anscombe writes:

> If the list and the things that the man actually buys do not agree . . . then the mistake is not in the list but in the man's performance . . . whereas if the detective's record and what the man actually buys do not agree, then the mistake is in the record.
>
> (ibid.: 56)

Our difficulty can be put like this. Anscombe envisages the husband buying the wrong items, and naturally enough calls this 'a mistake *in performance*': there is, and cannot sensibly be any mistake here until the husband actually *makes* one by buying the wrong items. Consider now what defenders of difference in 'direction of fit' wish to say about desire. It is, they claim, the very fact that the desire is unrealized – whether or not anyone has yet tried or failed to realize it – which constitutes the mistake. It is this mistake, or failing, which they then go on to locate in the *world*, rather than in the desire, so reversing the situation (as they see it) with belief.

Moreover it seems that they have to say that the mere fact that the desire is unrealized is a failing – an indication that something is lacking – because their problem is to move the agent from a state of inertia to action via desire. Their idea is that the failing which exists in the world by virtue of the desire's not yet being realized is to be *put right* in action. But with Anscombe any mistake that occurs only occurs *once the action is underway*, and lies in the *performance* itself, not in any antecedently existing state of affairs.

Anscombe's aim, far from being to contrast desire and belief in their relation to action, is to contrast two kinds of *knowledge*: that practical knowledge which we have of our own intentional actions, as *agents*, and the knowledge which other people have of our actions, as *observers*. Let us think again of the man on the shopping errand. Let us suppose that he knows perfectly well that he has to buy apples, but takes pears from the stall thinking that they are apples. Now suppose a friend comes up to him and asks him what he is doing. He replies, 'Buying apples.' But the friend corrects him, 'You aren't buying apples, you're buying pears.' And now Anscombe's point is that the mistake the husband makes is not in *'judgement'* – not in what he says, or judges, that he is doing – as it would be were the friend to get what the husband is doing wrong – but in *'performance'*. She writes:

> And here . . . the mistake is not one of judgement but of performance. That is, we do *not* say: What you *said* was a mistake, because it was supposed to describe what you did and did not describe it, but: What you *did* was a mistake, because it was not in accordance with what you said.
>
> (ibid.: 57)

That is to say, if the friend was wrong, the mistake would be in what she said – in her judgement. But if the man is wrong, the mistake is not in what he says, but in what he does.

Above I have attempted to expose the weaknesses, on several possible interpretations, of the various claims and assumptions which together constitute Platts' by now seminal argument for the conclusion that belief and desire have different directions of fit. But supposing this conclusion had been demonstrated, would it even then entail that *other* difference between the two attitudes which is our real concern here: that desire is necessarily, or as it is sometimes put, internally, motivating whereas belief is only contingently so? Certainly, it is thought that it would. Dancy (1993: 3), for instance, describing the position, writes that, given desire's 'world-to-mind' (as opposed to belief's 'mind-to-world') direction of fit, 'it seems that desires must [unlike beliefs] be internally motivating states'. As, however, we have seen, according to Platts, belief and desire have different directions of fit in that whereas beliefs should be changed to fit with the world, the *world* should be changed to fit with our desires. But to state that something *should* be done is to contemplate the possibility that it might not be done. But if desires are intrinsically, or internally, motivating, then motivation cannot but occur.

4 Smith's dispositional account of direction of fit

So far, we have mentioned Smith's dispositional account of difference in direction of fit only to make two points. First, it is predicated, like Platts' normative account, on that common but dubious assumption concerning the identity of propositional content across relevant pairs of desires and beliefs. Second, it involves a similar distortion of our ordinary way of thinking about desire. However, even if we were to accept the assumption and ignore the distortion, we might still find fault with it. Recent critics (Humberstone, 1992: 63–5; Sobel and Copp, 2001: 46–9) have pointed, for instance, to the ambiguity of Smith's reference to a 'perception with the content that not p' in the presence of which, according to him, the belief that p 'tends to go out of existence'. They argue as follows. If we are to understand by Smith's remark that the agent tends to cease to believe that p when she comes to believe that not p, then the claim appears to be vacuous. Suppose, however, we seek to avoid the circularity by taking it that the agent tends to cease to believe that p when it merely *appears* to her that not p. But this is false since there is no guarantee that she will take the appearance to be veridical. As Sobel and Copp observe, the appearance of puddles on a hot road has no tendency at all to undermine a driver's belief that the road is actually dry. Perhaps, however, Smith has in mind the conceptual truth that 'the belief that p tends to disappear in the face of the obviousness that not p'.

More fundamentally, we may question whether this account of the difference in direction of fit is dispositional at all. As we shall recall, the relevant difference lies in the fact that whereas my belief that p 'tends to go out of existence' in the presence of a perception that not p, the corresponding desire 'tends to endure', disposing me to act in the relevant way. But precisely what is the relation here posited between a desire *enduring* (or tending to endure) in the perceived absence of the state of affairs that would satisfy it and the desirer being *disposed* to bring this state of affairs about? Is it *by* tending to endure in these circumstances that the desire disposes us to act? But, if so, how exactly? By not having (or not tending to have) gone out of existence? But that is hardly the same thing as disposing us to act. By continuing (or tending to continue) to be around? But 'continuing to be around' and 'disposing us to act' still express separate ideas. The difficulty might even be rephrased in Platts' metaphorical language thus: surely for a desire to aim at realization is more than for it to merely endure in face of non-realization.

Perhaps the thought is that my continuing to have the desire *leads* to my being disposed to act upon it? But if so there is no longer any attempt to prevent the two ideas from coming apart. But if a desire's tending to endure is not the same as its disposing me to act, and if a desire's having the direction of fit it does is just its tendency to endure where the belief would have gone out of existence, difference in direction of fit is not being 'cashed' dispositionally. That desires do dispose us to act, if they do, is an additional feature to their tending to endure in the relevant circumstances, and hence to their having the particular direction of fit they do. (We should note, however, that many, including Hume himself, have held that *belief* can only be distinguished from imagination if it is also held to dispose us to act.)

Someone might, however, attempt to sidestep this critique by pointing out that since dispositions are mere tendencies, appeal to them would not in any case ensure the requisite necessary connection between desire and motivation. Picking up another strand in Smith's argument, they might now go on to suggest that what really accounts for the difference in direction of fit, and yields the requisite necessary / contingent distinction is the status of desires, and only desires as *goals* (Smith,1994: 116: 'having a goal is desiring'). For the reference to a goal, they will argue, is crucial to the explanation of any and every action.[5]

Perhaps if you have a particular goal you are relevantly motivated. However, it does not follow at least where 'goal-directed' is plausibly defined (Anscombe, 1957: 20–2) as directed towards 'some further thing [to be] obtained by the action', that you cannot be motivated unless you have a goal. Anscombe draws in this context a distinction which is useful here between what she calls 'forward-looking motives' where we do something, as she puts it, 'lest or in order that . . . [something] should not happen' and 'backward-looking' ones, where something that has happened is given as the ground of one's acting or refraining from acting. Some of the commonest examples of actions with backward-looking motives are, of course, moral ones, such as keeping a promise. Here merely pointing to the fact that I have, e.g. made a promise, and showing how my action makes sense in the light of it, provides my action with a complete explanation. It would be odd to add: 'I also want to keep the promise.'

Even where mention of a desire seems appropriate, it is frequently (as McNaughton, 1988: 112, plausibly argues) only because it is a common one that it may seem enough to state that the agent possesses it. When the desire is so bizarre that we are none the wiser for being told – McNaughton gives the example of a desire for a saucer of mud – or so eccentric that we don't understand how anyone could possess it – say, the desire to have one's healthy limb amputated – the explanandum remains similarly puzzling until the agent's perspective is spelt out. As we may recall, McNaughton maintains that to state the description under which an agent sees an action as attractive is to attribute to her a desire to perform it. He goes on to conclude that we can therefore talk about an internal link between such beliefs and her desires or motivations. To retort that one can share a conception of a situation with another person yet find oneself with quite different desires, that (as the slogan goes), any belief can go with any desire, seems little more at this point than a recital of hollow dogma: that of Humean 'distinct existences'.

Given its evident weaknesses on both the normative and dispositional interpretations, one may well wonder why the appeal to direction of fit has become such an orthodoxy that even cognitivist critics tend to make an initial genuflection toward it. It is tempting to speculate whether there does not lie behind it a reliance, conscious or unconscious, on another quite different type of justification, from which it has not been fully disentangled. This is also a justification for the existence of a special link between 'desire' and motivation. Here, however, 'desire' does not refer to one distinct kind of psychological state, which, in being linked necessarily, rather than merely contingently, to motivation, is to be contrasted with another distinct kind, belief. Rather, it signifies an agent's *subjective states and attitudes in general* (including beliefs) which are now canvassed as the only conceivable source of motivation, in sharp contrast to those facts or properties which lie outside the agent and are merely the objects of his rational apprehension.[6]

This last justification for the special link between desire and motivation already points forward to the 'extreme' version of the practicality argument, whose second premiss entails that reason, far from having a role in motivation, cannot move us to action at all. In the context of the 'intrinsicality' reinterpretation however, which is a reinterpretation of the 'moderate' version, the justification trades on an illicit confla-tion, similar to that we noted in the deployment of the traditional defence. This is a conflation of belief as a substantive psychological state which can, as the proponents of this reinterpretation require, causally interact with desire to produce action, with reason as it figures in the 'extreme' version: namely, as reason so construed as to be incapable of any causal impact whatsoever.

Suppose it had been possible satisfactorily to defend the claim that desires are necessarily motivating, whereas beliefs are only contingently so, by appeal to their different directions of fit to the world. There would still remain the problem of fitting together the apparently incompatible claims that desire is necessarily moti-vating and that belief is also required if motivation is to come about. We will end this chapter by considering and rejecting the various solutions on offer.

5 A symmetrical as well as an asymmetrical relation

The problem is apparent in Dancy's attempt (1993: 2–3) to expound this confusing position. On the one hand, desire and belief are said to resemble each other in each being a state which 'needs the contribution of the other' if motivation is to take place. On the other, the difference between desire and belief as a necessarily as opposed to a merely contingently, motivating state is explained in this way. Whereas desire is unable to exist without motivating, belief 'requires the help of desire', or again 'borrow[s] [its] ability to motivate from [its] relation to [desire]'. Dancy's examples only serve to obfuscate matters further. It is perfectly easy to see why, if 'a complete motivating state . . . must be a combination of belief and desire', the desire for an orange, in the absence of beliefs 'about the probable whereabouts of oranges', must remain (motivationally) 'impotent'. But it is not at all easy to see how this desire can remain so if it is in the essence of a desire to be motivating.

Perhaps the thought is that a desire can be motivating without its following that *the person who possesses the desire is actually motivated,* and hence the desire remains in this sense impotent. So though it is perfectly intelligible to attribute a desire to a person when she is asleep or temporarily unconscious, this desire is incapable at the time of motivating her. But this possibility is explicitly ruled out since it is claimed that for a desire to be motivating is for the person whose desire it is to be motivated. When she is incapable of being motivated, her desires will not be motivating.

Perhaps the thought is that a desire can be motivating yet unable on a particular occasion to get an action going, and so in this sense remains impotent. But it is diffi-cult to see what justification there could be here for distinguishing between being motivated to, say, cut oneself another slice of cake, and actually setting about doing so,unless it were to allow for certain kinds of constraints. These could be external constraints (suppose my arm were suddenly to become paralysed) or internal ones (suppose my abhorrence at the idea of becoming fat suddenly reasserted itself). But no such constraints are presupposed here, merely the absence of a relevant belief.

Is the thought that a desire can be motivating yet unable to provide a reason for action? But Humeans identify having a reason for action, and being motivated to act. Where, however, it is acknowledged that a person can be motivated to act in a given way, though she accepts that she has no reason to, or even has a reason not to, act that way, this would typically be construed as a case of weak will or even psychological compulsion. But here, the desire to act in this way is thought of as having somehow overwhelmed the agent's better judgement; it is not that the desire to refrain from so acting has failed to become effective on account of the absence of the relevant belief.

One possible solution might be to adopt the suggestion (which we considered in Chapter 1) made by Basson (1958) in his interpretation of the original Humean text. According to this, to say that a desire cannot exist without motivating is just to say that 'motive' is a description that applies exclusively to desire. It has no implications for whether on a given occasion a desire will actually lead to action, since this requires a relevant belief which may or may not be present. But this seems merely to repeat the claim that a belief isn't a desire, and does not influence action in the way that a desire does. There seems to be a similar difficulty with Baillie's more opaque description (2000: 89) of the difference as 'about the *structure* of motivation' (his italics). We are still left with the problem of explaining how the two attitudes diverge in such a way that only one of the two can be said to be necessarily, or intrinsically, motivating, though both are required for motivation.

Writers sympathetic to Basson's approach often respond to this objection by appealing a second time round to the metaphors involved in the original appeal to direction of fit, and from which metaphor we have just tried unsuccessfully to loose them. Dancy (1993: 13), for instance, arguing that desire and belief have, for Humeans, to differ as they do in the asymmetrical aspect of their relationship, in order to be the partners they are in the symmetrical aspect, describes them as on this view 'made for each other'. He has elucidated this 'partnership' by suggesting that desire influences action through its possession of a kind of 'latent energy', akin to a 'hydraulic thrust' which, in the absence of a relevant belief 'has no means of escape' but which, once such a belief is present, is released, enabling the belief to become 'ert'. McNaughton (1988: 108), on the other hand, likens our beliefs to maps that are only accurate so long as they 'reflect the way things are on the ground', but our desires to preferences for go[ing] one way rather than another'. Still other writers, such as Penelhum (1975: 125) think it will help us to see how reason, or belief, can be necessary for motivation, and yet at the same time 'wholly subordinate' to desire as the 'predominant' motivational force, if we think of the relationship between master and slave. As he puts it: 'There are many things that we can do with the aid of a slave that we cannot do without him; but that does not mean he is in charge.'

But if the appeal to these bewilderingly heterogeneous types of metaphor seems in all three cases to be ultimately obscure, this third seems to be particularly ill-chosen in that typically the slave contributes the brute force and the master the intelligence and direction. But certainly when Hume talked of 'direction' in this context it is reason which is said to 'direct' passion or desire, not vice versa. Admittedly, he famously states that 'reason is, and ought only to be the slave of the passions'. But this does not mean that appeal to a social relationship between a superior and his inferior is either appropriate or illuminating in trying to account for the asymmetrical relations of each of two states of affairs to a third, for whose occurrence they are at the same time claimed to be the individually necessary and jointly sufficient conditions.

I think it is hard not to conclude that the kind of desire–belief asymmetry which is required for the validity of the 'moderate' version of the practicality argument, even were we to have a plausible non-metaphorical account of it, would sit uncomfortably with according to belief a necessary role in motivation.

8 A Riddle and a Buried Assumption

1 Williams' example from *Owen Wingrave*

The negative findings of the last two chapters ought to puzzle anyone who has not distinguished more than one version of the practicality argument. For it would seem that this argument in its only fully extant form in contemporary literature – the form in which it is claimed to drive us towards non-cognitivism – hardly warrants its formidable reputation. But (unless we posit another version) this must leave it unaccountable how certain recent writers have managed to deploy the argument, or at least its second premiss, with such apparently devastating effect against their opponents. I have chiefly in mind here Bernard Williams.

Referring in his famous paper 'Internal and external reasons' (1981: 108) to the 'old question, of how reason can give rise to a motivation', he makes it seem that any answer other than Hume's 'famously . . . negative' one would be nonsensical. Of course, Williams' independent demonstration of this conclusion is important, as is his choice of Owen Wingrave's plight (in Britten's opera) to illustrate it. Lacking all desire to join the army or any other disposition from which this desire could rationally be derived Owen, Williams persuasively argues, cannot conceivably be moved to become a soldier, even by the fact that family tradition demands it. However, the additional power Williams draws from his allusion to Hume's second premiss cannot but strike us. Nor is it simply mention of Hume that carries authority. It is the denial itself that reason can move us that is in some obscure way intuitively compelling. But how can this be, it might be asked, when our attempts in the previous chapter to corroborate the second premiss of the practicality argument only resulted in its plausibility being progressively diminished.

Now we deliberately confined ourselves in the last chapter to a consideration of the second premiss of the 'moderate' version of the practicality argument. But on this reading premiss 2 acknowledges a role for reason or belief in motivation – indeed a necessary one – it simply denies it the pre-eminence ascribed to desire. Williams' categorical dismissal, however, of any kind of positive answer to the question whether reason can motivate action suggests, on the contrary, the 'extreme' reading: that reason has no role at all. Far, therefore, from being puzzled by the appeal of Williams to the second premiss, his success should encourage us to turn our attentions to this other version, seeking there the real source of the argument's power.

But, it will be objected, this is too swift. For the difference between the 'moderate' and 'extreme' readings of premiss 2 turns, as we have just reiterated, on whether reason is being denied merely a particularly crucial role in motivation, or any role at all. But if it is questionable to deny it even this particularly crucial role, how much more questionable to deny it *any* role. Moreover, the implication of Williams' remarks is not just that this categorical denial is more plausible than the qualified one, but that its contradictory – that reason is not, in Hume's famous words, *perfectly* inert, *utterly* impotent – is unthinkable. Thus, Williams (1981: 106) makes it seem inconceivable that Owen Wingrave, 'all [of whose] desires lead in another direction' could yet be moved to join the army simply by dispassionately reflecting upon the family tradition of military honour which, his family claims, demands this very action.

But we can both dismiss premiss 2 on the 'moderate' reading as unconvincing, yet also tentatively endorse it on the 'extreme' reading, so long as we recognize that the difference between the two cannot merely be one of scope. It must be the radically different way in which 'reason' itself is being construed. But this could be put again by saying that those cognitivists who can properly be regarded as the target of the 'extreme' version must have a radically different conception of reason from those at whom the 'moderate' version is aimed. At this point, however, a new doubt surfaces. It is all well and good, it will be said, in the context of Hume's original practicality argument to distinguish between different conceptions of reason – a metaphysical and a naturalistic conception. But is it really either plausible or useful to distinguish between today's cognitivists in this way?

Of course, it will be admitted, they fall into two groups depending on which of the premisses they contravene. One group, among them the utilitarians, can, however, immediately be dismissed as possible targets on the 'extreme' reading. It is precisely because they share the view, entailed by the 'moderate' reading, of a belief as only able to motivate if a desire happens to be present, that they must be content to claim that moral judgements are similarly dependent on desire. Thus, it is that they come to contravene premiss 1.

The other group – the 'necessitarians' – agree with premiss 1 that a moral judgement can on its own motivate us straightaway and so, unlike the 'accidentalists', find themselves in conflict with premiss 2. Thus, they assert against this premiss that a belief *can* all on its own, and without waiting upon a desire, motivate us. If, however, they were to be targets on the 'extreme' reading of the premiss, the very coherence of their assertion would have to be in question, not merely whether it is correct or mistaken. Moreover, it would have to be apparent why a belief, as they understand it, and despite their endorsement of premiss 1, is in fact a dubious candidate for having any impact whatsoever on motivation, even the limited one granted by the 'moderate' reading. But the evidence suggests otherwise.

Consider first those necessitarians who claim that a belief causally suffices for motivation either directly (Scheffler, 1992),[1] or indirectly, by itself producing the relevant desire (Smith, 1994). But their dispute with defenders of the relevant premiss 2 is ultimately just *factual*.

Consequently, even if it turned out that an independent desire was in fact always present alongside belief, in every instance of motivation, they could hardly be charged with incoherence for having brought the challenge. Still less does there seem to be anything about the particular way they construe belief that might lead to puzzlement as to how they can then go on to credit it with *any* motivational role.

Those necessitarians, on the other hand, who (like McNaughton, 1988) adopt an 'intrinsicality', rather than a 'sufficiency', interpretation of Hume's premisses, will claim that it is nothing less than a conceptual error to treat desire as a distinct psychological state that must be 'added' to belief if motivation is to ensue. But even this critique is still perfectly intelligible to adherents of premiss 2 on the 'moderate' reading, who will simply retort (with whatever limited success) that a proper investigation of our linguistic practices will show that the links between belief and desire, or belief and motivation, are after all only contingent. It is not, for instance, as if the cognitivists were here attempting to assert, absurdly, a logical link between two distinct psychological states; on the contrary, they are merely claiming that the one state can be brought under two descriptions. But if neither accidentalists nor necessitarians could possibly be the objects of attack on the 'extreme' reading of premiss 2, to what other type of cognitivist, it will sceptically be inquired, could this version of the argument be addressed today? Indeed, Williams himself, it will be observed, not only pronounces the position of the 'external reasons' theorists almost unstateable but treats it as largely hypothetical, leaving us to speculate who might most nearly resemble these shadowy inchoate figures.

This scepticism will, however, probably only be exacerbated when we respond with the names of moral rationalists of the early twentieth century, such as the moral intuitionist, Prichard. For if these writers are mentioned at all in the context of the practicality argument today – and in our dominantly post-Humean climate they have, as we shall see, become largely invisible except as historical figures – they are unthinkingly assimilated to either the accidentalists or the necessitarians. In light of this explanation, our task becomes clear: to restore to these writers a definite conceptual profile of their own. Only then will it be feasible to point to their type of cognitivism as that against which the 'extreme' version of the practicality argument is directed or sketch similarities with Williams' otherwise spectral 'external reasons' theorists.

The method to be used is unusual. It consists in recovering, and recombining, elements of their neglected position which have become fragmented and dispersed into the other now more familiar positions, in particular into accidentalism and necessitarianism. Our source will be examples of this dispersal in the literature. Our investigation of these examples will show that dispersal often occurs in contexts where a powerful naturalistic assumption has been made: that the source of action necessarily lies in the subjective or internal states of agents. I shall therefore bring this 'subjectivist assumption' out into the open so that both its rejection and its acceptance can become legitimate moves in the debate.

I begin with W.D. Falk who, in 'Obligation and rightness' (1945), treats the moral rationalists and intuitionists as not relevantly different from the *accidentalists* for the purposes of his critique of theories of moral obligation. Later, I will scrutinize and resist attempts to assimilate them to the *necessitarians*.

2 Dispersal into accidentalism

(i) Résumé of Falk's argument

Falk, renowned[2] for having introduced into contemporary moral debate those now ubiquitous terms 'internal' and 'external', uses them with the meaning internal or external *to an agent,* to distinguish between two types of analysis of moral obligation. Those offering an 'internal fact' analysis hold that a moral agent must look inside herself – to her state of mind, feelings, motives – to discover whether she is obliged to act. 'External fact' analysts, however, require her to look outside herself – to an objective state of affairs. Falk illustrates the former by reference to Butler for whom, he states (1945: 129), to know that an act is our duty is to 'realize that our nature demands it of us'. Falk observes, however, that the 'external fact' analysts will differ as to how they identify the relevant objective state of affairs. Moral rationalists, such as Clarke, and moral intuitionists, such as Ross, will point to the possession by the required action of the peculiar and not further analysable property of 'fittingness' to the circumstances. Prichard, also an intuitionist, prefers to speak directly of an action's 'rightness' or 'obligatoriness' (coming later to regard it as mistaken to apply even these predicates to the action itself). Utilitarians by contrast will point to the action's capacity to maximize overall happiness or welfare.

Now a genuine account of obligation, Falk maintains (ibid.: 139–42), must do justice to certain familiar features of morality, such as, for instance, the close link between failing in a duty and feeling remorse. One of these, however, seems more fundamental than the rest. This is that we cannot believe ourselves, or indeed be, bound by a duty which we know we cannot reasonably be expected to fulfil. However, he claims, we can only reasonably be expected to fulfil a duty, if we have a motive, or 'incentive', for doing so. Now according to him only an 'internal fact' analysis can provide one. This is apparently because, if someone has an obligation to perform an action – say, to pay her bills or keep her promise – yet does not admit this, it will nevertheless, on the 'internal fact' analysis, already be true of her that she possesses a relevant 'inward disposition'. Indeed, having an obligation is, on the 'internal fact' analysis, a 'read[iness] on reflection' to do the required act. Until, however, an agent does reflect – perhaps at the instigation of others who merely serve to 'remind' [her] of what 'on reflection [she] must be prompted to do' – she will not experience this 'readiness', and so will lack the requisite motive. Consequently, it is not, for the internalists, the agent's belief that she has a duty to pay her bills, or keep her promise, which, all by itself, generates the action (how ever much it may superficially seem to be), but the 'inner' motive she has all along possessed, and whose discovery is her recognition of her duty.

By contrast, the 'external fact analysis', Falk argues (ibid.: 143), by severing the link with this (inner) motive, cut off an agent's recognition of his duty from 'the internal conditions which determine to action'. Falk has already (ibid.: 139) traced what he takes to be the disastrous and spiralling implications of this divorce for the externalists. To hold that an agent is not inwardly determined to action is to hold, he claims, that she is without a 'sufficient cause' for action. But if there exists no sufficient cause for her to act then, he claims, 'the thought of doing [her duty must] leave [her] totally unaffected' and so quite 'incapable of exerting [herself] in any particular direction'. But if she is really incapable of fulfilling her obligation no-one can reasonably expect her to, and so she is not *genuinely* obligated at all.

Nor, Falk claims (ibid.: 130–40), does it help for the externalists to remind us (as he claims does H.A. Ross) that a separate desire to keep her promise is also required. For surely, he argues, it is undeniable that she might lack this desire, and therefore that in these circumstances knowing that she ought to keep her promise will just leave her cold. But this is just to admit that it is not *essential* for an agent's judgements to influence her actions, and so to open the door for people to complain that they know they ought to keep their promise, and yet are still without any incentive to do so. In other words either the agent will have no motive, and so lacking a 'sufficient cause' for acting, she will be incapable of doing so, or she will have an extraneous motive resulting from her happening to have the relevant desire. Falk rejects such talk as completely at odds with ordinary moral discussion which, he writes (ibid.: 141), is 'commonly carried on in the belief that in proving our point, and having it assented to' we shall 'necessarily affect [each other's] inward attitude', and 'provide one another with motives'. Only the 'internal fact' analysis makes sense of that.

But in Falk's attack this accidentalism is never fully disentangled from another and deeper source of Humean concern which it obscures. This obscured feature, however, only belongs to some of the 'external fact' analysts whom Falk cites, in particular to moral intuitionists like Prichard, and is paradoxically bound up with their opposition to accidentalism. Though crucial for the coherence of his critique, it can only be brought to light by digging down beneath the surface of Falk's discussion, as I now proceed to do.

(ii) The 'subjectivist assumption' brought to light

At the core of Falk's attack appears to be the view that someone without an inner, or subjective, motive lacks a 'sufficient cause' to act, and so is incapable of doing so. Let us call the assumption made here, that the source of action must lie in the inner, or subjective, states of an agent, the 'subjectivist assumption'. Now two distinct responses towards it would seem possible on the part of the externalists.

More radically, they could reject the assumption. They would then assert that sometimes, as in the moral sphere, an action can be performed without the agent's having any relevant inner or subjective motive, and simply as a result of her having become aware of the (objective) property the action would possess if performed. She might have realized, for instance, that helping a friend down on her luck would be right or 'fitting' in the circumstances because it would repay an earlier act of kindness by the friend. Her motive for action therefore, residing wholly in this perceived rightness or 'fittingness' is, they would say, external. Less radically, they could accept the 'subjectivist assumption', pointing to a separate desire that happens to be present alongside the moral judgement when action occurs.

These different types of externalists could therefore be expected to draw down upon themselves correspondingly different types of objection from Falk. The more radical externalists would be taxed with being unable to explain how moral actions can come about at all (indeed, of coming perilously close to countenancing the absurdity of supposing that they could occur in the absence of a 'sufficient cause'). The less radical ones, however, would invite only the more moderate criticism that they cannot account for moral actions coming about necessarily. But of course it is a distinction precisely along these lines between just these two types of failure which would enable us to single out those cognitivists, who can qualify as targets of the practicality argument on the 'extreme' reading of premiss 2 from the accidentalists who are merely targets on the 'moderate' reading.

We must, however, do more than merely show that Falk's remarks provide, in the manner described above, a logical basis for discriminating between two types of externalist, each vulnerable to a different kind of objection. For it is a striking feature of his attack, as should be apparent from our résumé, that the more radical position we have described never emerges as fully distinct from the less radical variety. Indeed, in so far as Falk can be taken implicitly to recognize the former, he apparently subsumes it *under* the latter, and with it the criticism it would attract of failing to be able to account for any link at all between moral judgement and motivation. Correspondingly, the only shortcoming he overtly dwells on is that of rendering as merely contingent a supposedly necessary link. But this of course is just the shortcoming which we saw that the accidentalists are charged with by proponents of the 'moderate' version of the practicality argument. If we are therefore to push forward our work of retrieval and reclamation, we must show that this subsumption is not defensible.

Consider this defence, however: what is important for a theory of obligation, such as Falk's, is that the link between accepting a duty and acting upon it should be represented as necessary. Since the less radical externalists, by representing the link as contingent, fail to meet this requirement, *a fortiori* do those more radical ones who cannot account for a link at all. Consequently there is no need to mention them separately. But this immediately raises the question why the necessary/contingent distinction should be singled out as the relevant point of reference. Why not, for instance, that more fundamental assumption that the source of all action lies in an agent's subjective states? After all, it is because Falk makes this more fundamental assumption that he judges that the externalists are unable to account for the necessity of the link in question. Now whereas the more radical externalists (by definition) do not accept this assumption, Falkian internalists are united with the less radical externalists in accepting it. Hence, from this angle, it might now seem more appropriate to *contrast* the more radical externalists with both these latter groups, rather than subsuming them within *one* of the two groups, which are then contrasted with each other.

This reply, though unsatisfactory as it stands, in that it substitutes one apparently arbitrary reference point for another, contains the seeds of a better reply. For precisely because they make the subjectivist assumption, the less radical externalists are, I will now suggest, unable even to attempt the kind of analysis of obligation which would allow them to be legitimately compared with Falk's internalists. The real counterparts of these internalists, I will argue, are the more radical ones – those who in attempting to offer such an analysis risk failing (for Humeans) in that spectacular way which would mark them out as targets of the practicality argument on the 'extreme' reading of premiss 2. By letting them fall out of the picture, Falk, I will claim, jeopardizes the coherence of his whole critique.

(iii) Intuitionists and rationalists: the real counterparts of Falk's internalists

For Falk, as we have seen, being genuinely obligated entails the existence of a specially close link between moral judgement and action: we do our duty because, and solely because, we recognize it as our duty. But this in turn, according to him, requires that the fact which makes our judgement true, and which we become aware of in making the judgement, be represented as *itself* our motive for action. Let us call this analysis an 'obligation-constitutive' one, and contrast it with a merely 'belief-content' one, where the writer, sceptical about whether our moral judgement can ever genuinely obligate us, though again spelling out the kind of fact which, on his view, would make it true, does so now merely in an attempt to illuminate the judgement's content.

A utilitarian, for instance, will clarify the kind of judgement I am making when I say that I ought to keep my promise to my friend as one which is really about the maximization of overall welfare: it will be true if, and only if, keeping my promise is in this way optimal. At the same time she could quite consistently hold that, since no such external fact could (on her view) supply me with the requisite motive, I could never be genuinely obligated by recognizing that keeping my promise would maximize welfare. A 'belief-content' analysis therefore is not the same as a failed 'obligation-constitutive' one. For the 'obligation-constitutive' analyst, failing to make the fact she cites plausible as a motive, fails to do what the 'belief-content' analyst, given her scepticism, could not coherently even aim to do.

With the help of these two definitions, we can now say more precisely why the internalists meet with Falk's approval. First, they aim to give an 'obligation-constitutive', and not a merely 'belief-content', analysis, the close link between moral judgement and action being secured by their identification of the (internal) fact, which makes the judgement true, with the relevant motive. But, second, this identification, according to Falk, actually *succeeds*. The fact cited – the agent's 'readiness on reflection' to act in the required way – a readiness which the agent *experiences* in recognizing her duty – is, Falk thinks (1945: 142), completely plausible as a motive. Let us now compare the more and less radical externalists in these respects.

It is of course precisely because the less radical externalists share with Falk's internalists the subjectivist assumption that they are obliged to maintain that no-one can do her duty, as distinct from knowing it, unless she also happens to have a relevant desire. But since whether an agent has this desire is a contingent matter, it becomes impossible, as we saw, for them, without patently contradicting their accidentalism, to represent moral judgements as entailing action, as do the internalists. For them the fact which, they would claim, makes these judgements true, simply *cannot* itself, however plainly recognized by the agent, supply her with the requisite motive. But then it is hard to see how they could coherently be said *even to aim* to represent it in this way. But then they are not failed 'obligation-constitutive' analysts, but merely successful 'belief-content' ones. Keeping these positions distinct, we must surely conclude that Falk, in comparing with his 'obligation-constitutive' internalists, externalists who can offer at best only a 'belief-content' analysis of moral judgements, is criticizing these externalists for something they could not even be *trying* to do.

Two observations are worth making here. First, many who would fall into our category of less radical externalists, such as certain recent utilitarians, openly admit that it is only 'after a manner of speaking', or 'courtesy of desire', that moral judgements can be said to give us reasons, or hence make the corresponding actions obligatory. They therefore seem to *invite* the interpretation that they aim merely to elucidate the content of these judgements, and accept what they take to be the negative implications for a genuinely 'obligation-constitutive' externalism. There are others, however, such as Ross (1939) – Falk's chief example of an externalist – who (as Falk portrays him) does not apparently think through these negative implications of his accidentalism. Here therefore, in so far as he can intelligibly be described as aspiring to provide an 'obligation-constitutive' analysis, he must seem, by Falk's own lights, confused.

Turning to the more radical externalists, the situation could scarcely be more different. Since they do not make the subjectivist assumption, they would be no more likely than Falkian internalists to perceive any need to interpose desire – a source of contingency – between the recognition of a duty and motivation. However, to leave it at that would misleadingly understate their radicalism. For, expressed positively, their rejection of the subjectivist assumption *is* the substitution, in the moral sphere, of an external motive for an internal, subjective one. Moreover, they locate this moral motive in that property of an action which they would cite in establishing the truth of the corresponding judgement. Thus, in our earlier example of the fulfilment of a duty, as interpreted by the more radical externalists, a person realizes that helping a friend down on her luck would be the only right or fitting response in the circumstances, because it would repay an earlier act of kindness by the friend. She is then (according to these externalists) directly moved by this perceived rightness or 'fittingness' to offer the help. Since, however, we have here the essential ingredients of an 'obligation-constitutive' analysis, we must surely conclude that attempting it is not merely logically open to a more radical externalist, but part of what it means to be one. Therefore, they are, and not the less radical externalists, the real counterparts of Falk's internalists.

But, it may now be objected, that the more radical externalists are necessarily committed to giving an 'obligation-constitutive' analysis is hardly surprising: it was built into our original definition of them. Are there, it will be asked, any actual writers falling into our hypothetical category? And if so, do they explicitly offer the more ambitious analysis, so inviting the charge that they are unable to account for any link at all between moral judgement and motivation? Or are they perhaps as confused about the implications of their more radical position, as Ross evidently was about his less radical externalism?

But our definition of the more radical externalism was already guided by features of actual writers, in particular moral rationalists, such as Clarke, and moral intuitionists like Prichard. We never made any secret of the fact. It is just, as was stated earlier, that these features have, in the context of recent discussions of the practicality argument, been largely lost sight of, with the consequence that the writers themselves have been erroneously assimilated to accidentalists, propounding a less radical externalism. It has been necessary therefore to spell out their distinctively more radical position in order to remedy the error.

(iv) Their dispersal into accidentalism prevented

(a) Prichard's 'external motive'

Prichard's more radical externalism is most clearly evident in possibly his best-known paper 'Does moral philosophy rest on a mistake?' ([1912] 1968) There, in the course of giving an affirmative answer to the title question, he describes an experience which he believes will be familiar to any reflective person who has reached a certain stage in his moral development. Struck by the peculiar irksomeness of carrying out his obligations and the sacrifice of interest involved, this person poses to himself these questions:

> Is there really a reason why I should act in the ways which hitherto I have thought I ought to act? May I not have been all the time under an illusion in so thinking? Should not I really be justified in simply trying to have a good time?
>
> (1968: 1)

But, says Prichard, he is also the kind of person who feels that somehow he ought to do what is right, and so asks for 'a *proof* that this feeling is justified'. In the part of his treatment relevant here, Prichard considers one typical response of moral philosophers to this self-questioning or questioning of moral philosophers. They try to convince the questioner that, once he fully apprehends the relevant facts, he will see that it is advantageous to him – even that it will lead to his happiness – to perform the required action. Prichard, however, exploits what he sees as the manifest irrelevance of this response in order to drive home the mutual exclusivity of the ideas of doing something because one has been brought to want to, and doing it because one is convinced one ought to. The questioner, he claims, is seeking reasons for accepting the validity of his sense of obligation, not inducements for doing his duty once he has acknowledged it. Thus even if the answer 'makes [her] want to keep [her engagements]' she might still complain that 'though [she has] lost [her] hesitation to act in these ways [she will] not recover [her] sense that [she] ought to do so' (ibid.: 3). Prichard rejects any answer which in 'substituting desire or inclination for the sense of obligation' (ibid.: 4), aims to point out some feature of the required action, even its intrinsic goodness, which will 'necessarily arouse the desire for it'. The questioner, he suggests, implicitly recognizes what the philosophers who give the answer fail to: that the sense of obligation, once restored, will if he is properly morally responsive, suffice on its own to move him to action. Of such a person, Prichard writes (ibid.: 7): 'To feel that [one] ought to pay [one's] bills is to be *moved towards* paying them' (Prichard's italics).

It is important to be clear that Prichard is suggesting here that there is something inimical to moral obligation in the whole notion of desire, and not just in
interested desires, but also in disinterested desires. Thus, he only ever speaks of the
'sense of duty' or 'sense of obligation' moving us to action. Still more crucially, he
marks off (ibid.: 3) a sense of duty or obligation, as belonging to the category of the
impersonal and objective, from desire. Indeed far from its resembling a desire of any
kind, he describes (ibid.: 4) recognizing a duty as 'feeling the imperative[ness] of an
action upon us'. He goes further (ibid.: 10–11). We have, he points out, when acting
from a sense of obligation 'no purpose or end'. But for him this is just to say that
there is nothing 'the existence of which we desire, and desire for which leads us to
act'. More generally, he rejects the view that any deliberate action must have a
purpose in so far as this just means that it must be done from some desire. He
substitutes the (for him) correct view that every deliberate action must have a
motive. But the implication of this is that not all motives are desires. He concludes
that the sense of obligation in prompting action is one such:

> . . . we mean by a motive what moves us to act. A sense of obligation does
> sometimes move us to act; and in our ordinary consciousness we should not
> hesitate to allow that the action we were considering might have had as its
> motive a sense of obligation. Desire and the sense of obligation are co-ordinate
> forms or species of motive.

But Prichard does not just resist what he calls (ibid.: 3) the 'resolution of obligation
into inclination', which as we have seen is a feature of *less* radical externalism. He
also resists the identification of the sense of obligation, despite its pivotal motivational role, with any distinctive subjective experience, such as that felt 'readiness to
act' on which in turn the Falkian internalists rely. Rather it is, for him, as for the
other more radical externalists, the apprehension of a self-evident truth concerning
the possession by the relevant action of the given relational predicate.

As far as the original question is concerned: it is only, Prichard maintains
(ibid.: 8–9, 15–17), legitimate at all where a particular obligation has been
incompletely stated. Suppose, for instance, that I am told that I ought to take my
aunt to the theatre, and when I ask why, I am reminded that I made a promise to
her to do so. I now turn back to moral rationalists, such as Clarke, and Hume's
critique of them.

(b) Clarke and Hume revisited

Having observed (3.1.1:4,17) that the moral rationalists locate 'the distinction
betwixt moral good and evil' in the 'eternal immutable fitnesses and unfitnesses of
things', Hume points out, as we saw, that they therefore take this distinction to be
'susceptible of demonstration'. Thus, he effectively assigns them to what we have
called (following Falk) the category of external, as opposed to internal, fact, analysts.
(Here, the relevant truth-making 'fact' is, of course, the 'eternal, immutable' relation
of 'fitness' or 'unfitness' of the required action to the circumstances.) To show,

however, that his criticism is precisely and narrowly relevant to them as *more* radical externalists, who aspire to give an 'obligation-constitutive', and not a merely 'belief-content', analysis of moral judgements, we must turn to the second prong of his attack on them.

In the more frequently discussed first prong (3.1.1:19–21), Hume has cast doubt on whether there could exist this relation of 'fitness' and 'unfitness' of actions to circumstances in which, for the moral rationalists, 'the essence of [virtue and] vice consists'. In the second prong, he argues (3.1.1:22) that, even were this conceded, even if indeed their 'fitness' or 'unfitness' was self-evident to any rational agent who contemplated the relevant actions, 'it will be still more difficult to fulfil [a] *second* condition, requisite to justify this system':

Hume thus turns his critical attention in this passage, as we shall recall from Chapter 3, to the moral rationalists' view concerning the necessary *practical* implications of affirming that an action has the requisite relation of 'fitness' or 'unfitness' to the circumstances. Crucial to his attack here is his assertion that knowing virtue and conforming the will to it are 'two particulars . . . evidently distinct'. As I pointed out earlier, it is tempting to take this as a refutation of the moral rationalists' claim that recognizing an action's fitness and being moved to perform it are bound together necessarily. How could this be, Hume would then be asking, when – and here we would supply the missing premiss – their distinctness precludes anything other than a causal, or contingent, link?

Significantly, however, when Hume *explicitly* refers, in this passage, to the necessary connexion, postulated by the moral rationalists, he speaks of it as holding, *not* between the agent's *recognition* of the relation of fitness and the will, but between *the relation of fitness itself,* and the will. But for the moral rationalists of course this relation (holding in its turn between an action and its circumstances) has an existence independently of the agent. It inheres, as Clarke put it, in 'the reason and nature of things'. Nor is their emphasis on its objectivity surprising when, as Hume himself points out, it is the relation on which, for them, 'the [eternal] measures of right and wrong' are 'founded'. Consequently, it would seem that the necessary connexion to which Hume is objecting is not one which holds, as his 'distinctness' claim might have led us to believe, between two subjective states of the agent's, one cognitive and one motivational. Rather, it holds between an objective fact – that very 'relation' of fitness of an action to its circumstances whose existence guarantees the truth of the corresponding moral judgement – and a subjective state.

Equipped with this revised, and more extreme, picture of the position that Hume is here seeking to refute, we can now appreciate the more oblique role actually played by his 'distinctness claim'. For Hume seems to be arguing as follows. Even if the moral rationalists had conclusively shown that an action's fitness to its circumstances was necessarily evident to any rational person, they would still not have shown that such a person would also *ipso facto* be moved to perform that action. For to recognize that something is the case – as they construe 'know[ing] virtue' – is not the same as 'to conform the will to it'. The first is a purely theoretical matter, the second practical, and the two cannot simply be conflated. If they wish therefore to convince us – and here I quote Hume again – that the 'connexion [betwixt the relation and the will] is so necessary, that in every well-disposed mind, it must take place and have its influence', they will have to establish this second claim, independently of the first. But since it is difficult to conceive of there being any direct connexion *at all*, let alone a necessary one, between such heterogeneous elements as an objective state of affairs and a subjective psychological state, their task looks insuperable.

In light of our earlier discussions, it would be hard not to conclude that the moral rationalists, as Hume (correctly) depicts them in this passage, belong within the category of more radical externalists, offering an 'obligation-constitutive' analysis of moral judgements. If the question is raised – but do they, as Hume represents them, deliberately aim to offer this more ambitious analysis – the answer is that they certainly seem to. For Hume not only attributes to them the express aim of demonstrating that morality is *'obligatory* on every rational mind' (his italics), but recognizes that they could only achieve this by placing the source of moral motivation beyond the vagaries of individual circumstance and temperament in an 'abstract rational difference', self-evident to such minds. It is this move, entailing as it does the rejection of what we earlier called the 'subjectivist assumption' – namely, the assumption that the source of all action lies in the inner or subjective states of an agent – which, it would seem, is what incurs Hume's scorn and incredulity.

Since the less radical externalists, as we saw earlier, accept the 'subjectivist assumption', we can only conclude that if they were the object of Hume's attack here, and if he thought that the moral rationalists belonged in this category, it would be impossible to explain the criticisms he brings against them in the above quotation. They would simply be inapplicable. But this is a finding of some importance. For it follows that Hume himself is here preoccupied with the more, not the less, radical externalism. It is only later Humeans who, apparently overlooking what Hume actually says, have somehow reversed this order of preoccupation, bringing the less radical externalism to the fore, and sidelining the more radical. At the same time, of course, they have switched round Hume's and his opponents' views concerning the link between moral judgement and motivation. Thus it is now frequently in Hume's name that contemporary non-cognitivists insist that moral judgements are intrinsically motivating against their accidentalist opponents. But this as we saw was as much to do with the constraints on showing that the argument was valid in the 'moderate' version as anything more reputable.

3 Dispersal into necessitarianism

(i) Morality's special authority again: 'distance' and 'directness'

The moral rationalists and intuitionists are, we have argued, more radical externalists aspiring to give an 'obligation-constitutive' rather than a merely 'belief-content' analysis of moral judgements. But this is just to say – again in our terminology – that they posit external motives. It is in giving credence to such motives that they become targets of the 'extreme' version of the practicality argument.

Now in order to distinguish these more radical externalists from the less radical ones with whom Falk confuses them it has been necessary to identify the two elements of which the notion of an external motive is composed, and which have been pulled apart in recent writings. One of these is the claim that a moral judgement is made true by an external fact, where 'external' is understood in the Falkian sense of external to the agent. Had moral rationalists and intuitionists stopped at this claim they would have qualified, like utilitarians and other accidentalists, as less radical externalists, offering a mere 'belief-content' analysis of moral judgements. Nevertheless the existence of that crucial normative gap between moral judgements and motivation (see Chapter 6) would already have been ensured: a gap which, as we saw earlier, widens in proportion as the agent finds the required action unappealing. The other element which, added to the first, qualifies these more radical writers as 'obligation-constitutive' externalists is their claim that the external fact, which makes a moral judgement true, can *directly* motivate the agent. It is thus that they violate the subjectivist assumption.

But we shall immediately recognize in these two claims the 'distance' and 'directness' requirements of Chapter 6. There we suggested that these requirements must be met by any account of the relation between moral judgements and motivation which aims to do justice to morality's special authority. Accidentalists, we shall recall, breach the 'directness' requirement by interposing an independent desire between moral judgements and motivation. Necessitarians, on the other hand, breach the 'distance' requirement. They do so, we argued, by construing moral judgement as itself a desire, or as a belief which is conceptually equivalent to a desire in that it is the agent's having this belief which explains why she finds a given course of action appealing. This appealing character, without which, on this view, it seems even a moral action cannot ultimately be explained, contradicts the idea that moral judgements have an essentially peremptory character.

Now, so far in this chapter, I have sought to restore to the rationalists' and intuitionists' conception of the relation between moral judgement and motivation that 'directness' ignored by Falk when conflating these more radical externalists with accidentalists. But we have seen how the rationalists and intuitionists also seek to meet the 'distance' requirement: how, that is, they endeavour to preserve the crucial normative gap between moral judgement and motivation. Can we find in recent literature an attempt to conflate their more radical position this time with necessitarianism, so ignoring their concern with the 'distance' requirement?

(ii) Has the 'extreme' version contemporary relevance?

Particularly germane here is M. Smith's rendering (in *The Moral Problem*, 1994) of the relation between moral judgement and motivation which, I shall argue, is at heart necessitarian. In his opening pages Smith describes a seemingly 'incoherent' position which, he suggests (ibid.: 11), we may find ourselves drawn to adopt in the attempt to hold on to our ordinary conception of moral judgements as beliefs while ascribing to them a direct motivational force. But this position, involving the postulation of 'a strange sort of fact about the universe: a fact whose recognition

necessarily impacts upon our desires', is unmistakably that of our more radical externalists seen through the eyes of an incredulous or scornful naturalist – a proponent of
the 'extreme' version of the practicality argument.

Now in attempting to answer the challenge which, according to him, the practicality argument poses for cognitivism, Smith first appears to be preparing to defend
this more radical version by showing that it is not so incoherent after all. However,
he actually answers a variant of the 'moderate' objection. Consequently he does not
quarrel fundamentally with what he calls (ibid.: 9) the 'standard [Humean] picture
of human psychology', which precludes such 'strange facts' with their direct motivating force, and apparent independence of an agent's subjective psychological states.
He merely quarrels over whether ordinary subjective motivation must involve a
belief *plus* an independent desire, maintaining that a belief can on its own produce
the requisite desire. (This of course is a view which, as we saw in Part I, Hume
almost certainly shared.)

The question for us concerns, just as it did with Falk's article, the legitimacy of
what is effectively a subsumption of the more radical cognitivism of the rationalists
and intuitionists under a less radical cognitivism, though one which this time has
more in common with necessitarianism than with accidentalism. Now Smith (ibid.:
136–7) sees as clearly as the rationalists and intuitionists (and more clearly than
many non-cognitivists and necessitarians) the importance of meeting the 'distance' as
well as the 'directness' requirement. Moreover, he takes this first requirement to be
integrally bound up with the claim that moral judgements are beliefs whose truth
depends upon (in Falk's sense) an external fact.

Plainly, therefore, if he succeeds in meeting both requirements, while holding
to the subjectivist assumption and resisting the introduction of external motives,
he will have at the very least made redundant the more radical cognitivism. But it
is precisely the more radical cognitivism which we have singled out as the target of
the 'extreme' version of the practicality argument. Of course, we could continue, if
we liked, to describe those who propounded it as targets of the 'extreme' rather
than the 'moderate' version. But who, it will be inquired, will bother except as a
historical exercise any longer to attack such a position? Our attempts then to
bring back into view a more radical cognitivism, rescuing it from philosophical
oblivion, and suggesting that it is precisely the attack on this kind of position
which accounts even today for the real power of the practicality argument, will
have been in vain.

I identify below some major difficulties with Smith's attempt to meet the two
requirements and so to do justice to the idea of morality's special authority. At the
same time I observe that the fact that he (like other notable writers) goes to such
ingenious lengths to recreate the conditions inside a naturalistic account for morality
to have this special authority is a remarkable testament to the seriousness with
which even naturalists approach this notion.

First, I pause to clarify the different uses of the term 'internalism' and 'externalism'. In particular, I relate Falk's use of the terms, which we have carried over
into our own discussions, and which will prove helpful again in expounding Smith,
to the way these terms are typically used today.

(iii) The terms 'internalism' and 'externalism'

Possibly the most common use of the terms today is in the expressions *moral belief* internalism and externalism. Here they signify no more than the views, respectively, that moral judgements are necessarily, and contingently, related to motivation. In other words they signify our necessitarianism and accidentalism. *Moral* internalism (or externalism) is the view that a necessary (or contingent) relation holds between an agent's *actually having* an obligation to act in a certain way (as opposed to just believing she has), and her being motivated (after the requisite deliberation) to do so.

When writers expound either of these types of internalism (or externalism) they standardly, as I pointed out in an earlier note, cite Falk as the source of their usage. But this we can already see is misleading. For though Falk may indeed have been the first philosopher in modern times to have used this terminology, he means something crucially different by it from these more recent writers. As we have seen when he speaks of an 'internal fact', or an 'external fact', analysis of obligation he means that the facts referred to are internal, or external, *to the agent.* In other words, for him the fact which makes a moral judgement true is on an 'internal fact' analysis a subjective psychological state of the agent whereas, on an 'external fact' analysis it is, an objective feature of the world outside her. Falk does not therefore use the terms, as writers now do, merely to characterize a relation holding between two terms (most typically moral judgement and motivation) as necessary or contingent. Just how easy it is to miss this vital difference, and how totally it has been missed, is plain from the absence of any acknowledgement of it in much recent writing, even where Falk is himself described as a moral internalist.

Now there *is* a relation between Falk's 'internal fact' and 'external fact' analyses of moral obligation, on the one hand, and, on the other, the various internalisms and externalisms which have in current discussion supplanted the original distinction. However, it is not a straightforward one. Crucially, our more radical 'external fact' analysts have been swallowed up in the transition from the earlier to the later usages. Nor is this surprising. As we saw Falk himself failed to appreciate that it is *their* position, and not that of the less radical accidentalists, with whom he conflated them, which is the real counterpart among 'external fact' analyses of his own 'internal fact' analysis. Accordingly, the only alternative to moral belief externalism – the view that moral judgements are merely contingently related to motivation – is now a moral belief internalism which makes the relation one of logical entailment. Accidentalism and necessitarianism, in other words, between them now apparently exhaust the possibilities.

It is true that if moral judgement logically entails motivation then, necessarily, the relation between the two is direct. One of the two requirements stipulated above for talk of morality's special authority is therefore met by those postulating such a link, namely, that motivation is not dependent on a relevant desire just happening to be present. However, the 'directness' requirement, as we have called it, can in principle be secured without going so far as to represent the relation in question as one of logical entailment. More radical 'external fact' theorists hold, as we have seen, that *if* we act on our moral judgement the external fact which makes this judgement true itself serves as our motive, while acknowledging that we may choose to act otherwise. Moreover, unless we detach 'directness' from logical entailment in this way, as we saw in Chapter 6, we destroy 'distance' – the other requirement for talk of morality's special authority.

Should we call these more radical 'external fact' theorists moral belief *internalists*? In so far as such writers are mentioned at all – Prichard is the one usually cited – current orthodoxy, making explicit the conflation implicit in Falk's account, seems to dictate that they be treated as moral belief externalists (see, for instance, Stratton-Lake, 1999). It is imperative, however, if we are to hold on to the distinction which we have recovered between them and the accidentalists that we contradict this orthodoxy and assert that they *are* moral belief internalists. We should nevertheless take care not to go to the other extreme and allow them to become conflated with the necessitarians. I propose therefore an amendment of current usage. Moral belief internalists will, properly understood, claim that a *direct* relation holds between moral judgements and motivation, one that does not require the interposition of an independent desire. One sub-group of these (the necessitarians) will, however, maintain that the relation involved is one of actual logical entailment.[3]

Once we admit moral intuitionists like Prichard among the ranks of moral belief internalists, we have to acknowledge that this type of internalism bears a different relation to the 'internal fact' analysis of obligation from that which moral belief externalism bears to the 'external fact' analysis. It does not follow, for instance, from the claim (of moral belief internalists) that there is a direct link between moral judgement and motivation that having a given obligation either does or does not involve reference to a subjective dispositional state of the agent's. The claim is thus far neutral between the 'internal fact' and 'external fact' analyses.

Moral belief externalists, on the other hand, hold that the relation between moral judgement and motivation is merely contingent precisely because they subscribe to an *'external* fact' analysis of obligation. They do not see how a belief about a state of affairs existing in the world outside the agent could without help from an independent desire influence action. Moral belief externalism is therefore more properly seen as the solution to a problem, whereas moral belief internalism is frequently regarded (at least by naturalists seeking to embrace it) as posing a problem.

Falk is himself typical of these naturalists in arguing thus: only if an agent's having an obligation were a matter of her already being, whether she knows it or not, psychologically disposed to act in the relevant ways could the necessary link between her accepting a moral judgement and acting upon it be explained. Otherwise a 'separate impulse' would be required, and so 'thinking ourselves obliged' could not *ipso facto* impel us 'to do what we think we ought to do' (Falk, 1945: 139), and moral belief externalism would have to be embraced. Falk is therefore a moral belief internalist who sees his 'internal fact' analysis of obligation as the only way of shoring up this position, though of course 'internalist' and 'internal' have here quite different senses.

As I observed, Falk has been described by some writers (Stratton-Lake, 1999: 79) as a moral internalist. As is easily deducible from the previous paragraph, he is a moral internalist as well as a moral belief internalist (as we are now using these terms). However, for him it is only by accepting an 'internal fact' analysis of moral obligation that he finds it possible to adopt either of these other stances, neither of which is identical with it. We shall not be tempted to forget this so long as we keep before our minds that for those – like e.g. Prichard – for whom their moral belief internalism is not a problem this very position is included within a larger 'external fact' analysis of moral obligation.

Let us finally note, returning now to current unamended usage, that some writers, replacing 'moral' in the expression 'moral internalism' with the broader term 'reasons', construe 'reasons internalism' and 'reasons externalism' in a parallel way to the more narrowly circumscribed moral internalism and externalism. Thus, 'reasons internalists' hold that the only reasons there are can be motivating reasons – or, put differently, that if I have a reason to perform a given action, then I have either an occurrent or a dispositional motive to do so. A 'reasons externalist', on the other hand, denies that there is any such close connection between having a reason and being motivated. Now Smith (1994) posits normative, as well as motivating, reasons, normative reasons being those which, even when the agent recognizes that she has them, are not necessarily matched by corresponding motivations. This characterization is, as we shall see, integral to his attempt to introduce 'distance' into the relation between moral judgement and motivation, where moral judgement is understood as a belief that one has a special sort of normative reason to act in the required way.

(iv) Why necessitarians cannot ensure 'distance'

Smith's notion of a normative reason is not, however, independent of his notion of a motivating one. For, first, this reason is normative for *imperfectly* rational agents only because it necessarily would motivate *perfectly* rational ones in similar circumstances. Second, its actually motivating, on the intermittent occasions when it does, imperfectly rational agents is itself a causal consequence of their realizing that it would motivate them if they were perfectly rational (Smith, 1994: 151–61, 177–81). We shall now see how, by switching in this way between perfectly and imperfectly rational agents, Smith might claim to be able to meet both the 'distance' and the 'directness' requirements. We will then consider some objections.

For Smith, to believe that one ought to keep a promise is, we noted above, to believe that one has a normative reason to do so. But this in turn is to believe that were one a perfectly rational agent one would necessarily, after the requisite deliberation, desire and so be motivated to keep the promise. The truth of such moral judgements thus seems to depend upon the possession by perfectly rational agents of the relevant psychological dispositions. But this is to endorse something like a Falkian 'internal fact' analysis of moral obligation for perfectly rational agents. But ordinary agents are imperfectly rational. The fact which makes *their* moral judgements true is consequently situated outside them in the psyche of perfectly rational agents. It would seem therefore that Smith can offer an 'external fact' analysis of moral obligation for imperfectly rational agents and so meet the 'distance' requirement for them.

An objection may now be raised concerning the fulfilment this time of the 'directness' requirement for these imperfectly rational agents. The fact which for Smith makes their moral judgements true is, we suggested, the possession by perfectly rational agents of the relevant psychological dispositions. But how can a fact about the psychology of a perfectly rational agent, even when an imperfectly rational one acknowledges it directly motivate her? Why, as one critic puts it (Hurka, 1995: 31), 'should a belief about a desire I do not have move me to action?' If, on the other hand, I could be moved to act directly by my moral judgement must I not already myself possess the requisite psychological disposition to do so? But wouldn't this now make it impossible to fulfil the 'distance' requirement?

An answer along these lines might be suggested. Merely idealized versions of ourselves, lacking any of our flaws and defects, are not in a certain sense us at all. Smith speaks of them metaphorically (1994: 151) as 'looking down on ourselves as we actually are from their more privileged position'. But this picture makes it natural to talk of our only reluctantly trying to live up to these idealized selves by acting morally as they would do. Why, we might ask rebelliously, should we do what we don't want to do whatever our fully rational selves might want us to do? In this way, it may seem that the 'distance' requirement can after all be safeguarded.

At the same time, however, these idealized agents are just more rational versions *of ourselves*. So we may also be inclined in cooler and more dispassionate moods to acknowledge them as (in Smith's words: ibid.: 151) 'the best people to give ourselves advice'. But this makes it plausible to suppose that sometimes our moral beliefs, just because they are beliefs about what we ourselves in our wiser, more circumspect, moments would want to do, can influence us. But if my belief that I ought to tell the truth can by itself arouse in me a desire to act in the relevant way, then no independent desire need be invoked, and the requisite 'directness' is also safeguarded.

Critics will feel, however, that this defence of Smith misses the point. They are mystified, they will say, at how any belief can just like that give rise to a desire. But this is surely because they are confusing an attempt to vindicate the naturalistic cognitivism at which the 'moderate' version of the practicality argument is directed with an attempt to vindicate the metaphysical cognitivism that is the object of the 'extreme' version. They have misinterpreted Smith's claim that certain beliefs, in particular moral ones, can engender desires as a plea for the recognition of – in his own striking description – that 'strange sort of fact about the universe . . . whose recognition necessarily impacts upon our desires'. But Smith spells out the content of moral beliefs precisely in order to make motivation by them seem psychologically credible. They are no longer about the objective 'fitness' of actions to circumstances posited by rationalists and intuitionists but rather about what we would desire if we were perfectly rational. He thus neither jettisons the naturalistic assumption nor invokes external motives (as he himself effectively points out, ibid.: 199–200, in his section: 'Mackie's objections').

Again, it is worth remembering that the claim that a belief can sometimes arouse a desire is no more than Hume himself was prepared on many occasions to accept. Of course for him belief and desire, as distinct existences, could not be necessarily connected. But with imperfectly rational agents Smith only posits a contingent connection between these distinct existences. Belief and desire are of course necessarily connected in the case of perfectly rational agents, but then they cease for Smith to be distinct existences.

It must be conceded that the confusion of the critics is to some extent understandable. For Smith never explicitly distinguishes, as we have done, between the practicality argument as a source of 'moderate' and 'extreme' objections to cognitivism. Mainly, as we have observed, he addresses himself to the former. Sometimes – not only on the occasion already noted, but even quite late in his book – he describes his position in terms which suggest that he is defending it against something much closer to the 'extreme' objection. So for instance he suggests (ibid.: 137) that to claim as he does that beliefs can produce action will be opposed on grounds that beliefs are 'simply inert representations of how things are'.

(v) Intuitionists and rationalists again: their dispersal into necessitarianism prevented

It is important for us to keep the two objections apart. We will not then be tempted to assume that Smith, in defending naturalistic cognitivism, has automatically incorporated into it anything worth saving from the metaphysical cognitivism of moral rationalists and intuitionists, which simply therefore drops out of the picture. On the contrary, we will keep before us this alternative account of how 'distance' and 'directness' can be met as a model against which to measure Smith's naturalistic solutions. But this will immediately reveal some striking disparities. For instance, as we have just suggested, Smith reconstructs the content of moral beliefs so as to show how the required course of action might in some sense appeal to the agent: if she were wiser, more perfect, she would want to pursue it. But this will remind us of the attempt by cognitivists such as McNaughton (1988) to point to the agent's beliefs in order to bring out the attractions for her of the required action. But we argued that he thereby made it difficult to fulfil the 'distance' requirement so crucial to the notion of morality's special authority.

It will be replied that 'distance' is preserved on Smith's account, as it is not on McNaughton's because, as was observed earlier, we only identify ourselves partially or intermittently with the selves we would be if we were perfectly rational. But surely this makes the fulfilment of the 'distance' requirement dependent upon an uneasy equivocation over whether or not we are our idealized selves? There is, however, a further still more important disparity. Integral to the idea of a moral judgement's peremptoriness is the possibility not merely of the agent being reluctant to obey it but of her actually disobeying it, and so incurring both blame and self-reproach. But this presupposes (see Chapter 6) a conception of the agent as in some sense free to have chosen otherwise than she does. But it is doubtful whether any such freedom can be accommodated within Smith's account.

Suppose I really believe that I morally ought (and so have normative reason) to behave in a certain way. Smith seems to envisage only two possibilities. One is that I am a fully rational agent in which case I necessarily will desire, and be motivated, to act in the required way. The other is that I will not desire or be motivated to act in that way, in which case I am apparently not 'a rational evaluator' (1994: 138). But for Smith those who are not 'rational evaluators' are 'depressives or compulsives or whatever whose depression or compulsion has caused them, irrationally, to desire other than what they think they have normative reason to do'. Moreover, he writes that:

> Desires are irrational to the extent that they are *wholly and solely* the product of psychological compulsions, physical addictions, emotional disturbances and the like; to the extent that they wouldn't be had by someone in a non-depressed, non-addictive, non-emotionally disturbed state.
>
> (ibid.: 155, Smith's italics)

His examples only emphasize this link between practical irrationality and pathology. One set illustrates the situation where agents are motivated to do what they believe they have normative reason *not* to do. Here he cites (ibid.: 154) Ayer's kleptomaniac, Frankfurt's heroin addict and Watson's mother who succumbs to a sudden urge to drown her screaming baby.[4] The other set illustrates the situation of those who are not motivated to do what they believe they have normative reason to do. Here he cites (ibid.; 155) Stocker's depressives who are variously suffering from 'spiritual tiredness, accidie or illness'. The ordinary morally weak person or the defiant amoralist whom, as we suggested earlier, are typically regarded (and regard themselves) as free to have chosen and done otherwise are no more in evidence here than in Hare's account (see Chapter 6).

This is not to say that Smith dismisses the importance of rational deliberation. On the contrary, he is keen to stress what a difference it can make. A person, for instance, who before she began deliberating, desired to act in a way which she would later have regretted now, after deliberation, desires and acts with the wisdom and foresight of a fully rational agent. But then her original desires were not presumably pathological ones. For if they had been, no amount of thinking through her situation, or coming to conclusions about what a fully rational agent would desire, and so what she herself ought to desire, could have altered her actual desires: only treatment would help.

Smith makes it clear (ibid.: 137) that the appeal to these 'deviant' cases is nevertheless not a merely peripheral matter but goes to 'the heart of the debate'. The existence of these cases show, he maintains (ibid.: 136), how 'accepting normative reason claims' – and more particularly moral judgements – though being '*bound up with* having desires', can '*come apart from* having desires' (Smith's italics). It is in this way that he evidently hopes to meet (what we have called) the 'directness' and 'distance' requirements, and so safeguard the idea of morality's special authority.

But the 'distance' for which he makes room by invoking these pathological behaviours is not the right kind of distance. It renders morality's inherent practical authority either redundant – the fully rational agent necessarily will desire and act in the required way – or ineffectual. For it is a foregone conclusion that the irrational agent – the agent who is suffering from a compulsion or crippling depression – is incapable of conforming his desires and actions to his moral judgements. 'The puzzle here,' says Smith (ibid.: 136) 'is a deep one'. But this is because 'directness' and 'distance' must be elements in the *same* relation. For Smith, however, it seems that either moral judgements logically entail motivating desires as with fully rational agents or, as with irrational ones, there is a total breakdown. Smith seeks nevertheless to incorporate both elements into the one relation. He does so by speaking (ibid.: 12) of there being a 'necessary connection of sorts' between moral judgements and motivation to indicate that it is sometimes broken. But it is difficult to see how such a compendious description is warranted. He speaks it is true of people being sometimes more, sometimes less, rational. But if we were to try somehow to incorporate pockets of irrationality into his picture of the otherwise fully rational agent it is difficult to see how these pockets could be anything else but just that.

(vi) Desperate mother and screaming baby

There is, however, another question which though bearing more indirectly on our concerns is so fundamental to Smith's strategy that something should be said about it. Smith's account of the relation between moral judgement and motivation is possibly best seen as resting on a form of reasons internalism. It is a reasons internalism, however, which, when qualified to cover deviations from the norm of rational conduct, permits indeed requires the postulation of normative reasons as a distinct category from motivating ones. (Moral judgements are then taken, as we have seen, to be a special kind of normative reason claim.) But does reasons internalism itself – the view that to have a reason to perform an action, S, is to have an occurrent or dispositional motive to S – really require, or even permit, this qualification to cover deviant cases? The question of whether the theory permits this qualification is really the question of how – unless it is just another way of talking about motivating reasons – a notion of normative reasons can be derived from *within* the theory and not merely imposed upon it from outside. The answer will become clear as we deal with the other question: whether the theory actually requires Smith's qualification.

Smith must first show that reasons internalism is in need of the revision he proposes. This he can only do if he can establish that the deviant behaviour he points to is a genuine counter-example to the original unrevised theory. If the theory can just as it stands cope with such behaviour there will be no rationale for undertaking the revisions. I now suggest that these deviant behaviours can only be represented as counter-examples to the theory by so altering it that its proponents can no longer be taken to posit a necessary relation even between the normative judgements of rational agents and motivation. However, as we saw, Smith needs to preserve intact this central part of the theory. For, according to him, it is the only way of guaranteeing that the normative judgements accepted by irrational agents can still be counted as reasons for them, or of maintaining a 'necessary connection of sorts' between these judgements and motivation. In developing my argument, I will concentrate on Smith's critique (ibid.: 137–41) of remarks made by Davidson in his article 'Actions, reasons and causes' (1963: 9).

Davidson, in these remarks, defines a 'primary reason' for an action as one given when the desires and beliefs which motivate it are stated. He further argues that this 'rationalization' of an action, as he calls it, is possible because, for any intentional action, we can always construct, 'corresponding to the belief and attitude of a primary reason for an action . . . the premises of a syllogism from which it follows that the action has some . . . "desirability characteristic"'. He finally defends the potentiality of these desires and beliefs for normative re-expression by arguing that there is always, from the agent's point of view, at the time when he acted, something, however rarified, to be said for the action.

The chief counter-example that Smith cites against Davidson is that of a woman who, brought to desperation by her screaming baby, has a sudden urge to drown it, and yields to this desire. All the while, however, she protests that the act is abhorrent to her, and afterwards continues to display an apparently quite genuine horror and revulsion at what she has done.

Smith considers it obvious to anyone contemplating this example that (1) though this woman desires to drown her baby, and acts on this desire intentionally, she cannot be said to regard her action as *desirable*. He considers it equally obvious that, conversely, (2) though she regards it as desirable *not* to drown her baby, she has no desire or inclination to desist from that course. But Davidson, he says, appears to be committed to contradicting both (1) and (2). If the woman desires to drown her baby, she must, according to him, find that course in some sense desirable. If she regards it as desirable not to drown her baby, she must lack any desire to do so. Smith concludes (1994: 138) that the example shows Davidson to be 'profoundly wrong'.

The question immediately arises: how is Smith using the term 'desirable' so that he is confident that we will be forced to draw these conclusions from the screaming baby example? It is not the case, for instance, that Smith identifies what a person regards as desirable exclusively with what she pursues as a goal or end, and then takes the example to show that mere desires cannot supply our goals or ends. On the contrary, Smith holds that our desires *can* supply us with ends or goals, and that the mother's drowning of her baby exemplifies this as well as any other example might. He explicitly describes (ibid.: 140) the mother, in yielding to her desire to act in this way as 'in pursuit of a goal that she has'. Indeed, his whole point seems to be that, given the mother's horror and revulsion at drowning her baby, neither her having desired this drowning, nor having pursued it as a goal – perhaps in her desperate state she saw it as the only way of stopping the baby screaming – could possibly, as Davidson seems to think, be sufficient for talk of her regarding the drowning as desirable.

Thus far, it looks as though Smith relies on our rough intuitions about what an agent can and cannot be said to regard as desirable. He does, however, attempt to make them more articulate. He looks for a way of construing 'desirable' which would fit in with these intuitions by making it false that the mother regarded drowning her baby as desirable. He finds it in the idea of what an agent *values*. He here endorses Watson's claim (1975: 101) that it is 'just false' that 'the mother values her child's being drowned'. Smith allows that we can say that she desires the drowning, and even that she pursues it as a goal, but only in spite of herself, since it is, as Watson puts it (in the quotation cited), without 'assign[ing it even] an initial value' that might then have been 'outweighed by other considerations'. Hence for the mother, this action is 'not even represented by a positive entry, however small on the initial "desirability matrix"'.[5] Davidson, by not respecting our ordinary intuitions in cases like this, has effectively reduced value to desire. The example, according to Smith, shows us that this is an error.

Although we have made precise the way in which Smith means the plight of the mother who drowns her screaming baby to serve as a counter-example to Davidson's position, a difficulty now arises. Davidson takes it as a necessary, and indeed sufficient, condition of an action's being capable of rational justification that the agent could be said to regard its performance as desirable. If therefore a proper appreciation of this example should lead him to relinquish talk about the mother's regarding drowning her baby as in any sense desirable, should it not also lead him to give up talk of that action's being in any sense rationally justifiable, at least from the mother's point of view?

But for Davidson to offer such a justification of an action from the agent's point of view, and to give its reasons, or rationalize it, are one and the same. If we cannot thus justify the mother's drowning her baby even from her own viewpoint then the action cannot have been done for *any* reason and cannot be rationalized. But *ex hypothesi* the drowning was an intentional action, and for Davidson it is a conceptual truth that any action, if it is intentional, is done for a reason, and so is capable of rationalization, namely, that distinct species of causal explanation appropriate to, and only to, intentional actions. Hence it would seem that for Davidson to accept that the mother's intentional action was without rational justification and so constituted a counter-example to his position would lead him into conceptual incoherence.

Now Smith agrees (1994: 140) that since the mother does not regard drowning her baby as desirable, it must also be true of her that she 'acknowledges that there is no rational justification for what she does [and that] . . . what she does is in no way responsive to her thoughts about what it is rational for her to do'. He also believes that there is an important sense in which it is correct to say that she has 'no reason for acting, and what she does is therefore not explicable, even by her own lights, as having been done for a reason'. He nevertheless maintains that this is another perfectly valid sense in which we *can* say that the mother 'both has a reason for acting, and acts for that reason'. For, as he puts it (ibid.: 140–1), she has a *motivating* reason, and this does not require talk, as Davidson 'assumes, wrongly' of her regarding her action as desirable or of our 'see[ing] her as having done something that is rationally justifiable at least by her own lights'.

Thus, it would seem that though Smith allows only one valid notion of desirability, namely, what an agent values, by being prepared to admit two valid notions of what it is to have a reason, he may hope to bring Davidson to acknowledge the mother with the screaming baby as a counter-example to his position, and yet at the same time to save him from incoherence in doing so.

It may be coherent for Smith, with his distinction between motivating and normative reasons, to talk of the mother finding the thought of drowning her baby not merely undesirable but abhorrent, yet having a reason for doing it. Moreover in this way he would fulfil Davidson's requirements for intentionality. But the question is: would it be coherent for Davidson to talk in this way? It would hardly seem so. Davidson's remarks make it clear that for him, unlike Smith, it is imperative even for the ascription to an agent of reasons exclusively based on her desires and beliefs that the latter be used to construct desirability characteristics for her action. Without this normative gloss, the species of causal explanation offered would not be that proper to intentional action, namely, rationalization.

It might be thought that the best thing Smith could do at this point would be to accept Davidson's account as far as it goes, at the same time stressing the narrowness of its remit. He could then simply assert the existence of a type of reason other than the type which Davidson discusses. The content of these *normative* reasons, he would explain, is determined unlike Davidson's *motivating* reasons independently of the agent's desires and beliefs, in a way that could even possibly conflict with them. He would finally insist that we need the concept of normative, as well as that of motivating, reasons if we are to respond in an adequate and appropriate way to examples such as that of the mother drowning her screaming baby.

But this is not the course Smith favours. He is not apparently content to withdraw to the position of someone already committed to other quite different assumptions than Davidson's. Nor is this surprising. Smith is trying in this very critique of Davidson to establish the legitimacy of *his* notion of normative reasons. Moreover, he shares with Davidson the conviction that the legitimacy of any reason as a reason for action must somehow ultimately rest on its connection with motivation. He thus tries to show that Davidson's claim that judgements of desirability can always be constructed out of an agent's motivating desires and beliefs is directly vulnerable to the screaming baby example, and hence fails *on its own terms*. But for this to be so, Davidson, rather than being solely concerned to provide a mere normative gloss for motivating reasons, would have himself to be offering thereby an account of normative reasons, in Smith's full-blooded sense.

But this is just, it would seem, what Smith takes him to be doing. He treats Davidson's judgements of desirability, despite the fact that they are merely, as we have seen, normative reconstructions of the agent's desires and beliefs, as themselves normative reason claims. More particularly, Smith attributes (1994: 139) to Davidson (though Davidson nowhere uses the expression 'normative reason claims') the view that our motivating reasons 'bring with them the acceptance of corresponding normative reason claims'. But as we have seen it is, for Smith, just the fact that certain kinds of reasons are not merely normative re-expressions of the agent's desires and beliefs, and so can come apart from these desires and beliefs, which marks these reasons out as normative and not motivating. Consequently Davidson must be interpreted as saying something along the following lines: 'Mismatches between normative reasons and motivating desires, though possible, never actually occur'. Davidson will then differ from Smith only to the extent that, whereas Davidson holds that an agent's motivating desires and beliefs always bring with them 'the acceptance of corresponding normative reason claims', Smith holds that they do so only intermittently. Smith is then in a position to cite the example of the mother drowning her screaming baby to illustrate how wrong Davidson is. If the concept of a normative reason is to have any sense distinct from that of a motivating one, Smith can now say, it must enable us to recognize the mother's abhorrence at drowning her baby as a reason for her not to do this, though she desires to drown it and acts on this desire. But then it cannot be, as Davidson holds, that our motivating desires and beliefs as a matter of fact unfailingly bring with them the acceptance of corresponding normative reason claims. It must seem (ibid.: 138) that 'Davidson's suggestion . . . simply ignores the possibility of [these] deviant cases'.

But Smith's reading of Davidson as already allowing that claims ascribing 'desirability characteristics' to actions could conceivably come apart from corresponding claims ascribing desires and beliefs to agents is surely erroneous. Certainly, Davidson (1963: 9), in acknowledging 'a certain irreducible – though somewhat anaemic – sense in which every rationalisation justifies' is admitting that the first type of claim does not have the same meaning as the second. However, he still clearly takes it that the normative fact reported by the former claim consists in the psychological fact which makes the claim true. He cannot therefore be thought of as even indirectly admitting the existence of a distinct category of reasons from motivating ones, which would not be tied to the agent's motivating desires. On the contrary, by being prepared to reformulate statements about an agent's desires in normative terms he deliberately leaves no conceptual space for this possibility.

So far we have only considered that part of Smith's account which stresses how normative reasons can come apart from motivating desires, and which appears to rely for much of its force on a flawed critique of Davidson. But Smith is also convinced, as we have noted, that the status of normative judgements as reasons for action depends finally upon their being as intimately bound up with motivating desires (if not necessarily those of the agent herself) as are Davidson's judgements of desirability.

Having opened up the gap between normative reasons and motivating desires, Smith is therefore obliged, if he is to preserve given his theoretical commitments their entitlement to be called 'reasons' to close it again. He attempts therefore to incorporate (with certain qualifications) Davidson's characterization of the link between an agent's motivating desires and the judgements of desirability that can be constructed out of them, into his own account of normative reasons, as no less than its central plank. But this leads him into still further difficulties.

Smith asks us to agree that had the mother who drowns her screaming baby been rational, she would have desired, and been motivated, in accordance with her normative judgements concerning the action's *un*desirability. Davidson's only mistake, Smith suggests, is to have 'incorrectly assume[d] that a feature of *rational* evaluators is a feature of *all* evaluators' (Smith's italics). In other words, according to Smith, we can after all endorse Davidson's claim that an agent's desires are appropriately expressed as claims about what she takes to be desirable, provided we restrict it to rational agents. The revised formulation is as Smith renders it: 'Rational agents desire in accordance with the normative reason claims they accept, irrational agents desire otherwise.'

However, it was only, as we saw, by construing the judgements of desirability to which Davidson refers as already effectively normative reason claims (in Smith's sense) that the situation of the mother drowning her screaming baby could plausibly be represented as a counter-example to Davidson. For Davidson then appears to be maintaining that our motivating desires and beliefs just *happen* to bring with them in every case normative reason claims. The example hence serves as an argument for restricting the scope of his assertion.

But the significance of this misconstrual for the admission of such counter-examples was that it implicitly prised apart judgements of desirability, even on Davidson's view, and the agent's motivating desires and beliefs. As a result, Davidson's claim would be, not that mismatch was impossible, but that though it was possible it just never occurred. All that Smith then has to do is come up with a case where, as he puts it (1994: 148) 'it actually happens', and so at last the mother's drowning her baby at last gets a grip as a counter-example.

Once their proper meaning is restored to Davidson's judgements of desirability as mere normative reconstructions of the agent's motivating desires and beliefs, the argument for restricting his claim to rational agents collapses. For if these judgements are merely such normative reconstructions then, since even irrational agents, such as the mother, have relevant desires and beliefs, corresponding judgements of desirability can be constructed out of these desires and beliefs also. The most that Smith can be taken to be doing in asserting that rational agents desire in 'accordance with the normative reason claims they accept' is signalling his intention to give the name 'normative reason' to those judgements of desirability which in rational agents are matched by corresponding motivating desires and beliefs, or again to call 'normative reasons' the motivating reasons of rational agents. But this leaves Smith's position as little more than an arbitrary verbal stipulation.

9 The Case of *Owen Wingrave*

1 Williams, the 'extreme' version and a dogma of naturalism

The 'more radical' externalists exemplified in recent times by Prichard in 'Does moral philosophy rest on a mistake?' ([1912] 1968) can, if the conclusions of the previous chapter are correct, survive assimilation both to accidentalists and necessitarians. They construe the relation between moral judgement and motivation in a way which enables them to meet, as these others cannot, the two requirements for talk of morality's special authority: 'distance' and 'directness'. But their success depends on the postulation of external motives, and thus on the rejection of the subjectivist assumption. But it is just these features of their position which fit them, it would seem, to be targets of the 'extreme' version of the practicality argument. How, it will scornfully be asked by the argument's proponents, can a mere fact such as an action's supposed objective 'fittingness' to or rightness in the situation itself furnish *any* motive for an agent?

In this chapter, I turn finally to Williams' paper 'Internal and external reasons' (1981) in which he deploys, with the help of his example of Owen Wingrave, what is effectively the second premiss of the 'extreme' version of the practicality argument against the so-called 'external reasons' theorists. I will point out how the latter, as Williams depicts them, propound a theory which corresponds at the level of reasons in general to that propounded by our 'more radical' externalists concerning *moral* reasons. I will draw attention to the crucial role that the subjectivist assumption plays in Williams' attack on them, and suggest why its rejection signifies for a naturalist like him a descent into absurdity. In this way, I will link Williams' critique back to Hume's original 'extreme' criticism of the moral rationalists. I will finally suggest, however, that James' story, *Owen Wingrave*, in which, we shall recall, the scion of an honourable military family shocks its members by refusing to join the army for reasons they find incomprehensible, can be so re-interpreted as to make a powerful case *for*, rather than (as Williams uses it) against, external reasons and motives.

The key distinction that Williams wishes to draw, as his title suggests, is that between 'internal' and 'external reasons'.[1] Thus, taking the sentence "A has a reason to φ' or 'There is a reason for A to φ' (where 'φ' stands in for some verb of action)', he states that on the 'internal interpretation':

> The truth of the sentence implies, very roughly, that A has some motive which will be served or furthered by his φ-ing, and if this turns out not to be so the sentence is false: there is a condition relating to the agent's aims, and if this is not satisfied it is not true to say, on this interpretation, that he has a reason to φ.
>
> (1981: 101)

On the 'external interpretation', however, 'there is no such condition, and the reason-sentence will not be falsified by the absence of an appropriate motive'.

Having stated that 'the simplest model' – which he also calls a 'sub-Humean model' – for the *internal* interpretation would be one in which 'A has a reason to φ if A has some desire the satisfaction of which will be served by his φ-ing', he adds crucially: 'Basically, and by definition, any model for the internal interpretation must display a relativity of the reason statement to the agent's *subjective motivational* set, which I shall call the agent's S' (ibid.: 102, Williams' italics).

Influenced by the prevailing concern in moral contexts with the difference between moral belief internalism and externalism, it is easy to take Williams' distinction here to correspond to *that* distinction, only now applied to reasons generally. He would then be stating something along these lines: if an agent judges correctly that she has an 'internal' reason to perform an action, *necessarily* she has an appropriate motivation, but this is not so with 'external' reasons. Thus, Owen Wingrave might correctly judge that he has an 'external' reason for joining the army though (as Williams puts it, ibid.: 106) 'he has no motivation to [do this] at all', though 'all his desires lead in another direction', and though 'he hates everything about military life and what it means'. If, therefore, Owen were to act on such a reason, his desires would have to be turned around, and he would have to gain a liking for the military life. But there is no guarantee that this would happen; indeed, it well may not. Accordingly, it is tempting to conclude that Williams objects to 'external' reasons because any relation between the judgement concerning such a reason and motivation will be *fortuitous*, or *accidental*. But then it would seem that Williams is really, despite his ostensibly 'extreme' reading of Hume's premiss, unexcitingly just reiterating the 'moderate' Humean objection – now applied to reasons generally – that non-cognitivists (Chapter 6) bring against the 'accidentalists'.

This is, for instance, broadly the way that Korsgaard (1986) understands Williams' distinction. She first draws the following distinction of her own between an 'internalist' and an 'externalist' theory:

> an *internalist* theory [is one] . . . according to which the knowledge (or the truth or the acceptance) of a moral judgement implies the existence of a motive . . . for acting on that judgement. If I judge that some action is right, it is implied that I have, and acknowledge, some motive or reason for performing that action. It is part of the sense of the judgement that a motive is present . . . On an *externalist* theory, by contrast, such a conjunction of moral comprehension and total unmotivatedness is perfectly possible: knowledge is one thing and motivation another.
>
> (ibid.: 8–9, her italics)

Her example of an 'externalist' theory is Mill's utilitarianism, where the link between moral judgement and motivation is fortuitous or accidental and so requires, she observes, mediation by an independent psychological 'sanction'. As she puts it: 'The reason why the principle of utility is true and the motive we might have for acting on it are not the same . . . the motives must be acquired in a utilitarian upbringing.' Referring to the internalist/externalist distinction that she has just drawn, she then goes on:

> This kind of reflection about the motivational force of ethical judgements has been brought to bear by Bernard Williams on the motivational force of reason claims generally. In 'Internal and External Reasons' Williams argues that there are two kinds of reason claims . . . Suppose I say that some person P has a reason to do action A. If I intend to imply that the person P has a motive to do the action A, the claim is of an internal reason; if not, the claim is of an external reason.
>
> (ibid.: 10)

It looks then as though she takes Williams, in espousing what he calls the 'internal reasons' theory, to be espousing something like her 'internalist' theory,[2] broadened to cover 'reason claims generally'. Likewise, it looks as though she takes him in rejecting the 'external reasons' theory to be rejecting something like her 'externalist' theory. But her example of that theory is, as we noted, utilitarianism where judgements and motivation are only contingently or fortuitously connected.

A warning bell should, however, have sounded for anyone tempted to take Williams' rejection of the 'external reasons' theory as really a rejection of the claim that my judgement that I have a reason to X is only externally – in the sense of *accidentally* or *fortuitously* – connected with the relevant motivation. For Williams, in applying the 'external reasons' position to Owen Wingrave, says things which absolutely rule out such an 'accidentalist' interpretation. He suggests, in fact, that there is an *internal* connection – in the sense that there is no need for a mediating desire – between an agent's judgement that she has an external reason to perform a given action and her being relevantly motivated. As Williams writes:

> We will take the case . . . in which an external reason statement is made about someone who, like Owen Wingrave, is not already motivated in the required way . . . The agent does not presently believe the external statement. *If he comes to believe it, he will be motivated to act.*
>
> (1981: 108, my italics)

Again, Williams says (ibid.: 109) that on the 'external interpretation', Owen would 'acquire the motivation *because* he comes to believe the [external] reason statement' (Williams' italics), and yet again that 'if the agent rationally deliberated then, whatever motivations he originally had, he would come to be motivated to [act in the relevant way]'.

Surely, it will be objected, Williams has earlier defined an 'external reason' state-ment as one that can be true of an agent precisely in the *absence* of her having a relevant motive. But in offering this definition Williams is clearly thinking of such a statement being made by a third party without reference to the agent's own beliefs about her reasons. (In what follows I will call this a 'third person' ascription of reasons.) Indeed, nothing is said or implied in this definition about the situation where the agent *herself* comes to believe that she has such a reason (let us call this a 'first person' ascription of reasons)[3]. Nothing, in other words, is said or implied about whether the conditions under which it would be true to say that the agent herself acknowledges such a reason must include a relevant motivation. However, in applying the 'external reasons' theory to Owen Wingrave, Williams switches to this viewpoint, that is, of the agent herself: suppose, he says, Owen Wingrave were to come to believe the external reason statement originally made by someone else about him, then he would have a motive to act.

It seems then that while, on Williams' construal, the *external* reason statement 'A has a reason to φ' can be true even though A has no motive to φ, if A *herself* comes to believe that she has this reason, she will *ipso facto* have a motive to φ. There is for Williams, therefore, a crucial asymmetry between 'internal reason' and 'external reason' theory. For there is no such disparity between (what I am calling) 'third' and 'first person' ascriptions of *internal* reasons. Thus, to state truly that 'A has an internal reason to φ' already implies that A has a relevant motive. Moreover, it is this same motive, implied by the 'internal reason' statement, which A discovers in herself through deliberation and which allows her truly to say of herself: 'I have a reason to φ'.

It looks already as though Williams' 'external reasons theorists' are far closer to our 'more radical' externalists than to Korsgaard's 'externalists' who are essentially acci-dentalists. But further confirmation is to be found in Williams' identification (see the quotation above) of 'motivation' exclusively with elements of what he calls 'the agent's *subjective* motivational set'. It is quite clear from this that, for him, the *only possible* kind of motive is subjective, and is entailed by an '*internal* reasons statement'; if such a motive is *not* present, or cannot be derived from one that is, the statement will be false or even senseless. There is, therefore, on Williams' account, a second striking asymmetry between the two types of reason. For whereas his 'internal' reason requires an appropriate *subjective*, or (in this sense) *internal*, motive, his 'external' reason, by definition, needs no such motive. 'External' reasons therefore are defined here in terms of motives *relevant to 'internal' reasons* – motives which they do *not* need – rather than in terms of a distinct kind of motive with which they might be associated: an external motive. Put again, when Williams says that the statement, that Owen Wingrave has an 'external reason' for joining the army, can be true independently of whether Owen has a relevant motive, he means that the statement can be true inde-pendently of whether Owen has a *subjective* motive. For Williams, no other motive is conceivable. But by thus making the 'subjectivist assumption', he has effectively proscribed the notion of an *external* motive as playing any role in action.[4]

Given our interest in reclaiming lost pieces of a larger conceptual picture, Williams, despite his negative treatment of external motives, represents a considerable advance on Falk. Indeed, it is illuminating to set what Williams says in the context of our earlier discussion. As we have noted, Williams is concerned with reasons in general and Falk with moral obligation in particular. Both, however, distinguish 'internalist' from 'externalist' interpretations of the relevant reasons. Moreover, both, in doing so, seem primarily concerned with whether (to use Falkian language) the fact which makes the reason statement true is held to be internal or external *to the agent*. Again, like Falk, Williams is only secondarily or derivatively concerned with whether the agent's beliefs about her reasons are necessarily or contingently connected with motivation. Falk, however, as we saw, contrasts the 'internal fact' analysts merely with (in our terms) the 'less radical' of the 'external fact' analysts to whom at the same time he automatically assimilates the 'more radical'. Williams, on the other hand, not only stops short of such an assimilation, but actually reverses it, making (in our terms) the *'more* radical' cognitivists his representative externalists. At the same time he still does not give credence to their position. It is rather, to speak metaphorically, as if he allows us, indeed invites us, to feel the pull or draw of their 'external reasons' while never allowing these supposed reasons to emerge into the plain light of day. It is as though he feels that unless he keeps his distance from them, he may be dragged down into incoherence with them.

The question, then, is how, for Williams, their lack of an associated (subjective) motive establishes the incoherence of 'external' reasons. Now Williams' remarks *can* be used to suggest that the concept of an 'external' reason is self-contradictory. Thus we might say, according to Williams, nothing can count as a reason unless it is logically tied to motivation but, by his definition, a reason only counts as 'external', if it is *not* so tied.

But this answer, at least as it stands, would again treat the problem that is posed for Williams by the 'external reasons' theorists as corresponding, at the level of reasons generally, to one that might be posed for a necessitarian by accidentalists. However, the accidentalists would even then only pose this problem – that is, they would only be using 'reason' in a contradictory way – if two things were the case. The first would be that they agreed that something could count as a reason only if it was logically tied to motivation. Second, they would have to insist that an agent's judgement that she ought to perform an action is itself her reason for doing so, while also accepting that this judgement can only lead to the action if a relevant desire or other motive happens to be present. But as we saw earlier, accidentalists typically concede that if such a judgement can be called a reason, it is only 'after a manner of speaking' or 'courtesy of desire'. (In our earlier terminology they do not pretend to be anything other than 'belief-content' externalists.)

But in any case the 'external reasons' theorists, by Williams' own account, hold as we have seen that an 'external reason' statement, once accepted by the agent, straightaway furnishes her with a motive. Williams, we might say, is not concerned with motives which *are* taken to be part of the agent's subjective motivational set, yet which are held not to be implicit in the relevant reasons claim (essentially the accidentalists' position). Rather he is concerned with motives which are declared *not* to be part of the agent's subjective motivational set. Such motives, he robustly maintains, simply cannot exist. In fact, the claim that, given Williams' definition, it is self-contradictory to talk of an 'external reason' is watertight only provided the 'subjectivist assumption' is accepted. If it is left open whether there may be other sources of motivation than an agent's subjective states, we get a different conclusion: that since 'external reasons' are unconnected in any way with *subjective* motives, they must furnish *their own* motives.

Moreover, Williams himself intimates that the difficulty with 'external reasons' is more than merely logical. He asks how Owen's having an 'external reason' for joining the army – which, on Williams' definition, is true as we have seen when he is *not* motivated to do so – could, as the 'external reasons' theorists suppose, explain Owen's doing so, when he *is* so motivated. He writes:

> Now no external reason statement could *by itself* offer an explanation of anyone's action. Even if it were true (whatever that might turn out to mean) that there was a reason for Owen to join the army, that fact by itself would never explain anything that Owen did, not even his joining the army. For if it was true at all, it was true when Owen was not motivated to join the army. The whole point of external reason statements is that they can be true independently of the agent's motivations. But nothing can explain an agent's (intentional) actions except something that motivates him to so act.
>
> (1981: 106, Williams' italics)

Here at last we begin to grasp the pivotal role that the move from (what I have called) 'third' to 'first person' ascriptions of 'external reasons' plays in Williams' argument for the incoherence of these reasons. At first, it looks as though Williams intends to nip in the bud the difficulty implicit in the last quoted observation concerning how we are to explain motivation by an 'external reason'. For he responds with the proposal that it is the *belief* that one has such a reason which, by supplying the required psychological link, accounts for the change from not being motivated to being motivated, and so 'help[s] to explain [the] action'. Thus, 'Owen Wingrave might come to join the army because (now) he believes that it is a reason for him to do so that his family has a tradition of military honour' (ibid.: 107). But Williams immediately retorts that this is now so plausible that it must seem that we are no longer dealing with an 'external reason statement' at all. He writes:

> this agent, with this belief, appears to be one about whom, now, an *internal* reason statement could truly be made: he is one with an appropriate motivation in his S. A man who does believe that considerations of family honour constitute reasons for action is a man with a certain disposition to action, and also dispositions of approval, sentiment, emotional reaction, and so forth.
>
> (ibid.: Williams' italics)

It is no use therefore considering the state of someone who already believes the 'external reason' statement for then he will already *have* the appropriate subjective motivation, and so the statement will have imperceptibly become an 'internal reasons' one. We must try therefore to isolate from the psychological process in which belief like any other subjective motivational state is embedded, that moment of transition, that *coming to* believe the 'external reasons' statement, and so the acquiring of the new motivation. It will not do, for instance, for Owen to acquire both the motivation and the belief as a result of being 'persuaded by his father's moving rhetoric' (ibid.: 108). For then any resultant action will have come about through the ordinary psychological channels. He must acquire the motivation because, and only because, he comes to believe the 'external reason' statement, and he must come to believe the statement because, and only because 'in some way, he is considering the matter aright' (ibid.: 109). But Williams now reminds us that in the case of 'internal reasons' the agent comes to acknowledge that she has such a reason in the only way possible: by deliberating from a (subjective) motivation that she acknowledges that she already has to the new one. The trouble with 'external reason' statements is that '*ex hypothesi* there is no motivation for the agent to deliberate *from*, to reach this new motivation'. Indeed, the new motivation 'must not bear to the earlier motivations the kind of rational relation which we considered in the earlier discussion of deliberation – for in that case an internal reason statement would have been true in the first place'. But then – and it is just at this point that Williams appeals for a second time to Hume's premiss concerning reason's inertia – it must seem that the new motivation erupts out of the blue. It is as though the fact which makes the 'external reason' statement true – in Owen's case the family tradition of valour in battle – under his impassive gaze (which of course must itself be without psychological reverberation) suddenly issued in a motivation. We are close here to Hume's criticism of the moral rationalists as I interpreted it: how could the eternal 'fitnesses and unfitnesses of things' possibly become agents of change when they remain themselves profoundly impervious to change, and when nothing else has changed around them? Like the moral rationalists on Hume's view, Williams 'external reasons' theorists, in insisting that these reasons *do* motivate us, apparently countenance an abrogation of ordinary causal laws, and so flout a fundamental principle of naturalism.

I conclude that, unless we take Williams' attack to be implicitly directed at the 'external reasons' theorists rejection of the 'subjectivist assumption' and their postulation of external motives, we shall fail to appreciate its force and impact.[5] On my interpretation, Williams seems to be staring, alongside the Hume of the 'extreme' objection, into the metaphysical abyss from which Smith and others shrink back. He then poses a question. How could any mere fact (e.g., to quote James himself, 'the general fact . . . of the paramount valour of [Owen's] family'), just by being recognized as true by an agent, suddenly and abruptly oppose, and supplant, those subjective dispositions of desire and belief which are the causally necessary and sufficient conditions of action? But in embracing this 'inert', and psychologically weightless, 'fact' as a motive, Williams' 'external reasons' theorists must be placed alongside those other anti-naturalists – the moral intuitionists and rationalists – as targets for the 'extreme' version of the practicality argument.

With the identity corroborated through our reading of Williams of the type of moral philosophers against whom the 'extreme' version (whether as represented by Hume himself or by more recent writers) can properly be said to be directed, I reach the main conclusion of my book. Only this 'extreme' version has a second premiss – that reason cannot conceivably move us to action – which, once properly analysed, might be held to be *obviously* true. Only this version therefore has any claim to be straightforwardly valid. It is therefore to this version that we must look, if anywhere, for the real source of the argument's power. However, the very obviousness of the second premiss of the 'extreme' version is itself a drawback, for as we have seen it turns out not to be that of a contentful empirical claim, but a piece of naturalistic dogma.

2 Henry James and a *literary* defence of external reasons

The practicality argument in its only tenable – 'extreme' – form is, if our fore-going conclusions are correct, an attack on the view that moral obligation constitutes an 'external reason' (in Williams' sense) for action. For such a view, as our original investigations had suggested, involves the – for naturalists absurd – idea that an 'inert' fact about the world – the fact which makes the corresponding moral judgement true – can prompt an agent to act independently of any subjective motivations she might have. Before we can consider further the merits of the naturalist case, it is necessary to clear up one point in our interpretation of Williams. Williams, we have noted, is concerned with reasons in general. So far we have assumed that we may take what he says and apply it without more ado to the moral context. However, he issues a caveat (1981: 106) to the effect that we should not just assume that his question about the status of 'external reasons' is 'undoubt-edly the same as' that concerning the status of the moral 'ought'. But it is not entirely clear why he issues this caveat. After all, by his own account (ibid.: 110) the 'external reasons' theorist 'wants any rational agent, as such, to acknowledge the requirement to do the thing in question'. In other words, the whole point about an 'external reason' seems to be that it applies categorically, or irrespective of an individual's desires or other subjective motivations; for these will typically differ from person to person depending on a whole variety of contingencies. It cannot therefore be the categorical nature of the moral 'ought' that is the obstacle to applying Williams' findings about reasons in general to morality in particular. In any case, we have our own independent grounds for maintaining that if morality is to have a special categorical force, the reasons it gives for action must be conceived as 'external' in precisely Williams' sense.

Williams seems to associate the claim that morality has a categorical force particularly with Kant. Perhaps he feels that in including *beliefs* as well as desires among an agent's subjective motivational states, and allowing that the agent may reach a new from an existing motivation by rational deliberation, he is to some extent cutting across Kant's distinction in the moral context between desire and reason. However, this special feature of Kant's account need not concern us here. The only other explanation of the caveat would seem to be that Williams wants to guard against a too narrow interpretation of 'external reasons' as only pertaining to morality. For he is concerned here with other requirements, whose content is not narrowly moral, but which are held (by their defenders) to be capable of exerting a binding force over the actions of anyone in the relevant situation once he 'considers the matter aright'. However, this would not be an argument for excluding moral judgement or obligation from the class of 'external reasons'. It would be an argument for including them as 'external reasons' within a wider class of requirements a few of which do not have a specifically – or traditionally – moral content. In any event, no dilution of the categorical force of the moral 'ought' would be entailed.

What are the prospects for doing justice to the special authority of such requirements when, as we have seen, this involves rejecting the subjective assumption and postulating external reasons and motives? I will first suggest that, when examined in more detail, Henry James' *Owen Wingrave*[6] (2001) does not, despite Williams' citing it, support his philosophical conclusions. In fact, I will argue, it is difficult to fully appreciate the complexity of the dilemma facing Owen without at some level, even if only informally, possessing the concept of an 'external reason', which Williams proscribes.

There are two ways in which Williams' brief presentation of the story is misleading. First, he does not adequately convey the *impersonality* of the requirement that Owen join the army and so uphold the family tradition of military honour. This requirement does not seem to qualify as an 'internal reason', as on Williams' account it must, at least for those members of the family who *actually* comply with it. For an 'internal reason' is by Williams' definition ascribed to an agent, as we have seen, ultimately on the basis of his particular subjective make-up. But it is not just that compliance with the requirement of family tradition involves (ibid.: 129) for the Wingraves a 'rigid indifference' – amounting to a 'defective sense of proportion' – in respect of all ordinary inclinations or desires from matters of the heart to physical comfort. It is that such compliance is not itself, in their case, an expression of individual personality at all. Rather, each member of the family, regardless of gender, is represented as an embodiment of the essentially masculine tradition of valour. Thus, Owen's aunt is described as 'somehow in her very person' (ibid.: 125) representing 'the might . . . the traditions and the exploits of the British army' and 'the genius of a military race' (ibid.: 128). 'Her very presence and each of her actions and glances and tones', are said (ibid.: 128–9) to be 'a constant and direct allusion' to 'the general fact – the paramount valour of her family'. She is 'military . . . because she [springs] from a military house' and she is 'a grenadier at bottom' (ibid.: 130). Of Owen's grandfather, James writes,

> It was impossible not to feel . . . beneath the surface a merciless old man of blood. The eye of the imagination could glance back into his crowded Eastern past – back at episodes in which his scrupulous forms would only have made him more terrible. He had his legend – and oh there were stories about him!
>
> (ibid.: 127)

It might be objected that the fact that it is Owen's *father*, and not these more distant relatives, who pleads with him to join the army suggests that there is after all ordinary fatherly pride at stake here. But in the original story (and also in Britten's opera) the father, contrary to what Williams says, is dead. James writes of him:

> like so many of his ancestors [he] had given up a gallant young life to the service of his country. Owen Wingrave the elder had received his death-cut, in close quarters, from an Afghan sabre; the blow had come crashing across his skull.
>
> (ibid.: 127)

It falls therefore to Owen's aunt and grandfather, as the sole surviving representatives of the family tradition, to impress on him (in interviews which tellingly we only learn of at second hand) the importance of carrying on this tradition. But they remain remote iconic figures concerned only with 'the forms [being] kept up' (ibid.: 146), with not 'putting a public dishonour on their family name' (ibid.: 136). If, indeed, there is 'an intensity of heartache' (ibid.: 146) over Owen's dereliction, it belongs rather to Paramore itself – 'that house of examples and memories' (ibid.: 134) – than to any *individual*.

The second way in which Williams' account is misleading concerns the nature of the conflict facing Owen. For he makes it seem that it is between, on the one hand, Owen's personal dispositions and temperament, which go in a totally different direction from the military, and give him apparently an 'internal reason' for defying his family, and on the other the family's wishes to which Owen is wholly unresponsive. But James does not portray the conflict in this simple way; it is altogether more complex and nuanced. First, Owen does not lack what it takes to be a soldier. On the contrary, he is said to possess 'the temperament of a soldier' (ibid.: 131). He is 'upright as a young hero' (ibid.: 135), 'noble', he has 'the natural carriage of a Wingrave' (ibid.: 130), 'he is the best of [the cadets]' (ibid.: 131). When at the end of the story he is found dead after spending the night in the White Room, reputedly haunted by the ghost of his terrifying murderous great-great grandfather who died there, and which no-one has since slept in, he is eulogized as 'all the young soldier on the gained field'.

But nor is he impervious to the demands of family tradition; on the contrary, he is acutely sensitive to them, and as a result they weigh heavily upon him. Thus in reply to Mr Coyle – the head of his military academy – who queries what it is that worries him about going against these demands, he confesses:

> Oh the house – the very air and feeling of it. There are strange voices in it that seem to mutter at me – to say dreadful things as I pass. I mean the general consciousness and responsibility of what I'm doing. Of course it hasn't been easy for me – anything rather! . . . I've started up all the old ghosts. The very portraits glower at me on the walls. There's one of my great-great grandfather . . . that fairly stirs on the canvas, just heaves a little, when I come near it. I have to go up and down stairs – it's rather awkward! It's what my aunt calls the family circle, and they sit, ever so grimly, in judgement. The circle's all

constituted here, it's a kind of awful encompassing presence, it stretches away into the past.

(ibid.: 138)

Moreover, he even acknowledges a certain complicity with this 'family circle' exclaiming sadly to Coyle, 'Ah, we're tainted all.'

Nor yet again is it that Owen has a taste for luxury and leisure which would be denied to him if he became a soldier, however much he might be suited in other ways to the military life. For James decisively rules this out: 'If he had thrown up the probability of a magnificent career it wasn't to dawdle along Bond Street nor parade his indifference in the windows of a club' (ibid.: 124). Nor does he 'care a rap for the loss of the money' (ibid.: 137) involved in his grandfather's cutting him out of his will. Still less may we put down his opposition to being a soldier to cowardice. After all 'marching up to the battery in spite of his terrors' (ibid.: 131) – that is to say, facing the onslaught of his grandfather who 'had denounced him in a way to make his hair stand up on his head' (ibid.: 136) – is 'a special exposure' that 'many a plucky youth would have funked'. Moreover, the manner of Owen's death (as we have just observed) bears this heroism out.

It is not, however, that James portrays Owen as having no reason or motive for going against family tradition, but his reason has to do (ibid.: 131) with 'ideas'. As his fellow cadet, Lechmere, explains to Coyle: 'He *has* done a lot of reading and he says it opened his eyes' (ibid.: 132). In fact, he has become, as a result of this protracted period of study and reflection, a pacifist whose 'conscientious scruples' are 'founded on an overwhelming conviction of the stupidity – the "crass barbarism" – of war'. He is now contemptuous of the military profession and considers it 'beneath him'. He has concluded that anyone who does not share this 'stand' has 'the wrong view'.

It seems that Owen refuses to submit to family tradition because then he would be committed to actions, in particular to killing and maiming on the battlefield, which are forbidden by another principle which he judges to take precedence over the first – that of pacifism. But in obeying this latter imperative, Owen is no more, James seems to be urging, following a set of individual proclivities than he would be were he to comply with family tradition. Indeed, he is portrayed as bringing to his championship of this (for his family) 'wrong cause' (ibid.: 131) exactly that grim resolution and personal detachment which would have so admirably fitted him to represent the family tradition. Thus, he exercises 'a great power of resistance' (ibid.: 136) against his grandfather for whom he is 'an unyielding match'. Again, 'the more [Coyle] insisted that the boy had a kind of intellectual independence the more this struck [Owen's aunt] as conclusive proof that her nephew was a Wingrave and a soldier' (ibid.: 130). It would seem that Owen's relation to his pacifist principles, *despite* his complying with them, is still not such as to make them (in Williams' sense) an 'internal reason' for him. But nor may we dismiss the family tradition of valour as giving him a reason at all because it does not give him an 'internal reason'. Rather, we seem to need the notion of an *external* reason precisely to distinguish Owen's relation to both these evidently objective yet conflicting requirements from the kind of ('internal') reason that would be given him by e.g. ingrained fear, or a natural streak of pugnacity or emotional enthralment to the family legacy.

The story, it is plausible to suggest, is an exploration of how far one can freely – that is as an act of 'intellectual independence' – go against a requirement – here that of family tradition – which one recognizes as, for good or ill, in some sense binding upon one, which is even perhaps 'in one's blood'. This question bears some resemblance to our philosophical question concerning whether any sense can be made of an agent's being bound by a moral judgement, the conditions for whose truth lie not in her possession of the relevant subjective dispositions and motives but outside her, and which judgement she can choose to disobey. James puts his doubts as to whether this kind of choice can exist in the mouths of two relatively minor characters. Thus, Lechmere repeatedly asks Coyle (ibid.: 133–4) such questions as 'Is he beastly afraid?', 'But do you think he funks it?', '[Is] he thinking of his own skin?' and considers that without such an explanation Owen's behaviour must seem 'awfully odd', even 'extraordinary' (ibid.: 149). But taking the story as a whole, and given its culmination, it seems that James' answer is that such freedom is possible, though at a price – in Owen's case his life.

3 Sketch for a Wittgensteinian approach

Henry James' story, then, is an extremely complex and subtle one, more so than Williams' use of it suggests. And, indeed, that motivations, especially moral ones, can be not merely subtle but elusive, is a constant theme in James' fiction. So much for a *literary* defence of external reasons. These reasons, as we have seen, are categorical in the sense that their ascription to an agent does not depend on her having (at some level) relevant psychological dispositions or motivations. Indeed, if these reasons do lead to action it is by, so to speak, furnishing their own (external) motives. Their *philosophical* defence therefore hangs on whether one can reject the subjectivist assumption (that all action has its source in the agent's subjective psychological states) without thereby countenancing, as Hume and Williams imply that one must, an abrogation of causal law.

Now it would be rash to deny that the idea of morality as a system of categorical requirements received its most celebrated exposition and defence – by Kant – against the background of an intense ongoing debate, originally prompted by Newton's scientific discoveries, concerning the philosophical implications of the thesis that all natural events have determining causes. It would be equally rash not to acknowledge that this debate was so dominating that it not only focused attention in a new way upon the key notions structuring the moral agent's relation to her actions – those of her power over and responsibility for them and of her freedom to have refrained from them – but also largely dictated the *content* of these notions. Thus, Kant argued that if there existed determining causes of which the moral agent's choices and actions were mere effects, then these determining causes wholly accounted for her moral conduct. But for an agent to be held responsible for her choices and actions, in the sense required for moral praise or blame, she must have been free to have refrained from these choices and actions. But such freedom,

according to Kant, required – indeed just was – 'independence from the determining causes of the world of sense'.

It is understandable how the impact of new scientific ideas and discoveries
might, at a particular historical period, lead to a reappraisal of the conceptual foundations of our moral practices, especially if these new ideas are seen – whether
correctly or incorrectly – as potentially threatening to the validity of these practices.
Furthermore, this reappraisal might be recognized as having sharpened awareness of
the conditions of validity of these practices in a way that no future commentator can
disregard. Thus we might agree that Kant has brought to our attention in a new
and compelling way the links that must hold, on the one hand, between the notions
of responsibility, power and freedom, and, on the other, between these and our
moral practice of praising and blaming people, if this practice is to have any
validity.

But it does not follow that we must concur with Kant in giving these notions a
similar metaphysical content, or even that we must adopt any particular stand at all
on the larger deterministic questions. Indeed, long before the advent of Newton,
certain Christian writers argued that moral meritoriousness required a construal of
the moral agent's power over her actions, which linked it with her freedom to
refrain from those actions. Thus, Meister Eckhard, as we noted earlier, held that if
the 'power' to resist temptation were, even for those 'in the right state of mind' a
foregone conclusion, it would rob them of the opportunity to 'exercise that power'.
But then they would remain 'untried in all things, and in all that they [did]'
unaware of the dangers of things, and so 'without the honour of battle, victory and
reward'.

It seems clear, however, that if we are to dissociate the rejection of the subjectivist assumption from that of the thesis that all natural events, including human
actions, are ineluctably governed by causal law we must reject the very terms in
which naturalists conduct the debate. We must that is, adopting an essentially
Wittgensteinian approach, reject their simple dichotomy: *either* naturalism *or* metaphysical obscurantism. Here I sketch a couple of ways in which this might be done.

(i) A metaphysics in the eye of the naturalist[7]

It is often possible to defuse the naturalists' attack on those who postulate external
reasons by pointing out that its success depends on the naturalists adopting, even if
only temporarily, the same illegitimate picture for which they upbraid their opponents. One can go further. Sometimes it seems to be the naturalists who, allegedly
to clear up its obscurity, deliberately *impose* upon their opponents' position that very
metaphysical picture which they then condemn. It is illuminating to look in this
light at Foot's influential article, 'Morality as a system of hypothetical imperatives'
(1972).

It is well known that Foot (addressing herself first to Kant, but later to modern
philosophers more generally who uphold the categorical nature of moral requirements) claims that there are certain *non*-moral statements, such as those about
etiquette or club rules, where 'should' is used in a non-hypothetical sense. Citing

(ibid.: 160) the rule of etiquette that 'an invitation in the third person should be answered in the third person', she states that it does not fail to apply to someone simply because they do not care about manners. Likewise she states that the club rule you 'should not bring ladies into the smoking-room' still applies to a person who does not care about such rules and is resigning his membership.

The first claim seems at least controversial. The second may seem less so because of the lack of clarity about the status of the person referred to since he appears to be in that twilight zone between membership and non-membership of the club. We can, however, get rid of this lack of clarity by asking whether Foot means her claim to be incompatible or compatible with such common remarks as 'I'm not a member of that club because I refuse to be subject to its ridiculous rules'. If her claim is meant to be incompatible with this kind of remark, then it must surely strike us as false. Suppose, however, that it is meant to be compatible with the remark. Then, since the remark presupposes that people are *not* subject to, nor bound by, the rules of clubs to which they have chosen not to belong, the 'non-hypothetical' status of the relevant 'should' must at best be superficial. This is precisely, we might say, what differentiates club rules and judgements of manners from the kind of non-moral requirement that Williams discusses. For this is held to bind Owen antecedently to and independently of any choice he might make as to whether to subscribe to it. (Owen has of course no choice but to be a member of his family – in particular the one on whose head, in James' words, 'all the hopes of the house . . . were gathered'.)

Foot, however, almost immediately (1972: 161) concedes that whatever she origi- nally meant by speaking of a non-hypothetical use of 'should' in the etiquette case, it is not that we cannot reasonably demand a reason why we should comply with a rule of etiquette and otherwise refuse to take notice of it. Moreover, she acknowledges that this represents a vital difference between the way we view etiquette and club rules, on the one hand, and moral requirements, on the other. For whether or not we are obliged to take notice of a moral requirement is not, as with these other types of requirement, held to be conditional upon whether we have, or can show, a good reason to do so. Moral considerations, she writes, are supposed 'necessarily [to] give reasons for acting to any man', and again to have, unlike considerations of etiquette, an 'automatic reason-giving force'.

There are, however, two divergent ways of taking this characterization of moral requirements. It may be taken as proscribing any attempt, on the grounds that it is inappropriate or senseless, to ask for or to offer reasons for complying with these requirements. Alternatively, and quite contrarily, it may be (or rather has been) taken as Foot takes it here as an invitation to explain the *special* kind of reason that moral judgements and requirements give us for action. In other words it may be taken as an invitation to provide an explanation of, so to speak, their superadded reason-giving power compared with club rules or judgements of manners.

Now the first alternative can be expressed in Wittgensteinian terms by saying that the moral *language game* is different from that which is played with etiquette or club rules. Since with these latter we are taken to have no reason to comply with the relevant judgements unless reason is given it is a legitimate move to demand a reason why we should comply. (Of course, the move will not be legitimate where we have already by, say, becoming a member of a club accepted its rules.) This move is precisely blocked in the moral language game. Nor will it do to say that the question still seems to make sense when raised in the new context. Wittgenstein will reply that we have carried over this 'sense' from the other contexts. He will explain: 'When a sentence is called senseless, it is not as it were its sense [borrowed from these other contexts] that is senseless. But a combination of words is being excluded from the language, withdrawn from circulation' (1958, Part. I: 500).

By adopting the second alternative therefore Foot has, in Wittgensteinian terms, illegitimately transferred a move from the language game of etiquette or club rules to that of morality. She has then asked (1972: 162) precisely the question that is in this context ruled out as a senseless 'combination of words', namely: 'why we should do what we are [morally] required to do'. She has done so moreover on the basis of a superficial, if not spurious, similarity between 'the moral "should"' and 'the "shoulds" appearing in normative statements of [these] other kinds': if the latter, she asks, do not have automatic reason-giving force, why should the former? (ibid.: 161).

Having gone this far, it now becomes impossible to preserve the supposed difference between moral requirements and rules of etiquette, or club rules, without claiming that the former must provide a special type of reason – so to speak, a super-reason. This is a reason that, as Foot puts it (ibid.: 162–3), we 'must' or 'have to' comply with, that is specially 'inescapable', and not just in the ordinary sense which attaches to the 'should' of club rules or judgements of manners (if we choose to accept them).

Foot, however, ascribing this 'obscure' claim to her opponents – those who assert that moral requirements are categorical – now represents them as casting around for a way of dispelling this obscurity. But she represents them as only getting further mired in confusion by trying to explain moral 'inescapability' in terms of a special *feeling* of compulsion.

For, she objects, we can talk of physical compulsion when one person is pulled by others, and mental compulsion when one person succeeds in getting another to do something by torture. But the compulsion or binding force of moral requirements only applies in the absence of such mental or physical compulsion, and whose presence typically absolves the agent of moral responsibility. Her diagnosis is that her opponents have taken the merely subjective feeling of compulsion for an objective reality. It is as if, to cite her analogy, a person, feeling as if she is falling were mistakenly to believe that she is actually 'moving downward'. But the categorical imperative therefore, according to Foot, involves the postulation of what is self-evidently absurd – a super-reason by whose sheer normative force agents are irresistibly moved to action. It is an attempt, she says (ibid.: 167), 'to give the moral "ought" a magic force'.

Now some writers have indeed drawn attention to the use in this attack on Wittgensteinian ideas. The above analogy, it has been said, suggests that proponents of morality's categorical nature, in trying to capture the peculiar 'mustness' of morality, are 'in the grip of a false picture'. And we can agree that anyone engaged in a search for a super-reason which leads them into the morass Foot describes would be vulnerable to Wittgensteinian strictures that they have 'interpret[ed] a grammatical movement made by [themselves] as a quasi-physical phenomenon which [they] are observing' (1958: Part I, 401). They have taken the question as one of 'explaining a language-game by means of our experiences [when it is one] of noting a language-game' (ibid.: 655). They would thus be open to a Wittgensteinian rebuke for giving credence to bogus 'super-concepts' or 'super-expressions' (ibid.: 192) and ordered to 'bring words back from their metaphysical to their everyday use' (ibid.: 116).

However, it is Foot herself, a Wittgensteinian might with some justice say, who in the first place illegitimately transfers a move (that of seeking to show why there is a reason to do what is required) from the one language-game to the other. It is she therefore to whom 'the sentence seems queer' because, as Wittgenstein might put it, she has 'imagin[ed] a different language-game for it from the one in which we actually use it' (ibid.: 195). It is she who makes 'the mistake of looking for an explanation where [she] ought to have said: this *language-game is played*' (ibid.: 654). It is she who in this way forces her opponents to appeal to a bogus super-reason at once legitimizing and making practically effective the ordinary requirements of morality. It is therefore she who concedes (at least temporary) sense to such an enterprise in order to declare it finally senseless.

It is worth noting that among Foot's opponents there are those like Prichard who would not make Foot's (Wittgensteinian) mistake. For they precisely reject the demand for reasons for complying with moral judgements as senseless. Thus Prichard, as we saw in an earlier chapter, repeatedly tells those who 'want to have it proved to [them] that [they] ought to do [it]' that their demand: 'cannot be satisfied because it is illegitimate' ([1912] 1968: 14–17). And of 'the knowledge that would satisfy this demand' he says with finality 'there is no such knowledge'. Those who make, and seek to satisfy, the demand are allowing their 'general thinking' to take over the work which should properly be done by their 'moral capacities of thinking'. It is thus perhaps more appropriate to describe Foot and the naturalists rather than writers such as Prichard as, in Wittgenstein's phrase, 'held captive' by a picture (1958: 115).

As it happens, Foot's original proposal as to how morality and etiquette might be distinguished did seem to imply that this rejection of the demand for reasons in the case of morality lies at the heart of the contrast. It made no such appeal to metaphysics, and yet seems able to distinguish morality from etiquette, once two questions are separated which seem to have become conflated. There is first the question whether a rule gives a reason to someone to perform a particular action which falls under it. Second, there is the question whether it is appropriate to demand reasons for *accepting* the rule in the first place, or the system of rules to which it belongs.

Now appeal to these two different questions, or levels of enquiry, may enable us to explain what Foot represents as puzzling, namely how rules of etiquette can be simultaneously non-hypothetical and hypothetical. The way is then open for them to be contrasted with morality which is ordinarily taken to be non-hypothetical at both levels, or in other words, *truly* categorical.

Thus, at the level at which rules give us reasons to act in particular ways, etiquette, for those who accept it, is a source of non-hypothetical imperatives. That is to say its imperatives apply, like moral imperatives, independent of the agent's desires or interests. Thus provided a person's not caring about etiquette is just a temporary lapse against a persistent background of adherence to the system, a particular rule of etiquette may be said still to apply to her, even though she lacks any momentary desire to follow or interest in following it. If our question is about the appropriateness of demanding reasons for adherence to a whole system, etiquette is only a source of hypothetical imperatives. Thus, an individual can coherently ask, as she cannot with morality, what is in favour of following etiquette's rules? Now if she agrees that etiquette is a good thing, e.g. serves her interests, or makes for social harmony, and is moved to seek these ends, its rules will give her reasons to act in the relevant ways.

(ii) Outsiders and participants again

Naturalists might object: but why should we let Wittgensteinians get away with turning a perfectly legitimate attempt to stand outside our language-games, and so say something 'objective', into something as self-referential as a 'grammatical move-ment made by [ourselves]'? But this raises the question whether we really can coherently adopt such an 'outsider's' perspective upon our moral practices, and also what force talk of 'objectivity' would have here. This brings us to a second way that the naturalistic enterprise might possibly be blocked – and again I merely sketch a direction of inquiry. It would involve trying to show that the things that the natu-ralist wants to say by adopting this outsider's viewpoint cannot be said. This would be either because she will find herself saying something different from what she intended to say – something that one of the participants might say – or because she will fall into incoherence. The outsider, it will be suggested, whether she likes it or not, can never fully disengage herself from the participants' viewpoint.

In Chapter 6 we considered an attempt by accidentalists to do justice, despite representing moral practice as dependent on contingent social facts, to the special authority, or categoricity, of moral requirements. This, as we saw, involved adopting precisely such an outsider's viewpoint upon this moral practice – a viewpoint which was then taken as dominant, with the participants seen as shielded from the outsiders' sceptical verdict on the nature and scope of moral norms. We considered in particular the almost insuperable difficulty of sealing off the participants' view-point from the outsider's. In dealing with the questions mentioned above, however, the focus would now be on the outsider's viewpoint rather than the participants'. We would want to know why the outsider's viewpoint should prevail over the participants', and still more fundamentally whether the idea is coherent of an outsiders' viewpoint which is genuinely independent of that of the participants.

The first question receives a partial answer since the outsider is claimed to be a non-committed observer making factual reports of the moral practice in a commu-nity. It is the presumed objectivity of such an investigator, free from the partial and biased perspective of members of the community in thrall to particular values and norms, that is perhaps responsible for the belief that this viewpoint must in the end prevail.

But this only raises the more fundamental question: can the outsiders' account be genuinely independent of the participants' own account? One drastic, traditional, way of ensuring its independence is to expunge from it any reference to the concepts in terms of which the participants themselves characterize their behaviour, and to introduce a new set of concepts, such as those belonging to the natural sciences. Thus we might try, following in the tradition of Mill (see Hart's critique, 1961: 87) substituting for talk of duties, obligations and norms that of 'observable regularities of conduct, predictions, probabilities and signs'.

The outsider, on this interpretation, notes that certain types of behaviour – those which from the participants' own perspective are either manifestations of, or associated with, their conformity with moral norms – are regularly followed by certain other types of behaviour. This leads her to take the former as 'natural signs' of the latter, rather as clouds are signs of rain (Hart, 1961: 86–8). She is thus able to predict later behaviours on the basis of earlier ones, and to explain them accordingly.

But this presupposes that she has a way of identifying instances of behaviour as belonging to the same general type. It cannot be that they are all examples of conformity, or non-conformity, with a particular moral rule since the concept not merely of a moral rule, but that of a rule more generally, belongs exclusively to the participants' viewpoint. In excluding reference to rules, however, it is not just that sophisticated notions like obligation and duty must be expunged from the outsiders' account. It would seem that the idea of meaningful action itself, because of its intrinsic connection with rule-following, could have no place in such an inquiry.

Indeed, it might seem that we have no grounds for assuming that the outsider has any level of familiarity at all with distinctively human activities. No-one brought up in society, it might be felt, could possibly take what is obviously rule-governed behaviour, for the occurrence of two phenomena related as clouds are to rain.

Even taking the observed phenomena to be, not mere sequences of movements, but actions under some description, there are insuperable difficulties. It has often been pointed out that actions which are exemplifications of a moral rule, such as keeping a promise, may have nothing else in common but their falling under this rule. Conversely a given action might, depending on context, signify either the keeping or the breaking of a promise. Again when we conform to a moral rule, there is rarely a relevant prior event, such as the issue of an order. Finally, where respecting a moral rule involves refraining from doing something, there is no positive action to be observed at all.

The outsider of course cannot really be ignorant of the idea of rule-following behaviour. After all, she is herself applying rules when she identifies certain kinds of behaviour as a natural sign of other kinds of behaviour. These are the rules which govern scientific practice. Whereas, however, with the study of natural phenomena, only her own set of concepts are available to explain them, with moral behaviour, there is a competing set of concepts, those of the agents or the participants themselves. The question thus arises once again: why should her set of concepts prevail over those of the participants? Have they a special fitness to do so lacked by the participants' own concepts? Does the outsiders' account stand over and against that of the participants' allowing a balanced 'objective' appraisal of their practices? It would hardly seem so. Indeed, just the opposite, as we now see, appears to be true.

The outsider, we may note, observes not only that participants typically perform certain actions consequent upon the enunciation of relevant statements of duty or obligation, but that there are unpleasant consequences when they do not do so. She in this way comes to take these statements as a basis for predicting that disobedience will be followed by unpleasant consequences.

But then her attitude to the existence of a moral rule, rather than standing over and against the participants', resembles that of just one type of participant in moral practice, namely, those who erroneously take an obligation only as a warning that failure to fulfil it would provoke hostility, and see such a failure as for this reason alone a bad thing, not because it is disobedience, which could itself be used to justify these hostile reactions. Such participants, who are described by Hart as ignoring 'the internal aspect' of rules, and concerning themselves solely with their 'external aspect', are thus moved to obey them merely by a desire to escape the unpleasant consequences of not doing so. In this way they – possibly cynically – treat being obligated as though it were a form of coercion. This hardly seems the basis for an objective account of moral practice.

According to an alternative interpretation, described by Hart as lacking the 'extreme externality' of the previous one, the outsider now grasps the rule-following nature of the participants' behaviour. Though he therefore acknowledges the 'internal aspect' of rules, in not seeking to conform his own behaviour to them, he does so from an 'external' point of view. The participants, by contrast, acknowledge (Hart, 1961: 88) the 'internal aspect' of rules 'from their own internal point of view'.

But in what sense can such a viewpoint be claimed to be more 'objective' than that of the participants? Well, it is the viewpoint from which the antecedent conditions can be fully spelt out for the coming into being and continued existence of morality, namely that individuals happen to have been in the first place moved to accept its norms as authoritative. But surely appeal to this prior psychological motivation as genuinely explanatory is spurious since there is no other evidence for it than the participants' actual adherence to moral norms? It thus seems to be little more than a reiteration of the naturalists' dogma that no action can come about except through the ordinary psychological channels.

We return finally to the naturalists' claim that the essentially social nature of morality entails its genesis in, and dependence, upon a particular factual setting. The supposed entailment is certainly not indisputable. Indeed, many draw an opposite conclusion from the observation that morality is social. It is precisely, they insist, its social nature that makes this kind of naturalistic reduction impossible. For it implies that individuals could independently of the whole practice of morality have happened to entertain certain ends, as a means to the accomplishment of which a system of rules was then devised, around which full-blown moral practice in turn developed. But many would object that no such ends can coherently be identified as 'moral' prior to the establishment of the practice. These ends are given relative to moral practice, and are complexly woven together with rules and particular judgements within it.

4 Final remarks

With these sketches of how Wittgensteinian ideas might be brought to bear on the challenge posed for those who posit external reasons and motives by naturalist proponents of the 'extreme' version of Hume's practicality argument, I reach the end of my inquiry. The case for non-cognitivism is, I have argued, fundamentally flawed in so far as it is made through the 'moderate' version of Hume's argument, whose precarious validity depends on its never being fully distinguished from the valid 'extreme' version. The cognitivist/non-cognitivist opposition itself gives way, once we unambiguously focus on the 'extreme' version of the practicality argument, to the opposition between naturalists, whether cognitivist *or* non-cognitivist, and *non*-naturalists.

Clearly, it would hardly be consonant with these findings to attempt to use the Wittgensteinian ideas sketched above to develop, in the manner of Lovibond (1983) or Johnstone (1989), a specifically cognitivist alternative to 'Humean' non-cognitivism.[8] Moreover, the strength of Wittgensteinian ethics would, I have intimated, lie in its rejection of the dichotomy: *either* naturalism *or* metaphysical obscurantism. Care would therefore have to be taken not to allow tell-tale signs of the naturalistic enterprise to creep back. (One would do well, for instance, to question the appropriateness of retaining, as Johnstone does, 1989: 82–4, 95, 105, the contrast between inert facts and dynamic values.) For then the new account will be no more capable than, I have argued, are naturalistic ones, whether cognitivist or non-cognitivist, of showing that the will legitimately, as Wiggins (1976: 341) has put it in another context, 'craves objective reasons'.[9] Nor will it be able to do justice to our profound sense of the unconditionality of our common moral precepts.

It is important, additionally, to point out that the espousal of any general theory at all in Wittgenstein's name would be misguided. Wittgenstein repeatedly insists that there is no substitute for paying the closest possible attention to our language games; they are simply more complex, more diverse, than can be anticipated in advance of such attention.[10] In an effort to comply with this, writers such as Winch (1965)[11] and Diamond (1996) have been led to explore certain concepts with nuanced moral connotations through literary examples. I did this myself (1983), and have done it again here in my reading of *Owen Wingrave*. But, far from being incompatible with traditional philosophical preoccupations, or requiring us, as it is too often supposed, to jettison the classical philosophical debates, with their hard-won insights, as either irrelevant, or some form of mental aberration, Wittgenstein's later thought should encourage us to pay even more painstaking attention to them. This is especially true where the debate is associated with a work of such unparalleled richness and prodigious creativity as Hume's *Treatise*.

Glossary

(Where the term is not mine I indicate the source.)

Accidentalism (common)

The view that moral judgements are beliefs which are dependent on the fortuitous or accidental presence of a desire if they are to lead to the requisite action.

'Belief-content' externalism

The view (of accidentalists) that, since there is only a fortuitous connection between moral judgements and motivation, these judgements cannot genuinely oblige us to act. In identifying the property or state of affairs on which their truth depends, one is merely therefore illuminating their content.

Cognitivism (common)

The view that moral judgements are beliefs about a given objective property of an action on whose presence their truth depends.

'External fact' analysis (Falk, 1945)

This holds that an agent must look outside herself to an objective property of the action in order to discover whether she is morally obliged to perform that action.

External motive

The idea that the objective property of an action which is held to make a moral judgement true *itself* provides the relevant motive.

'Internal fact' analysis (Falk, 1945)

This holds that an agent must look inside herself – to her state of mind, feelings, motives – to discover whether she is morally obliged to act.

Moderate version of the practicality argument

The (invalid) version whose second premiss states that *reason moves us to action, but only with the help of an independent desire*. I distinguish three different reinterpretations, aimed at making this version valid, of which the respective first premisses state that moral judgements are *sufficient on their own for*, that they *compel*, and that they are *intrinsically related to*, motivation.

More radical 'external fact' analysis (my adaptation from Falk, 1945)

This holds that in the moral sphere an action can be performed without an agent having a relevant subjective motive and simply as a result of her rational awareness of the relevant objective property of the action. External motives are therefore posited (see above).

Necessitarianism

The view that moral judgements are beliefs which are nevertheless in some way necessarily connected to motivation.

Non-cognitivism (common)

The view that moral judgements are expressions of feeling or desire, not beliefs.

'Obligation–constitutive' externalism

Moral judgements can genuinely oblige us to act in the relevant way. This is because the property or state of affairs on which the truth of our judgement depends, though outside us, itself provides our motive.

Subjectivist assumption

That the source of all action lies in the subjective, or internal, states of agents.

Sufficiency reinterpretation

See the 'moderate' version of the practicality argument, above.

Notes

Introduction

1 For present purposes, I treat the phrases 'influencing action' and 'having a motivational role' as equivalent. I assume, however, that someone motivated to perform an action, X, will only perform that action, or only attempt to do so, in the absence of countervailing motivations.

2 My remarks here apply much more to the *Treatise* than the *Enquiry,* and no doubt this accounts for my preference for the earlier work. As Pears (1990: Postscript) eloquently points out: 'In his first presentation of his system paradoxical implications are never blunted to reduce the shock of their impact.'

1   A contradiction not an ambiguity

1 W. Empson, *Seven Types of Ambiguity*, Chatto and Windus, London, 1949: x.

2 But this will be dealt with at much greater length in Chapter 5.

3 The word 'mere' is meant to capture the somewhat dismissive attitude towards rhetoric implicit in Baillie's 'once we get past the rhetoric'. I would stress, however, that it is only in recent times that rhetoric has come to seem a rather empty, or even disreputable, art or skill; it would not have been regarded thus by Hume.

4 Generalizing about this latter type of situation, he writes: 'a person may be affected with passion, by supposing a pain or pleasure to lie in an object, which has no tendency to produce either of these sensations, or which produces the contrary to what is imagin'd'.

5 Radcliffe, for instance (in Cohon, 2001: 381, note 37) acknowledges that 'the claim that we are motivated by the prospect of pleasure raises some difficult questions about the priority of passion over reason'. She explains: 'If my belief that an object or an action will be pleasurable generates motivating passions toward that action or object, then it appears that reason is motivating, since that belief is a product of reason', and concludes that: 'Hume certainly writes as though the existence of a motive can depend upon belief.' However, she rejects this reading as 'unlikely' on grounds that it contradicts his characterization elsewhere of passions as original existences. But she offers no reason for giving precedence in this way to the latter characterization in determining a correct interpretation, nor indeed for not just allowing the apparent contradiction to stand at least pending further investigation. Darwall, however, (1995: 225, note 32), thinks that, given such claims as that 'the prospect of pain or pleasure' can arouse in us an 'emotion of aversion or propensity', Hume must be overstating his case elsewhere when he speaks of the inertness of reason.

6 Brown (in Cohon, 2001: 346) deals in this way with Hume's talk of it being 'the prospect of pain or pleasure from any object' that arouses desire and so leads to action. 'Objects' she writes explaining Hume's view, 'affect us because we have pre-existing feelings about them . . . [it is these that] make the difference.'

2 Validity and the 'moderate' version

1   Examples of other writers who, assuming a 'moderate' reading, draw attention to the argument's invalidity when the first premiss is taken as stating no more than that morality has an influence on action are Brown (2001: 349) and Radcliffe (2001: 385). However, the only exhaustive attempt I know to try out different formulations of the first and second premiss, consistently with a 'moderate' reading, in order to secure the argument's validity, is Snare (1991: 34–83). But he does not consider the possibility of distinguishing as we do between this 'moderate' version of the argument, and an 'extreme', valid, one.

2   Superficially, Hume uses the terms 'reason' and 'belief', or 'judgement', interchangeably. Since we have no clear warrant so far for ascribing different underlying meanings to them, I shall for the time being follow both him and recent writers in also treating them as interchangeable. I shall, however, use 'belief' more frequently than 'reason' since it has a more natural ring with our contemporary illustrations. I stress though that the decision not to distinguish between 'reason' and 'belief' in the Humean context is only provisional. As we shall see towards the end of the chapter, it soon runs up against severe difficulties.

3   There are a number of others. Compare the following statements of the conclusion by Stroud: 'we can never arrive at moral views by reason or reasoning alone' (1977: 172) and '[moral conclusions or moral judgements] could not be arrived at by reason' (ibid.: 173). Again, compare Baillie's claim that Hume thought he had 'refut[ed] the grounding of morality in reason alone' (2000: 121) and his claim that, for Hume 'the "discovery of morality" cannot be the sole preserve of reason' (ibid.: 123) with his claim that, for Hume, 'rightness cannot consist in conformity to reason' (ibid.: 123).

4   See, for example, Harrison (1976: 110, 112) where he calls this view 'the crude view'.

5   See, for example, Stroud (1977: 184).

6   Harrison (1976: 111) recognizes that inductive reasoning would be out of place here, but differs from us in allowing sense to the idea of getting to know what one's feelings, or sensations, are by introspection.

7   See, for example, Stroud (1977: 182–3).

8   That Hume intends, despite occasionally giving the impression that he is collapsing them, to keep distinct two levels of analysis is surely clear from passages like that at 3.3.1:30. The first level is that of ordinary moral responses, to which his description of individuals, as 'reap[ing] a pleasure from the view of a character' belongs, and to which talk of virtue, and vice must, for him, if it is to have a sense at all, be exclusively confined. The second level is that pertaining to the ultimate 'source' of this pleasure in objective properties, such as social usefulness, and primarily to be investigated by philosophers, with the ordinary moral responses as their data.

9   Norton (1982: 120) is one of the few notable writers (perhaps the only one) to claim that Hume is a moral objectivist, holding that 'there are moral distinctions grounded in real existences that are independent of the observer's mind'. But Norton supports his claim with a one-sided diet of quotations, and interprets even these in an idiosyncratic, implausible, and often patently erroneous way. I point to just one example. Consider again Hume's famous remark at 3.1.1:26:

> Take any action allow'd to be vicious . . . examine it in all lights, and see if you can find that matter of fact, or real existence, which you call *vice* . . . In which-ever way you take it, you find only certain passions, motives, volitions, and thoughts . . . The vice entirely escapes you, as long as you consider the object.

Now Norton (1982: 116, note 21) abbreviates the remark, at the same time substituting 'moral qualities' for Hume's 'vice', and 'action' for Hume's 'object'. He writes: 'Moral qualities entirely escape us so long as we consider the action'. He goes on to link the remark, as he has it, with Hume's later point (3.2.1) that actions function merely as 'signs' of virtuous, or vicious, motives (Norton's 'qualities of the agent's mind'). He thus gives the impression that Hume, in the first remark (at 3.1.1:26), is contrasting actions, as the mere sign of virtue, or vice, with motives, or 'qualities of the agent's mind', as their objective source. But, in this remark, Hume classifies the 'action' with those 'passions, motives, volitions, thoughts' (Norton's 'qualities of the agent's mind'), which lead up to it, as together 'the *object*'. He then contrasts the 'object', thus compendiously understood, with the *subjective* feelings of pleasure, or pain, of the spectator viewing the 'object'. It is here, Hume goes on to stress, in the spectator's own breast that virtue and vice reside, not in any real qualities either of the action, or of the agent's mind. In calling an action (or more properly an agent's motives, or 'qualities of mind') virtuous, or vicious, the spectator is therefore, according to Hume, merely projecting on to these actions, or 'qualities of mind', his own, subjective, feelings. Norton, by thus derailing Hume's intended contrast, attempts – unsuccessfully – to turn one of Hume's most uncompromising statements of moral subjectivism into one evincing a thorough-going objectivism, in which (1982: 118) 'the qualities of the agent's mind are the objective correlate[s] of the [spectator's] moral feeling'.

10 Stroud (1977: 183) canvasses this suggestion but likewise rejects it.

11 The term comes from Stroud (ibid.: 185) but, as he observes (2001: 143), it was originally coined by Paul Grice writing on Hume in the early 1970s. Clearly it is an application to the moral context of a metaphor Hume uses when discussing necessary connexion (1.3.14:25) where he writes: 'the mind has a great propensity to *spread itself* on external objects' (my italics).

12 But I discuss secondary qualities in more detail in Chapter 4.

13 See, for instance, Stroud (1977: 190–2).

14 Baillie (2000: 139) who adopts, more self-consciously, and deliberately, than most writers, what we would call a 'moderate' reading of the practicality argument's second premiss, also seems untroubled by the role Hume here grants to reason.

15 But Hume provides one such metaphor when he speaks in the *Enquiry* of reasoning merely 'paving the way for' sentiment. It may be this metaphor which Penelhum (1975: 142) has in mind when he refers to 'the cognitive preliminaries that lead to [the moral sentiments]'. See also Baillie (2000: 190) who points to the role Hume grants to the imagination, alongside reason, in the adoption of a disinterested and impartial standpoint. He emphasizes (again assuming the 'moderate' reading mentioned in note 14 above) that the reasoning involved is no more than what Hume would see as being involved in motivation generally.

16 Stroud (1977: 157) suggests this thought.

17 There are those who clearly recognize that Humeans must ultimately be committed to the asymmetry claim, and yet do not apparently recognize that it, together with the claim that moral judgements are linked to motivation in the same close way as desires, must *already* be among the Humean premises, if they are to yield this stronger conclusion. For instance, Dancy (1993: 3) mistakenly takes this stronger conclusion to be established (provided one accepts the premises as true) by a 'sufficiency' version of 'the classic Humean argument' in which *neither* of these claims apparently figure. Indeed the premises, as he renders them are merely these: 'No set of beliefs alone is sufficient to generate an action [premiss 2]. But if we add to such a set a moral judgement, we have a new set which could be sufficient for action [premiss 1]'. He goes on to maintain that, *given* that these premises (if true, as Humeans believe they are) entail the identification of moral judgements with desires, it *follows* that such judgements must (for Humeans) be necessarily motivating. This is because, according to him, Humeans *already* independently maintain that *desires* (unlike beliefs) are necessarily motivating.

18 Not all writers use the terms 'sufficient' and 'intrinsic' to refer to different types of relation as I do. Some use 'sufficient' to refer to the very relation that we have called 'intrinsic'. Others, however, while using the terms interchangeably, have in mind a relation which does not quite coincide with either of those I describe, and allows therefore for a certain equivocation between the two, which I have sought to get rid of. See particularly Radcliffe (2001: 363–87).

19 I have taken the word 'mandatory' from Smith's characterization of how, on the Humean view, reason, or belief, is deficient compared with moral judgement as a motivating force, making it impossible for the latter to be, for Humeans, purely cognitive. Thus, Smith writes that, according to the Humeans,'a change in my desires [cannot be] mandated by reason'(1994: 8), though he represents them as allowing that a belief can have a 'non-rational' impact on desire, and hence on motivation. He goes on to observe, however, (ibid.: 10) that the practicality of moral judgements (asserted in premiss 1) entails, by contrast, that if we judge that an action is right then, all things being equal, 'we *must* be motivated' to act in accordance with our judgement (my italics).

20 Stroud (1977: 200). He is here quoting Hume.

21 It is not uncommon with the 'moderate' version to find Hume's original contradictory formulations incorporated within its second premiss (and so *within* the theory of motivation which it expresses and which Hume has bequeathed to us) as though these were just two different ways of saying the same thing. To take one example, Smith (1994) would have us believe that, for Humeans, desires are both the 'only states' (ibid.: 125) that can motivate action (with the implication that beliefs do no motivational work at all) and also (ibid.: 91, 97, 126) that they are merely *among* the sources of motivation, with means-end beliefs as further necessary conditions. In this way, Hume's contradiction breaks out again not merely between those favouring a 'moderate' and an 'extreme' reading but inside the ostensibly 'moderate' reading itself where it is reproduced, one suspects, almost unthinkingly as an odd kind of orthodoxy.

Below, however, I put the validity of the 'moderate' version to one side, and concentrate on the question whether its premisses are true.

22 Stroud (1977: 173).

23 But Hare (1963: 67) is an exception in acknowledging that Hume does not claim that moral judgements are necessarily linked with action. See also Brown (in Cohon, 2001) below.

24 Brown (in Cohon, 2001: 351–2) holds that the 'intrinsicality' reinterpretation of the first premiss secures the argument's validity, but rejects it as not coherent with Hume's intentions. Radcliffe (2001: 365) agrees with Brown that Hume needs the stronger claim, but argues that it is coherent with the text (see below).

25 Whether or not the necessity of the relation between the pleasurable sentiment of moral approval and the inclination to act can be upheld, a problem will still arise as to the *kind* of action to which this sentiment is, on Foot's account, supposed to incline us. On her interpretation, after all, it is not merely that this sentiment inclines us to *some* action, it inclines us to the *very* action, whose contemplation in others gave us this pleasurable sentiment. But why shouldn't we, for instance, try to prolong the pleasure of contemplation – if that is the idea – by trying to get the *agent* herself to repeat the action, rather than ourselves endeavouring to perform it? If there is to be any justification for preferring the first to the second interpretation, this also will have to be found in the 'self-hatred' example.

26 Moore ([1903] 1966: 135) seems to be referring to this idea when he writes: 'It may be maintained . . . that it is only because certain things were originally willed, that we ever came to have ethical convictions at all'. But he links it with the fallacy of supposing that 'to shew what was the cause of a thing is the same thing as to show what the thing itself is'. See Radcliffe (2001: 369, note 16).

27 The amount of space I give to my refutation of Radcliffe's arguments may still seem disproportionate to their significance. But looking no further than a 'moderate' reading of the argument, she is eloquent on the pressures she – and many others – feel under to defend the 'intrinsicality' reinterpretation. As she writes (ibid.: 365)

Why not give up the . . . account, where approbation motivates directly, in favor of the story Hume explicitly offers, where a desire to avoid pain is the relevant motive to behave morally? The reply is that Hume needs the former account if his crucial argument against the moral rationalists, based on the motivating force of our moral distinctions . . . is to survive. That argument . . . commits him to the view that morality is inherently motivating.

28 See Smith (1994: 14): 'I will argue that we can and should accept Hume's claim that belief and desire are distinct existences, states with distinctive roles to play in the explanation of human action'. See also Copp (1997: 35) who represents Smith's claim (1994: 12) that for Humeans, or in a Humean psychology, belief and desire are 'distinct existences' as a claim about belief and desire being 'different kinds of psychological state, and any action [being] the result of states of both kinds'.

29 I have derived this formulation of the first premiss from the *denial* of the premiss that Mackie (1980: 54) puts into the mouth of Harrison, who wishes to challenge it. I have also here constructed an equivalent formulation of premiss 2.

30 For a more recent attempt along Mackie's lines to read premiss 1 as entailing a metaphysically necessary connection, but to distance Hume from it, see Darwall (2001: 389–422). Radcliffe (in Cohon, 2001: 371) who mentions Darwall's interpretation is right, I believe, to reject it. But she is wrong to say that there is no evidence of Hume having thought the moral rationalists were committed to *a priori* internalism (as well as to the view that moral judgements were discerned *a priori*). In fact, Hume ridicules them precisely for positing an *a priori* link between moral judgements and the will.

31 Mackie's endorsement of this is somewhat qualified. He thinks that in order to be plausible premiss 2 must be read as denying the requisite practicality only to 'demonstrative reasoning, causal knowledge and factual information of ordinary sorts', not to 'knowledge, beliefs and reasoning of any kinds'. He observes, however, that the argument will then fail to rule out cognitivists who, like the moral intuitionists, hold that moral knowledge is a special sort of knowledge supplied by a moral sense.

32 However, I will argue later (Chapter 6) that these cognitivist naturalists themselves undermine this contrast, and so are finally as incapable as non-cognitivists of capturing the essentially peremptory character of moral judgements.

3 Metaphysics and the 'extreme' version

1 This work by Clarke was originally published in 1706. Selections are reprinted from the 1728 edition in D.D. Raphael (ed.) (1969) *British Moralists 1650–1800, I. Hobbes–Gay*, Oxford: Clarendon Press, 191–225 or paragraphs 224–61. References in the text are to these paragraphs. Prior (1956: 30) suggests that Hume's (and Hutcheson's) arguments 'were directed against Clarke more than anyone else'.

2 This work by Wollaston was originally published in 1724. Selections are reprinted in Raphael (ed.) (1969), 239–58 or paragraphs 272–302. References are to these paragraphs.

3 This work by Cudworth was originally published in 1731. Selections are reprinted in Raphael (ed.) (1969), 105–19 or paragraphs 119–53. References are to these paragraphs. For an interpretation of Cudworth which stresses his differences from, rather than, like mine, his similarities with, Clarke, see Darwall (1995). On Darwall's reading, there is for Cudworth a separate faculty of practical reason distinct from theoretical reason, moral motives being given by the former rather than by the latter.

4 Significantly, this 'inward anticipation of the mind' is, Cudworth tells us, matched by an 'inward and vital principle whereby [rational beings] have a natural determination in them to do some things, and to avoid others, which could not be, if they were mere naked passive things'. However, for us today, even to begin to take on board this metaphysical hinterland of ideas would require an imaginative leap into a way of thinking, partly at least theological, that has now – largely due to Hume – slipped below our conceptual horizon Indeed it is this larger metaphysical context which, in his criticisms of moral rationalism, Hume strips away.

5 Prior (1956: 33) points out that the adjective was originally used of Hume's passage by D.D. Raphael (in *The Moral Sense*).

6   Moore ([1903] 1966: 40) here gives a clear account of what he means by 'naturalistic'. He writes: 'I do mean . . . that which is the subject-matter of the natural sciences and also of psychology.'

7   Derivatively, Nature also comes to be contrasted by Clarke, with what is unnatural, in the sense of corrupt or perverted, since men sometimes try to gainsay Nature by asserting that something is good which is by nature indifferent, and so attempt to deny the truth that a thing can only be good *by goodness*.

8   Prior (1956: 26) points out that:

> the tendency to fall into fallacious modes of reasoning is rather like an epidemic that breaks out during a war. It strikes one side first, giving a temporary advantage to the other; but it has a way of drifting across the lines of battle and infecting those who formerly had the satisfaction of being free from it.

9   So far, to commit the naturalistic fallacy seems, even in the metaphysical context, to consist simply in the reduction itself of ethical propositions to propositions of another kind. As before, Moore adduces considerations as to why this reduction itself is unacceptable, and again they concern its counter-intuitive implications. Here, however, he introduces a novel and powerful consideration which has come to be known as Moore's 'open argument' ([1903] 1966: 125–6). Despite this, the same ambiguity arises, as before, over whether the naturalistic fallacy is just the reduction of 'good' to these other terms, or the further step of continuing to try to make significant moral claims. It is worth noting that, in so far as Moore's target is now not naturalism per se, but also non-naturalism, our earlier objection to taking the is–ought passage as anticipating Moore – that Hume himself is a naturalist – is eased. In so far, however, as Moore's objection is to *any* definition of 'good' (1966: 77) Hume's remark at 3.1.1:26 is still an obstacle to a Moorean interpretation of the is–ought passage.

10 Thomas Reid, *Essays On the Active Powers*, v–vii, quoted by Prior (1956: 33–4).

11 Hare (1952: 84) offers what he calls a restatement of Moore's argument, yielding the conclusion that a naturalistic definition of 'good' obstructs its 'commendatory', or prescriptive, function.

12 Nowell-Smith anticipates the following retort: 'I just don't believe you. You are propounding a philosopher's paradox, playing with words', and replies:

> Of course you are right. Of course the question, 'Why should I do what I see to be right . . . [is] an absurd one. In ordinary life we should be puzzled by a man who said 'Yes, you have convinced me that it is the right thing to do; but ought I to do it?' We shouldn't know how to answer him . . . because, in conceding that it is the right thing to do, he has already conceded that he ought to do it.

13 See also Baillie's remark (2000: 122):

> Hume's target is any form of moral rationalism claiming that when we act from a sense of moral obligation – doing something because we judge it to be the right thing to do – our action is both caused and rationally explained by the presence of beliefs alone.

4   Sentimentalism, secondary qualities and sensations

1   This work was published in 1725, its full title being *An Inquiry into the Original of our Ideas of Beauty and Virtue, II An Inquiry concerning the Original of our Ideas of Virtue or Moral Good*. Selections are reprinted from the 1738 edition in Raphael (ed.) (1969) 261–99, paragraphs 303–54. Citations in the text are by paragraph number except where I state otherwise.

2   This work was published in 1728, its full title being *An Essay on the Nature and Conduct of the Passions and Affections. With Illustrations on the Moral Sense.* Selections are reprinted from the 1742 edition in Raphael (ed.) (1969) 300–21, paragraphs 355–73. Citations are by paragraph.

3   On just this ground Harrison (1976, 115–16) points to the inappropriateness of calling Hume a moral sense theorist. He writes:

> There is an important difference between sense and sentiment . . . My senses give me information about the things I see, or hear or feel . . . if there were a moral sense, its function would be precisely to discover such facts about an action as that it was right or wrong. Indeed, one would have supposed that it would discover to us properties of the action itself . . . enabl[ing] us to arrive at true beliefs about actions.

4   Hutcheson's statement that one of his main purposes in undertaking the *Inquiry* was 'to prove what we call the *Reality of Virtue*' has been said to indicate that he believed that there was a moral reality independent of the perceiver. But this is much too swift.

Certainly, whether virtue was 'real' was furiously debated by Hutcheson's predecessors. Moreover, when Shaftesbury allied himself with the 'Realists' for whom virtue was 'really something in-itself, and in the nature of things', he was affirming a form of moral objectivism. However, the virtue whose 'reality' Mandeville denied, calling the search for it 'a wild goose chace', was something quite different: the possession by human beings of genuinely altruistic motives. Mandeville cynically explained away apparently virtuous behaviour by suggesting that it was simply their self-regarding desire to think well of themselves that led people to try and live up to the ideals propounded by their rulers precisely for this purpose, and concluded by describing ([1714] 1969: 269) 'The moral virtues' as 'the political offspring which flattery begot upon pride'. We cannot just assume therefore that Hutcheson, in asserting virtue's 'reality', is re-affirming Shaftesbury's (meta-ethical) objectivism rather than opposing Mandeville's psychological egoism. But suppose we were sure that Hutcheson was addressing the meta-ethical issue concerning the nature of moral judgements, as well as the psychological issue concerning the nature of human motivation, and suppose we were also sure that his talk of 'virtue's reality' pertained to the former. It is doubtful whether even then, *purely on the strength of his use of this expression,* that we could be certain that his stance was, like Shaftesbury's, objectivist. When Shaftesbury sided with 'the Realists', he was opposing conventionalism: the meta-ethical expression of Hobbes' moral scepticism (egoism being its psychological dimension). Thus, Shaftesbury (1714) spoke of those 'nominal moralists' for whom 'virtue is nothing or a name of fashion', and again of those for whom moral distinctions are a matter of 'force and power', 'fashion and vogue' or 'fancy or will'. But his specific target here was the Hobbesian view that moral judgements lacked any fixed or consistent content. But it is not clear that this fluctuation of content can only be repaired by going all the way to moral objectivism. There are at least three possible solutions. One of these is indeed moral rationalism, according to which the truth of moral judgements depends on nothing less than the existence of certain eternal and immutable relations of actions to circumstances. But another, though also grounding moral judgements 'in the object', takes the relevant moral property to be identical with a given natural property, such as, for instance, an action's having beneficial consequences. However, Humean subjectivism, according to which human beings are so naturally constituted as to have regular and uniform responses to particular types of actions, or their motives, can also be construed as providing moral judgements with an invariable content, and so as a response to Hobbesian conventionalism. As I argue, Hutcheson's analogy between the moral sense and sense perception is a better indication of his moral objectivism.

5   It is, however, still sometimes suggested, see Stafford (1985: 136), that Hutcheson was primarily concerned to counteract the egoistic psychology of Hobbes and Mandeville. See also Winkler (1985: 191–2) who takes 'the reality of virtue' to apply mainly to this

motivational question., and signifies Hutcheson's rejection of Hobbesian egoism. While I
agree with Sprague (1954) and Norton (1982) that Hutcheson was concerned with both
the meta-ethical and the motivational question, I do not agree with either that he also
maintained that the moral sense was *itself* a source of motivation, independently of ordinary natural motivations (see below pp. 111–12). Rather, Hutcheson seeks to show, by
pointing to examples of our appreciation of unselfish actions, that we have a moral sense
distinct from our other senses. Since such an appreciation, he argues, is not motivated by
self-love (it is not subject to the will at all and in any case we have nothing to gain by this
appreciation) and does not have as its object the self-love of the agent (for what is admired
is the agent's selflessness), he concludes that there must be a natural source of motivation
other than self-love. In fact, it is the genuine benevolence of the agent to which we are
responding in such cases.

6 I agree with Darwall (1995:215) that the debate between Norton, Stafford and Winkler
has been "marred by some unclarity about what moral realism must be". Stafford
(1985:136) unjustifiably charges Norton with representing Hutcheson as "postulating
moral (as opposed to natural) facts and entities, non-natural qualities or other metaphysical fictions" or "ontological fripperies". He seems to have reached this view, despite
Norton's insistence that Hutcheson was a naturalist, on the strength of Norton's suggestion that for Hutcheson "the moral sense is a faculty capable of apprehending
independently existing, intersubjective features.. of the world about us, just as the other,
ordinary senses presumably do". Stafford clearly takes it (ibid.: 137) that any claim to the
effect that the moral sense was, for Hutcheson, cognitive, that (as Norton puts it) "virtue
and vice [were for Hutcheson] genuine features of reality", attributes to him a metaphysical realism. Ironically it is Stafford himself, in interpreting Norton and Hutcheson, and
not as Stafford claims (ibid.:135) Norton, who cannot allow a mid-way position between
"nihilistic scepticism and [this] metaphysical realism".

7 Perhaps they are impressed by the fact that Hutcheson, in the preceding paragraph, adds
"pleasure" and "pain" to a list of secondary qualities, including "colours, tastes [and]
smells". But it should not be forgotten that he is talking here as elsewhere of the ideas of
secondary qualities, not of secondary qualities themselves. Moreover all that he denies
concerning them is that they are " images of any like external quality". But this is
compatible with them representing (unlike pain) external qualities in a non-resembling
way (see below). Some defenders of the subjectivist interpretation (Stafford 1985:140;
Winkler 1985:188) have also pointed to the following remark: "But let none imagine,
that calling the ideas of virtue and vice perceptions of a sense . . . does diminish their
reality, more than the like assertions concerning all pleasure and pain, happiness or
misery". They have argued that any impression given by the reference to "reality" that
vice and virtue are objective qualities is immediately cancelled out by the ensuing
comparison with "assertions concerning.. pleasure and pain". But again it must not be
forgotten that, for Hutcheson, sense–perception in general is accompanied by, indeed
inextricably bound up with, perceptions of pleasure and pain. In fact we are reminded of
this by the last sentence of the originally quoted passage, where he speaks of the "pleasures of harmony, of taste, of smell".

8 I am indebted here to Bennett's enlightening account (1971:106–11) of why Locke in
some passages assimilates secondary qualities to sensations, and so contradicts what he
says elsewhere. I also learnt a great deal from Bennett's illuminating discussion
"Berkeley's conflation" (1971: 112–23).

9 Indeed as such they are not "qualities" at all by Locke's strict definition, according to
which an object's qualities are "inseparable from it in whatever state". See here Jackson in
Martin, C.B. and Armstrong D.M. (eds) (1968): 66.

10 See particularly McGinn, (1983) chapters 2 and 6; also McDowell (1985:110–29).

11 See also Penelhum (1975: 136) who writes that Hume presents his "most fundamental
argument against the rational basis of evaluation" when "he passes to consider the view
that reason does not function in morality by demonstrating moral truths, but by discov-

ering moral matters of fact in some non-demonstrative way". The final negatively framed adverbial phrase leaves it ambiguous as to whether he wishes to reflect here Hume's stated aim or what he actually tries to prove. However, in quoting from Treatise 3.1.1:26, he like Mackie proceeds directly to the thought-experiment. He then offers this paraphrase: "If you examine any virtuous or vicious actions, all you find are the agent's deeds, plus his passions, motives, volitions or thoughts. You do not find his virtue or his vice".

12 See McDowell's discussion (1985:110–29) of Mackie's construal of secondary qualities as qualities incorrectly taken for primary qualities.

13 In the following I am indebted to Darwall's excellent discussion of these issues (1995: 223–33).

14 The quotations in these two sentences are from the facsimile reproduction of the third edition of the Essay, with an introduction by Paul McReynolds (1969): 28–30. See also: 34, 39.

5   The inconsolable sceptic

1 We should not assume that when Hume uses the term 'metaphysical' he is doing so in the sense in which we are expounding it here, and in which it characterizes the position of his rationalist opponents. In fact, he uses the adjective or its cognates, 'metaphysician' and 'metaphysics', on perhaps a dozen occasions in Book 1. On some four of these he applies it directly to 'reasoning' or 'reflection' but in three different senses. He describes (Introduction: 3) that reasoning as 'metaphysical' which is exclusively concerned with the traditional questions of philosophy putting thereby no restriction on the kind of answers which might be offered or accepted. Indeed, he sees himself – a naturalist – as nevertheless engaged in metaphysical reasoning in *this* sense. He does not even object – and here we come to the second sense of 'metaphysical' – to these philosophical questions being addressed in a metaphysical way where this just means 'abstruse' or 'refin'd or 'difficult to understand' or 'profound'. He sides with those who bear such 'strain'd' reasoning rather than with those who, betraying 'common prejudice', turn impatiently away to seek something more 'natural and entertaining'. He appears to bring together these two senses of 'metaphysical' when he suggests (1.4.1:11) that the topics treated by philosophers are necessarily difficult, and so require complicated reasoning and argument. The only time that he is certainly using 'metaphysical' to refer to the kind of ideas propounded by his rationalist opponents is where he attempts (1.3.14:35) to refute the view that everything must necessarily have a cause, concluding that 'there is no absolute nor metaphysical necessity, that every beginning of existence shou'd be attended with such an object'.

2 It is not enough, in trying to encapsulate in a single phrase what from Hume's viewpoint is wrong with the moral rationalists, to pick up on his claim that we cannot go *beyond experience*. This is because (see below) there is, for him, a perfectly legitimate sense in which we all can, and do, go beyond experience, namely in causal inference. Thus he describes 'the mind' (1.3.4:1) in such operations as 'carr[ying] its view beyond those objects, which it sees or remembers'. It would therefore become necessary to distinguish this legitimate 'going beyond experience' from that which he dismisses as 'presumptuous and chimerical' (Introduction: 8). It would have to be pointed out that in causal inference we only, for Hume, go beyond those *current* sense impressions which initiate the process. It would have to be emphasized that we are still reliant on a variety of memory impressions to ensure both that the inferred idea is a genuine one and the object of this idea is properly the effect of the object of the original sense-impression.

3 The naïve empiricists, however, as well as postulating additional fictitious impressions, agree with Hume that experience is composed of distinct particulars. He is therefore able to argue against them thus: even if there were a separate impression of power in the flame, one would still have the same problem of connecting it with the sensation of heat, as one had before with the impression of flame. He concludes that, so long as they claim (1.3.14:24) that causal power is 'perceived externally in bodies', they will be unable to

give a satisfactory objective account of '[that] efficacy of causes . . . which makes them to be follow'd by their effects (1.3.14:3).

4 Hume's use of the terms 'reason' and 'belief' does not correspond in any neat way to the distinction between demonstrative reasoning on the one hand and probabilistic, or causal, reasoning on the other. In fact, he uses 'reason' or 'reasoning' on its own to refer to both, though attention to the context can usually get rid of any ambiguity. For instance when (Abstract 15 and 16) he contrasts 'reason' with 'custom' he clearly does not mean by 'reason' causal inference. Sometimes, however, he uses 'reasoning' in the two different senses in a single sentence. He writes (1.3.14:36): 'For . . . all our reasonings concerning existence are deriv'd from causation, and . . . all our reasonings concerning causation are deriv'd from the experienc'd conjunction of objects, not from any reasoning and reflection.' As regards 'belief', though he uses the term for the most part to refer to the outcome of causal inference, he does not always do so: on one occasion, for instance, he speaks of the outcome of a demonstration as 'belief'. A common feature of both demonstrative and probabilistic reasoning, as he understands them, and which seems to account for his usage, is that both involve chains of inference.

5 I am indebted here to Owen's discussion of these issues (1999: 93).

6 Though causal generalizations, according to Hume, rely on past experience, their scope of application is not confined to it. They are not just, that is to say, codifications or summaries of that experience, but moving 'audaciously' (Pears, 1990: 82) from 'the known to the unknown' cover 'indefinitely many' new instances. They involve 'transferring . . . [a] past experiment to the future (1.3.12:19) or again 'transfer[ring] our experience to instances of which we have no experience', or yet again (1.3.6:11) 'extend[ing] that experience beyond those particular instances, which have fallen under our observation'. They seem therefore (in today's terminology) to be capable of sustaining, unlike mere codifications or summaries, counterfactual and subjunctive conditionals. An example would be the inference from the statement that 'All gases expand when heated under constant pressure' to the statement not just that 'this gas, presently being heated under constant pressure, will expand', but to the statement that 'were another gas to have been similarly heated, it also would have expanded'.

7 'The observation', writes Ferreira, expounding this view (1995: 274), 'that we do not have a particular kind of backing for a particular kind of claim . . . may indicate only a sensitivity to differences in subject-matter, with no sceptical intention or implication.'

8 See Penelhum (1975: 26) who expresses Hume's prevarication thus:

> Even when inculcating his sceptical doubts about induction . . . Hume frequently confuses us by talking as though he accepts the very beliefs which he is questioning. This is especially true when he is describing . . . those psychological mechanisms whereby nature, in spite of the absence of justifying reasons, persuades us into accepting them: he seems unable to hold fast to the contention that nature is consolidating an *unjustified* belief, and talks as though it is a justified one.

9 In fact, Hume expects ordinary non-philosophical people to be 'astonished' and affronted by his attempt to excise causal necessity and power from the world and place them in 'the mind that considers them'. These people will denounce such a move as 'a gross absurdity and contrary to the most certain principles of human reason'. They will cling indeed so tenaciously and pugnaciously to their illusory beliefs that, Hume thinks, an explanation is called for which he gives as follows: ''Tis a common observation that the mind has a great propensity to spread itself on external objects, and to conjoin with them any internal impressions which they occasion . . . We transfer the determination of the thought to external objects' (1.3.14:24–7).

6 Morality's dynamism

1 To give two examples – for Smith (1994: 13) the argument, recast in the form of three propositions which cannot all be true, is no less than 'the central organizing problem in meta-ethics'. Snare (1991: 35) cites the argument, together with one other from *Treatise* 3.1.1, as showing that 'Hume is the ultimate source of whatever good arguments there are for non-cognitivism.'

2 Commentators on the *Treatise*, such as Brown (1988) or Radcliffe (1996), draw attention, as we have seen, to the argument's invalidity as formulated by Hume, where the first premiss says quite loosely that that moral judgements 'influence' action. However, participants in today's cognitivist / non-cognitivist debate frequently assume that the argument has always been formulated with a first premiss stating that moral judgements have some kind of specially tight link with motivation.

3 See Chapter, 8, p. 193–5 for a critical discussion of this term and its use (or over-use).

4 Dancy (1993: 3), reversing our first and second premisses, gives the argument as follows:

> Premiss 1: No set of beliefs alone is sufficient to generate an action.
>
> Premiss 2: If we add to such a set a moral judgement, we have a new set which could be sufficient for action.
>
> Conclusion: So a moral judgement must either be, or at the least contain, a desire.

This conclusion in fact, despite what Dancy says, is not strictly non-cognitivist since it leaves open the possibility that a moral judgement, merely 'contain[ing] a desire', is a combination of desire and belief, even possibly in equal proportions. Nor is this result surprising. For Dancy does not have the requisite claims amongst his premisses – in particular the claims that desire and belief are asymmetrically related to motivation, and that moral judgements are linked to motivation in the same close way that desires are – for them to entail an unequivocally non-cognitivist conclusion. However, having set out the argument as above, he goes on to claim that, since Humean non-cogni-tivists – presumably independently – maintain that desires are 'internally' [i.e. necessarily] motivating states', they must also hold that 'moral judgements are inter-nally motivating states'. Presumably he thinks that the argument does, despite his own formulation of it, yield an unequivocal non-cognitivist conclusion. It would then be a corollary of the argument, together with the further claim that desires are necessarily motivating, that moral judgements (being identical with desires) are also necessarily motivating.

5 Of premiss 1, S. Svavarsdottir (1999: 163) states:

> the necessity at stake is supposed to be conceptual necessity . . . the idea is that the ascription conditions for moral judgements are such that an agent could not be considered to have made a specific moral judgement unless he were motivated in a specific way.

and again (ibid.: 165) 'moral judgements are of conceptual necessity connected to moti-vation'.

Of premiss 2, and the conclusion, she states (168) 'if moral judgements manifest cona-tive states of mind they will necessarily have some motivational force, whereas if they manifest beliefs, it needs to be explained why they would – unlike most beliefs – be necessarily motivating'. See also Lockie (1998) and Tenenbaum (2000).

6 I have taken the word 'mandatory' from Smith's characterization (1994) of how on the Humean view reason, or belief, is deficient compared with moral judgement as a

motivating force, making it impossible for the latter to be, for Humeans, purely cognitive. Smith maintains that, according to the Humeans, a change in my desires [cannot be] mandated by reason (8), though he represents Humeans as allowing that a belief can have a 'non-rational' impact on desire, and hence on motivation. He goes on to observe, however, (ibid.: 10) that the practicality of moral judgements (asserted in premiss 1) entails, by contrast, that if we judge that an action is right then, other things being equal, 'we *must* be motivated' to act in accordance with our judgement (my italics).

7   Parfit considers the argument stronger on this formulation:

(A) If we have some moral conviction, we must be motivated to act upon it.

(B) If moral convictions were beliefs, (A) could not be true.

Therefore

(C) Moral convictions cannot be beliefs (1997: 106)

and weaker on this formulation:

(D) When moral convictions motivate us, they can do that without the help of any independent desire.

(E) No belief could have this property.

Therefore

(C) Moral convictions cannot be beliefs, but must themselves be desires.

(1997: 107)

8   See my discussion of Kierkegaard's notion of 'tragic guilt' as applied to Greek tragedy, Botros (1987: 123–31).

9   In fact, Hare already takes this claim to entail something much stronger: that we cannot in the fullest sense accept moral judgements without conforming to them.

10   But Smith's view, and in particular his restriction of the claim to rational persons, is discussed in Chapter 8 below.

11   Duties, as Prichard (1968: 1) puts it, can be 'irksome' and are often carried out where an end is only adopted reluctantly. As Mackie (1978: 171) tells us, they are typically things we don't want to have, though we are selfishly glad that others have them, and psychologists have spoken of the experience of duty as of something 'imposed upon our reluctant selves by some relatively extraneous force'. The intrinsic 'irksomeness' of duty has led many to reject *self*-regarding duties as a contradiction in terms. It is not, however, their *content* which presents the difficulty. Rather, it is that we wouldn't need to be commanded or exhorted to perform self-regarding duties in the way we often have to be commanded or exhorted to perform other-regarding acts. Typically, self-regarding acts are, as Larmore (1978: 86) aptly puts it, 'attractive' rather than 'imperative'. Indeed we may not have to have them drawn to our attention at all since, being so inclined towards them anyway, we just do them.

12   Scheffler (1992: 68), seeking to embed his cognitivism in a psychological naturalism, points to what he regards as the obvious fact that certain attitudes such as gratitude are, despite being based on moral beliefs, capable of motivating us without the interposition of an independent desire. He then goes on to suggest that a type of naturalistic theory, such as psychoanalysis, with its picture of human personality as a complex structure, and of motivation as involving the interplay of radically different elements, has the resources to explain how this can be so, at least for some individuals. They are those who have

successfully developed superegos which, as internal repositories of moral standards, can provide a motivating force which is genuinely independent of desire. Scheffler concedes that this way of avoiding the non-cognitivist conclusion rests upon the convincingness either of psychoanalytic theory or some other similar theory.

7 Desires, beliefs and 'direction of fit'

1 See W. Kneale and M. Kneale (1962) *The Development of Logic*, Oxford: Clarendon Press, pp. 52–3.
2 See G. Pitcher (ed.) (1964) *Truth*, Englewood Cliffs, NJ: Prentice-Hall Inc, p. 6.
3 See T. Sprigge (1970) *Facts, Words and Beliefs*, London: Routledge and Kegan Paul Ltd, p. 141, for orders as expressions of desire; also A.N. Prior (1971) *Objects of Thought*, Oxford: Clarendon Press, pp. 69–70, and S. Haack (1978) *Philosophy of Logics*, Cambridge: Cambridge University Press, pp. 84–5 for related discussions.
4 Zangwill though (1996: 177) seems to think that we shall all know what he means when he remarks of the case where a desire is unsatisfied: 'That's a fault in the world'.
5 On the resort to desires as goals in the interpretation of Hume, see Baillie (2000: 89).
6 This seems to be what D. Hubin (1999: 30–45) has in mind when he defends Hume's desire-based reasons by stating that 'reasons for action should turn out to be the sort of things that typically do motivate people', and characterizes opponents of this view as treating the *faculty of reason* as a source of reasons, those, in other words, who base reasons on something other than, as he puts it, 'the subjective, contingent, conative states of the agent'. It seems to be this assumed identification of a desire-based theory of motivation with naturalism to which Scheffler (1992: 60, 63) is also referring. For he suggests as a possible defence of the Humean view that 'only sentiments or desires are ultimately capable of moving a person to action' (a view which in fact he rejects) that 'it is not easy to see how there could be such a thing as motivation independent of one's natural attitudes and inclinations' (a view that he endorses).

8 A riddle and a buried assumption

1 I classify Scheffler here with the necessitarians. He might well be thought, however, to qualify with Foot as an accidentalist in that, for him as for Foot (as was pointed out in an earlier chapter), an independent desire ultimately comes into the explanation of action. However, just as with Foot, the desire only enters the picture in, so to speak, a roundabout way, permitting talk of motivation occurring as a direct result of the relevant belief.
2 It is perhaps Nagel (1970: 7) who is responsible for bringing Falk to prominence on account of having introduced the terms 'internalism' and 'externalism' into contemporary moral debate. In fact, Nagel is indebted to Frankena ([1939] 1958), but he points out that Frankena himself derives the terms from Falk's (1948) paper '"Ought" and motivation'. Since Nagel, it has become customary for writers discussing internalism and externalism to cite the 1948 article by Falk as the source of this terminology. However, Falk first used the terms in an earlier article – 'Obligation and rightness' (1945) – which is the focus of our interest here. His use of the terms, however, does not substantially differ in the later paper. See below for a discussion of this use compared to that of more recent writers.
3 One may continue to talk of the relation being 'necessary' in both cases, provided this is taken to mean only that motivation does not require the imposition of an independent desire.
4 Ayer's kleptomaniac is from 'Freedom and necessity' (1954) reprinted in Watson (1982: 20). Frankfurt's heroin addict is from 'Freedom of the will and the concept of a person' (1971). Watson's example of the mother is in 'Free agency' (1975). Both these latter articles are also reprinted in Watson (1982).
5 This is again a quotation from Watson.

9 The case of *Owen Wingrave*

1 For consistency's sake I will, like Williams, use the masculine pronoun in this discussion.

2 It should not be supposed that Korsgaard herself endorses unqualifiedly this 'internalist' theory. In fact, she defines (1986: 15) an 'internalism requirement' to which she subscribes, and which restricts the claim, linking moral judgement and motivation, to rational agents.

3 Clearly a third person could state that the agent *himself believed* that he had reason to act. However, I here define a 'third person' ascription of reasons precisely so as to exclude this case, and to cover only the case where a statement is about the agent's *having* such a reason. Though Korsgaard mentions (1986: 11) something like my distinction when comparing Williams' and Nagel's views, she seems wholly to miss its significance. In fact, she thinks that the two are making the same point only from the different perspectives of explainer and agent.

4 That Williams' 'subjective motivational set' can include beliefs as well as desires shows once more that he is not relying on any special distinction between these two psychological attitudes as would a proponent of the 'moderate' version of Hume's argument.

5 A point, however, that seems to have been consistently missed. Korsgaard, for instance, only gets round to mentioning Williams' claim that 'internal reasons are by definition relative to something that he calls the agent's 'subjective motivational set' towards the end of her discussion (1986: 19), and even then does not grasp the significance of this restrictive definition.

6 I cite the page numbers of the text mentioned in the bibliography.

7 I am here freely adapting for use in the present context Strawson's remark (1982: 79), 'But the metaphysics was in the eye of the metaphysician'.

8 Johnstone can be considered a cognitivist in that he allows sense to talk of moral judgements' objectivity, truth, validity. He nevertheless stresses (1989: 100, 111, 146) that, since these judgements concern decisions to act, they cannot be said to be objective, true, etc. in the same sense as empirical propositions.

9 I do not wish to suggest that Wiggins would share my general position here.

10 See Diamond's (1996) critique of Lovibond (1983) as failing to fully appreciate the extent to which Wittgenstein turned his back on all general theories. Indeed, what Lovibond calls 'Wittgensteinian realism', Diamond suggests, contains a misunderstanding of Wittgenstein since it assumes that every proposition that is descriptive in form has a descriptive function. But see Lovibond's response (2002) discussed by Mulhall (2002).

11 Winch's philosophical use of literary examples has never been bettered.

Bibliography

Anscombe, G.E.M. (1957) *Intention*, Oxford: Blackwell.

Ardal, P.S. (1976) 'Some implications of the virtue of reasonableness in Hume's *Treatise*', in D. Livingstone and J. King (eds) *Hume: A Re-Evaluation*, New York: Fordham University Press.

Ayer, A.J. (1954) 'Freedom and necessity', reprinted in G. Watson (ed.) (1982) *Free Will*, Oxford: Oxford University Press, pp. 15–23.

Baillie, J. (2000) *Hume on Morality*, London: Routledge.

Basson, A.H. (1958) *David Hume*, Harmondsworth: Penguin.

Bennett, J. (1971) *Locke, Berkeley, Hume*, London: Oxford University Press.

Berkeley, G. ([1710] 1945) *Principles of Human Knowledge*, ed. T. Jessop, London: Thomas Nelson and Sons.

Botros, S. (1983) 'Acceptance and morality', *Philosophy* 58: 433–53.

—— (1987) 'Precarious virtue', *Phronesis* XXXII(1): 101–31.

Brink, D.O. (1997) 'Moral motivation', symposium on Michael Smith's *The Moral Problem*, *Ethics* 108: 4–32.

Brown, C. (1988) 'Is Hume an internalist?', in R. Cohon (ed.) (2001) *Hume: Moral and Political Philosophy*, Dartmouth: Ashgate, pp. 343–61.

Campbell, K.J. (ed.) (1991) *German Mystical Writings*, New York: Continuum.

Clarke, S. (1728) *A Discourse of Natural Religion*, selections reprinted in D.D. Raphael (ed.) (1969) *British Moralists 1650–1800, I: Hobbes–Gay*, Oxford: Clarendon Press, pp. 191–225, paragraphs 224–61.

Cohon, R. (ed.) (2001) *Hume: Moral and Political Philosophy*, Dartmouth: Ashgate.

Copp, D. (1997) 'Belief, reason and motivation: Michael Smith's *The Moral Problem*', *Ethics* 108: 33–54.

Cudworth, R. (1731) *A Treatise Concerning Eternal and Immutable Morality*, selections reprinted in D.D. Raphael (ed.) (1969) *British Moralists 1650–1800, I: Hobbes–Gay*, Oxford: Clarendon Press, pp. 105–19, paragraphs 119–35.

Dancy, J. (1993) *Moral Reasons*, Oxford: Blackwell.

Darwall, S. (1995) *The British Moralists and the Internal Ought 1640–1740*, Cambridge: Cambridge University Press.

Davidson, D. (1963) 'Actions, reasons and causes', reprinted in D. Davidson (1980) *Essays on Actions and Events*, Oxford: Oxford University Press, pp. 3–20.

—— (1980) *Essays on Actions and Events*, Oxford: Oxford University Press.

Diamond, C. (1996) 'Wittgenstein, mathematics, and ethics: resisting the attractions of realism', in H.D. Sluga and D.J. Stern (eds) *The Cambridge Companion to Wittgenstein*, Cambridge: Cambridge University Press, pp. 226–60.

Empson, W. (1949) *Seven Types of Ambiguity*, London: Chatto and Windus.

Falk, W.D. (1945) 'Obligation and rightness', *Philosophy* XIX: 129–48.
—— (1948) '"Ought" and motivation', *Proceedings of the Aristotelian Society* 1947–8: 111–38.
Ferreira, M.J. (1995) 'Hume's naturalism: "proof" and practice', in S. Tweyman (ed.) *David Hume Critical Assessments*, London: Routledge, vol. III, pp. 271–83.
Foot, P. (1963) 'Hume on moral judgement', in D. Pears (ed.) *Hume: A Symposium*, London: Macmillan, pp. 67–76; reprinted in P. Foot (1978) *Virtues and Vices*, Oxford: Basil Blackwell, pp. 74–80.
—— (ed.) (1967) *Theories of Ethics*, Oxford: Oxford University Press.
—— (1972) 'Morality as a system of hypothetical imperatives', reprinted in P. Foot (1978) *Virtues and Vices*, Oxford: Basil Blackwell, pp. 157–73.
—— (1977) 'Approval and disapproval', reprinted in P. Foot (1978) *Virtues and Vices*, Oxford: Basil Blackwell, pp. 189–207.
—— (1978) *Virtues and Vices*, Oxford: Basil Blackwell.
Frankena, W.K. (1939) 'The naturalistic fallacy', reprinted in P. Foot (ed.) (1967) *Theories of Ethics*, Oxford: Oxford University Press, pp. 50–63.
—— (1958) 'Obligation and motivation in recent moral philosophy', in A.I. Melden (ed.) *Essays in Moral Philosophy*, Seattle: University of Washington Press, pp. 40–81.
Frankfurt, H. (1971) 'Freedom of the will and the concept of a person', reprinted in G. Watson (ed.) (1982) *Free Will*, Oxford: Oxford University Press, pp. 81–95.
Haack, S. (1978) *Philosophy of Logics*, Cambridge: Cambridge University Press.
Hare, R.M. (1952) *The Language of Morals*, Oxford: Clarendon Press.
—— (1963) *Freedom and Reason*, Oxford: Oxford University Press.
—— (1992) 'Weakness of will', in L. Becker and C. Becker (eds) *Encyclopaedia of Ethics*, New York: Garland, pp. 1304–7.
Harrison, J. (1976) *Hume's Moral Epistemology*, Oxford: Clarendon Press.
Hart, H.L.A. (1961) *The Concept of Law*, Oxford: Clarendon Press.
Holmes, R. (1998) *Coleridge: Darker Reflections*, London: HarperCollins.
Hubin, D.C. (1999) 'What's special about Humeanism?' *Nous* XXXIII(1): 30–45.
Humberstone, L. (1992) 'Direction of fit', *Mind* 101: 59–83.
Hume, D. (1739–40) *A Treatise of Human Nature*, D.F. Norton and M.J. Norton (eds) (2000), Oxford: Oxford University Press.
—— (1777) *Enquiries Concerning Human Understanding and Concerning the Principles of Morals*, L.A. Selby-Bigge and P.H. Nidditch (eds) (1975), Oxford: Clarendon Press.
Hunter, G. (1962) 'Hume on is and ought', *Philosophy* 37: 148–52.
Hurka, T. (1995) 'Between belief and desire: review of Michael Smith's The Moral Problem', *Times Literary Supplement* 4830, October 27 1995, p. 31.
Hutcheson, F. (1738) *An Inquiry Concerning Moral Good and Evil*, selections reprinted in D.D. Raphael (ed.) (1969) *British Moralists 1650–1800, I: Hobbes–Gay*, Oxford: Clarendon Press, pp. 262–99, paragraphs 303–54.
—— (1742) *An Essay on the Nature and Conduct of the Passions and Affections with Illustrations on the Moral Sense*, 3rd edn, selections reprinted in D.D. Raphael (ed.) (1969) *British Moralists 1650–1800, I: Hobbes–Gay*, Oxford: Clarendon Press, pp. 300–21, paragraphs 355–73; see also the facsimile reproduction of this edition, with an introduction by P. McReynolds (1969), Gainsville, FL: Scholars' Facsimiles and Reprints.
Jackson, R. (1929) 'Locke's distinction between primary and secondary qualities', reprinted in C.B. Martin and D.M. Armstrong (eds) (1968) *Locke and Berkeley: A Collection of Critical Essays*, New York: Doubleday & Co, pp. 53–77.
James, H. (2001) *Ghost Stories*, Ware: Wordsworth Classics.
Johnstone, P. (1989) *Wittgenstein and Moral Philosophy*, London: Routledge.

Kant, I. (1785) *The Groundwork of the Metaphysic of Morals*, reprinted in H.J. Paton (1958), *The Moral Law*, London: Hutchinson & Co. Ltd.

Kierkegaard, S. (1843) 'Ancient tragical Motif', *Either/Or*, Vol. 1 (1959) trans. by D. F. Swenson and L.M. Swenson, New York: Doubleday & Co, Inc., pp. 137–62.

Kneale, W. and Kneale, M. (1962) *The Development of Logic*, London: Oxford University Press.

Korsgaard, C. (1986) 'Skepticism about practical reason', *Journal of Philosophy*, 83(1): 5–25.

Locke, J. (1690) *An Essay Concerning Human Understanding*, J. Yolton (ed.) (1961), London: Dent & Sons Ltd.

Lockie, E. (1998) 'What's wrong with moral internalism?' *Ratio* 11 (0034–0006): 14–36.

Lovibond, S. (1983) *Realism and Imagination in Ethics*, Minneapolis, MN: University of Minnesota Press.

—— (2002) *Ethical Formation*, Cambridge, MA: Harvard University Press.

McDowell, J. (1985) 'Values and secondary qualities', in T. Honderich (ed.) *Morality and Objectivity: A Tribute to J.L. Mackie*, London: Routledge and Kegan Paul, pp. 110–29.

McGinn, C. (1983) *The Subjective View: Secondary Qualities and Indexical Thoughts* Oxford: Oxford University Press.

Mackie, J.L. (1977) *Ethics*, Harmondsworth: Penguin.

—— (1978) 'Can there be a right-based moral theory?' in J. Waldron (ed.) (1984) *Theories of Rights*, Oxford: Oxford University Press, pp. 168–81.

—— (1980) *Hume's Moral Theory,* London: Routledge and Kegan Paul.

McNaughton, D. (1988) *Moral Vision*, Oxford: Blackwell.

Mandeville, B. (1714) *An Enquiry into the Origin of Moral Virtue*, selections in D.D. Raphael (ed.) (1969) *British Moralists 1650–1800, I: Hobbes–Gay*, Oxford: Clarendon Press, pp. 229–36, paragraphs 262–71.

Martin, C.B. and Armstrong, D.M. (1968) *Locke and Berkeley: A Collection of Critical Essays*, New York: Doubleday & Co.

Mill, J.S. (1861) *Utilitarianism*, reprinted in M. Warnock (ed.) (1966) *Utilitarianism John Stuart Mill*, London: Collins: 251–321.

Millgram, E. (1995) 'Was Hume a Humean?' *Hume Studies* 21(1): 75–93, reprinted in R. Cohon (ed.) (2001) *Hume: Moral and Political Philosophy*, Dartmouth: Ashgate, pp. 43–57.

Moore, G.E. (1903) *Principia Ethica*, reprinted (1966) Cambridge: Cambridge University Press.

Mulhall, S. (2002) 'Ethics in the light of Wittgenstein', *Philosophical Papers*, 31(3): 293–321.

Nagel, T. (1970) *The Possibility of Altruism*, Oxford: Clarendon Press.

Norton, D.F. (1982) 'Hutcheson's moral realism', *David Hume: Common-sense Moralist, Sceptical Metaphysician*, Princeton, NJ: Princeton University Press, pp. 55–93.

—— (1985) 'Hutcheson's moral realism', *Journal of the History of Philosophy* 23(3): 397–418.

—— (1993) *The Cambridge Companion to Hume*, Cambridge: Cambridge University Press.

Nowell-Smith, P. (1954) *Ethics*, Harmondsworth: Penguin.

Owen, D. (1999) *Hume's Reason*, Oxford: Oxford University Press.

Parfit, D. (1997) 'Reasons and motivation', *Aristotelian Society Supplementary Volume* 71, 99–130.

Pears, D. (1963) *David Hume: A Symposium*, London: Macmillan.

—— (1990) *Hume's System*, Oxford: Oxford University Press.

Penelhum, T. (1975) *Hume*, London: Macmillan.

Pitcher, G. (1964) *Truth*, Englewood Cliffs, NJ: Prentice-Hall Inc.

Plato (1976) *Protagoras,* trans. C.C.W. Taylor, Oxford: Clarendon Press.

Platts, M. (1979) *Ways of Meaning*, London: Routledge and Kegan Paul.

Price, K.B. (1995) 'Does Hume's theory of knowledge determine his ethical theory?', in S. Tweyman (ed.) *David Hume Critical Assessments*, London: Routledge, vol. IV, pp. 3–11.

Prichard, H.A. (1912) 'Does moral philosophy rest on a mistake?', reprinted in *Moral Obligation* (1968), Oxford: Oxford University Press.

Prior, A.N. (1956) *Logic and the Basis of Ethics*, Oxford: Clarendon Press.

—— (1971) *Objects of Thought*, Oxford: Clarendon Press.

Radcliffe, E. (1996) 'How does the Humean sense of duty motivate?' reprinted in R. Cohon (ed.) (2001) *Hume: Moral and Political Philosophy*, Dartmouth: Ashgate, pp. 363–87.

Raphael, D.D. (ed.) (1969) *British Moralists 1650–1800, I: Hobbes–Gay*, Oxford: Clarendon Press.

Ross, W.D. (1939) *Foundations of Ethics*, Oxford: Clarendon Press.

Sayre-McCord, G. (1997) 'The meta-ethical problem': Symposium on Michael Smith's *The Moral Problem*, *Ethics*, 108: 55–83.

Scheffler, S. (1992) *Human Morality*, Oxford: Oxford University Press.

Searle, J. (1964) 'How to derive "ought" from "is"', reprinted in P. Foot (ed.) (1967) *Theories of Ethics*, Oxford: Oxford University Press, pp. 101–14.

Shaftesbury, Third Earl of (1714) *Characteristics of Men, Manners, Opinions, Times*, London: J. Darby.

Smith, M. (1994) *The Moral Problem*, Oxford: Blackwell.

—— (1997) 'In defence of *The Moral Problem*: A reply to Brink, Copp, and Sayre-McCord', *Ethics* 108: 84–119.

Snare, F. (1991) *Morals, Motivation and Convention: Hume's Influential Doctrines*, New York: Cambridge University Press.

Sobel, D. and Copp, D. (2001) 'Against direction of fit accounts of belief and desire', *Analysis* 61: 44–53.

Sprague, E. (1954) 'Francis Hutcheson and the moral sense', *Journal of Philosophy*, 51: 794–800.

Sprigge, T. (1970) *Facts, Words and Beliefs*, London: Routledge and Kegan Paul.

Stafford, J.M. (1985) 'Hutcheson, Hume and the ontology of morals', *Journal of Value Inquiry* 19: 133–51.

Stocker, M. (1979) 'Desiring the bad: an essay in moral psychology', *Journal of Philosophy* 76: 738–53.

Stratton-Lake, P. (1999) 'Why externalism is not a problem for Ethical Intuitionism', *Proceedings of the Aristotelian Society*, 99, Part 1: 77–90.

Strawson, P. (1962) 'Freedom and resentment', reprinted in G. Watson (ed.) (1982) *Free Will*, Oxford: Oxford University Press, pp. 59–80.

Stroud, B. (1977) *Hume*, London: Routledge and Kegan Paul.

Svavarsdottir, S. (1999) 'Moral cognitivism and motivation', *The Philosophical Review* 108(2): 161–219.

Tenenbaum, S. (2000) 'Ethical internalism and Glaucon's question', *Nous* 34(1): 108–30.

Tweyman, S. (ed.) (1995) *David Hume Critical Assessments*, London: Routledge.

Watson, G. (1975) 'Free agency', reprinted in G. Watson (ed.) (1982) *Free Will*, Oxford: Oxford University Press.

—— (ed.) (1982) *Free Will*, Oxford: Oxford University Press.

Williams, B. (1981) 'Internal and external reasons' in *Moral Luck*, Cambridge: Cambridge University Press, pp. 101–13.

Winch, P. (1965) 'The universalizability of moral judgements', in *Ethics and Action* (1972) London: Routledge and Kegan Paul, pp. 151–70.

Winkler, K. (1985) 'Hutcheson's alleged realism', *Journal of the History of Philosophy* 23(2): 79–94.

Winters, B. (1995) 'Hume's argument for the superiority of natural instinct' in S. Tweyman (ed.) *David Hume Critical Assessments*, London: Routledge, vol. III, pp. 262–70.

Wittgenstein, L. (1958) *Philosophical Investigations*, trans. G.E.M. Anscombe, Oxford: Blackwell.

Wollaston, W. (1724) *The Religion of Nature Delineated*, selections reprinted in D.D. Raphael (ed.) (1969) *British Moralists 1650–1800, I: Hobbes–Gay*, Oxford: Clarendon Press, pp. 239–58, paragraphs 272–302.

Zangwill, N. (1996) 'Direction of fit and normative functionalism', *Philosophical Studies* 91: 173–203.

Index